LIBRARY OF HEBREW BIBLE/
OLD TESTAMENT STUDIES
447

Formerly Journal for the Study of the Old Testament Supplement Series

WORD AND SPIRIT IN EZEKIEL

James Robson

t&t clark

NEW YORK • LONDON

T & T Clark International, 80 Maiden Lane, New York, NY 10038

T & T Clark International, The Tower Building, 11 York Road, London SE1 7NX

T & T Clark International is a Continuum imprint.

Library of Congress Cataloging-in-Publication Data
Robson, James E.
    Word and spirit in Ezekiel / James Robson.
        p. cm. -- (Library of Hebrew Bible/Old Testament studies ; 447)
    Includes bibliographical references and index.
    ISBN-13: 978-0-567-02622-4 (hardcover)
    ISBN-10: 0-567-02622-1 (hardcover)
    1. Bible. O.T. Ezekiel--Criticism, interpretation, etc. I. Title. II. Series.

    BS1545.52.R63 2006
    224'.406--dc22

                                        2006024405

06 07 08 09 10   10 9 8 7 6 5 4 3 2 1

Printed and bound in Great Britain by Biddles Ltd., King's Lynn, Norfolk

CONTENTS

Part II
WORD, SPIRIT AND INSPIRATION

Chapter 3
INSPIRATION AND EZEKIEL

Chapter 4
DIACHRONIC PERSPECTIVES ON PROPHETIC INSPIRATION

Part III
WORD, SPIRIT AND TRANSFORMATION

PREFACE

This book is the revision of a thesis submitted to Middlesex University for which the degree of Ph.D. was awarded in 2004. I am glad to be able to express my gratitude to Thomas Renz, who supervised my doctoral research with great wisdom and meticulous care. He has proved an inspiring example and has become a good friend. I am also grateful both to Max Turner, who willingly shared his expertise and his encouragement, and to Gordon Wenham, Paul Joyce, Ronald Clements and Andrew Mein for reading and commenting on earlier versions of this work. The faculty and students at Oak Hill College have been consistent in stimulating thinking and providing encouragement. I owe a particular debt of gratitude to the Principal, David Peterson. There have been many others who have assisted me. Although necessarily nameless here for fear of omitting one, I thank each one. This book is dedicated to my wife, Bridget, who has been a constant source of love, encouragement and support, and to our daughters, Anna and Naomi, who help keep everything in perspective.

ABBREVIATIONS

AB	Anchor Bible
ABD	*The Anchor Bible Dictionary.* Edited by D. N. Freedman. 6 vols. New York: Doubleday, 1992
AnBib	Analecta biblica
ANET	*Ancient Near Eastern Texts Relating to the Old Testament.* Edited by J. B. Pritchard. Princeton, 1954.
AOAT	*Alter Orient und Altes Testament*
ASTI	*Annual of the Swedish Theological Institute*
ATANT	Abhandlungen zur Theologie des Alten und Neuen Testaments
ATD	Das Alte Testament Deutsch
AUSS	*Andrews University Seminary Studies*
BBR	*Bulletin for Biblical Research*
BDB	Brown, F., S. R. Driver, and C. A. Briggs. *A Hebrew and English Lexicon of the Old Testament.* Oxford, 1907
BHS	*Biblica Hebraica Stuttgartensia.* Edited by K. Elliger and W. Rudolph, Stuttgart, 1983
BibOr	Biblica et orientalia
BJRL	*Bulletin of the John Rylands University Library of Manchester*
BN	*Biblische Notizen*
BO	*Bibliotheca orientalis*
BZAW	Beihefte zur Zeitschrift für die alttestamentliche Wissenschaft
CahRB	Cahiers de la Revue biblique
CBC	Cambridge Bible Commentary
CBR	*Currents in Biblical Research*
CBQ	*Catholic Biblical Quarterly*
COS	*The Context of Scripture.* Edited by W. W. Hallo. 3 vols. Leiden, 1997–2003
DCH	*The Dictionary of Classical Hebrew.* Edited by D. J. A. Clines. Sheffield, 1993–
DSB	Daily Study Bible
EncJud	*Encyclopaedia Judaica.* Jerusalem: Macmillan, 1971
ESV	English Standard Version
ET	English translation
ETL	*Ephemerides theologicae lovanienses*
EvT	*Evangelische Theologie*
GKC	*Gesenius' Hebrew Grammar.* Edited by E. Kautzsch. Translated by A. E. Cowley. 2d. ed. Oxford, 1910
HALOT	Koehler, L., W. Baumgartner, and J. J. Stamm. *The Hebrew and Aramaic Lexicon of the Old Testament.* Translated and edited under the supervision of M. E. J. Richardson. Study edition. 2 vols. Leiden, 2001
Heb.	Hebrew
HAR	*Hebrew Annual Review*

HS   *Hebrew Studies*
HSM   Harvard Semitic Monographs
HUCA   *Hebrew Union College Annual*
IBHS   *An Introduction to Biblical Hebrew Syntax.* B. K. Waltke and M. O'Connor.
            Winona Lake, Indiana, 1990
ICC   International Critical Commentary
Int   *Interpretation*
ISBE   *International Standard Bible Encyclopaedia.* Edited by G. W. Bromiley. 4
            vols. Grand Rapids, 1979–1988
ITC   International Theological Commentary
JBL   *Journal of Biblical Literature*
JETS   *Journal of the Evangelical Theological Society*
JNSL   *Journal of Northwest Semitic Languages*
Joüon   Joüon, P. A. *Grammar of Biblical Hebrew.* Translated and revised by T.
            Muraoka. 2 vols. Subsidia biblica 14/1–2. Rome, 1991
JPS   Jewish Publication Society
JPTSup   Journal of Pentecostal Theology Supplements
JQR   *Jewish Quarterly Review*
JSNTSup   Journal for the Study of the New Testament: Supplement Series
JSOT   *Journal for the Study of the Old Testament*
JSOTSup   Journal for the Study of the Old Testament: Supplement Series
JTC   *Journal for Theology and the Church*
JTS   *Journal of Theological Studies*
LXX   Septuagint
MOT   Mastering the Old Testament
MT   Masoretic Text
NAC   New American Commentary
NASV   New American Standard Version
NCB   New Century Bible
NIB   *The New Interpreter's Bible.* Edited by L. E. Keck. 13 vols. Nashville, 1994–
            2004
NIBC   New International Biblical Commentary
NICOT   New International Biblical Commentary on the Old Testament
NIDOTTE   *New International Dictionary of Old Testament Theology and Exegesis.*
            Edited by W. A. VanGemeren. 5 vols. Grand Rapids, 1997
NIV   New International Version
NIVAC   New International Version Application Commentary
NJB   New Jerusalem Bible
NRSV   New Revised Standard Version
OAN   Oracles Against the Nations
OBT   Overtures to Biblical Theology
OTG   Old Testament Guides
OTL   Old Testament Library
OtSt   *Oudtestamentische Studiën*
PRSt   *Perspectives in Religious Studies*
RB   *Revue biblique*
RelS   *Religious Studies*
RSPT   *Revue des sciences philosophiques et théologiques*
RSV   Revised Standard Version
SBJT   *Southern Baptist Journal of Theology*

SBLDS	Society of Biblical Literature Dissertation Series
SBLMS	Society of Biblical Literature Monograph Series
SBLSymS	Society of Biblical Literature Symposium Series
SBT	Studies in Biblical Theology
SJT	*Scottish Journal of Theology*
STJ	*Stulos Theological Journal*
TDNT	*Theological Dictionary of the New Testament*. Edited by G. Kittel and G. Friedrich. Translated by G. W. Bromiley. 10 vols. Grand Rapids, 1964–1976
TDOT	*Theological Dictionary of the Old Testament*. Edited by G. J. Botterweck and H. Ringgren. Translated by J. T. Willis, G. W. Bromiley, and D. E. Green. 14 vols. Grand Rapids, 1974–
ThWAT	*Theologisches Wörterbuch zum Alten Testament*. Edited by G. J. Botterweck and H. Ringgren. 10 vols. Stuttgart, Kohlhammer, 1973–2000
TLOT	*Theological Lexicon of the Old Testament*. Edited by E. Jenni, with assistance from C. Westermann. Translated by M. E. Biddle. 3 vols. Peabody, Mass., 1997
TOTC	Tyndale Old Testament Commentaries
TWOT	*Theological Wordbook of the Old Testament*. Edited by R. L. Harris, G. L. Archer, Jr., and B. K. Waltke. 2 vols. Chicago, 1980
TynBul	*Tyndale Bulletin*
TZ	*Theologische Zeitschrift*
VT	*Vetus Testamentum*
VTSup	Vetus Testamentum Supplements
WEC	Wycliffe Exegetical Commentary
WBC	Word Biblical Commentary
WTJ	*Westminster Theological Journal*
ZAH	*Zeitschrift für Althebräistik*
ZAW	*Zeitschrift für die alttestamentliche Wissenschaft*
ZTK	*Zeitschrift für Theologie und Kirche*

Part I

GATHERING THE DATA

The goal of divine action is to maintain and to create life; to achieve this aim Yahweh chiefly avails of himself of two means which we encounter in varying intensities in all the realms of his manifestation: the Spirit and the Word.

—Edmond Jacob[1]

---

1. Edmond Jacob, *Theology of the Old Testament* (trans. A. W. Heathcote and P. J. Allcock; London: Hodder & Stoughton, 1958), 121.

Chapter 1

INTRODUCTION

In the Old Testament, two fundamental experiences of God are these: an encounter with the "word" of God, often rendered, particularly in prophetic literature, by דבר,[1] and an encounter with the "spirit" or "wind" or "breath" of God, almost always represented by רוח.[2] If one were to select the Old Testament character and book where these are most prominent, there is little doubt that the choice would be Ezekiel the prophet and Ezekiel the book. Encounters with Yahweh's word and Yahweh's רוח are central to the prophet Ezekiel and to the book that bears his name.

The surface structure of the book of Ezekiel reveals how it is dominated by the prophetic "word of Yahweh." Apart from five visionary encounters with Yahweh, in which the "hand of Yahweh" is significant (1:1–3:15; 3:22–5:17; 8:1–11:25; 37:1–14; 40:1–48:35), Zimmerli identifies forty-seven other units.[3] Of these, forty-five are introduced by

---

1.   The semantic range of דבר is very great. The closest synonyms (in terms of function and syntagmatic relations) that speak of Yahweh's prophetic word are פה (used metonymically), נאם, and three poetic nouns, אמר, אמרה and מלה. פי יהוה can speak of Yahweh's prophetic word (e.g. 1 Kgs 13:21 [cf. v. 9]; Num 24:13); see further C. J. Labuschagne, "פֶּה *peh* mouth," *TLOT* 2:976–78. אמר speaks of Yahweh's prophetic word in Hos 6:5 (באמרי־פי) (cf. Num 24:4, 16); it also speaks of Yahweh's word more generally (e.g. Josh 24:27; Job 22:12 [//תורה]; 23:12; Ps 138:4). אמרה speaks of the prophetic word in Isa 28:23 and 32:9; it, too, speaks of Yahweh's word more generally (e.g. nineteen times in Ps 119). A third poetic word, found particularly in wisdom literature, is מלה. It never occurs in a construct relationship with "Yahweh" or "God"; it is only used for the divine prophetic word in 2 Sam 23:2 (ומלתו); the other occurrence where it speaks of Yahweh's words is in Job 23:5 (מלים). The final synonym that should be mentioned is נאם. I shall be examining it and its occurrence in the phrase נאם יהוה below.

2.   The principal alternative is נשמה. In Isa 30:33, נשמת יהוה; in Job 4:11, מנשמת אלוה; in Job 32:8 and 33:4, ונשמת שדי; in Job 34:14, ונשמתו; in Job 37:10, מנשמת־אל; in 2 Sam 22:16, מנשמת רוח אפו (cf. Ps 18:16 [ET 18:15], מנשמת רוח אפך).

3.   Walther Zimmerli, "The Special Form- and Traditio-Historical Character of Ezekiel's Prophecy," *VT* 15 (1965): 515–16.

the phrase (or a variation of the phrase), "the word of Yahweh came to me saying…" (ויהי דבר־יהוה אלי לאמר).[4] Rarely are there narrative comments (e.g. 20:1; 24:18); instead, the words that Ezekiel is to utter, the sign-acts he is to perform, even the reaction of his audience, are all subsumed within what Block calls "the prophetic event,"[5] the prophet receiving a "word" from Yahweh. As Zimmerli comments, "the message in this prophet is dominated completely by the event of the divine word to which he refers in the first person."[6]

This emphasis on the "word of Yahweh" is matched by the prominence of רוח. Within the book, there are fifty-two references to רוח, a number that has led Block to call Ezekiel "the prophet of the spirit."[7] While Block is quick to qualify such a statement, since רוח can have meteorological ("wind") and anthropological ("spirit," "mind," "breath") meanings, as well as theological ones ("spirit," "Spirit"), it is striking to notice the contrast between Ezekiel and the two works to which Ezekiel is most similar both in thought and language, Jeremiah and Leviticus.[8] Leviticus has no reference to רוח of any kind, and Jeremiah never uses רוח theologically.[9] It is against such a background that the present study

---

4. Zimmerli accounts for the other two instances: Ezek 33:21–22 gives the year, the day and the month on which not Yahweh but an escapee from Jerusalem brings Ezekiel news of Jerusalem's destruction. This unique "narrative without a word of proclamation" exploits the prominence of the "word of Yahweh" and emphasizes the announcement of the fall. The other is the "lament" (קינה) of ch. 19. For further discussion, see Zimmerli, "Special Form- and Traditio-Historical Character," 515–16.

5. Daniel I. Block, *The Book of Ezekiel Chapters 1–24* (Grand Rapids: Eerdmans, 1997), 18.

6. Zimmerli, "Special Form- and Traditio-Historical Character," 516.

7. Daniel I. Block, "The Prophet of the Spirit: The Use of *RWḤ* in the Book of Ezekiel," *JETS* 32 (1989): 28.

8. Cf. John Woodhouse, "The 'Spirit' in the Book of Ezekiel," in *Spirit of the Living God Part One* (ed. B. G. Webb; Explorations 5; Sydney: Lancer, 1991), 5. Paul-Eugène Dion notes, "Le matériel législatif de l'Ancien Testament paraît donc totalement imperméable aux emplois théologiques de la notion de souffle" ("La *rwḥ* dans l'Heptateuch," *Science et Esprit* 42 [1990]: 168).

9. Of the eighteen occurrences in Jeremiah, fourteen refer directly to רוח as "wind" (Jer 2:24; 4:11–12, 5:13; 10:13; 13:24; 14:6; 18:17; 22:22; 49:32, 36 (×2); 51:1, 16), of which the most significant is 5:13, where "the prophets are nothing but wind" (והנביאים יהיו לרוח); one refers to an extension of this meaning, "side" (52:23), two to the "breath" that idols do not have (10:14 = 51:17), and one to the "spirit" of the kings of the Medes (51:11). רוח as "wind" is under Yahweh's control (e.g. 10:13), and often a simile or metonymy for Yahweh's judgment (e.g. 4:11; 13:24; 22:22).

examines the theological relationship between Yahweh's word and Yahweh's spirit/wind/breath, exclusively rendered as רוח within the book of Ezekiel. A study of this relationship will take us right to the heart of a number of significant topics.

At a more general level, there is the controversial question of רוח-inspiration within the diverse phenomenon of Old Testament prophecy. An examination of רוח-inspiration in the book of Ezekiel requires an analysis of this wider question, and we shall be looking further at it below in this opening chapter. This study will enable us to address a number of significant issues within the contemporary interpretation of the book of Ezekiel.

First, there is the vexed question of the tension between divine sovereignty, expressed in God's declaration that he will give Israel "a new heart and a new spirit" (Ezek 36:26; cf. 11:19), and human responsibility, expressed in the call for Israel get for themselves "a new heart and a new spirit" (18:31), as well as in other calls to repentance.

Secondly, there is the question of the marked prominence of רוח in the book of Ezekiel, and, in particular, the prominence of theological uses. This surely requires an explanation, particularly in the light of the striking absence in Jeremiah and Leviticus.

Thirdly, there is the place of the prophetic persona. Almost everything within the book is subsumed within the experience of the prophet Ezekiel. This in itself is not unique. The persona of Habakkuk, and, more significantly, that of Jeremiah, are both prominent in the books that bear their names.[10] What is different about the book of Ezekiel is the fact that the narrative as a whole is presented with Ezekiel as the speaker (apart from 1:2–3).

Finally, there is the rhetorical function of the book as a whole. The careful structuring of the book, combined with the striking similarity in style throughout, suggests some kind of intentional unity.

Although these issues might appear to bear little relation to one another, this study will show that an examination of the theological relationship between Yahweh's word and Yahweh's רוח (spirit) within the book of Ezekiel provides a coherent perspective and contributes to current thinking on each of these areas.

---

10. Brevard S. Childs, *Introduction to the Old Testament as Scripture* (London: SCM, 1979), 349–50; Donald E. Gowan, *Theology of the Prophetic Books: The Death and Resurrection of Israel* (Louisville, Ky.: Westminster John Knox, 1998), 91, 100.

1. *Questions of Method*

Before, however, proceeding to outline in more detail these and some of the other issues within the study of Old Testament prophecy and, more particularly, within the book of Ezekiel, I want to explain the three dimensions of my approach to these questions.

1.1. *Synchronic*

First, by speaking of "the book of Ezekiel," I mean to make clear that I am working synchronically, from the standpoint of regarding the book as an intentional, if redactional, unity. A brief retelling of the story of Ezekiel research illuminates what I mean by this.

The scholarly study of Ezekiel can be characterized as having three phases.[11]

The first phase, up until the beginning of the twentieth century, was marked by a broad agreement on the authorial unity and general integrity of the book.[12]

This peace was shattered soon afterwards, although the cracks had already appeared.[13] Significant in this was the work of Hölscher,[14] who

---

11. For more detailed reviews of literature until 1950, see in particular H. H. Rowley, "The Book of Ezekiel in Modern Study," in idem, *Men of God* (London: Nelson, 1963), 169–210; repr. from *BJRL* 36 (1953–54): 146–90; Walther Zimmerli, *Ezekiel 1: A Commentary on the Book of the Prophet Ezekiel Chapters 1–24* (trans. R. E. Clements; Hermeneia; Philadelphia: Fortress, 1979), 3–8; Henry McKeating, *Ezekiel* (OTG; Sheffield: Sheffield Academic Press, 1993), 30–42. For reviews of scholarship after 1950, see McKeating, *Ezekiel*, 43–61; Katheryn Pfisterer Darr, "Ezekiel Among the Critics," *Currents in Research: Biblical Studies* 2 (1994): 9–24; and most recently Risa Levitt Kohn, "Ezekiel at the Turn of the Century," *CBR* 2 (2003): 9–31. Other notable reviews are those by Joyce, who tackles questions of unity and authorship by examining the different criteria that have been used, and Renz, who deals lucidly and comprehensively with the particular question of the location of the prophet. See Paul M. Joyce, *Divine Initiative and Human Response in Ezekiel* (JSOTSup 51; Sheffield: JSOT Press, 1989), 21–31; Thomas Renz, *The Rhetorical Function of the Book of Ezekiel* (VTSup 76; Leiden: Brill, 1999), 27–38.

12. G. B. Gray, *A Critical Introduction to the Old Testament* (Studies in Theology 10; London: Duckworth, 1913), 198: "No other book of the Old Testament is distinguished by such decisive marks of unity of authorship and integrity as this… [I]t forms a well-articulated whole." S. R. Driver, *An Introduction to the Literature of the Old Testament* (9th ed.; Edinburgh: T. & T. Clark, 1913), 279: "No critical question arises in connexion with the authorship of the book, the whole from beginning to end bearing unmistakably the stamp of a single mind."

13. Zimmerli (*Ezekiel 1*, 4) notes how in the 1897 commentary of Bertholet, some parts of the book only arrived later in their present context, and how in 1900

drew a sharp distinction between authentic poetry, on the one hand, and secondary prose, on the other. After removing all hopeful material (chs. 33–48), because Ezekiel was a prophet of doom, and any passages redolent with the language of (later) Deuteronomy and the Holiness Code, he was left with around 150 verses that were genuine. In the years that followed, it was, according to Torrey, "as though a bomb had been exploded in the book of Ezekiel, scattering the fragments in all directions."[15] Issues revolved around three interlocking topics: *when* the book was composed, *how* (if at all) the book is a unity, and *where* the prophet (if there was one) had carried out his ministry.[16] The emphasis on Jerusalem in the first twenty-four chapters led a number of scholars to argue that part or all of Ezekiel's ministry had taken place there.[17] Other views, such as Torrey's, were more radical.[18]

The shift to the third phase started around 1950. Howie, although arguing that the "collection of Ezekiel's teachings" was made by others,

---

Kraetzschmar thought he could find "parallel recensions" on the basis of the shift between first and third person found in Ezek 1:1–4, and subsequently at different points throughout the book. Howie notes that the earliest shift from the traditional view is to be found in the late eighteenth-century work, G. L. Oeder's *Freye Untersuchung über einige Bücher des Alten Testaments*. According to Howie, Oeder claims that chs. 40–48 are a "spurious addition" to Ezekiel's prophecy. See C. G. Howie, *The Date and Composition of Ezekiel* (JBL Monograph Series 4; Philadelphia: Society of Biblical Literature, 1950), 1–2.

14. Gustav Hölscher, *Hesekiel, der Dichter und das Buch* (BZAW 29; Giessen: Töpelmann, 1924).

15. Charles C. Torrey, "Notes on Ezekiel," *JBL* 58 (1939): 78. The "fact" that precipitated the destruction of the "unity and harmony" was the editing of "the original Palestinian prophecy…in such a way as to transfer it to Babylonia" (*ibid.*).

16. Cf. Rowley, "Book of Ezekiel," 171.

17. So, for example, Herntrich, who regarded most of chs. 1–39 as coming from Ezekiel's ministry in Jerusalem prior to 586. The rest of the book comes from a Babylonian redactor, who also reshaped the first thirty-nine chapters so as to give an apparent Babylonian provenance for the prophet. See Volkmar Herntrich, *Ezechielprobleme* (BZAW 61; Giessen: Töpelmann, 1932). Bertholet, however, ascribed the dual focus of the book, on both Jerusalem and Babylon, to a dual ministry. Ezekiel was not deported in 597 but in 586. See Alfred Bertholet, *Hesekiel, mit einem Beitrag von Kurt Galling* (HAT 13; Tübingen: J. C. B. Mohr [Paul Siebeck], 1936).

18. Charles C. Torrey, *Pseudo-Ezekiel and the Original Prophecy* (New Haven, Conn.: Yale University Press, 1930). For him, "The original 'Ezekiel'…was a pseudepigraph purporting to come from the reign of Manasseh, but in fact composed many centuries later. It was converted into a prophecy of the so-called 'Babylonian Golah' by an editor" as part of a "literary movement" starting "in the middle of the third century B.C." whose "purpose" was "the vindication of the religious tradition of Jerusalem" (p. 102).

contended for a solely Babylonian ministry for the prophet, drawing on historical, linguistic, and archaeological data which corresponded with the book of Ezekiel.[19] Fohrer recognized the problem the book presents by seeming to portray Ezekiel as a prophet to Jerusalem although he lives in Babylon. He, however, examined rigorously the arguments used to defend a Palestinian sphere of ministry for the prophet and a late date, and systematically refuted them.[20] Rowley, after reviewing the recent scholarship of his day (1953–54), concluded, "The ministry of Ezekiel I would place wholly in Babylonia in the period immediately before and after the fall of Jerusalem."[21] The transition to the third phase was given further, one might even say conclusive, impetus by the publication of the first part of Zimmerli's major commentary on Ezekiel. His work was marked by comprehensive form-critical and traditio-historical analysis, and by a systematic attempt to trace the journey from the prophet himself, whose ministry he located exclusively in Babylon, to the final form of the text.

The first characteristic of the third phase could be described as the *reinstatement of the prophet*. For the last fifty years, it has been without doubt the majority opinion that the prophet Ezekiel was a real figure with a real ministry in Babylon during the early part of the exile, and that significant parts of the book of Ezekiel reflect accurately his words and his ministry.[22]

---

19. Howie, *Date and Composition*. Examples include (a) the term לבנה in Ezek 4:1, which Howie regards as a "sun-dried brick," and therefore Ezekiel's action reflects a practice common in the Neo-Babylonian empire, but unusual in Judah (p. 18); (b) "mud brick" walls, which were the only walls used in Mesopotamian house-building and through which it would have been possible to dig (Ezek 12:5), unlike the stone walls common in pre-exilic Palestine, which would have immediately collapsed (p. 18). Howie also makes the important point that the prophet need not "face his audience directly" if he is to be a prophet (p. 100). This then removes one of the main arguments in favour of a ministry in Jerusalem.

20. Georg Fohrer, *Die Hauptprobleme des Buches Ezechiel* (BZAW 72; Berlin: Töpelmann, 1952). He observes that the command to Ezekiel to speak to his addressees orally (*mündlich*) is mirrored in the OAN (Oracles Against the Nations), yet that does not mean Ezekiel should be thought to have preached to those nations. Thus, based on the form of oracles alone, the location of the prophet cannot be deduced (pp. 204–5).

21. Rowley, "Book of Ezekiel," 210.

22. Though there have been, of course, some dissenting voices, particularly among German scholars such as Garscha and Pohlmann. See Jörg Garscha, *Studien zum Ezechielbuch: eine redaktionskritische Untersuchung von 1–39* (Europäische Hochschulschriften 23; Frankfurt: Lang, 1974); Karl-Friedrich Pohlmann, *Das Buch des Prophet Hesekiel (Ezechiel) Kapitel 1–19* (ATD 22/1; Göttingen: Vandenhoeck

There is a sense, though, in which the reinstatement of the prophet did not lead directly or necessarily to the reinstatement of the *book* of Ezekiel. Allen summarizes my point succinctly:

> Zimmerli, while concerned with the whole book, was inclined to stand *beside* Ezekiel and then look *beyond* to the redactional sequel to which the book bears witness. This is a natural procedure, especially since the book urges us to look back at Ezekiel's prophesying. Yet its real invitation is to engage in a re-reading of the record *from a later standpoint*, and it is only as we endeavor to respond to that invitation that we honor the book.[23]

Certainly some scholars have repudiated diachronic approaches to the book, without subscribing either to a pre-critical or to an ahistorical literary reading. The leading exponent has been Moshe Greenberg. He has mounted a sustained critique of some of the preconceptions and methods used to distinguish between what is authentically Ezekielian and secondary material,[24] and in his two commentaries has demonstrated the value of a synchronic reading.[25] It, however, has not been essential to follow Greenberg unequivocally in order to focus on the book of Ezekiel from the perspective of recognizing its essential unity. It is this perspective, recognizing not just the essential accuracy of the book's portrayal of the prophet's words and Babylonian location, but also the essential (usually redactional) unity, that has marked almost all of the monographs published in English in the last thirty years.[26] This methodological perspective, of a synchronic reading based on a redactional unity, has proved

---

& Ruprecht, 1996); idem, *Das Buch des Prophet Hesekiel (Ezechiel) Kapitel 20–48* (ATD 22/2; Göttingen: Vandenhoeck & Ruprecht, 2002). For Garscha, only 17:1–10 and 23:2–25 are the authentic words of Ezekiel. For Pohlmann, the Babylonian setting that pervades the book does not derive from the oldest material. Only 134 verses in the first nineteen chapters derive from the oldest layer.

23. Leslie C. Allen, *Ezekiel 1–19* (WBC 28; Waco, Tex.: Word, 1994), xxvi (my emphasis).

24. See in addition to Greenberg's commentaries the trenchant article, "What Are Valid Criteria for Determining Inauthentic Matter in Ezekiel?," in *Ezekiel and His Book: Textual and Literary Criticism and Their Interrelation* (ed. Johan Lust; BETL 74; Leuven: Leuven University Press, 1986), 123–35.

25. Moshe Greenberg, *Ezekiel 1–20* (AB 22; New York: Doubleday, 1983), and idem, *Ezekiel 21–37* (AB 22A; New York: Doubleday, 1997).

26. It should also be noted that the three major English commentaries published in the last twenty years similarly focus on the unity of the book: Greenberg, *Ezekiel 1–20* and *Ezekiel 21–37*; Allen, *Ezekiel 1–19*; idem, *Ezekiel 20–48* (WBC 29; Dallas, Tex.: Word, 1990); Block, *Ezekiel 1–24*; idem, *The Book of Ezekiel Chapters 25–48* (Grand Rapids: Eerdmans, 1998).

fruitful in recent research, and I have adopted it neither uncritically nor in an ahistorical literary manner.[27]

1.2. *Recognizing Communicative Intent*

The second dimension to my methodological approach also arises from the phrase "the book of Ezekiel," though it is not implicit in it. I am approaching Ezekiel not simply as a collection of the words of a prophet, but as a book written with a purpose, to a set of addressees. This focus on the communicative intent of the book of Ezekiel (or of part of it) has characterized a number of recent monographs on Ezekiel.

In her book *Swallowing the Scroll*, Ellen Davis takes account of parts of the book "which violate our preconceptions about prophetic speech" while at the same time "taking seriously" Ezekiel's "own claim to stand in the line of Israel's prophets."[28] She outlines what she calls a new "mode of interpretation" of the book, whereby the prophet, in a radical departure from what has preceded him, confronts his audience by means of text in order to create a new community.[29]

Thomas Renz, in his book *The Rhetorical Function of the Book of Ezekiel*, argues that the book of Ezekiel "received its final shape to function in a specific way for the second generation of exiles."[30] That is, the book of Ezekiel is not so much an anthology as an argument. In his study, Renz explores both the function of the book and the means used to achieve that function. For him, the book was "designed to shape the self-understanding of the exilic community," in particular to persuade them to "dissociate themselves from a communal vision in which Yahweh is not central," "to find their identity neither in Babylon nor in the Jerusalem of the past" that has now been judged by Yahweh and destroyed, and to align themselves with a different, new, vision of "a nation centred on Yahweh's sanctuary."[31]

Kalinda Stevenson's work, *The Vision of Transformation*, can also be placed here, although she deals with Ezek 40–48 alone.[32] Stevenson looks at these chapters through the lenses of human geography, regarding them

---

27. On a related matter, I have chosen to work with the MT, with an eye in particular on the LXX where the MT is awkward syntactically or semantically.

28. Ellen F. Davis, *Swallowing the Scroll: Textuality and the Dynamics of Discourse in Ezekiel's Prophecy* (JSOTSup 78; Bible and Literature Series 21; Sheffield: Almond, 1989).

29. Ibid. The phrase "mode of interpretation" comes from p. 127.

30. Renz, *Rhetorical Function*, 1.

31. Ibid., 229.

32. Kalinda R. Stevenson, *The Vision of Transformation: The Territorial Rhetoric of Ezekiel 40–48* (SBLDS 154; Atlanta: Scholars Press, 1996).

as rhetoric concerning space, rather than an elaborate blueprint for building. The mass of details is in no sense irrelevant but is there "to give hope to a community in exile."[33] The book generates hope "by creating a vision of a future restructured society, a society centered around the temple of YHWH"[34] with Yahweh as the only king, a vision evident from Yahweh's territorial claim.

Using insights from these three works, I shall be considering the communicative intent of the book, recognizing that it is designed to shape its addressees. I shall be drawing also on insights that can be derived from speech act theory in my analysis.

According to speech act theory,[35] "speaking a language is engaging in a rule-governed form of behaviour. To put it more briskly, talking is performing acts according to rules."[36] There are three aspects of speaking. First, there is the *locutionary utterance*, "which is roughly equivalent to uttering a certain sentence with a certain sense and reference, which again is roughly equivalent to 'meaning' in the traditional sense."[37] Secondly, there is the *illocutionary utterance*,[38] which is an utterance that does not describe anything, but "is, or is a part of, the doing of an action."[39] A typical example is that of a person declaring, "I hereby name this ship 'Josephine.'" No other action needs to be performed for the ship to acquire the name Josephine, though it is of course true that there need to be certain conditions in place for the naming to be "happy"[40] or

33. Ibid., 163.

34. Ibid.

35. Developed first in J. L. Austin, *How to Do Things With Words* (ed. J. O. Urmson; Oxford: Oxford University Press, 1962), then by John R. Searle in works such as John R. Searle, *Speech Acts: An Essay in the Philosophy of Language* (Cambridge: Cambridge University Press, 1969); idem, "What is a Speech Act?," in *The Philosophy of Language* (ed. John R. Searle; London: Oxford University Press, 1971), 39–53; idem, *Expression and Meaning: Studies in the Theory of Speech Acts* (Cambridge: Cambridge University Press, 1979); John R. Searle and Daniel Vanderveken, *Foundations of Illocutionary Logic* (Cambridge: Cambridge University Press, 1985).

36. Searle, *Speech Acts*, 22.

37. Austin, *How to Do Things*, 108.

38. Also known as a "performative utterance."

39. Austin, *How to Do Things*, 5.

40. Since illocutionary acts are actions, they are not so much true or false, but are carried out properly or not. The term Austin used was "happy" if the appropriate conventions were in place. Conventions for naming a ship would include, as one example, that the one who does the naming has the publicly recognized right to name that ship. For Austin's list of conventions for the "happiness" of a particular illocutionary act, see ibid., 14–15.

"successful."[41] The focus here is on the *force* of the utterance, and answers the question, "What are you doing *in* saying that?" or "What *kind* of speech act is it?" Finally, there is the *perlocutionary utterance*. This answers the question, "What are you doing *by* saying that?" and explains what is the result, or effect, of saying these words. It can cover both intentional and unintentional effects. Cohen summarizes Austin's short formula to distinguish the three clearly: "a locution is an act *of* saying something, an illocution is an act done *in* saying something, a perlocution is an act done *by* saying something."[42]

Since Austin's and Searle's early work, the study of speech acts has moved on significantly.[43] Nonetheless, still fundamental is the difference between locutionary acts, "acts of uttering or inscribing words,"[44] and illocutionary acts, "acts performed *by way of* locutionary acts, acts such as asking, asserting, commanding, promising, and so forth."[45] The significance of such a distinction will be apparent at a number of different points in this study, as, for example, I examine how the prophet Ezekiel's oracles uttered against Jerusalem can function in the book that bears his name after Jerusalem itself has fallen.

---

41. Searle and Vanderveken, *Foundations*, 13.

42. Ted Cohen, "Illocutions and Perlocutions," *Foundations of Language* 9 (1973): 493 (original emphasis). Cohen (p. 493) points out that this is inadequate, because the " 'in'/'by' distinction…will not underwrite the illocution/perlocution distinction…for it does not unfailingly mark a distinction between what is conventional and what is not." Nonetheless, the formula generally seems to have been accepted as an approximation.

43. See, e.g., Hugh C. White, "Introduction: Speech Act Theory and Literary Criticism," *Semeia* 41 (1988): 1–24; John Lyons, *Linguistic Semantics: An Introduction* (Cambridge: Cambridge University Press, 1995); George Yule, *Pragmatics* (Oxford: Oxford University Press, 1996); Nicholas Wolterstorff, *Divine Discourse: Philosophical Reflections on the Claim That God Speaks* (Cambridge: Cambridge University Press, 1995); the essays by Kevin J. Vanhoozer ("From Speech Acts to Scripture Acts: The Covenant of Discourse and the Discourse of the Covenant," 1–49), Dan R. Stiver ("Ricoeur, Speech-Act Theory, and the Gospels as History," 50–72) and Nicholas Wolterstorff ("The Promise of Speech-act Theory for Biblical Interpretation," 73–90) in *After Pentecost: Language and Biblical Interpretation* (ed. Craig Bartholomew, Colin Greene and Karl Möller; Scripture and Hermeneutics Series 2; Carlisle: Paternoster, 2001); Richard S. Briggs, *Words in Action* (Edinburgh: T. & T. Clark, 2002). For some recent cautionary words, see Brevard S. Childs, "Speech-Act Theory and Biblical Interpretation," *SJT* 58 (2005): 375–92. In my judgment, his wholesale rejection of "Woltersorff's application of speech-act theory to biblical interpretation" as "deeply flawed" (p. 391) is unwarranted.

44. Wolterstorff, *Divine Discourse*, 13.

45. Ibid., 13 (original emphasis).

1.3. *Theological*

The third dimension to my methodological approach is highlighted in the phrase, "the theological relationship between Yahweh's word and Yahweh's רוח." There are three points that need to be made concerning this phrase.

First, the word "theological" highlights that the focus of this study is not the psychology of the prophet, even in his experience of רוח; nor is it the role of the prophet in society; nor is it historical questions surrounding either the social situation of exile or the relationship between the preaching of Ezekiel and the prophetic book that bears his name; nor, finally, is it hermeneutical questions concerning the ideology (ideologies) of the redactor(s) portraying the character and words of Ezekiel that so dominate the book. Rather, my focus is intra-textual, focusing on the theological relationship found in the text(s).

Secondly, this focus on theology accords with the book of Ezekiel itself. Although I shall be exploring what the book of Ezekiel asks from its readers, and slightly modifying the following statement, essentially the book asks of its readers not a plan of action, but a change of belief. Restoration lies in the hands of Yahweh, and Yahweh alone.[46]

Thirdly, the phrase "the theological relationship" might suggest that I regard the prominence of both Yahweh's word and Yahweh's רוח in the book of Ezekiel as entailing a self-evident relationship between them. I posit no such self-evident relationship. There is, however, after all, a natural association between "breath" and "word"—it is a person's breath that carries his or her word. Such an association is quite common in the ancient Near East. For example, in the Egyptian *The Legend of Isis and the Name of Re*, "Isis came, bearing her effective magic, her speech being the breath of life, her utterance dispelling suffering, her words revivifying one whose throat is constricted."[47] This connection is sometimes exploited in the Old Testament. In Isa 11:4, the shoot from the stump of Jesse, on whom the spirit of Yahweh shall rest, shall kill the wicked "with the breath of his lips" (ברוח שפתיו), a phrase that occurs in parallel with him striking the earth "with the rod of his mouth" (בשבט פיו). Such an association is also predicated of Yahweh. This is particularly apparent in Ps 33:6:

---

46. See Renz, *Rhetorical Function*, 246–47.
47. "The Legend of Isis and the Name of Re," translated by Robert K. Ritner (*COS* 1.22:33–34). For other ancient Near Eastern texts, see Johannes Hehn, "Zum Problem des Geistes im Alten Orient und im Alten Testament," *ZAW* 43 (1925): 218–19.

By the word of Yahweh (בדבר יהוה) the heavens were made, and all their
host by the breath of his mouth (ברוח פיו).

Eichrodt, in commenting on "the association of the spirit of life with the
creative word," affirms "the inner homogeneity of the two concepts."
This homogeneity is evident from the fact that "the same expression" is
"used to designate both the spirit of God as the breath of life going forth
from him and the word of God as the breath of his mouth."[48]

This near-interchangeability of the two concepts is seen very clearly in
the postexilic book of Judith 16:14, "Let all your creatures serve you, for
you spoke (εἶπας), and they were made. You sent forth your spirit (τὸ
πνεῦμά σου), and it formed them; there is none that can resist your voice
(τῇ φωνῇ σου)." It is against this kind of background that Woodhouse has
argued of רוח in Ezekiel that language "usually understood to refer to the
'Spirit' of God is better understood when it is seen to be a transparent
anthropomorphism to be rendered by an English expression such as 'the
breath of God.'"[49]

The way in which Yahweh's word and, more particularly, Yahweh's
רוח are conceived will shape the resultant understanding and framing of
the theological relationship. This study, therefore, sets out to explore
every dimension of the possible relationship between Yahweh's word
and Yahweh's רוח. I am not simply interested in the "prophetic spirit" or
the "prophetic word," but in relating Yahweh's רוח, wherever it may be
found, to Yahweh's word, wherever it may be found.

1.4. *Summary*
The method that I am adopting in examining the relationship between
Yahweh's word and Yahweh's רוח, then, is synchronic, recognizing a
redactional unity that arises out of a communicative intent, and principally theological.

2. *Putting this Study in Context*

This is the first systematic examination of the theological relationship
between Yahweh's word and Yahweh's רוח in Ezekiel. It takes place
against a number of different contexts, and needs to be understood against
those contexts.

---

48. Walther Eichrodt, *Theology of the Old Testament* (trans. J. A. Baker; 2 vols.;
London: SCM, 1961–67), 2:49.
49. Woodhouse, "'Spirit,'" 20.

2.1. רוח *in the Old Testament*

In the Old Testament as a whole, there are 389 occurrences of רוח; eleven of these occur in the Aramaic sections of Daniel.[50] The semantic range of the word is wide. It can serve as a meteorological term, speaking of the "wind." Thus in 1 Kgs 18:45, the heavens are said to have grown black "with cloud and wind (רוח)." It can also serve as an anthropological term, speaking of the "breath of life" or the emotions or disposition in a person. Thus, in Gen 6:17, Yahweh declares that he will "destroy from under heaven all flesh in which is the breath (רוח) of life," and in Judg 8:3, after Gideon has mollified the Ephraimites, the narrator reports that "their anger (רוחם) subsided." רוח can also function as a theological term, referring to Yahweh's רוח. In Judg 3:10, "the spirit of Yahweh" (רוח־יהוה) came upon Othniel and he judged Israel. Such a wide semantic domain is reflected in the variety of words used by the LXX to translate it, including πνεῦμα ("breath," "wind," "spirit," 277 times), ἄνεμος ("wind," 52 times), θυμός ("anger," 6 times) and πνοή ("breath," 4 times).[51]

2.2. *Study of* רוח *in the Old Testament*

The second context is that of scholarly study of רוח in the Old Testament. In view of the fact that רוח is essentially invisible, and generally refers to the unseen cause of a wide variety of effects, it is neither surprising that Neve comments, "Probably nothing in the Old Testament so eludes comprehension as the spirit of God,"[52] nor that the study of רוח in the Old Testament has given rise in the last one hundred years to only a small number of monographs dedicated to the subject in English, French and German.[53]

---

50. See Daniel Lys, *Rûach: Le Souffle dans L'Ancien Testament* (Études D'Histoire et de Philosophie Religieuses; Paris: Presses Universitaires de France, 1962), 15; Rainer Albertz and Claus Westermann, "רוח *Rûaḥ* Spirit," *TLOT* 3:1202.

51. For these figures, see Friedrich Baumgärtel, "Spirit in the Old Testament," *TDNT* 6:367. Baumgärtel also lists other, less frequently occurring words with references. See further Muraoka's Appendix 4, "Hebrew/Aramaic Index to the Septuagint," p. 344, and the corresponding entries in the Concordance itself in Edwin Hatch and Henry A. Redpath, *A Concordance to the Septuagint* (2d ed.; Grand Rapids: Eerdmans, 1998).

52. Lloyd Neve, *The Spirit of God in the Old Testament* (Tokyo: Seibunsha, 1972), 1.

53. English: in addition to Neve, there is George T. Montague, *Holy Spirit: Growth of a Biblical Tradition* (New York: Paulist Press, 1976), 3–15; Wilf Hildebrandt, *An Old Testament Theology of the Spirit of God* (Peabody, Mass.: Hendrickson, 1995) (I have excluded the more popular book, Leon J. Wood, *The Holy Spirit*

Alongside these monographs are general articles or sections on רוח in journals,[54] dictionaries,[55] Old Testament theologies[56] and other books.[57]

in the Old Testament [Contemporary Evangelical Perspectives Series; Grand Rapids: Zondervan, 1976], because it does not interact with critical works).

French: Lys, *Rûach*; an influential series of articles by Paul van Imschoot, "L'action de l'esprit de Jahvé dans l'Ancient Testament," *RSPT* 23 (1934): 553–87; idem, "L'esprit de Jahvé, source de la vie dans l'Ancient Testament," *RB* 44 (1935): 481–501; idem, "L'esprit de Jahvé et l'alliance nouvelle dans l'Ancient Testament," *ETL* 13 (1936): 201–20; idem, "Sagesse et esprit dans l'Ancient Testament," *RB* 47 (1938): 23–49; idem, "L'esprit de Jahvé, principe de vie morale dans l'Ancient Testament," *ETL* 16 (1939): 457–67; idem, "L'esprit de Jahvé, source de la piété dans l'Ancient Testament," *Bible et Vie Chretienne* 6 (1954): 17–30.

German: Paul Volz, *Der Geist Gottes und die verwandten Erscheinungen im Alten Testament und im anschließenden Judentum* (Tübingen: J.C.B. Mohr [Paul Siebeck], 1910); Robert Koch, *Geist und Messias* (Freiburg: Herder, 1950); idem, *Geist Gottes*; Manfred Dreytza, *Der theologische Gebrauch von RUAḤ im Alten Testament: Eine wort- und satzsemantische Studie* (Giessen: Brunnen, 1990).

54. E.g. Charles A. Briggs, "The Use of רוח in the Old Testament," *JBL* 19 (1900): 132–45; William R. Schoemaker, "The Use of רוח in the Old Testament, and of πνεῦμα in the New Testament," *JBL* 23 (1904): 13–67; Hehn, "Zum Problem des Geistes"; Claus Westermann, "Geist im Alten Testament," *EvT* 41 (1981): 223–30.

55. "רוח," *BDB*, 924–26; Baumgärtel, *TDNT* 6:359–67; Albertz and Westermann, *TLOT* 3:1202; F. W. Horn, "Holy Spirit," *ABD* 3:260–80; S. Tengström, "רוח *rûaḥ*," *ThWAT* 7:385–418; M. V. Van Pelt et al., "רוח," *NIDOTTE* 3:1073–78; "רוח," *HALOT*, 1197–1201.

56. Ludwig Koehler, *Old Testament Theology* (trans. A. S. Todd; London: Lutterworth, 1957), 111–18; Jacob, *Theology*, 37–42, 121–34; Eichrodt, *Theology*, 2:46–68, 131–34; Paul van Imschoot, *Theology of the Old Testament* (trans. K. Sullivan and F. Buck; Tournai: Desclée, 1965), 172–88 (inevitably not as comprehensive as his journal articles); Gerhard von Rad, *Old Testament Theology* (trans. D. M. G. Stalker; 2 vols.; Edinburgh: Oliver & Boyd, 1962–65), 1:94–104; 2:56–57; Rolf P. Knierim, *The Task of Old Testament Theology* (Grand Rapids: Eerdmans, 1995), 269–308; Horst D. Preuss, *Old Testament Theology* (trans. L. G. Perdue; 2 vols.; Edinburgh: T. & T. Clark, 1995–96), 1:160–63. There is surprisingly little in Walter Brueggemann's stimulating volume, *Theology of the Old Testament: Testimony, Dispute, Advocacy* (Minneapolis: Fortress, 1997), in which the most significant discussion is at pp. 292–93.

57. Important treatments include those in Norman H. Snaith, *The Distinctive Ideas of the Old Testament* (London: Epworth, 1944), 143–58; Aubrey R. Johnson, *The One and the Many in the Israelite Conception of God* (Cardiff: University of Wales Press, 1961), esp. 14–17; idem, *The Vitality of the Individual in the Thought of Ancient Israel* (2d ed.; Cardiff: University of Wales Press, 1964), 26–39; Hans W. Wolff, *Anthropology of the Old Testament* (trans. M. Kohl; London: SCM, 1974), 32–39; Max-Alain Chevallier, *Souffle de Dieu: Le Saint-Esprit Dans le Nouveau Testament* (Le Point Théologique 26; Paris: Editions Beauchesne, 1978), 22–35; Henri Cazelles, "Prolégomenes à une étude de l'esprit dans la Bible," in *Von Kanaan*

There are also a number of articles, chapters or monographs on רוח in the Old Testament with a more specific focus. Some examine רוח with particular reference to a time-period[58] or a restricted corpus such as the Heptateuch[59] or the historiographic writings.[60] Perhaps not unexpectedly, however, it is in the discussions about the prophets that רוח has particular prominence.

Most significant in this regard is the book by Wonsuk Ma on the spirit of God in the book of Isaiah.[61] Although he recognizes that there is a degree of potential oversimplification to his approach, in that further redactional layers may be obscured, he splits his work into four chapters reflecting his "four-stage reading" of Isaiah, to preserve clarity. His first stage is the "Pre-exilic Isaianic Spirit Tradition"; his second is "Exilic Isaianic Spirit Traditions"; his third is "Postexilic Isaianic Spirit Tradition"; finally, he "takes a more holistic approach by reading the passages [already discussed] in the literary and theological context of the entire book."[62] He categorizes spirit traditions in the Old Testament under headings such as "Leadership Spirit," "Prophetic Spirit," "Creation Spirit," and "The Spirit as God's Independent Agent," and explores how each one is portrayed within each stage. The strengths of the book are his painstaking examination of the individual texts, his relating the conclusions from close exegesis to the ongoing development in the conception of רוח, and his attempt to integrate both a diachronic and a more holistic reading.

Discussions about the relationship between רוח and prophecy are also found in a number of books exploring Old Testament prophecy, in particular the works by Wilson,[63] who explores the spirit's role in mediation in the light of contemporary sociological and anthropological

---

bis Kerala (ed. W. C. Delsman et al.; AOAT 211; Neukirchen–Vluyn: Neukirchener, 1982), 75–90; Benjamin B. Warfield, "The Spirit of God in the Old Testament," in idem, *Biblical Doctrines* (Edinburgh: Banner of Truth, 1988 [1929]), 101–29.

58. E.g. Richard J. Sklba, "'Until the Spirit from on High is Poured Out on Us' (Isa 32:15): Reflections on the Role of the Spirit in Exile," *CBQ* 46 (1984): 1–17; Helen Schüngel-Straumann, *Rûaḥ bewegt die Welt: Gottes schöpferische Lebenskraft in der Krisenzeit des Exils* (Stuttgarter Bibelstudien 151; Stuttgart: Katholisches Bibelwerk, 1992).

59. Dion, "*rwḥ* dans l'Heptateuch."

60. Daniel I. Block, "Empowered by the Spirit of God: The Holy Spirit in the Historiographic Writings of the Old Testament," *SBJT* 1 (1997): 42–61.

61. Wonsuk Ma, *Until the Spirit Comes: The Spirit of God in the Book of Isaiah* (JSOTSup 271; Sheffield: Sheffield Academic Press, 1999).

62. Ibid., 158.

63. Robert R. Wilson, *Prophecy and Society in Ancient Israel* (Philadelphia: Fortress, 1980).

research, Heschel,[64] who argues that the dimension of רוח as expressing pathos or emotion is often omitted, and the wide-ranging Lindblom.[65] In addition, there are also a number of articles that explore the relationship between רוח and the prophetic word. I shall return to this shortly.

2.3. *Study of* רוח *in the Book of Ezekiel*

When we turn to the book of Ezekiel, although there has been no work comparable to Ma's, there are four journal articles that focus on רוח in Ezekiel,[66] and three books which give particular attention to the subject beyond the ones already mentioned.[67] In most of the works mentioned in this section and in the previous one, the approach is essentially one of isolation, categorization and analysis of each occurrence. The categories vary slightly.

The three categories of meteorological, theological and anthropological are the most general ones.[68] These should not be understood to be imprecise, though. Lys, for example, subdivides each category carefully. Within the meteorological category of "wind," he detects five distinct aspects: wind as the announcer of God, wind and historical disasters, wind and cosmic disasters, the east wind, and wind as orientation. Within the theological category, he discerns three subcategories: the spirit of God's chariot, the spirit and the prophet, and the spirit and renewal (after 586 B.C.). Finally, within the anthropological category, he notes two subcategories for uses before 586 B.C.: the spirit of a particular person designating that person's behaviour on a particular occasion, and the spirit of every child of God. This latter subcategory is closely related to the anthropological usage of רוח after 586 B.C., which speaks of what will be brought into effect in the people's renewal.

Different categorization characterizes the work of Zimmerli, Joyce, Block and Hosch. Zimmerli divides the occurrences into four categories:

---

64. Abraham J. Heschel, *The Prophets* (2 vols.; New York: Harper & Row, 1962; repr., Peabody, Mass.: Prince, 2000), 2:95–97.

65. Johannes Lindblom, *Prophecy in Ancient Israel* (Oxford: Blackwell, 1962).

66. Block, "Prophet of the Spirit"; Woodhouse, " 'Spirit' "; Harold E. Hosch, "*RÛAḤ* in the Book of Ezekiel: A Textlinguistic Analysis," *JOTT* 14 (2002): 77–125; Pamela E. Kinlaw, "From Death to Life: The Expanding רוח in Ezekiel," *PRSt* 30 (2003): 161–72.

67. Keith W. Carley, *Ezekiel Among the Prophets: A Study of Ezekiel's Place in Prophetic Tradition* (SBT 2nd Series 31; London: SCM, 1975); Walther Zimmerli, *Ezekiel 2: A Commentary on the Book of the Prophet Ezekiel Chapters 25–48* (trans. J. D. Martin; Hermeneia; Philadelphia: Fortress, 1983), 566–68 (Excursus: "רוח in the Book of Ezekiel"); Joyce, *Divine Initiative*, 109–11.

68. Lys, *Rûach*; Neve, *Spirit of God*; Dreytza, *Der theologische Gebrauch von RUAH*.

"wind," "breath of life," "the world of the divine" and "prophetic experience of a call."[69] Joyce suggests six categories for the use of רוח in the Old Testament, and identifies occurrences of all six in Ezekiel: "wind," "God-given breath of life," "dynamic power of Yahweh," "the medium... of understanding" in humans, "the medium...of feeling" and "the moral will."[70] Block regards the foundational meaning of רוח as "wind" and suggests a bifurcation from this meaning.[71] One fork leads to the meaning of רוח as "side," which in turn gives way to "direction." The other fork has five sub-categories: רוח as "agency of conveyance," as "agency of animation," as "agency of prophetic inspiration," as "mind," by which Block means "the seat of the emotions, the intellect and the will," and, finally, as "sign of divine ownership." Hosch analyzes all of the occurrences from the perspective of discourse analysis into one of eight different semantic domains: "movement of air; vigor of life; attitudes and emotions; psychological faculties; thought; punishment, reward; spatial orientation; supernatural beings."[72]

For the most part, the work of analysis is considered complete when each instance has been allocated to a particular category and discussed. A notable exception to this is the recent article by Kinlaw.[73] She explores the use of רוח in Ezekiel from the perspective of what can be gleaned by an ideal reader engaging with the "expanding symbol" of רוח that gains meaning with each occurrence.[74] In the article, she works through the text through the lenses of רוח, charting each occurrence in order, and examining how this symbol is functioning for the reader in this context. Her work can be illustrated by observing what she concludes that an ideal reader would derive from the opening three chapters of Ezekiel:

> the רוח, an essence as powerful as a stormy wind that conveys a vision of God from an open heaven, can enter not only into inanimate objects to provide movement, but can also enter into a human being. Yet, some tension rises from a series of paradoxes. How can something like a stormy wind enter into a human being? What is this רוח already present in the prophet? Also, in what direction will this movement take God's presence, associated with רוח by the close occurrence to it of both hand [*sic*] and the glory of God? Does the prophet's message of judgment say to the reader that the repetition of רוח should evoke only associations of condemnation? The reader's tension builds.[75]

69. Zimmerli, *Ezekiel 2*, 566–68.
70. Joyce, *Divine Initiative*, 109–11.
71. See the diagram in Block, "Prophet of the Spirit," 29.
72. Hosch, "*RŪAḤ* in the Book of Ezekiel," 83.
73. Kinlaw, "From Death to Life."
74. Ibid., 163.
75. Ibid., 166.

Although her aim of synthesizing and relating all the occurrences is a creative and important attempt at integration, it is doubtful whether רוח would be the dominant symbol upon which a reader would be focusing. There is a danger by concentrating analysis on רוח that wider concerns of the book are not allowed to affect interpretation of רוח as a symbol. In addition, would an ideal reader naturally relate all the occurrences in this way? For example, is the shift in gender in ch. 1 a clue to difference, not merely similarity? Further, the literary approach that she adopts is more imperialistic than a reading strategy, for she believes that the book's "textual history is complex enough to effectively obscure the actual author and the original audience."[76] This necessarily ahistorical approach enables her effectively to ignore her ideal reader's pre-understanding of רוח. Speaking, however, of an ideal reader demands an understanding of how one would know what the ideal reader would have gleaned. This in turn demands a particular historical context.

2.4. *Study of Word and* רוח *in Ezekiel*
When we turn our attention to those works that give particular attention to the relationship between Yahweh's word and Yahweh's רוח in Ezekiel, broadly speaking, they do so from one of two perspectives.

2.4.1. *Ezekiel and the prophetic spirit.* First, there is the perspective of
Ezekiel and the prophetic רוח. Several studies look at רוח-inspiration in Ezekiel against the wider backdrop of רוח-inspiration within Old Testament prophecy. Some draw attention to the continuity between Ezekiel, on the one hand, and the pre-classical prophets, on the other, in the emphasis on רוח within their prophetic ministry.[77] Others highlight the discontinuity between Ezekiel, with his experience of רוח, and the classical prophets, with their remarkable reticence in speaking of רוח.[78]

---

76. Ibid., 164 n. 21.
77. Zimmerli, "Special Form- and Traditio-Historical Character"; idem, *Ezekiel 1*, 42–43; Carley, *Ezekiel Among the Prophets*.
78. Volz, *Der Geist Gottes*, 62–69; Sigmund Mowinckel, "The 'Spirit' and the 'Word' in the Pre-Exilic Reforming Prophets," *JBL* 53 (1934): 199–227; repr. in *The Spirit and the Word: Prophecy and Tradition in Ancient Israel* (ed. K. C. Hanson; Minneapolis: Fortress, 2002); idem, "A Postscript to the Paper 'The Spirit and the Word in the Pre-Exilic Reforming Prophets,'" *JBL* 56 (1937): 261–65. A similar view has been put forward more recently by both Scharbert and Couturier; see Josef Scharbert, "Der 'Geist' und die Schriftpropheten," in *Der Weg zum Menschen: Zur philosophischen und theologischen Anthropologie* (ed. Rudolf Mosis and Lothar Ruppert; Freiburg: Herder, 1989), 82–97; Guy Couturier, "L'Esprit de Yahweh et la Fonction Prophétique en Israël," *Science et Esprit* 42 (1990): 129–65.

All of these studies contribute in different ways to the controversial question of the place of רוח within Old Testament prophetic activity. Certainly later theology places all the activity of a prophet wholly under the influence of the divine רוח, whether in the Old Testament (Neh 9:30), in the New Testament (2 Pet 1:20–21) or in Church history. Aquinas writes:

> in prophetic revelation, the mind of the prophet is moved by the Holy Spirit, just like an instrument deficient in view of its principal agent. Moreover, the mind of the prophet is not only moved towards something to be laid hold of, but also towards something to be said, or towards something to be done; and sometimes indeed to all three at the same time; sometimes, however, to two of these; sometimes, in fact, to one only.[79]

The matter, however, is not straightforward. Among scholars, there is divergent opinion on the nature of the relationship, and the reasons for that relationship (if there is one). Kaufmann has commented, particularly with reference to word, spirit and prophecy, that "there is no biblical doctrine of the relationship between the word and the spirit."[80] For him, there is no direct relationship between the working of the divine רוח and the prophetic reception or delivery of the divine word. More specific, and more influential, has been the article of Mowinckel, in which he argues that the pre-exilic classical prophets repudiated רוח and attributed their prophetic consciousness and message to Yahweh's word.[81] Ma, on the other hand, asserts that "the prophetic inspiration of the spirit of God throughout the Old Testament is for the preaching of Yahweh's word"[82] and that, after a relative absence of such prophetic inspiration in the pre-exilic classical prophets, "it is only after the fall of Jerusalem that the idea receives a revived emphasis as seen in Ezekiel."[83] Such an emphasis in Ezekiel is usually then seen as part of the prophet's conscious echoing of pre-classical prophecy, in order to authenticate his own inspired ministry.[84]

---

79. *Summa Theologiae* IIaIIae, q.173, a.4. "…in revelatione prophetica movetur mens prophetae a Spiritu Sancto, sicut instrumentum deficiens respectu principalis agentis. Movetur autem mens prophetae non solum ad aliquid apprehendum, sed etiam ad aliquid loquendum, vel ad aliquid faciendum; et quandoque quidem ad omnia tria simul; quandoque autem ad duo horum; quandoque vero ad unum tantum."

80. Yehezkel Kaufmann, *The Religion of Israel: From Its Beginnings to the Babylonian Exile* (trans. and ed. Moshe Greenberg; London: George Allen & Unwin, 1961), 101.

81. Mowinckel, "The 'Spirit' and the 'Word.'"

82. Ma, *Until the Spirit Comes*, 121.

83. Ibid., 135; so too Tengström, *ThWAT* 7:394.

84. Zimmerli, "Special Form- and Traditio-Historical Character"; idem, *Ezekiel 1*, 42–43; Carley, *Ezekiel Among the Prophets*.

2.4.2. Ezekiel and the transforming spirit. The other perspective exploring the relationship between Yahweh's word and Yahweh's רוח examines the role of Yahweh's רוח in the transformation of the recipients of Yahweh's word from being despondent and lifeless exiles in Babylon to being a believing people, back in the land, obedient to Yahweh's word. Generally speaking, these studies integrate discussions of רוח with wider reflection on the book of Ezekiel and its theology or anthropology. In particular, they reflect on the contrast between the promise of a new רוח as a gift from Yahweh (11:19; 36:26) and the call to the exiles to get for themselves a new רוח (18:31). Not all, though, have explicit focus on the relationship between word and רוח, focusing instead more on the contrast than the role of רוח.

For Raitt, in his study on the preaching of Jeremiah and Ezekiel, this contrast is best explained in terms of a development over time in the preaching of Ezekiel from the preaching of repentance to inevitable annihilation to unconditional salvation.[85]

For Matties, in his study on the ethics of Ezekiel, there is particular emphasis on human responsibility as seen in the call to repentance in 18:31, which he regards as an ongoing call that needs to be heard alongside the promise of divine salvation. Ezekiel 18 speaks of the "liminal moment between Ezekiel's harsh announcements of judgment and his bold eschatological vision."[86] At this moment, it is "an attempt to shape a moral community...it envisions the possibility for transformation and reconstitution. Its task is to nurture the formation of a peoplehood."[87]

Joyce, on the other hand, in his study of the relationship between divine sovereignty and human responsibility in Ezekiel, concludes, after lucidly rebutting the notion that Ezekiel's prime contribution is as the innovator of individual responsibility, that the book exhibits "radical theocentricity" such that "the responsibility of Israel has been subsumed in the overriding initiative of Yahweh."[88] If Matties concludes by giving significant place to human responsibility, Joyce ends by accentuating divine sovereignty.

For Renz, calls to repentance cannot be consigned to a different stage in the prophet's ministry, but are explicable in terms of different addressees.[89] Within Ezekiel the book, these calls remain in force, but not

85. Thomas M. Raitt, *A Theology of Exile: Judgment/Deliverance in Jeremiah and Ezekiel* (Philadelphia: Fortress, 1977).
86. Gordon H. Matties, *Ezekiel 18 and the Rhetoric of Moral Discourse* (SBLDS 126; Atlanta: Scholars Press, 1990), 224.
87. Ibid., 219.
88. Joyce, *Divine Initiative*, 89, 127.
89. Renz, *Rhetorical Function*, 73.

in such a way that human responsibility displaces Yahweh's "initia-tive."[90] In his discussion of Ezek 37, Renz makes clear that רוח comes in and through the divine word spoken through Ezekiel, bringing life.[91]

Mein, in his study of ethics in Ezekiel, argues that a study of biblical ethics needs to take account of social context.[92] The "dual focus" on both Jerusalem and Babylon found in the book makes sense when it is recog-nized that Ezekiel's addressees are the Jerusalem élite. The élite's con-cern for, and past involvement in, foreign policy and the cult account for oracles proclaiming judgment on Jerusalem, while oracles focusing on the disempowered exiles "ritualize" ethics by extending the language associated with the temple and "domesticate" sin, focusing particularly on the individual and the family. This "dual focus" enables Mein to see the calls to repentance in chs. 14 and 18, in particular, as genuine calls. Nonetheless, the life that is envisaged here should not be confused with the life that is promised in the later salvation oracles.

Lapsley explores precisely the same tension between calls to repen-tance, on the one hand, and declarations that Yahweh will act unilaterally to bring about salvation (compare 11:19; 36:26 with 18:31).[93] Instead of focusing on issues of theology, though, she concentrates instead on what she sees as two conflicting views of human moral identity. On the one hand, there is what she terms "virtuous moral selfhood," whereby "people are assumed to be inherently capable of making moral decisions that accord with a vision of the good, which for Ezekiel is always cotermi-nous with Yahweh's will (most often manifested by *torah*)."[94] This is evidenced by the language of repentance in several chapters (chs. 3; 14; 18; 33). On the other hand, there is what she terms "neutral moral self-hood," whereby "people are inherently incapable of acting in accord with the good."[95] This is apparent from the language of determinism, espe-cially in chs. 16; 20; 23; 24. Within the book of Ezekiel, she discerns a shift in Ezekiel's conception of human moral identity, which cannot be reduced to a simple chronological shift within the book, and which has two aspects. First, there is a shift in origin of this identity, "from being inherent in human beings to existing only as a potential gift from God."[96]

---

90. Ibid., 113.
91. Ibid., 199–209.
92. Andrew Mein, *Ezekiel and the Ethics of Exile* (Oxford Theological Mono-graphs; Oxford: Oxford University Press, 2001).
93. Jacqueline E. Lapsley, *Can These Bones Live? The Problem of the Moral Self in the Book of Ezekiel* (BZAW 301; Berlin: de Gruyter, 2000).
94. Ibid., 185.
95. Ibid.
96. Ibid., 186.

Secondly, there is a shift in form, from a moral selfhood focused on action to a moral selfhood focused on knowledge.

While these studies make a particular contribution to the vexing question of calls to repentance in the context of declarations of Yahweh's monergistic action, a slightly different perspective is provided by those studies that focus particularly on the (re-)creative dimension of רוח, and how that relates to moral renewal.[97] Some of these begin to make connections between the prophetic רוח and the transforming רוח,[98] but there has been no thorough exploration. This study aims to fill this gap.

3. *The Central Argument*

Having surveyed the current scene, I am now in a position to articulate clearly the central claim of this book. The relationship between Yahweh's רוח and Yahweh's word in the book of Ezekiel is to be understood not so much in terms of the inspiration and authentication of the prophet but in terms of the transformation of the book's addressees.

The claim is both negative and positive. Negatively, the relationship between Yahweh's רוח and Yahweh's word in the book of Ezekiel is to be understood not so much in terms of the inspiration and authentication of the prophet. In other words, I shall be arguing that perhaps the dominant paradigm for explaining the emphasis on Yahweh's רוח and its relation to Yahweh's word within the book of Ezekiel is inadequate. According to this paradigm, the prophet Ezekiel is recovering an emphasis on רוח in prophecy from the pre-classical prophets, or even pioneering an emphasis that has been conspicuously absent from the classical, writing prophets. Such an emphasis on in Ezekiel is usually understood, on this reading, in terms of the self-authentication of the ministry of the prophet.

Positively, the relationship between Yahweh's רוח and Yahweh's word in the book of Ezekiel is to be understood...in terms of the transformation of its addressees. In other words, the emphasis on Yahweh's רוח, even the "prophetic spirit," is best understood within the overall function of the book, which is concerned for the transformation of the addressees. In particular, I shall be arguing that the prophet Ezekiel's experience of Yahweh's רוח and his own obedience to Yahweh's call are clearly contrasted with the disobedience of the prophet's addressees in order to present Ezekiel as a model for the addressees of the book. His

---

97. See, e.g., Lys, *Rûach*, 128–42; Schüngel-Straumann, *Rûaḥ bewegt die Welt*; Sklba, "Until the Spirit."

98. E.g. Schüngel-Straumann, *Rûaḥ bewegt die Welt*, 65; Sklba, "Until the Spirit," 14; Kinlaw, "From Death to Life," 170.

experience will illuminate for them not just *that*, but also *how* the dramatic vision of the future can become a reality in their experience. This proposal for the function of the book also provides a different perspective on the conundrum of the presence of calls to repentance within the book being found alongside Yahweh's apparently unilateral actions to bring about the salvation of the exiles. Yahweh's רוח has a fundamental role in the envisaged obedient response to Yahweh's word. The action of Yahweh's רוח is the bridge between the present and the future. This approach serves to integrate many of the occurrences of רוח in the book which are usually kept separate. Further, it illuminates the role of the prophetic persona, not merely as the vehicle through which Yahweh's words come to the people, but also as the embodiment of those words.

The present study will therefore proceed in three main parts. In the rest of Part I, I shall look in detail at where Yahweh's word can be found within the book of Ezekiel, and at how it should be conceived. I shall also look, more briefly given the fact that some occurrences will be treated in greater depth in Part II and Part III, at the different occurrences of רוח within the book, with a view to categorizing them and identifying those instances where interpreters disagree.

In Part II, I shall examine what is probably the dominant paradigm for interpreting the relationship between word and spirit in the book of Ezekiel— that of the inspiration and authentication of the prophet. Since such a paradigm is typically associated with a particular perspective on the relationship between word and spirit through Israel's history, Part II will explore the relationship between word, spirit and the inspiration of the prophet, in terms of possible historical developments. I shall argue that the book of Ezekiel, in its emphasis on רוח, is less concerned with authenticating the prophet than is often supposed.

In Part III, I shall propose a different conceptual framework for the link between Yahweh's word and spirit within the book. In particular, I shall maintain that the prophet portrayed in the book has, in addition to the customary proclamatory role, a paradigmatic one to the readers of the book. Through examining the role of Yahweh's רוח in the programmatic 36:26–27, 37:1–14 and 39:21–29, I shall argue that the prophet himself is a prescriptive paradigm of the transformation necessary for the addressees of the book. The book of Ezekiel, and the emphasis on Yahweh's רוח within the book, is more concerned with the transformation of the people in obedience to the word of Yahweh. Yahweh brings about the transformation of his people through the cooperation of word and רוח.

I shall finish by reviewing the main arguments and conclusions, and by considering the contribution that this study makes both to the study of Ezekiel and to the study of רוח in the Old Testament.

Chapter 2

EXPLORING WORD AND SPIRIT IN EZEKIEL

In this chapter, I explore two principal foci for my study. First, I shall examine the different possible communication situations in which the word of Yahweh can be discerned, exploring in the process some issues surrounding the different possible relationships of different groups to the word of Yahweh. If we are to see how Yahweh's רוח is related to Yahweh's word, we need to see where that word is found, and how it should be understood. We will look at the dating and provenance of the book of Ezekiel, since Part II explores the contribution of the book of Ezekiel within the framework of historical development. Secondly, I shall look at the different instances of רוח in the book of Ezekiel chiefly through the lenses of four writers to provide a necessary orientation to the debate that will follow in the subsequent chapters, and to discuss in more detail those occurrences which will not be prominent in the rest of the book.

With regard to the first, I shall argue that it is possible to discern four distinct communication situations in which Yahweh can be said to be the speaker. I shall argue that the final communication situation envisaged is that of the book of Ezekiel to its addressees in exile in Babylon. Further, I shall also seek to demonstrate that insights from speech act theory can help illuminate some of the different possible relationships to the (same) word of Yahweh that different groups might have.

With regard to the second, the distinction between theological, anthropological and meteorological senses of רוח is not always as easy to maintain as some studies might suggest. Works that look only at the theological use of רוח can miss some of the force and interplay of the other instances.

1. *Yahweh's Word in Ezekiel*

Although it is possible to take Yahweh's word in the sense of the *message* of the book of Ezekiel, a summary of the argument or theology,[1] our

---

1. Walther Zimmerli, "The Word of God in the Book of Ezekiel," in *History and Hermeneutic* (ed. R. W. Funk; JTC 4; New York: Harper & Row, 1967), 3–13.

task is to focus more closely on places where Yahweh's word functions as a "speech event"[2] with Yahweh as the speaker. Thus, I am using the "word" of Yahweh in a narrower sense than "message," but I am also using it in a broader sense, for my focus is not limited to prophetic discourse, but embraces every communication situation in which a speech event features Yahweh as the speaker. There are four communications, four possible "speech events," which require our attention:

1. Yahweh addressing Ezekiel;
2. Ezekiel addressing his audience;
3. Yahweh's ordinances and statutes;
4. the book of Ezekiel itself.

For each of these possible speech events, I shall look at how these different communications can be understood as speech events, and to what extent Yahweh can be understood as the speaker. After exploring each one of these four, I shall turn my attention to the question of the recipients of these speech events, in order to illuminate further our understanding of each event as a whole. It is only when we have explored the different speech events in which Yahweh can be said to be the agent that we will be in a position to see how Yahweh's רוח relates to each of those events.

1.1. *Yahweh Addressing Ezekiel*
Ezekiel the book is dominated by Yahweh's dealings with the prophet, both in the giving of visions, and in the giving of his word. Central to an understanding both of what it means for Yahweh to address Ezekiel, and of the significance of that address, is the word-event formula, "the word of Yahweh came to me, saying…" (and variations on this), which dominates the book's articulation of the coming of Yahweh's word to the prophet.[3] After assessing this formula, I shall look at how the visions

---

2. Yule, *Pragmatics*, 57: "A speech event is an activity in which participants interact via language in some conventional way to arrive at some outcome."

3. For more on דבר יהוה in general, and on the "word-event" formula in particular, see J. Bergman, et al., "דְּבַר *dābhar*; דָּבָר *dābhār*," *TDOT* 3:84–125; Frank R. Ames, "דְּבָר," *NIDOTTE* 1:912–15; G. Gerleman, "דָּבָר *dābār* word," *TLOT* 1:325–32; Klaus Koch, "The Language of Prophecy: Thoughts on the Macrosyntax of the *děbar YHWH* and Its Semantic Implications in the Deuteronomistic History," in *Problems in Biblical Theology: Essays in Honour of Rolf Knierim* (ed. Henry T. C. Sun et al.; Grand Rapids: Eerdmans, 1997), 210–21. For a nuanced discussion of introducing direct discourse in Ezekiel and the "word-event" formula, see especially Samuel A. Meier, *Speaking of Speaking: Marking Direct Discourse in the Hebrew Bible* (VTSup 46; Leiden: Brill, 1992), 230–42, 314–19. For discussion of the theology of the "word of God," see von Rad, *Old Testament Theology*, 2:80–98; Eichrodt, *Theology*, 2:69–79; Preuss, *Old Testament Theology*, 1:195–200; 2:73–81.

Ezekiel receives relate to Yahweh's word, in order to develop a coherent picture of what it means for Yahweh to address Ezekiel.

1.1.1. *The word-event formula.* In this section, I shall focus the discussion around two questions: first, the question of what it means to speak of "the word of Yahweh" (דבר יהוה) as found in the formula, and, secondly, the question of what the significance of the formula itself is. Under this second question we shall look at the distribution of the formula within prophetic literature and some explanations of this distribution, the question of in what way this formula speaks of an "event," the related question of whether the "word" is to be regarded as an hypostasis, and, finally, issues around the reception, audibility and form of the word.

The word-event formula occurs fifty times within the book, exclusively in chs. 1–39. It almost always introduces "a new speech section."[4] Apart from 1:3, where it is a redactional description in the third person of what happened to Ezekiel, it is always a first-person account of Ezekiel's reception of Yahweh's word, and it precedes direct discourse by Yahweh. In what we might call its purest form (ויהי דבר־יהוה אלי לאמר), the same phrase occurs thirty-nine times. There are another ten instances, with some variation. Some of these include a date (in particular those which introduce the introduce some of the oracles against the nations[5]); another instance includes a time (12:8, "in the morning"); on one occasion, 24:20, the phrase is set in a narrative context, with Ezekiel explaining his behaviour to the exiles after his wife has died.

Central to the word-event formula is "the word of Yahweh" (דבר יהוה). The phrase occurs around 225 times in the Old Testament, and has been characterized as "a technical term for the prophetic word of *revelation.*"[6] Internal evidence within the book of Ezekiel for understanding the phrase as a technical term can be derived from the lack of variation in wording. The robustness of the formulaic saying as a whole, and in particular the phrase "word of Yahweh," against variation is apparent from the fact that two other major formulae, the "citation" formula (כה אמר יהוה, "Thus Yahweh declares") and the "signatory" formula (נאם יהוה, "the declaration of Yahweh"), both have a distinctive wording in the book of Ezekiel, with יהוה אלהים usually replacing יהוה.[7] On no

4. Zimmerli, *Ezekiel 1*, 144.

5. Ezek 26:1; 29:1, 17; 30:20; 31:1; 32:1, 17; other dated instances of Yahweh's word coming are 1:3; 3:16; 20:1–2; 24:1; 33:21–23.

6. O. Grether, *Name und Word Gottes im alten Testament* (BZAW 64; Giessen: Töpelmann, 1934), 66, 76, cited in Bergman et al., *TDOT* 3:111 (my emphasis).

7. Cf. Zimmerli, *Ezekiel 2*, 556–62 (Appendix 1). He comments (p. 558) that the distinction between Jeremiah and Ezekiel "shows that the two books in their present

occasion, however, in the book of Ezekiel (or in the Old Testament as a whole) does the word-event formula have the double designation of the divine name, "the word of *the Lord Yahweh* came to me…saying…"[8] The same effect is also observable in Jeremiah. The phrase "Yahweh of Hosts" (יהוה צבאות) occurs more than seventy times, but never in connection with Yahweh's word, yielding "the word of Yahweh of Hosts" (דבר יהוה צבאות). On the other hand, the phrase "the word of Yahweh" (דבר יהוה) occurs more than sixty times in Jeremiah, but it remains untouched by the distinctive Jeremianic divine appellation.

Two cautions, though, need to be levelled against the characterization above. First, in view of the limited occurrence of the word-event formula (and the phrase דבר יהוה) in many prophetic books, an understanding of דבר יהוה as a technical term should clearly be carefully circumscribed. It is a characteristic mark only of some prophets in some prophetic books. Further, the phrase "word of X" is not exclusive to prophets or prophetic books, but is a commonplace for the word of a king (e.g. 2 Kgs 18:28, "'Hear the word of the great king, the king of Assyria!'"), or indeed of a person with authority in the Old Testament (e.g. 1 Sam 4:1, "And the word of Samuel came to all Israel"). Meier notes how "other cultures elsewhere in the ancient Near East also employed the same figure of speech to describe the dictates of gods and kings."[9] Its usage as a technical term is illuminated by its use in more ordinary contexts, where it "connoted an authoritative communication."[10]

Secondly, the "word of Yahweh" should not be associated more with "revelation" as a theological category than with divine speech.[11] Thiselton points out that the concept of revelation "*directs attention to propositional content*, but so pervasively as to leave no room for questions about propositional *force*."[12] In the book of Ezekiel, the focus is very much on "propositional *force*." The word is Yahweh's speech *addressed to the prophet*, or, in the case of the call-to-attention formula, "hear the word of

form come from quite different tradition circles and, in spite of all the points of contact, are not to be attributed overhastily to related editing."

8.   There are only three instances of the phrase "the word of the Lord Yahweh" (דבר־אדני יהוה), all in Ezekiel (6:3; 25:3; 36:4). They all occur in the phrase "hear the word of the Lord Yahweh."

9.   Meier, *Speaking of Speaking*, 316.

10.   Ibid., 319.

11.   For a cogent argument on the difference between the two, see Nicholas Wolterstorff, *Divine Discourse: Philosophical Reflections on the Claim That God Speaks* (Cambridge: Cambridge University Press, 1995), 19–36 (Chapter 2).

12.   Anthony C. Thiselton, "Speech-Act Theory and the Claim that God Speaks: Nicholas Wolterstorff's *Divine Discourse*," *SJT* 50 (1997): 101 (original emphasis).

Yahweh," it is the prophet addressing his audience.[13] The word of Yahweh is Yahweh's particular word to a particular situation, as is emphasized by the dates given throughout the book, a word of address which
cannot be reduced to the concept of revelation.[14] The book of Ezekiel
makes clear that what follows is nothing other than what Yahweh says.

The word-event formula is not unique to the book of Ezekiel. If the
significant elements are the phrase דבר יהוה, the verb היה and the marker
of direct discourse, לאמר, there a number of parallels and distinctions
from other Old Testament books.[15]

In some of the books, these three elements do not appear at all
together; indeed, the verb היה is not used with דבר יהוה to describe the
prophetic event (Amos, Obadiah, Nahum, Habakkuk, Malachi). In some
of the books, the phrase דבר יהוה and the verb היה occur together only
in the third person and only in the redactional headings (Hos 1:1; Joel
1:1; Mic 1:1; Zeph 1:1); they do not introduce individual oracles (i.e. the
third element, marking direct discourse, is absent). The only prophetic
books apart from Ezekiel where the three elements combine to introduce
direct discourse to a prophet are Jeremiah, Haggai[16] and Zechariah (though
they do occur in Jonah 1:1 and 3:1, but Jonah is narrative; see below for
Isaiah). Of these, the first person form that is almost universal in Ezekiel is to be found on ten occasions in the book of Jeremiah.[17] Subsequently, the only occurrences of the first person form are in the book of
Zechariah.[18]

13. Though this too is subsumed within the word of Yahweh to the prophet, since
the voice of Ezekiel is rarely heard in the book as an independent element, other than
as the narrator.

14. See Claus Westermann, *Elements of Old Testament Theology* (trans. D. W.
Scott; Atlanta: John Knox, 1982), 24–25. See also Zimmerli, *Ezekiel 1*, 145, and
Mowinckel, "A Postscript to the Paper," 264. All three writers stress this historical
and particular nature of the divine word. Westermann (*Elements*, 24) goes so far as
to say that the word "cannot be separated out of this history as something God said.
The Old Testament knows nothing of an abstracted, objectified word of God, and
that is why the word of God in the Old Testament cannot become a doctrine." Were
he correct, then there would be no justification for the word being retained, edited
and reapplied for subsequent generations.

15. See especially Meier, *Speaking of Speaking*, 314–19, for what follows.

16. Though in only two of the five occurrences is the word said to come *to*
Haggai, as opposed to *through* him (ביד־חגי) (Hag 2:10, 20). The other three
instances (1:1, 3; 2:1) stress the agency of Haggai in speaking to Haggai's
addressees, merging the prophetic and rhetorical events.

17. Jer 1:4, 11, 13; 2:1; 13:3, 8; 16:1; 18:5; 24:4; 32:6 (cf. 25:3). There are thirty
instances altogether within Jeremiah of the word of Yahweh coming to the prophet.

18. Zech 4:8; 6:9; 7:4; 8:18; cf. the third person forms in 1:7; 7:8; 8:1.

In the book of Isaiah, there are two instances where the phrase דבר יהוה and the verb היה occur together in the context of the word of Yahweh coming to people, followed directly by Yahweh's speech. In 28:13, strikingly, the word comes not to prophets, but to the people as a whole. Meier plausibly suggests that "its appearance in this isolated piece of poetry…points to the actual significance the phrase had before it became a stereotypical marker used by some prophets to identify a communication from God. Here it simply refers to an authoritative directive issued to insubordinate Israelites."[19] In 38:4, the three elements *are* present in a situation where Yahweh's word comes to a prophet (Isaiah), but it is likely that they occur here because the section is borrowed from Kings, where the formula is often to be found (e.g. 1 Kgs 13:20, of the northern prophet who invited home the man of God who came from Judah; 1 Kgs 16:1, of Jehu;[20] 1 Kgs 17:2, of Elijah; 2 Kgs 20:4, of Isaiah).[21]

Outside the prophetic literature identified above and Kings, these three elements are hardly to be found together. Within Genesis to Judges, they only occur together in Gen 15:1 (though Gen 15:4 should be noted, where there is the deictic והנה instead of היה). In Samuel, they occur together in three places (1 Sam 15:10, of the word coming to Samuel; 2 Sam 7:4, to Nathan; 2 Sam 24:1, to Gad, David's seer). These elements are also sparingly present in Chronicles, from sources in 1 Chr 17:3 (parallel to 2 Sam 7:4, though with רוח־אלהים) and 2 Chr 11:2 (parallel to 1 Kgs 12:22), but otherwise in only two places (1 Chr 22:8, of David; 2 Chr 12:7, of Shemaiah).[22]

Thus, this way of speaking about Yahweh addressing a prophet is by no means universal, even within prophetic literature. At the same time, the prominence of this way of speaking in the particular works identified above should not be surprising given the similar "temporal horizon" of the sixth century when the phrase "word of X" was used "as the introductory (and not repeated) words in official communiques [*sic*]."[23]

---

19. Meier, *Speaking of Speaking*, 319.

20. Though strikingly in 1 Kgs 16:7, Jehu becomes the invisible mediator, as the word of Yahweh (דבר־יהוה) comes (היה) to King Baasha and his house by the hand of Jehu.

21. So Meier, *Speaking of Speaking*, 315. Other instances in Kings where the main elements occur, marking divine speech, are 1 Kgs 6:11 (to Solomon); 1 Kgs 12:22 (to Shemaiah; with דבר האלהים); 1 Kgs 17:8; 18:1; 19:9 (with והנה instead of היה); 21:17, 28 (to Elijah); 1 Kgs 18:31, to Jacob.

22. Ibid.

23. Ibid., 319.

This largely socio-temporal explanation for the profile of occurrences has not been the only one. Wilson, in particular, has advanced a socio-geographical explanation which has significant bearing on the relationship between word and רוח.[24] For him, the particular emphasis on the "word of Yahweh" characterized Ephraimite prophetic tradition, and serves as evidence that they "regarded spirit possession as the most common means of inspiration."[25] In other words, the use of such modes of expression entails a prophetic self-understanding of רוח-possession, without רוח ever necessarily being mentioned. Were this true, there would be a conspicuous, continuous link between Yahweh's רוח and word running throughout much of the prophetic literature. Wilson reaches this conclusion by extrapolating from the observation that within "contemporary intermediation, possession theories are usually characterised by the belief that the possessing spirit takes control of the intermediary and speaks directly through him, with the result that the speech of the intermediary is actually the speech of the spirit,"[26] though ultimately he insists his understanding is based on exegesis, not contemporary sociology or anthropology.[27] Since there is a similar emphasis on "direct divine speech" within the Ephraimite prophetic tradition, as evidenced by "the tendency to describe prophecy as the reception and delivery of the word of God,"[28] this is, for him, conclusive evidence that "the Ephraimites regarded possession involving God's speaking as the normal form of intermediation."[29] Certainly רוח-inspiration is found explicitly among Ephraimite prophets, such as Elijah and the prophets in 1 Kgs 22. One difficulty, however, with such a conception is the fact that the difference between Ephraimite and Judaean traditions with regard to רוח-inspiration is not as clear as Wilson portrays. The most obvious exception to his viewpoint is Ezekiel, where, as we have seen, emphasis on the "word of Yahweh" is great. It is true that he recognizes and tries to account for the book of Ezekiel's Deuteronomic characteristics.[30] There is, though, only

24. Wilson, *Prophecy and Society*.

25. Ibid., 144; cf. also Susan Niditch, "Ezekiel 40–48 in a Visionary Context," *CBQ* 48 (1986): 208–24. For Niditch (p. 208), Ezekiel is like "a spirit medium" because in so many of his actions he "looks like those whom traditional societies consider to be possessed by the divine, a mouthpiece for the deity, a bridge between heaven and earth."

26. Wilson, *Prophecy and Society*, 145.

27. Ibid., 16.

28. Ibid., 145.

29. Ibid., 146.

30. He does not attribute these to a Deuteronomic redaction of Ezekiel, since he regards the Ephraimite portrayal of Ezekiel (i.e. a prophet like Moses to whom

one reference beyond the superscription to "the word of Yahweh" in the Ephraimite Hosea (Hos 4:1). Further, Jeremiah is very reticent to speak about the role of רוח within prophecy, so it is rather too speculative to regard the opening formula in Jer 1:2 as a "typical Ephraimite superscription indicating that the prophet received his revelations when he was possessed by Yahweh's spirit."[31]

Although the presence of dates and other modifiers to the word-event formula indicates a narrowing of the speech event to a particular point, this does not mean the event should be over-dramatized or over-interpreted. So again Meier observes that "the use of 'word' in conjunction with the verb 'to be' is actually quite underwhelming in its banality in the light of usage in Akkadian and Hebrew," because many more colourful fientive verbs, such as "seize" or "arrive" or "reach," are predicated of "word."[32] Indeed, in 1 Sam 4:1, the verb-form ויהי and the phrase דבר־שמואל occur together to describe the event of *Samuel's* word going to all Israel.

Consequently, we should not see in the word-event formula the hypostatization of the word. Zimmerli's claim that, "instead of a direct encounter by the personal address of God, the 'word' is understood almost as an objective entity with its own power of entry,"[33] reads too much into the phrase, given what we have observed above about the "banality" of the verb "to be."[34] In addition, in Ezekiel there is not always a consistent mediation of the word between Yahweh and the prophet. On occasions, Yahweh speaks directly with the prophet, without "the word" mediating (2:2, 8; 3:10, 24; cf. 22:28).[35]

---

elders come and inquire; intercession is forbidden to him) as present in every layer. Thus, for Wilson (ibid., 284–85), Ezekiel had Deuteronomic influence on him before being exiled, though he retains a distinctive Zadokite element. What is found is Ezekiel's "own personal synthesis."

31. Ibid., 235; cf. p. 226 for a similar statement about Hosea. Carroll questions the "appropriateness of fit between spirit possession cults and biblical prophecy" because "spirit possession seems to be a minor element in the prophetic texts." See Robert P. Carroll, "Prophecy and Society," in *The World of Ancient Israel: Sociological, Anthropological and Political Perspectives* (ed. R. E. Clements; Cambridge: Cambridge University Press, 1989), 218. See Part II below for the relationship between word, רוח and inspiration.

32. Meier, *Speaking of Speaking*, 317.

33. Zimmerli, *Ezekiel 1*, 145. For the question of hypostatization, see Bergman et al., *TDOT* 3:120–21; Gerleman, *TLOT* 1:331–32.

34. For the question of the inherent power of a word, as opposed to hypostatization, see further Chapter 6 below.

35. See Greenberg, *Ezekiel 1–20*, 83–84.

Speaking of the word coming "directly" to the prophet, or of Yahweh "addressing" the prophet, raises questions about the mode of reception, audibility, and the form which the word took.

It appears that the word was a private word, in the sense it was not immediately publicly available. When the elders visited the prophet (14:1; 20:1), the "word of Yahweh" came to Ezekiel. There is no evidence that the elders heard it before Ezekiel addressed them; indeed, Yahweh's address is explicitly to Ezekiel in the first person, instructing him on what to say to the elders (14:3–4; 20:3). Such a perspective is reinforced by the reticence inherent in the word-event formula, for, "although the content is specified as verbal (דבר יהוה)," the phrase "retreats from the position that God's voice is heard, for it obscures any precision—God's word simply happened."[36] While the word was inaudible to onlookers, the book characterizes Ezekiel's subjective impression of the words of Yahweh as objective speech.[37] Such characterization is not restricted to Ezekiel "hearing" Yahweh's voice in the context of visions, though it is present there (1:28b; 2:2; 3:24; 8:5, 9). In 3:17, Ezekiel is told that he will hear a word from Yahweh's mouth, and that he, as a watchman, is to utter it. Further, his certainty in the face of hardheartedness (2:7), unbelief (12:21–28), scorn (21:5 [ET 20:49]) and apathy (33:30–33) points to a profound experience of something that, though probably internal, must have *seemed to him* to have been objective. If the prophet did not believe that the words were objective, his critique of the false prophets, that they prophesy out of their own "imagination" (מלבם, 13:2) or "follow their own spirit" (הלכים אחר רוחם, 13:3) would have been both duplicitous and erroneous.[38]

1.1.2. *Summary*. It is preferable to see in the book's use of the "word of Yahweh," and, in particular, the word-event formula, the self-conscious awareness on the part of Ezekiel, as narrator, of Yahweh *speaking* to him *within history* as an *objective event*. This mirrored both "the old tradition of the prophetic schools,"[39] as seen in the narratives of the early

---

36. Meier, *Speaking of Speaking*, 232.

37. Cf. Lindblom, *Prophecy*, 110; Heschel, *The Prophets*, 2:211: "To the consciousness of the prophet, the prophetic act is more than an experience; it is an objective *event*." For Heschel here, "the prophetic act" is "the act of inspiration," that is, the act of the word coming to the prophet.

38. Cf. Geerhardus Vos, *Biblical Theology: Old and New Testaments* (Grand Rapids: Eerdmans, 1948), 230–48 (especially 232), and Heschel, *Prophets*, 2:190–26.

39. Zimmerli, *Ezekiel 1*, 145; cf. John F. Kutsko, *Between Heaven and Earth: Divine Presence and Absence in the Book of Ezekiel* (Biblical and Judaic Studies 7; Winona Lake, Ind.: Eisenbrauns, 2000), 10.

monarchical prophets (e.g. 1 Sam 15:10; 2 Sam 7:4; 1 Kgs 13:20), and the contemporary practice found in official communiqués. This "word" is not a hypostatic entity, nor is a focus on the "word of Yahweh" necessarily evidence of an underlying belief in spirit possession.

1.1.3. *Visions*. We now turn to Ezekiel's visions. These are important for an analysis of the relationship of Yahweh's רוח to the word of Yahweh coming to the prophet, since Yahweh's רוח at points in the book is explicitly linked with the visions. Kaufmann distinguishes between spirit-inspired visions and the word that comes to the prophet within them: "The spirit of prophecy also prepares him [the prophet] to receive the divine word—to see visions, to hear the divine voice in dreams or ecstatic slumber. But the source of prophecy proper is other than these activities. It is in the revelation of God."[40] In this section, I argue that Ezekiel's visions are not simply vehicles for Yahweh's word to come, but can in themselves be understood as "speech events." Before I can make the case for this, we need first to identify the visions.

Three of the visions, the longest vision complexes, are introduced with the phrase מראות אלהים (1:1–3:15; 8:1–11:25; 40:1–48:35).

The opening vision complex is marked off by the word-event formula in 3:16, and is made up of a report of the vision *per se* in 1:4–28bα, followed by a report of the words Yahweh spoke to commission Ezekiel (though with a brief reversion to visionary encounter in 2:8–3:3 and again in 3:12–15).

The second of these vision complexes introduced by מראות אלהים occurs in chs. 8–11. Although there are clear signs of disjunction within these chapters (e.g. formally, the word-event formula in 11:14; in terms of content, the survival of twenty-six prominent men who ought to be already dead [11:1, 13; cf. 9:3–11]), the chiastic order apparent in 8:1–4 and 11:22–25 clearly marks out the complex as one literary unit.[41]

The third vision occurs in chs. 40–48. Again, there are clear signs of discontinuity, notoriously, one might say, around the pro-Zadokite material in ch. 44 and around the organization of the text in chs. 45–46. Such discontinuities led Tuell to observe, "Attractive as it may be to hold for a single interpretive principle explaining all of chapters 40–48, the text

40. Kaufmann, *Religion of Israel*, 99.
41. Cf. Allen, *Ezekiel 1–19*, 129–37; Block, *Ezekiel 1–24*, 272–76; also Paul M. Joyce, "Dislocation and Adaptation in the Exilic Age and After," in *After the Exile: Essays in Honour of Rex Mason* (ed. John Barton and David J. Reimer; Macon, Ga.: Mercer University Press, 1996), 49–50.

itself is too vague, too disparate in nature, too haphazardly presented for such a single-theme approach to be relevant."[42]

Stevenson, however, observes rightly that "interpreters evaluate the visionary character of the text on the basis of their own assumptions about what an 'authentic vision' is supposed to be, whether the vision was a real experience or a literary fiction, whether authentic visions contain legislation, and so on."[43] As it stands, the text has been put together as a narrative account of a vision. It is with this perspective, rather than with an emphasis on its redactional history, that chs. 40–48 need to be understood as "visions given by God." Within this, there are descriptions of what the prophet saw and what the prophet heard.

The fourth visionary encounter to be identified, the second that occurs in the book, is in 3:22–5:17.[44] The end of the unit is marked by the word-event formula in 6:1. Allen observes that the pattern followed here mirrors that in 1:1–3:15, with an "introductory divine vision (3:22–24a)... followed by a divine speech (3:24b–5:17)."[45] Although a number of scholars see 4:1 as the start of a new section,[46] the formulaic markers noted above, and the presence of the "hand of Yahweh" (3:22), which is characteristic of visions in Ezekiel, mark this out as a vision complex, with the vision proper limited to a brief description of Yahweh's glory in v. 23, but within which Yahweh's word comes.[47]

---

42. Steven S. Tuell, "The Temple Vision of Ezekiel 40–48: A Program for Restoration?," *Proceedings Eastern Great Lakes Biblical Society 2* (1982), 98, cited in Stevenson, *The Vision of Transformation*, 6. It is evident from his later book (*The Law of the Temple in Ezekiel 40–48* [HSM 49; Atlanta: Scholars Press, 1992]) that Tuell subsequently changed his mind significantly.

43. Stevenson, *Vision of Transformation*, 157.

44. Zimmerli, "The Special Form- and Traditio-Historical Character," 515. In his commentary, Zimmerli does not identify the unit specifically as a *visionary* encounter, and regards the unit as starting with 3:16a, while 3:16b–21 he treats separately, as a "redactional insertion" (*Ezekiel 1*, 154).

45. Allen, *Ezekiel 1–19*, 55. He regards the unit as starting in v. 16, but notes the difficulties surrounding the first section of the literary unit (3:16b–21).

46. E.g. Walther Eichrodt, *Ezekiel* (trans. C. Quin; OTL; London: SCM, 1970), 80; Ronald E. Clements, *Ezekiel* (Louisville, Ky.: Westminster John Knox, 1996), 20; Block, *Ezekiel 1–24*, 162.

47. Odell questions whether "oral speech forms continue to govern the development of literary forms," and has reservations about treating 1:1–3:15 and 3:16–5:17 as "two separate units because they were crafted from two separate genres." See Margaret S. Odell, "You Are What You Eat: Ezekiel and the Scroll," *JBL* 117 (1998): 230. The sharp lines marking direct discourse in Ezekiel, however, do argue for treating them as in some sense independent units.

The fifth vision which can be identified in the book, the fourth to occur, is that in 37:1–14. The incident with the dry bones clearly takes place within a vision, since the introduction closely mirrors that of the vision in ch. 40,[48] the events that are described could not be conceived as literal events, and "the frequent use of והנה throughout the passage as well as ואראתי in v. 8 give additional support to such a reading."[49]

The five visions in Ezekiel are not introduced by the word-event formula but by the "hand of Yahweh" upon the prophet,[50] by Ezekiel seeing (1:1, 4; 8:2; cf. 3:23), and in particular by והנה followed by a description of what Ezekiel saw.[51] This does not mean, though, necessarily that a vision event *in toto* cannot be understood as Yahweh's speech or discourse, nor that there are not close links between individual visions within a vision event and Yahweh's word. In 11:25, for example, the vision that Ezekiel has seen is described at the close as "all the דברי יהוה that he had shown me." Yahweh's communication is not simply restricted to words uttered; the visions within the vision event can also be understood as divine speech. Critical in this expansion of understanding is speech act theory. Speech act theory maintains a distinction between the locutionary utterance, an act of saying something, and the illocutionary utterance, an act done in saying something. This distinction means that, as Wolterstorff observes,

> though of course such actions as asking, asserting, commanding, and promising, can be performed by way of uttering or inscribing sentences, they can be performed in many other ways as well. One can say something by producing a blaze, or smoke, or a sequence of light-flashes. Even more interesting: one can tell somebody something by deputizing someone else to speak on one's behalf. In short, contemporary speech-action theory opens up the possibility of a whole new way of thinking about God speaking.[52]

In this sense, it is quite legitimate to regard a vision as a "word" of Yahweh, as an illocutionary act, or, better, an illocutionary event of God "speaking." Such a view is confirmed by other instances in Ezekiel, and in other parts of the Old Testament, where the close links between divine visions and the word of Yahweh are apparent.

---

48.   In particular, the phrase "the hand of Yahweh was upon me" and the striking use of הֵנִיחַ (usually "he gave rest to") in the sense of הִנִּיחַ ("he set down"). An alternative is that MT "misvocalizes" (Block, *Ezekiel 25–48*, 367).

49.   Renz, *Rhetorical Function*, 201.

50.   Ezek 1:3; 3:22; 8:1; 37:1; 40:1.

51.   Ezek 1:4, 15; 2:9; 3:23; 8:2, 4 and frequently in ch. 8; 9:2, 11; 10:1, 9; 11:1; 37:2, 7, 8; 40:3, 5, 17, 24; 42:8; 43:2, 5; 44:4; 46:19, 21; 47:1, 2, 7.

52.   Wolterstorff, *Divine Discourse*, 13.

In 12:21–8, visions seem almost interchangeable with the word of Yahweh. This is apparent in the response Yahweh gives to two current proverbs. In 12:22, the proverb of the people lampoons the ineffectiveness, even falsehood, of the divine visions relayed by Ezekiel or perhaps by Jeremiah, "The days are prolonged, and every vision comes to nothing."[53] Yahweh declares there will be an end to such cynicism by asserting that he will speak the *word* that he will speak, and will fulfil it (12:25). A parallel is implicit between the divine vision (חזון) in the past that has not come to anything, and the word (דבר) which will come to pass in the future. Such a parallel is reinforced by the slightly awkward phrase ודבר כל־חזון (12:23b).[54] However it is to be rendered, the explicit link between word and vision is established. In 12:27, the second proverb relates more explicitly to Ezekiel. The house of Israel has been bemoaning the fact that the vision Ezekiel had received was for the distant future, "The vision that he sees is for many years ahead; he prophesies for distant times." Ezekiel is told to reply, "none of my words will be delayed any longer (לא־תמשך עוד כל־דברי)" (v. 28).[55]

Such links between word and vision are also found elsewhere in the book. In ch. 13, the opening charge against the false prophets is that they say "hear the word of Yahweh" (שמעו דבר־יהוה), when they have not "seen" (ראו) anything (13:2–3). Finally, in 7:26, a prophet is clearly expected to have visions (cf. Jer 18:18, where a prophet is marked by a "word"). This pattern is reflected elsewhere in the Old Testament. As Block notes, "several prophetic books that consist largely of oracles are formally introduced as 'the visions' of the respective prophets (Isaiah,

53. That the "yours" in the first part of 12:22 ("'Mortal, what is this proverb of yours about the land of Israel, which says…'") is not simply Ezekiel is clear from לכם. Whether this first oracle relates to words that are being said *in* the land of Israel" or "*about* the land of Israel" is debated. The phrase in MT is על־אדמת ישראל. Arguments in favour of "in" include the preposition ב in v. 23, which is more probably locative ("in Israel"), and the parallel with 33:24, where the same expression (על־אדמת ישראל) occurs locatively and Ezekiel similarly has access to the words of those left behind in Jerusalem. On this reading, the unfulfilled visions are perhaps those of Jeremiah. On the other hand, the inclusion of Ezekiel in the phrase points strongly to the saying being prominent in exile (so Allen, *Ezekiel 1–19*, 196), and the phrase can also mean "concerning the land of Israel" (Ezek 36:6).

54. Zimmerli, *Ezekiel 1*, 279: "That which every vision proclaims"; Allen, *Ezekiel 1–19*, 185: "the content of every revelation"; Greenberg, *Ezekiel 1–20*, 226: "the event of every vision." Some scholars emend the MT here, making וְדָבָר into a verb (cf. Syriac) to ensure a verb clause. For a concise list of attempts, see Zimmerli, *Ezekiel 1*, 279.

55. For the plural subject with the feminine singular verb, see GKC 145k; see also Allen, *Ezekiel 1–19*, 188.

Obadiah, Nahum). Others speak of words or oracles that the individual 'saw' (Amos, Micah, Habakkuk)."[56] The "word of Yahweh" could come equally through a vision or through a direct "word" (cf. 1 Sam 3:1).[57]

In summary, Yahweh addresses the prophet both by vision and by word. Both should be conceived as Yahweh's speech to the prophet which takes place at a particular historical point. The divine word in visions is not to be restricted simply to divine speech *within* visions, but encompasses the visions themselves. Such an address, while not audible to onlookers, is perceived to originate in Yahweh.

1.2. *Ezekiel Addressing His Audience*

The second place in the book where Yahweh's word is to be found is in Ezekiel's being instructed to address his audience. Narrated interaction between the prophet and his audience is negligible within the book, since almost everything is subsumed within Yahweh addressing Ezekiel, the rhetorical event.[58] Nonetheless, it is possible to isolate such speech, since the book of Ezekiel makes strenuous efforts to mark the different voices. As Meier notes, "A number of prophetic texts are simply uninterested in the marking of divine speech and speech in general... At the other extreme stands the book of Ezekiel with the most extensively standard-ized marking of DD [Direct Discourse] in the entire Bible."[59] Significant attention is necessary here because it is possible that any relationship between רוח and the prophetic word uttered in the rhetorical event may simply be a product of the role of רוח and the prophetic event.

In this section, I shall focus specifically on three formulae, the citation formula (more usually known as the "messenger formula"), the signatory formula and the call-to-attention formula. I shall argue that the "messen-ger formula" is not necessarily an indicator that the prophets saw them-selves as messengers. I shall also argue that all three formulae indicate that what the prophet is saying in the rhetorical event is not simply a report of what Yahweh has said, but an instantiation of Yahweh speak-ing in the present. Finally, I shall argue that the words Ezekiel is to utter

---

56. Block, *Ezekiel 1–24*, 111.

57. Jeremiah's critique of the false prophets in Jer 23:16 was not that they saw visions, but that the visions they saw came from their own minds (מלבם), and not from the *mouth* of Yahweh. It was possible not merely to *see* Yahweh's word, but to *hear* Yahweh's visions. For the prophet "seeing" Yahweh's word, see Wilson, *Prophecy and Society*, 261; Preuss, *Old Testament Theology*, 2:73.

58. A notable exception is 11:25, where Ezekiel comments, "And I told the exiles all the things that Yahweh had shown me." The book's addressees have just been given, therefore, the content of what Ezekiel told the exiles.

59. Meier, *Speaking of Speaking*, 324.

are *verbatim* with the words he has received. This direct relationship between Ezekiel's words and Yahweh speaking makes it conceivable that Yahweh's רוח is intimately related to the rhetorical event.

The book of Ezekiel as a whole first marks the words that Ezekiel is to utter by the command of Yahweh to "say."[60] This is expressed either by the imperative אמר,[61] by the imperative דבר,[62] or, when preceded by the imperative of another verb enjoining Ezekiel to speak, by the *w*^e*qatal*, ואמרת.[63] Preceding imperatives include דבר ("speak"),[64] הנבא ("proph- esy"),[65] הודע ("make known"),[66] חוד חידה ומשל משל ("propound a riddle and speak an allegory"),[67] שא קינה ("raise a lamentation").[68] In the MT, there are a number of occasions where there is no explicit command for Ezekiel to speak, even though what follows is clearly Yahweh's speech, introduced by the formulaic כה אמר (אדני) יהוה.[69]

---

60. Much of these data are replicated in ibid., 230–42, but Meier omits some examples (such as the lamentation in 19:1) and his primary scope is only Ezek 11:14–39:29.

61. Ezek 6:11; 11:5, 16, 17; 12:10, 11, 23, 28; 13:11; 14:6; 17:9, 12; 20:30; 21:14 (ET 21:9) (though this is preceded by a command to "prophesy and say" [הנבא ואמרת] and the citation formula); 22:24; 24:21; 28:2; 31:2; 33:10, 11, 12, 25; 36:22; 39:17.

62. Ezek 12:23; 37:19, 21.

63. Note that in Ezek 11:5, the imperative אמר introducing the words Ezekiel is to say is preceded by the imperative הנבא. The sequence, however, is broken by a narrative report of Yahweh's רוח falling on the prophet. Note also that on occasions ואמרת is preceded not by an imperative enjoining speech, but by a participle ("I am sending you," Ezek 2:4), by another finite verb form ("I will open your mouth," 3:27; "You shall eat…and drink," 12:18–19), by a (projected) report of the words of Ezekiel's addressees (21:12 [ET 21:7]), by another *w*^e*qatal* form of a verb of speak- ing, which in turn is preceded by an imperative (3:11), or by an imperative which does not enjoin speech ("mark well and look closely," 44:5–6).

64. Ezek 14:4; 20:3, 27; 33:2; the instance in 29:3 is also preceded by the imperative הנבא.

65. Ezek 6:2; 11:4; 13:2, 17; 21:2 (ET 20:46), 7, 14, 19, 33 (ET 21:2, 9, 14, 28); 25:2; 28:21; 29:2; 30:2; 34:2; 35:2; 36:1, 3, 6; 37:4, 9; 37:12; 38:2, 14; 39:1. Of these, the imperative הנבא is preceded by "set your face" in Ezek 6:2; 13:17; 21:2 (ET 20:46), 7 (ET 21:2); 25:2; 28:21; 29:2; 35:2; 38:2 (cf. 4:7, where there is the same motif, without direct discourse following).

66. Ezek 16:2–3; 20:4–5 (הודיעם); 22:2–3 (והודעתה, preceded by a direct question, "will you judge?").

67. Ezek 17:2–3; cf. 24:2–3 (ומשל...משל, preceded by a command to "write").

68. Ezek 19:1; 27:2–3; 28:12; 32:2.

69. Ezek 5:5–17; 7:2–4, 5–27; 14:21–23; 15:6–8; 21:29–32 (ET 21:24–27); 22:19–22; 23:22–35; 26:3–6, 7–14, 15–18, 19–21; 39:17–20; 43:18–27. Observing that in some of these instances (7:2; 15:6; 39:17) the LXX includes the command to

Such a command by Yahweh for Ezekiel to speak does not necessarily mean, of course, that Ezekiel is to mark as *Yahweh*'s words the words he is to say. Indeed, in some cases it is debatable whether they should be understood as Yahweh's words, even though Yahweh has instructed Ezekiel to speak them, because Yahweh is not marked as the speaker when they are uttered. For example, in Ezek 21:12bα (ET 21:7), Ezekiel is told how to respond to the question asked by his addressees about his moaning: "And when they say to you, 'Why do you moan?' you shall say, 'Because of the news that has come...'" Although Ezekiel is commanded to speak these words, and Yahweh gives them to him, the words cannot be understood to be the words of Yahweh in the same way as the words that Ezekiel is said to relay to his addressees specifically as Yahweh's words. This is because they are marked differently.[70] Presumably, the author of the book of Ezekiel would have his readers understand these words as the (future) words of the prophet, although within the book they are subsumed within the word coming to the prophet.

After the command to speak there comes on ten occasions the call-to-attention formula. On each of these occasions, and in the vast majority of instances where Ezekiel is given the words of Yahweh to utter, such words are introduced by the formulaic כה אמר (אדני) יהוה. This serves to identify Yahweh's voice in the (hypothetical) rhetorical event in a very consistent fashion.[71] The only places where Yahweh's words that Ezekiel is told explicitly to utter are not prefaced by this formula are 17:12, where Ezekiel is instructed to give an explanation for the riddle found in 17:3–10; 21:12bβ (ET 21:7), where Yahweh's words are explicitly identified as such by the signatory formula at the end of the verse; 22:24, where Ezekiel is commanded to speak against the land; 33:2, where Yahweh reintroduces the watchman motif; and 33:11–12, where Yahweh reaffirms his lack of pleasure in the death of the wicked and the

speak, Zimmerli (*Ezekiel 1*, 194) takes the omission to be an "original ellipse" subsequently filled out in the versions. Cf. Block, *Ezekiel 1–24*, 247. Block observes the same data, but does not draw specific conclusions.

70. Other instances include 19:2, where Ezekiel is told what to say in his lament for the princes of Israel; 32:2b, where Yahweh, having instructed Ezekiel to raise up a lamentation over the king of Egypt, does not introduce his own verdict until the citation formula at the start of v. 3. Care should be taken here, however, since such precise demarcation of divine speech based on the citation formula is not always followed in the Old Testament. The most striking example is found in 2 Kgs 1:2–6, where the location of the citation formula shifts as the narrative moves from the commissioning of Elijah to his fulfilment of that commission. See Meier, *Speaking of Speaking*, 295–96.

71. Cf. Meier, *Speaking of Speaking*, 231–34.

ineffectiveness of the righteousness of the righteous to save the people when they transgress.

Given the high degree of consistency in the marking of divine speech throughout the rest of the book, we must look at how the book portrays the rhetorical event by examining in particular the citation (or messenger) formula, the signatory formula and the call-to-attention formula.[72]

1.2.1. *The citation formula*. The citation (or messenger) formula (כה אמר [אדני] יהוה) occurs over four hundred times in the Old Testament. Without the double divine designation, it occurs almost three hundred times in the Old Testament; over half of those occurrences are in Jeremiah. Only three occurrences are in the book of Ezekiel (11:5; 21:8 [ET 21:3]; 30:6). The expanded phrase, "Thus has the Lord Yahweh declared" occurs more than 130 times in the Old Testament. Of these, over 90 per cent are in the book of Ezekiel. Other occurrences occur in Isaiah (eight, of which five are in chs. 1–39), Jeremiah (7:20), Amos (3:11; 5:3) and Obadiah (1:1). Neither version appears in Hosea, Joel, Habakkuk or Zephaniah, and there is only one occurrence in each of Obadiah, Nahum and Malachi. Though the author of the book of Ezekiel does not coin the expanded version, nor is it unique to the book, yet he makes the phrase his own. Though it does point to "the subservient role of the prophet,"[73] it speaks also of the rebelliousness of the people against the one who *is* the Lord Yahweh even though they do not acknowledge him as such.[74]

On most occasions, the formula occurs within a unit introduced by the word-event formula. It can occur, though, within a vision unit (e.g. 11:5). It can function either at the outset of the message that the prophet is to declare, or it can punctuate the message itself, often introducing a new oracle that Ezekiel is to utter within the word that has come to Ezekiel (e.g. 13:3, 8, 13). Further, on some occasions Ezekiel is told to say, "Thus has the Lord Yahweh declared," while on other occasions the citation formula suddenly appears within a unit without any hint that the situation

72. See especially the work by Meier, *Speaking of Speaking*, 230–42 on Ezekiel, and pp. 273–322 on marking divine speech in general. Meier's work on Ezekiel is hampered by a focus almost exclusively on 11:14–39:29, given that divine speech is also found outside these chapters. It is not surprising that divine speech is marked somewhat differently *within* divine visions (though I note that, within the book, 11:14–23 is subsumed within the divine vision). Where the formal units are not divine visions, the pattern discernible in 11:14–39:29 is also present (i.e. in chs. 6 and 7).

73. Block, *Ezekiel 1–24*, 34.

74. Cf. Greenberg, *Ezekiel 1–20*, 64–65.

has moved from Ezekiel hearing material which explains a situation to his hearing material he is to proclaim and announce. For example, after the word-event formula in 15:1, vv. 2–5 appear to convey Yahweh explaining to Ezekiel how charred wood (i.e. the destroyed Jerusalem) is useless. Only in v. 6 does the citation formula come. There is no instruction for Ezekiel to speak anything, yet the presence of the citation formula, along with the "you" plural in v. 7, shows that these words are meant for an audience wider than Ezekiel. The citation formula refers to the putative rhetorical event but does not have the explicit command, "say," presumably because this ellipsis serves to strengthen the links between the word that came to the prophet and the word that the prophet uttered. The gap between the prophetic event and the rhetorical event is systematically eliminated by such a strategy. Here is evidence of the book itself serving a rhetorical purpose. The focus is not so much on an account of Ezekiel's life and ministry, as to make the force of that word present to the readers and hearers of the book.

There are two somewhat different perspectives on the formula in current scholarship, particularly over the putative *Sitz im Leben*, which in turn lead to different conclusions about how much theological freight it can carry. Of particular concern for us are three issues. If the formula indicates that the prophet saw himself as conveying Yahweh's words as a messenger, then this may well, first, exclude (certain kinds of) רוח-inspiration, and, secondly, indicate a particular kind of relationship between the words originally spoken to the prophet, and the words spoken by the prophet. Thirdly, there is the issue of whether the formula speaks of a past event, of words relayed to the prophet, or of a present event, of the original speaker (Yahweh) somehow being present in the words of the prophet. Conclusions on these three issues will shape our discussion concerning the relationship between word and רוח.

On the one hand is the view that the formula is a messenger formula. This has been most extensively expressed by Westermann, who states,

> If one can begin the inquiry about the speeches of the prophets with the basic knowledge that they are messengers who bring a message and speak in the style of a message, then there is a foundation of formulas, speech forms, and speeches which have been passed down, where one can be assured of encountering the self-understanding of the prophets and of being on solid ground.[75]

---

75. Claus Westermann, *Basic Forms of Prophetic Speech* (trans. H. C. White; London: Lutterworth, 1967), 39. Westermann acknowledges he is building on the work of Köhler and Lindblom.

For him, this is "nothing more than a methodological starting point; but this basis should now be confidently accepted."[76]

Westermann has used this "starting point" as one strand in his argument that the prophetic "announcement of judgment" (*Gerichtsankündigung*) "is something essentially different from the threat" because "a threat is transmitted very poorly by a messenger."[77] He has also used the same "starting point," that the prophets were messengers, to argue that, since "it is impossible for a message to be received in a state of ecstasy…in no case may one assume that the reception of the messenger's speech occurred in ecstasy."[78]

More significant for our purposes are two other possible implications of regarding the formula as a messenger formula, and the self-understanding of the prophets as messengers. First, it is possible to treat the relationship between the words spoken in the prophetic event and the rhetorical event in a similar fashion to the relationship between the words that a messenger received and the words which the messenger delivered. That, of course, would potentially raise interesting questions about the relationship between Yahweh's רוח and the word of Yahweh in the prophetic event, on the one hand, and the relationship between Yahweh's רוח and the word of Yahweh in the rhetorical event, on the other. Secondly, and related to this first point, within this viewpoint of the prophet as messenger, the formula is sometimes translated in the present tense, "Thus says PN," despite the perfect אָמַר.[79] So, for example, Schmid observes

76. Ibid., 39. Such a viewpoint has been accepted by most Old Testament scholars, as seen, for example, in Klaus Koch, *The Growth of the Biblical Tradition: The Form-Critical Method* (trans. S. M. Cupitt; London: A. & C. Black, 1969), 189–90; Walther Zimmerli, *Old Testament Theology in Outline* (trans. D. E. Green; Edinburgh: T. & T. Clark, 1978), 102; also in the dictionary articles by Jerome A. Lund, "אמר," *NIDOTTE* 1:444–45; H. H. Schmid, "אמר *'mr* to say," *TLOT* 1:159–62; and in the glossary of "genres" in Marvin A. Sweeney, *Isaiah 1–39* (FOTL 16; Grand Rapids: Eerdmans, 1996), 524.

77. Westermann, *Basic Forms*, 66–67.

78. Ibid., 63.

79. Such a comment is not intended to show my understanding of the Hebrew verbal system as anchored within the confines of a narrow, tense-based approach. Nonetheless, there needs to be an explanation of why אמר is translated as "says" or "said." For work on the Hebrew verbal system to 1990, see the summary in *IBHS* §29; see also Yoshinobu Endo, *The Verbal System of Classical Hebrew in the Joseph Story: An Approach from Discourse Analysis* (Studia Semitica Neerlandica 32; Assen: Van Gorcum, 1996); Tal Goldfajn, *Word Order and Time in Biblical Hebrew Narrative* (Oxford Theological Monographs; Oxford: Clarendon, 1998); and, more recently, John A. Cook, "The Semantics of Verbal Pragmatics: Clarifying the Roles of *Wayyiqtol* and *Weqatal* in Biblical Hebrew Prose," *JSS* 49 (2004): 247–73.

how with verbs of speaking, there is the possibility of "expressing the coincidence of statement and behavior" with the *perfectum declarativum* ("I state hereby"), and he suggests that, "the formula *kōh ʾāmar yhwh* 'thus says Yahweh (herewith, through me)' may also belong here."[80] In other words, at the moment the messenger relays the message, the sender of the message is *also* speaking, through his messenger. On such an understanding, when Ezekiel speaks as Yahweh's messenger, he is not simply reporting words that Yahweh has uttered, but Yahweh is uttering them at that moment through him. Here again there is potential significance for an understanding of a relationship between Yahweh's רוח and Yahweh's word.

Greene and Meier offer the two most comprehensive recent disagreements with this perspective. Greene takes issue with the notion that prophets are messengers, not least because "'messenger speech' [the form-critical category] was neither equal to nor the equivalent of message."[81] Meier's thesis on this point is that the so-called messenger formula "PN כה אמר is not diagnostic of messenger speech and cannot be used in support of the metaphor of prophet as a messenger" since "there is no speech form for the introduction of messages in the Hebrew Bible that unequivocally points to messenger activity."[82] Instead, the formula needs to be understood within a rather less theologically rich framework as introducing the "quoting" of "another's words that have already been spoken."[83] Therefore, "as a citation of another's words which have already been spoken, we can be spared the over-theologizing of the verb tense when applied to God's speech."[84]

Evidence usually garnered for the designation "messenger formula" comes from two places. First, in the Old Testament, there are clear

---

80. Schmid, *TLOT* 1:160. Without using the technical terms associated with speech act theory, Schmid observes how verbs of speaking can also *do* something. They are a particular kind of performative utterance.

81. John T. Greene, *The Role of the Messenger and Message in the Ancient Near East* (Brown Judaic Studies 169; Atlanta: Scholars Press, 1989), 226. Although his observation is apposite that form-critical scholars sometimes are sloppy in applying the term "message" to categories broader than is warranted on the basis of an analysis of ancient Near Eastern messages (pp. 139–46), his work suffers from his own admission (p. 207) that the sources for his research were letters rather than narratives. Meier points out that the perspective that is received from letters is very different from that received from study of messengers embedded within narrative. See Samuel A. Meier, *The Messenger in the Ancient Semitic World* (JSM 45; Atlanta: Scholars Press, 1988), 60.

82. Meier, *Speaking of Speaking*, 278.

83. Ibid., 290.

84. Ibid., 291.

instances where an intermediary is commissioned with to take a message to take to a third-party. One of the most striking examples is in Gen 32:3–5, where Jacob sends messengers before him to Esau. He instructs them to say upon encountering Esau, "Thus you shall say (כה תאמרון) to my lord Esau: Thus says your servant Jacob (כה אמר עבדך יעקב)…"[85] Secondly, there are examples in the ancient Near East of a similar pattern. Zimmerli cites an example of this "memorandum," "a letter from the governor Kibridagan to King Zimrilim of Mari begins: 'To my lord [i.e. Zimrilim] say: Thus says Kibridagan…].' "[86]

Meier argues strongly for a different interpretation of the data.

First, he observes that the almost total lack of occurrence of the formula in many of the prophetic books points to the fact that "even within prophetic circles (or circles depicting prophetic activity) there was not a uniform understanding of this phrase and its significance, or…prophecy is a considerably variegated phenomenon."[87] That is, if it be granted that the formula indicates the self-understanding of those who used it, "these prophets who did not use the term must not have perceived of themselves as messengers from God, or, if they did, they did not underscore this perception as of great import."[88]

Secondly, the use of the phrase by messengers is optional.[89] Meier comments that while it is certainly true that Old Testament narratives depict messengers using this phrase, most messengers do not use it.[90] There are broadly two kinds of absence. First, there are those instances where the messengers do not explicitly identify the source of their words

85. See also Num 20:14 (Moses sending messengers from Kadesh to the king of Edom); 22:16 (officials from Balak coming to Balaam); Judg 11:15 (Jephthah sending messengers to the king of the Ammonites); 2 Kgs 1:11 (a captain conveying the king of Samaria's command to Elijah); 18:19, 31 (Rabshakeh's announcement to Hezekiah and then the people of the words of the king of Assyria); 2 Kgs 19:3 (Eliakim, Shebna and the senior priests convey Hezekiah's words to Isaiah).

86. Friedrich Ellermeier, *Prophetie in Mari und Israel* (Herzberg: Jungfer, 1968), 29, cited in Zimmerli, *Old Testament Theology*, 102.

87. Meier, *Speaking of Speaking*, 274.

88. Ibid., 278.

89. Meier is not wholly consistent here. In *Messenger*, 186, he comments, "In biblical literature, one may assume from commands to messengers and from actual performance that they prefaced their message with the formula 'Thus says PN,'" while on p. 191, he comments, "The biblical literature, due to its variety, spontaneity and total lack of adherence to any consistent forms (even 'Thus says PN' is more often than not omitted and on one occasion occurs twice), may provide the best insight into actual messenger performance." In other words, there is variety in "*actual* messenger performance," not consistency.

90. Meier, *Speaking of Speaking*, 278–79.

(e.g. Num 22:5). Since "messengers function in a communication process where a source A (the sender) employs a channel B (the messenger)
to reach a target C (the addressee),"[91] they would have needed some form
of self-identification. Without such a self-identification, "the target C has
no clue as to who the message is from."[92] Therefore its general absence
shows that "it is an optional narrative feature that biblical story-telling
found largely irrelevant for the purposes of its art."[93] It is not possible to
make clear judgments on the basis of these absences. There is, however,
a second, and more significant, kind of absence. This is where the messengers do identify themselves, but not with the "messenger formula." In
1 Sam 25:40, messengers (cf. v. 42) sent by David identify themselves as
sent by David, but there is no messenger formula. It is true that the words
they utter do not contain the direct speech of David, but this example
makes it clear that the "messenger formula" is not a necessary condition
for a messenger.[94]

Thirdly, the messenger formula is not the exclusive preserve either of
messengers, or indeed of situations where there is an intermediary. Meier
argues that "the phrase has a prehistory antedating its appearance in
Hebrew texts where messengers use it."[95] A correlation between occurrences in the messenger speeches in the Old Testament and in the
prophets' speeches does not imply a causal link between the two. There
can be, and is, in Meier's view, an antecedent causal link. He observes
that, in diverse genres in Akkadian, the cognate phrase *kīam iqbi* "never"
describes "a message delivered by a messenger on behalf of another. It is
simply a citation formula that marks a statement, often formal, made by
an individual."[96] Further, the citation formula is used in other situations
where there is no intermediary between two communicating parties, and
therefore no message is being relayed. For example, in narrative, in 1
Sam 9:9, "the narrator quotes the typical words Israelites used to say
when consulting a prophetic oracle: 'Formerly in Israel thus said the man
(כה אמר האיש) on his way (בלכתו) to inquire of God, "Come, let us

91. Meier, *Speaking of Speaking*, 281.
92. Ibid.
93. Ibid., 279.
94. Cf. also 2 Kgs 5:22, and the fabricated words of Gehazi, Elisha's servant,
to Naaman, introduced by "Greetings! My master sent me, saying…" (שלום אדני
שלחני לאמר). Meier, *Messenger*, 186–87, notes another example, 1 Sam 4:16–17,
where the self-identification is not by means of the "messenger formula." Here,
though, the runner with news of the Israelites' defeat is not actually despatched by
anyone.
95. Meier, *Speaking of Speaking*, 279.
96. Ibid., 280.

go…"''"[97] This is simply a citation, not a situation involving messengers or intermediaries.

Perhaps more striking, the phrase occurs in the prophets without any link to messenger activity. Meier points out how "words of Yahweh depicted as specifically addressed to the prophet may be introduced with the phrase, 'Thus said the Lord to me' (כה אמר אלי אדני; Isa 21:6)."[98] Again, this is no A→B→C situation here, with the messenger as B relaying the words of A to C. Isaiah is quoting what Yahweh has said to him.

Further, Meier argues that there is no need for the phrase "to me" to demarcate this as different from a messenger situation. He observes a number of examples in Jeremiah where the phrase כה אמר יהוה occurs in an address meant for the prophet alone: "In Jer 30:1–3, Jeremiah is told to write in a book all the words that God had given to him. This is not a message from God for Jeremiah to pass on to others, but it is a command that he alone is to hear and obey. But it is introduced with the words, 'Thus said Yahweh' (כה אמר יהוה; 30:2)."[99]

In these occurrences, the citation formula speaks not of the rhetorical event, but of the prophetic event. On one occasion in the book of Ezekiel, it is possible that the formula introduces words meant for Ezekiel alone as part of the prophetic event. On occasions in the book of Ezekiel, the formula occurs without an antecedent command to "say." One rhetorical function of such instances, where in addition the words are clearly ultimately to be addressed to Ezekiel's addressees, was to narrow the gap between prophetic and rhetorical event. In Ezek 39:17, Ezekiel is told, "As for you, mortal, thus says the Lord Yahweh: Speak to the birds of every kind…" The LXX characteristically includes a second command to "say" (εἰπόν) before the citation formula.[100] There is some evidence within the MT of a second command to "say" after the citation formula (21:14, 23 [ET 21:9, 18]), but as it stands, the MT in 39:17 is an example within Ezekiel of the citation formula being used in a situation where no message is involved, its context being the prophetic, not the rhetorical, event.

Meier then refutes the suggestion that these last two sets of examples are variations of or derivations from the formula, כה אמר יהוה, because

97. Ibid., 282. Meier gives other examples (2 Sam 16:7; 19:1) and other places with the *yiqtol* form of אמר in the phrase כה + אמר (Gen 31:8; 1 Sam 14:9, 10; 20:7, 22; 2 Sam 15:26).

98. Ibid. He also notes Isa 8:11; 18:4; 21:16; 31:4; Jer 17:19.

99. Ibid., 283. Other places he notes are Jer 26:2; 33:1–3, 23–26; 34:1–2a; 35:12–13; 37:6–7. To these can be added Hag 2:10.

100. Cf. n. 69 above.

"the unanimous evidence from the cognate phrase in Akkadian demonstrates that the phrase's citation function is standard and demonstrably prior to any function as a 'messenger formula' in the Bible."[101]

Fourthly, he argues that the ancient Near Eastern parallels have not been understood correctly, because "scholars have unfortunately confused a written epistolary style with the oral despatching of messengers."[102] There are a number of strands to his argument, but the main point is that, even if it be granted that the parallel in Akkadian is not with the cognate *kīam iqbi*, but with the particle *umma*, characteristic of the introduction of Mesopotamian letters, this particle "typically introduces in Babylonian any quotation made by anyone, whether messenger or not."[103]

Finally, "the repetition" of the phrase "within single units," as found particularly in Ezekiel, Haggai and Zechariah, "has no counterpart in messenger activity."[104] Rather, it "is attested as a literary phenomenon in royal inscriptions of the Persian period."[105]

In summary, Meier concludes that this phrase does not by its very presence point to messenger activity. Usually it does not have a messenger function. "One must look to the context to determine if messengers are using this formula as a part of their commission to identify the one who sent them. The formula is simply used to make citations of other's words."[106] Meier's powerfully argued conclusions mean that Ezekiel cannot be assumed to be Yahweh's messenger merely by the use of this formula. In addition, he also insists that the translation of the verb must be "past" because what is introduced is simply the citation of the words of another, uttered in the past.[107]

This in turn leaves us with two main tasks or questions. The first one is whether Ezekiel is portrayed as Yahweh's messenger, given that the "messenger formula" is better rendered "citation formula." The second is whether we are compelled by the designation "citation formula" to regard the tense as past, such that the words spoken by the prophet in the rhetorical event are merely a *report* of words spoken to the prophet by Yahweh, or in fact Yahweh speaking *through* the prophet.

One problem with arguing that the prophets *en bloc* regard themselves as messengers is that many seem unconcerned to distinguish the words of

101. Meier, *Speaking of Speaking*, 283.
102. Ibid., 284.
103. Ibid., 285–86. He notes the exceptions of poetic myth and epic, where "*umma* is eschewed" (p. 286).
104. Ibid., 297.
105. Ibid., 298.
106. Ibid., 284.
107. Ibid., 290.

Yahweh from their own. A further concern is that only in the post-exilic period are prophets clearly acknowledged as messengers.[108] While Ezekiel explicitly speaks of himself as a prophet, a נביא (Ezek 2:5; 33:33), he is nowhere explicitly designated a messenger of Yahweh. Nonetheless, there are three strands of evidence that would support the conclusion that Ezekiel is in some sense Yahweh's messenger.

First, there is in the book of Ezekiel the same care to identify and distinguish Yahweh's voice as that found in Haggai, a book that clearly speaks of Haggai as Yahweh's messenger (Hag 1:13). Secondly, there is the temporal proximity of Ezekiel to Haggai. Given the points of similarity above about identifying Yahweh's speech, such proximity makes it more likely that Ezekiel should be understood as Yahweh's messenger. Thirdly, Meier, in his study on the messenger in the ancient Semitic world, observes that "characteristic of West Semitic literature was the phrase, 'Thus says PN', while characteristic of Akkadian was the statement, 'I will send you.'"[109] This background accords well with the picture that is found in Ezekiel. Three times within Ezekiel's commission (2:4; 3:11, 27), Ezekiel is told that he will say to the people, "Thus has the Lord Yahweh declared." Four times, he is described as "sent" (שׁלח) by Yahweh (2:3, 4; 3:5, 6). It is therefore not an unreasonable working assumption that the prophet Ezekiel is indeed Yahweh's messenger.

The second question is over the precise relationship of the words to be uttered by the prophet, or messenger, to the God who has given them to him.

Zimmerli, Meier, Schmid and others provide two contrasting views. The first, that the tense must be "past," and the translation must be "thus has Yahweh said," comes from Zimmerli and Meier. Zimmerli comments,

> It points back to the moment when he [the messenger] received the message and was used at the time of delivery in order to appeal back to this moment. From this the perfect tense of the messenger formula becomes

---

108.   In Hag 1:13, Haggai is described as "the messenger of Yahweh" (מלאך יהוה) who spoke "with Yahweh's message" (במלאכות יהוה); in Mal 3:1, the messenger going ahead of Yahweh is probably a prophetic figure. See David L. Petersen, *Zechariah 9–14 & Malachi* (OTL; London: SCM, 1995), 209–10; cf. Koch, *Growth of the Biblical Tradition*, 216. See also 2 Chr 36:15–16.

109.   Meier, *Messenger*, 248. Meier consciously avoids relating his work to the question of whether the prophets were messengers, however: "The perception of the prophet as a messenger sent from God (Hag 1:13) is a subject which can also benefit from this study but is not appropriate as a primary source for this investigation. We wish to remain precise and deal with messengers *per se* and not with possible permutations of the social reality as employed by the prophets who may have used the notion as a metaphor for their social status and message" (p. 9).

intelligible. At the moment of delivery of his message the messenger identifies himself with the time when he was entrusted with it by the person who commissioned him.[110]

The clear implication is that there is some distance between Yahweh, the sender of the message, and the words actually spoken. The words the prophet utters are the reported speech of Yahweh, not Yahweh actually speaking in the present in and through the prophet's words.

The second view, that it ought to be translated as a present tense, "Thus says Yahweh," is expressed by a number of scholars. Schmid, as we saw above, links it to the *perfectum declarativum*, linking "statement and behavior."[111] Koch comments that "the sender of the message is brought as near to the recipient of it, and speaks to him in just the same tone, as if the two were face to face."[112] Thus for him, "the Hebrew perfect does not in this case refer back to a particular point in time when the originator of the message first spoke to the messenger alone. Here the perfect is intended to express the absolute validity of the pronouncement. Thus it can only be used by a man of superior or of equal rank."[113]

Two intermediate positions between these two can be found in Westermann and Bjørndalen. Westermann observes two occasions for using the "messenger formula," and so discerns two possible translations:

> In the process of sending a message, then, the messenger formula has a twofold place; it occurs two times: the sender first introduces his speech with it—that means that in the presence of the messenger whom he sends he authorizes the speech that is introduced with this formula as *his* speech; then when the messenger has arrived, he introduces the message that has been entrusted to him with the formula, and in this way authorizes it as the speech of the person who had sent him. Because of these two places in which the messenger formula occurs, the Hebrew perfect *ʾāmar* cannot be clearly rendered by our present or perfect tense. If we are thinking of the moment of the commissioning, then we must say, "Thus says NN"; but if we are thinking of the moment of the delivery, then it is more exact to say, "Thus said NN."[114]

He does not, however, take adequate account of the fact that in the vast majority of cases the citation formula occurs *within* direct speech that the messenger, or prophet, is to utter, and therefore, even at the point of

110. Zimmerli, *Ezekiel 1*, 133; cf. Meier, *Speaking of Speaking*, 290.
111. Schmid, *TLOT* 1:160.
112. Koch, *Growth of the Biblical Tradition*, 190; cf. R. Rendtorff, "Botenformel und Botenspruch," *ZAW* 74 (1962): 167: "sie [die Botenformel] macht ihn in seiner Botschaft gegenwärtig."
113. Koch, *Growth of the Biblical Tradition*, 190.
114. Westermann, *Basic Forms*, 102

commissioning, the timeframe envisaged by the phrase is no different from that at delivery.

Bjørndalen, on the other hand, regards the presence of the vocative as the key element in determining a translation in the present tense: "Where the citation formula introduces a message with the vocative of the recipient, and the sender is identical with the cited person, the citation formula must have a present timeframe."[115] Meier, however, regards such a view as "remarkable" given the citation function both of the Akkadian, *kīam iqbi*, and the cognate phrase in Hebrew, כה אמר יהוה.[116]

The formula is best spoken of as the "citation formula," rather than the "messenger formula." Nonetheless, we are faced with the disputed question whether the particular usage in this situation should extend beyond mere citation to describe the coterminous act of prophet and sender speaking in the present.

The use of the citation formula with the prophetic event points towards this as a possibility. For example, in Jer 30:1–3, the citation formula in v. 2 clearly occurs within direct speech of Yahweh to Jeremiah marked by לאמר in v. 1.[117] The context of the citation formula is not the reporting by B of words spoken in the past by A, whether the words were for B or for C. Rather, it introduces words spoken in the *present* by Yahweh to Jeremiah. Although this is an extension of the citing of the words of another, it demonstrates the necessity of sometimes translating the citation formula in the present tense.[118]

Further, Bjørndalen highlights the significance of the vocative in the relaying of A's speech by B to C. It is not as if the identity of the prophet has been lost in the delivering of the words. Rather, the implication is "that the speech *of the messenger should be regarded as the speech of the sender*, in the vocative: *as his actual address to the recipient*."[119]

---

115.   A. J. Bjørndalen, "Zu den Zeitstufen der Zitatformel...כה אמר im Botenverkehr," *ZAW* 86 (1974): 397: "Wo die Zitatformel eine Botschaft im Vokativ des Empfängers einleitet, und der Absender mit der zitierten Person identisch ist, muß die Zitatformel die Zeitstufe Präsens haben." Bjørndalen discusses five different groups of texts involving the "*Zitatformel*." His chief exception is the fifth of these, where the formula also has אלי.

116.   Meier, *Speaking of Speaking*, 291.

117.   For further examples, see nn. 98 and 99 above. For the significance of לאמר in introducing direct speech, see Cynthia L. Miller, *The Representation of Speech in Biblical Hebrew Narrative: A Linguistic Analysis* (HSM 55; Atlanta: Scholars Press, 1996), 163–232.

118.   Cf. Bjørndalen, "Zeitstufen der Zitatformel," 400–1.

119.   Ibid., 402: "daß die Botenrede *als Rede des Absenders gelten darf*, bei Vokativ: *als seine aktuelle Anrede an den Empfänger*" (original emphasis).

Finally, there are a number of places in (the exilic, and so nearly con-temporary) Isa 40–55 where the imperfect, יֹאמַר, and the perfect, אָמַר, are used interchangeably to introduce Yahweh's word in the present.[120] Although it is true in these cases that כֹּה is not present, nonetheless the flexible use of perfect and imperfect is further evidence that a rendering of the citation formula as "Thus says Yahweh" in these instances is correct.

To assist with a conceptual understanding, we need to revisit again speech act theory and performative utterances. Talstra has criticized a definition of "performative" that embraces this formula on two grounds.[121] First, he observes that usually a performative can be discerned when "the one who speaks is identical with the subject of the verb," but in this case "the speaker (the messenger) is not the subject of the verb (the sender)."[122] Secondly, the identification of a performative is confirmed by the possi-bility of adding "hereby."[123] Talstra states that "*kh* does not refer to the very moment of speaking and acting, but introduces a quotation."[124] Nonetheless, speech act theory can assist us, for the notion of "deputized discourse" enables a conception of Yahweh's spokesperson speaking words that "count as" Yahweh's words.[125] It is my contention that the citation formula introduces words of the prophet that count as the words of Yahweh, in the present.

To summarize and conclude, the messenger formula is better spoken of as the "citation formula," but this does not preclude the notion that Ezekiel himself implicitly appropriated the metaphor of Yahweh's messenger. Such a possibility should be borne in mind when comparing, for example, the words spoken to Ezekiel in the prophetic event, and those to be spoken in the rhetorical event. Further, although on certain occasions the citation formula does simply introduce words spoken in the past, when the vocative, in particular, is present, there is a strong indica-tion that the words of the prophet are to count as the words of Yahweh in the present. Though the citation formula, like other formulae, may have served in one way as a means of aligning the prophet with a particular

---

120. Imperfect: Isa 40:1, 25; 41:21; perfect: 45:13; 48:22; 49:5; 54:1, 6, 8, 10.
121. E. Talstra, "Text Grammar and Hebrew Bible. II: Syntax and Semantics," *BO* 39 (1982): 28.
122. Ibid.
123. *IBHS* §30.5.1d n. 17, in speaking of this test, notes the contrast between "I hereby renounce title to the estates" and "I renounce title to the estates by marry-ing the woman I love." Only in the first instance are the speaking and the acting "identical."
124. Talstra, "Text Grammar," 28.
125. Wolterstorff, *Divine Discourse*, 42–51.

tradition (and the false prophets clearly used the same formula, too; see 13:6), its primary function was to assert the authenticity of the prophet and his message.[126] It asserts that, at that moment, what the prophet says, Yahweh says. It serves to mark divine speech, whether, for example, announcing the grounds for judgment (e.g. 13:3–7, 18–19) or the actual judgments themselves (13:8–12, 13–16, 20–23). By not merely introducing the report of a past speech event, the possibility remains that Yahweh's רוח is directly related to the rhetorical event.

1.2.2. *The signatory formula.* The signatory formula (נאם [אדני] יהוה, "the declaration of [the Lord] Yahweh"), like the citation formula, occurs in two forms.[127] The first, "the declaration of Yahweh," occurs only four times in the book of Ezekiel (Ezek 13:6, 7; 16:58; 37:14), of which two are citing the claims of the false prophets (13:6, 7). It occurs more than 250 times in the Old Testament, with more than 160 instances in Jeremiah. The second, "the declaration of the Lord Yahweh" occurs eighty-one times in Ezekiel, and a further eleven times in the rest of the Old Testament.[128] Here again, as with the citation formula, there is a difference between Ezekiel and Jeremiah in usage. Ezekiel stresses the sovereignty of the Lord Yahweh in a way that is characteristic of the book as a whole.

There have been debates about the etymology, morphology and semantic and syntactic functions of the key element of this formula, נאם.[129] With regard to etymology, most scholars link it with the Arabic *n'm*, meaning "whisper,"[130] while Meier argues that a more satisfactory derivation is from the "convergence of two Akkadian particles,"[131] *umma* and *anumma*. Of course etymological links alone are not significant, but

126. Block, *Ezekiel 1–24*, 33.
127. The rendition of נאם is that of Block, *Ezekiel 1–24*, 33. For other translations, see Meier, *Speaking of Speaking*, 98–99.
128. In Isaiah, twice (3:15, "the Lord Yahweh of hosts"; 56:8), in Jeremiah, four times (2:19; 49:5; 50:31, "the Lord Yahweh of hosts"; 2:22), and in Amos, five times (3:13; 4:5; 8:3, 9, 11).
129. For a discussion of the phrase's history and details of its usage, see D. Vetter, "נאם *ne'um* utterance," *TLOT* 2:692–94, and Meier, *Speaking of Speaking*, 298–314.
130. Vetter, *TLOT* 2:692.
131. Meier, *Speaking of Speaking*, 303. His principal arguments against links with the Arabic verb are threefold. First, the "quality of the utterance" is different (p. 300), since "one refers to speech while the other refers to sound." Secondly, "the evidence for this root in biblical Hebrew is overwhelmingly nominal and not verbal" (p. 300). The only occurrence of the verb is in Jer 23:31. Thirdly, the uniform vocalization of the word in what he argues at this point is a reliable Masoretic tradition points more to it as "a particle" (p. 301).

Meier observes that these are reinforced by a "syntactic and semantic connection as well."[132] In particular, *umma* in Akkadian is "the particle identifying quoted speech."[133] Although "rarely repeated" within an utterance "in Old Babylonian," "in Middle Babylonian, and particularly in the peripheral dialects," it "may be repeated within a lengthy quotation or discourse apparently as a reminder that the quotation has not yet terminated."[134] Such a pattern can also be seen in Old Testament texts, though the usage of נאם is by no means either identical with the Akkadian particles, nor indeed consistent throughout the Old Testament.[135]

Some have tried to locate the function of the phrase within the book of Ezekiel in the marking of the structure of utterances, and in particular, with ending a section or an oracle.[136] Its precise location within the oracles, however, is hard to systematize, although the introductory function that it has, for example, in Num 24:3–4 has been wholly superseded by the citation formula.[137]

What is striking for our purposes is that its usage in the Old Testament in general, and in Ezekiel in particular, clearly reinforces the picture of the rhetorical event as Yahweh speaking, thus confirming our understanding of the citation formula above.

There is not a necessarily retrospective glance in the use of this marker of direct discourse. It does not even automatically point to previously uttered words that are now being related as if in the present. It can be used by a speaker, *within* his speech, to alert his hearers that what follows *are* indeed his words. In Num 24:3–5, one of the rare occasions when the utterance that follows is not Yahweh's, נאם occurs within Balaam's speech, identifying the words that follow as his own words: "and he uttered his oracle, saying (ויאמר): 'The oracle of Balaam son of Beor (נאם בלעם בנו בער), the oracle of the man whose eye is clear (ונאם הגבר שתם העין), the oracle of one who hears the words of God (נאם שמע אמרי־אל), who sees the vision of the Almighty, who falls down, but with

---

132. Ibid, 303.
133. Ibid.
134. Ibid., 303–4.
135. Ibid., 309.
136. E.g. Ronald M. Hals, *Ezekiel* (FOTL 19; Grand Rapids: Eerdmans, 1989), 361: the formula is "usually…placed at the end of a unit or a major section within a unit."
137. Greenberg, *Ezekiel 1–20*, 114 outlines the different occurrences. Meier (*Speaking of Speaking*, 309), however, criticizes some of the categories ("marking 'a change of topic within an oracle,'" "heightening effect" and "anticipatory, false ending") as "*ad hoc*," since many changes of topic are not marked in this way. Further, its usage is "highly variable and optional" (p. 238).

eyes uncovered: How fair are your tents…'" Such an observation makes probable an interpretation of those occurrences in the rest of the Old Testament and in Ezekiel where the quoted words are indeed to be understood in the present.[138] This is strengthened by the fact that there is no counter-example where the formula must be understood as functioning with a clear time lapse between the speaker of the formula and the words introduced by the formula. Meier also points to the contemporary nature of the discourse marked by נאם: "Not only does נאם introduce speech that follows, precisely like Akkadian *umma*, but one of the peculiar features of the particle נאם is its frequent appearance within a quotation, re-identifying the person who *speaks*."[139] In other words, the words the prophet utters *are* the words that Yahweh utters. Meier does not, however, seem to recognize the significance of his argument, for it serves to reinforce the *contemporary* nature of Yahweh's words introduced by the citation formula.

Although their location within Yahweh's speeches in the book of Ezekiel is different, the rhetorical function of the citation formula and the signatory formula is equivalent, and the false prophets use both to try to authenticate their message (Ezek 13:6–7; 22:28): "this formula adds solemnity to the prophetic pronouncement by pointing to its divine source."[140] Further, the signatory formula seems to have displaced over time the concluding truncated citation formula, אמר יהוה.[141] What the prophet says, Yahweh also says.

1.2.3. *The call-to-attention formula.* The call-to-attention formula (שמעו [את־[דבר [אדני] יהוה) accounts for the remaining instances of דבר יהוה in the book of Ezekiel, apart from those occurring in the word-event formula. The phrase occurs seven times in the book of Ezekiel without אדני, and a further three times with it.[142] The phrase also occurs throughout the prophetic literature of the Old Testament, though it is not nearly as widespread as the first three formulae examined.[143] It closely resembles

138.   E.g. 2 Sam 23:1–2 (David); Prov 30:1–2 (Agur); Ps 36:2 (transgression); of Yahweh, see e.g. 2 Kgs 19:33; Isa 56:8.

139.   Meier, *Speaking of Speaking*, 306 (my emphasis).

140.   Block, *Ezekiel 1–24*, 33.

141.   Vetter, *TLOT* 2:693–94.

142.   Without אדני: 13:2; 16:35; 21:3 (ET 20:47); 34:7, 9; 36:1; 37:4; with אדני: 6:3; 25:3; 36:4.

143.   Once in 1 Kings, in 22:19 (Micaiah) (paralleled in 2 Chr 18:18); twice in 2 Kings, in 7:1 (Elisha) and 20:16 (Isaiah); four times in Isaiah, in 1:10; 28:14; 39:5; 66:5; thirteen times in Jeremiah, in 2:4; 7:2; 17:20; 19:3; 21:11; 22:2, 29; 29:20; 31:10; 34:4; 42:15; 44:24, 26; once in Hosea, in 4:1; once in Amos, in 7:16.

the introduction to an official proclamation made by a herald,[144] or the call of a singer about to start.[145] This call-to-attention can be directed to a wide variety of addressees. In 1 Kings, it is addressed to an individual (1 Kgs 22:19). Within the book of Ezekiel, it can be addressed to groups (e.g. false prophets (Ezek 13:2), shepherds/leaders (34:7, 9), the people (e.g. 18:25; 37:4; cf. 25:3), to the city of Jerusalem (16:35), to the land or the earth (mountains (6:3; 36:1, 4), to the forest (21:3 [ET 20:47]—a probable metonymy for Jerusalem[146]) and to dry bones (37:4). Within Ezekiel, the only instance of the formula introducing a message of hope, rather than of judgment, is that of 37:4, where the prophet addresses the dry bones.

On each occasion that it occurs, it is followed by the citation formula. The clear implication again is that the word that Ezekiel is to utter is indeed the word of Yahweh, not merely a report or citation of that word. Further, the gap between what the prophet receives and what the prophet is to utter is further reduced by the usage of the same phrase, "word of Yahweh," to describe both the essence of the prophetic event and the rhetorical event.

1.2.4. *Verbatim speech.* In the discussion of the rhetorical event, I have made three main points. First, these three formulae all stress that what the prophet utters is what Yahweh is saying. When put alongside the repeated assertions by Yahweh that "I have spoken," there is little doubt that what Ezekiel is to say, Yahweh also says, not *said*. This picture is reinforced by the presence in Isa 66 of all three formulae mentioned (citation formula, v. 1; signatory formula, v. 2; call-to-attention formula, v. 5 alongside the imperfect of אמר, יאמר, v. 9), which clearly designates the present speech of Yahweh. Secondly, there is some good evidence supporting the notion that Ezekiel is Yahweh's messenger. Thirdly, the gap between prophetic event and rhetorical event is reduced in a number of ways: by subsuming everything within the prophetic event; by the

144.   Cf. 2 Kgs 18:28, "Hear the word of the great king (שמעו דבר־המלך הגדול), the king of Assyria!"

145.   Cf. Judg 5:3, "Hear, O kings (שמעו מלכים); give ear, O princes; to Yahweh I will sing."

146.   Scholars disagree over the referent, principally because there is no evidence of trees in the Negeb, the desert land south of Jerusalem. Craigie argues that Ezekiel was speaking using "allegory," since there was hardly going to be a forest fire in the desert; see Peter C. Craigie, *Ezekiel* (DSB; Edinburgh: The Saint Andrew Press, 1983), 154. Block (*Ezekiel 1–24*, 663) notes support for seeing Jerusalem here from the LXX, and from the second half of the oracle that shows "the correctness of this approach" by making Jerusalem explicit.

occasional ellipsis of the command to "say" before the citation formula; by the presence of the citation formula which "is styled as a literal repetition of the words that were given to the messenger at the time that the messenger was commissioned by the sender."[147]

There is also a fourth way in which the gap is all but eliminated, and that is by the explicit depiction of the words that Ezekiel is to utter as identical with the words received. There is no gap between the word that the prophet receives, and the word that he is to speak.

Elsewhere in the Old Testament, the relationship between the word that comes to the prophet and that which he delivers as Yahweh's word is not necessarily verbatim (e.g. the word that comes to Elijah in 1 Kgs 21:19, and that which he delivers in 1 Kgs 21:20b–24).[148] Similarly, a messenger did not always simply deliver a message verbatim, but could respond to queries and even be creative in how to frame a particular instruction.[149] In Ezekiel, visions cannot, of course, be reported verbatim. Nonetheless, there are four pieces of evidence in Ezekiel that point to a verbatim relationship between what he is portrayed as hearing, on the one hand, and uttering, on the other.

First, there is the unusual phrase in 3:4, ודברת בדברי אליהם ("use my very words in speaking to them"[150]). According to *The Dictionary of Classical Hebrew*, דבר ב (Piel) followed by the noun דבר can mean "speak concerning" (e.g. Deut 6:7; 11:19) or speak "in, with, by means of," with the preposition designating "accompaniment, method, means, instrument."[151] The former meaning makes no sense here.[152] The latter is less likely than a third view, "recite," as Weinfeld argues in his commentary on Deut 6:7. Noting parallels with *qrʾ b* (Deut 17:19) and *hgh b* (Josh 1:8; Ps 1:2), and from the comparison with Exod 13:9, "where the sign and reminder (compare v 8 here) should serve the purpose, 'that the teaching of YHWH shall be in your mouth,'" he maintains that the phrase "involves *recitation* and reading or murmuring."[153] Although the LXX, the Syriac and the Vulgate reduce the force of the MT here (LXX renders

---

147. Sweeney, *Isaiah 1–39*, 524.

148. Though, of course, such a shift could be a narratorial device, highlighting Elijah's unreliability or the twin aspects of Ahab's sin, murder (v. 19) and idolatry (vv. 20–21).

149. Cf. Exod 5:6–13; 2 Sam 11:7, 20–21, 25. See Meier, *Messenger*, 205, 250.

150. Allen, *Ezekiel 1–19*, 4.

151. *DCH* 2:392. Ezek 3:4 is placed under the second of these categories.

152. Cf. G. A. Cooke, *A Critical and Exegetical Commentary on the Book of Ezekiel* (ICC; Edinburgh: T. & T. Clark, 1936), 40.

153. Moshe Weinfeld, *Deuteronomy 1–11* (AB 5; New York: Doubleday, 1991), 333 (my emphasis).

בדברי with τοὺς λόγους μου), suggesting an original את־דברי (cf. 2:7), they are more likely to reflect a free rendering of the MT, for there is no reason why the more difficult MT reading should have arisen. Zimmerli renders the phrase "speak (with the authority of) my words to them," deriving such an interpretation from "the stereotyped language of prophetic schools" which is reflected in 1 Kgs 13.[154] Such an interpretation, however, requires דבר to be singular. Greenberg, followed by Allen[155] and Block,[156] is right when he says that "the nuance…seems to be verbatim repetition of the message."[157] The force of this phrase is that Ezekiel is to speak with the *very words* which Yahweh had spoken to him. Ezekiel's personality is not to obtrude. He is to speak precisely and only what Yahweh speaks to him.

The second piece of evidence that Ezekiel is to utter verbatim what Yahweh says to him is the incident within the commissioning vision of Ezekiel swallowing the scroll (2:8–3:3). This links closely with the observations above about 3:4. Yahweh's word coming to Ezekiel "*as a text*"[158] serves to limit and constrain the freedom of the prophet to modify or reshape the words. The scroll having writing on both sides symbolizes a complete message to which Ezekiel may not add.[159] "This gloomy scroll is full; it contains *nothing but* desolation and there is no leftover space. No amendments will be made; no codicil will be added; the sentence is final."[160] The exclusivity of the words, and the exhaustive nature of them is further reinforced by the image of "filling" (3:2) his stomach with them. The words that Ezekiel has swallowed, he is to utter, using precisely those words that he has been given (3:4).

Such an interpretation, linking the scroll with the *message* that Ezekiel is to utter, though popular with most commentators, has been challenged

154. Zimmerli, *Ezekiel 1*, 92–93.
155. Allen, *Ezekiel 1–19*, 4.
156. Block, *Ezekiel 1–24*, 128.
157. Greenberg, *Ezekiel 1–20*, 68; so too his "On Ezekiel's Dumbness," *JBL* 77 (1958): 103: "The *b* of *bidebārî* is…unexampled…but it would seem far better to regard it as written with a special purpose, than as a mistake: The prophet may speak only what God has put into his mouth, in the very words that God has spoken. This is also the meaning of the remarkable image of eating the scroll of prophecy, which immediately precedes these words."
158. Davis, *Swallowing the Scroll*, 51 (original emphasis).
159. Cf. William H. Brownlee, *Ezekiel 1–19* (WBC 28; Waco, Tex.: Word, 1986), 30; Block, *Ezekiel 1–24*, 124.
160. Baruch J. Schwartz, "Ezekiel's Dim View of Israel's Restoration," in *The Book of Ezekiel: Theological and Anthropological Perspectives* (ed. Margaret S. Odell and John T. Strong; SBL Symposium Series 9; Atlanta: Society of Biblical Literature, 2000), 44.

by Odell.[161] She argues that the event with the scroll should be understood as a test of the prophet rather than as the legitimation of his message, seen in the consuming of the contents of the message. She advances a number of arguments to support her view.

First, she argues that the parallelism in the phrases "hear," "do not be rebellious" and "open your mouth and eat" (2:8) "emphasizes Ezekiel's obedience, not the synonymity of eating and hearing."[162] Secondly, in 3:1, the command "eat...eat" and "go, speak" (3:1) "simply outlines a series of actions Ezekiel is to perform,"[163] rather than entailing that what is eaten is what should be spoken. Thirdly, the noun דבר is absent from this section, though very prominent in 3:4–11. Fourthly, the sequence of the narrative, in which the scroll-event precedes instructions outlining to Ezekiel what he is to do when he hears Yahweh's word, suggests that he has not yet received that word. Fifthly, the internalizing of the divine message is expressed in 3:10 by taking into the heart and ears, not into the belly.[164] Finally, her interpretation resolves, she says, the "apparent conflict that has long been noted between Ezekiel's message of judgment and the description of the scroll as lamentations."[165]

Her alternative, which forms part of her thesis that the whole call vision from 1:1–5:17 marks the transition of Ezekiel from a priest to a prophet, is that "what Ezekiel eats...is not the message of divine judgment but the judgment itself."[166] He does this as a priest, bearing the guilt in a way parallel to the ordination ceremony in Lev. 8–9: "By eating the scroll, Ezekiel takes into his inner being the fate of his people."[167] The phrase "words of mourning and lamentation and woe" (קנים והגה והי)[168] speaks of the consequences, not the essence, of the message, and this precludes an understanding of the scroll as Ezekiel's message.

161. Odell, "You Are What You Eat." Eichrodt (*Ezekiel*, 70) criticizes the notion that there is a "theory of prophetic inspiration" enshrined in the procedure. What the scroll-event indicates to him is "on the one hand, a proof of the obedience of the person who has been chosen and, on the other hand, an assurance that the message with which he is entrusted is independent of his own subjective judgments, and is divine in origin."
162. Odell, "You Are What You Eat," 242.
163. Ibid.
164. Ibid., 243.
165. Ibid., 244.
166. Ibid.
167. Ibid.
168. There are a number of textual issues here—LXX (and Targum) read the singular of קנים (θρῆνος); the final word is a *hapax*, which LXX confuses and reads καὶ οὐαί. See Zimmerli, *Ezekiel 1*, 91–92.

Odell's arguments concerning the scroll are not conclusive, however. First, although it is true that the terms used to describe what is written on the scroll speak more of the anticipated *consequences* of the message that Ezekiel is to utter than the content itself, it is possible that "mourning and lamentation and woe" are instances of metonymy for the events that bring about these effects (cf. Ezek 7:27, where the king shall "mourn" [קנה]), or synecdoche, where the whole of Ezekiel's message is spoken of by means of a part of it.[169] Such figures of speech are not alien to the book of Ezekiel, for in 23:24, the prophet speaks of "wheel" (וגלגל) as a synecdoche for "wheeled vehicles."

Secondly, while it is true that there is a dimension of "obedience" that is emphasized here,[170] this does not preclude the scroll being the divine message.[171] Within the framework of Ezekiel receiving God's word and then speaking it in 2:8–3:3, the eating of the scroll (3:1) most naturally functions as receiving God's word. This is reinforced by two observations. First, these verses are at the centre of what Schwartz calls "the concentric structure" of the verses from 2:1–3:15, framed by words of encouragement (2:6–7; 3:4–9), the charge to speak (2:3–5; 3:10–11) and assistance given by רוח (2:1–2; 3:12–15).[172] Since the "focus" lies in 2:8–3:3, it

---

169. Cf. Zimmerli (ibid., 135), who follows Koch and Fahlgren in adopting an interpretation based on the "synthetic view of life" for the close link between cause and effect; Allen (*Ezekiel 1–19*, 40), who comments that "the title refers not to the content of the prophetic revelation but obliquely to its effect"; Block (*Ezekiel 1–24*, 125), who comments that, "the words…describe the effects of the judgments he will pronounce upon his people."

170. See further Chapter 5 below.

171. Note particularly the discussion in Gregory Y. Glazov, *The Bridling of the Tongue and the Opening of the Mouth in Biblical Prophecy* (JSOTSup 311; Sheffield: Sheffield Academic Press, 2001), 226–74.

172. Baruch J. Schwartz, "The Concentric Structure of Ezekiel 2:1–3:15", in *Proceedings of the Tenth World Congress of Jewish Studies, Jerusalem, August 16–24 1989* (ed. David Assaf; Jerusalem: The World Union of Jewish Students, 1990), 107–14. Lind similarly regards the swallowing of the scroll as central, but for him it is central in the commissioning narrative, from 1:1–3:1. See Millard C. Lind, *Ezekiel* (Believers Church Bible Commentary; Scottdale, Pa.: Herald, 1996), 25–26, 381–82. Certainly the *inclusio* provided by Yahweh's hand and the location by the Chebar river is striking (1:1–3; 3:14–15). The next "ring," of the movement of the chariot and the glory of Yahweh, is tenuous, partly because of the difference in length between the two descriptions (1:4–28; 3:12–13), and partly because the action of רוח is in the foreground in 3:12–13, not the movement of the glory of Yahweh (see Schwartz, "Concentric Structure," 110). Finally, the correspondence between the two commissioning narratives is much clearer with Schwartz's divisions (2:6–7//3:4–9; 2:3–5//3:10–11) than with Lind's "ring" units (1:28b–2:7//3:4–11).

makes greatest sense if this section contains "both charge and encouragement." "The Scroll-eating both orders the prophet what to say and at the
same time relieves him of the responsibility of figuring out how to say it,
since he has been infused with God's own words."[173] The second observation is the fact that throughout the book, Ezekiel is a prophet, priest
and lawgiver like Moses.[174] In these verses it is Ezekiel who is a prophet
"among them" (Ezek 2:5; cf. Deut 18:18) in whose "mouth" Yahweh has
placed his "words" (Ezek 2:8–3:3; cf. Deut 18:18).[175]

The other objections outlined above, based on a comparison between
2:8–3:3 and 3:4–11, fail to account for the fact that what is figuratively
expressed in the scroll-event is then literally expressed in 3:4–11.

Finally, Odell's own interpretation contains a significant shift in the
referent of the words on the scroll. Initially, "the scroll contains something that is decreed, fixed by having been written."[176] This she takes to
be "the judgment itself."[177] However, it is difficult to see precisely how
words of "lamentation, mourning and woe" are "the judgment itself." So
Odell then asserts that what he eats is "the judgment itself *and its consequences*."[178] Her analysis speaks more of the consequences of the
judgment than the judgment itself. Although her interpretation is aimed
at avoiding the "conflict" as she sees it between the message that Ezekiel
is to utter and the description of the scroll, her interpretation involves a
similar conflict.

Before concluding that the scroll is indeed a metaphor for the message
the prophet is to utter, there is, though, a third possibility that should be
considered, and another objection to the notion of the scroll as Ezekiel's
message.

A third way of understanding the scroll is to see the words of "lamentation, mourning and woe" as relating to Ezekiel's experience resulting

---

173.   Schwartz, "Concentric Structure," 112.
174.   Cf. Zimmerli, *Ezekiel 2*, 432; Jon D. Levenson, *Theology of the Program
of Restoration of Ezekiel 40–48* (HSM 10; Missoula, Mont.: Scholars Press, 1976),
38–39; J. Gordon McConville, "Priests and Levites in Ezekiel: A Crux in the Interpretation of Israel's History," *TynBul* 34 (1983): 28–29; Henry McKeating, "Ezekiel
the 'Prophet Like Moses'?," *JSOT* 61 (1994): 97–109; Risa Levitt Kohn, *A New
Heart and a New Soul: Ezekiel, the Exile and the Torah* (JSOTSup 358; London:
Sheffield Academic Press, 2002), 109.
175.   See Levitt Kohn, *New Heart and a New Soul*, 109. It should be noted that
there is not a verbal but a conceptual link with the notion of "among" (מקרב אחיהם,
Deut 18:18; בתוכם, Ezek 2:5).
176.   Odell, "You Are What You Eat," 243.
177.   Ibid.
178.   Ibid., 244 (my emphasis).

from his commission. They describe neither the message that he is to utter (most commentators), nor Ezekiel's embodying of the judgment on Israel and its consequences (Odell), but the experience of the prophet in his ministry. With this interpretation, the fact that the scroll is covered on both sides with writing points to the fact that his ministry from beginning to end will be marked by difficulty ("lamentation, mourning and woe"). This is true whether his message is one of judgment, or of reassurance and hope. Ezekiel needs to be willing to undergo unremitting hardship in his ministry. His swallowing the scroll is a test of that willingness.

The fact that this narrative occurs within the commissioning of the prophet makes it very clear that Ezekiel's ministry is going to be marked by stubborn resistance and hostility. Further, later in Ezekiel's ministry he is told to take up a lament (קינה; ch. 19), echoing 2:10.[179] Again, the experience of the death of his wife and the command not to mourn or weep (בכה, ספד) in one sense encapsulates the "lamentation, mourning and woe" which is to be his lot. The lack of public mourning in 24:15–24 does not preclude inward mourning. In addition, the experience of frustration, of hostility, of rejection seems to have been the reality, as portrayed in the book, from the beginning to the end of Ezekiel's ministry, hence both sides of the scroll are covered with the writing.

There are two difficulties with this third view. First, there are almost no verbal allusions or indicators that the scroll relates to Ezekiel's own experience. This is not insuperable, since there are almost no verbal allusions that link the contents of the scroll to his message. The gap, however, between the words on the scroll and Ezekiel's own experience is greater than that between the words on the scroll and the judgment announced. Secondly, the structure of the unit highlights the scroll-eating not just as an act of obedience, but also as an act of equipping the prophet with the message he needs to bring.

A possible further objection to the notion that the scroll speaks of Ezekiel's message is the observation that Ezekiel's message was not exclusively one of doom and destruction. Hölscher resolves this by arguing that the real Ezekiel only announced judgment.[180] Schwartz highlights and then resolves it in a different fashion.[181] He believes that there is no

179.   Cf. Lawrence Boadt, "Rhetorical Strategies in Ezekiel's Oracles of Judgment," in Lust, ed., *Ezekiel and His Book*, 195; Renz, *Rhetorical Function*, 62. Allen (*Ezekiel 1–19*, 40) observes that Ezekiel's laments, apart from ch. 19, all relate to other nations. As a result, he does not think there is a connection between 2:10 and ch. 19.

180.   Hölscher, *Hesekiel, der Dichter und das Buch*, 40–42.

181.   Schwartz, "Ezekiel's Dim View," 43.

basis within the book for the shift in Ezekiel's ministry from oracles of judgment and doom to oracles speaking of Yahweh's purposes to restore and prosper the exiles. Given that the scroll is indeed the message to proclaim, the message of the restoration of Israel is of a piece with the oracles of judgment, wholly and unchangeably melancholic:

> For Ezekiel, the future restoration of Israel is not something distinct from and subsequent to YHWH's punishment of his people, but rather a direct outgrowth of it. According to Ezekiel, YHWH's ultimate decision to restore his people's fortunes is not the result of any change in their feelings or behavior towards him or in his disposition toward them. And since Israel's unregenerate evil and YHWH's wrathful resolve to requite them for it remain unaltered, Ezekiel never really alters his message.[182]

It is not necessary to go with either Hölscher or Schwartz. The most common view, often linked with Ezekiel's dumbness, is that the fall of Jerusalem, or news of the fall of Jerusalem, precipitates a shift in the thrust of the message.[183] At one level, that is of course true, since the balance of the message clearly shifts. However, it naturally raises questions about the place and function of oracles of salvation in chs. 1–24. Those scholars who regard such oracles as post-587 additions do not have a difficulty regarding the scroll as Ezekiel's message, since until the fall Ezekiel's message was unremitting "lamentation, mourning and woe."[184] There is, however, then a danger of losing synchronic coherence because the book of Ezekiel contains words of hope before the fall. A second view, suggested by Odell, is that a transition in the book is evident in Ezek 24:15–24.[185] For her, the prohibition against mourning is not concerned with limiting expressions of grief. Rather, it has a social function, expressing dissociation from the one who has died.[186] In similar fashion, the putting on of a turban has a wider social function. She notes that it occurs in contexts unrelated to mourning, and serves principally to mark a change in the status of the one who puts the turban on.[187] For her,

---

182. Ibid., 55.
183. Cf. especially Davis, *Swallowing the Scroll*, 56–58.
184. So, e.g., Hals, *Ezekiel*, 70–71; Allen, *Ezekiel 1–19*, xxviii–ix.
185. Margaret S. Odell, "Genre and Persona in Ezekiel 24:15–24," in Odell and Strong, eds., *The Book of Ezekiel*, 195–219.
186. Ibid., 201.
187. Ibid., 203. Instances where it occurs include "in the description of the clothing worn by priests" (Ezek 44:8; Exod 39:28), "or in accounts of election or restoration to high office" (Zech 3:5), "or in wedding imagery" (Isa 61:10). This wider perspective concerning change of status explains how turbans can be associated with mourning.

Ezek 24:15–24 "signifies…that God has chosen the exilic community over Jerusalem, and that Ezekiel's actions are a sign of this election."[188]

Odell's arguments about the social function of the prohibition against mourning and of the putting on of the turban are well made. Her suggestive thesis, however, needs further development. In Ezekiel, it is the exiles who are to put on turbans (24:23); yet, in Isa 61:10, as Odell herself notes,[189] it is the *bridegroom* who puts on a turban as a mark of the change in his status, so the parallel is not exact. It is not easy to see how the exiles are to act like a bridegroom, and yet be Yahweh's "betrothed" after his wife, Jerusalem, has died. Secondly, given that the exiles remain rebellious until the end of the book, the change in status needs to be some kind of proleptic change.

The best solution is to recognize that in view of the anticipated hardheartedness of Ezekiel's addressees, and the anticipated forty years in exile (cf. 4:6), even messages of hope and salvation that, within the narrative timeframe, predated the fall of Jerusalem were not messages of hope and comfort for that generation. For Ezekiel's addressees, the message until the fall of Jerusalem that Jerusalem was finished was a message of misery.

The second piece of evidence, then, pointing to the verbatim communication of Yahweh's words is the motif of the prophet swallowing the scroll and subsequently speaking Yahweh's words.

The third piece of evidence that points towards the verbatim nature of the relationship between the words Ezekiel receives and those he utters is the only instance recorded of the prophet actually speaking to his exilic audience (24:20–27). There, in response to the people's question in v. 19 about Ezekiel's lack of mourning, Ezekiel replies to them by relaying to them his experience of the prophetic event, and the words he received in that prophetic event: "Then I said to them, 'The word of Yahweh came to me…'" Thus the "rhetorical event" consists of Ezekiel simply repeating verbatim the prophetic event. There is no gap between them.

The fourth and final piece of evidence is the form of the book itself. The readers of the book are not presented with the rhetorical event, of the prophet delivering his words, but with the prophetic event, of the prophet receiving Yahweh's words. Such an approach leaves no gap between the two events. What the prophet received is what confronts the reader (and, presumably, the prophet's audience). The word of Yahweh does not just come to the prophet; it comes to the readers of the book.

188. Ibid., 196.
189. Ibid., 205.

1.2.5. *Summary*. Though the book of Ezekiel hardly ever records the prophet actually speaking, the use of the different formulae introducing speech indicates a clear distinction between the prophetic event and the rhetorical event. Such a distinction, however, should not obscure the point that Ezekiel was essentially to utter verbatim what he received. Further, the rhetorical event is not simply a repetition of words that Yahweh said to him, and instructed him to relay. Rather, the rhetorical event is Yahweh speaking in the present. This, then, leaves open the possibility of a more direct relationship between Yahweh's רוח and Yahweh's word in the rhetorical event.

1.3. *Yahweh's Ordinances and Statutes*
Until now, our focus on Yahweh's word in the book of Ezekiel has been exclusively on the prophetic word. It is a mistake, however, when study-ing the relationship between the word of God and the spirit of God from a theological perspective, to limit Yahweh's word to the "prophetic word." Vriezen notes, when writing about revelation by the word, that besides the "word" to the prophet, there is "revelation to the priest, who receives *torah* (instruction) from God."[190] Throughout the book of Ezekiel, Yah-weh speaks of "my ordinances/judgments" (משפטי)[191] and "my statutes" (חקתי),[192] "my teaching" (תורתי, Ezek 22:26) and "my teachings" (תורתי, Ezek 44:24). Thus Yahweh stands behind these words in the same way that he stands behind the prophetic word; he is the author and speaker of both. This broadening of the field of study is not invalidated either by the fact that דבר יהוה is a technical term for the prophetic word, or Gerle-man's contention that the seven passages[193] where the noun דבר, in con-struct relationship with "Yahweh," indicates unequivocally God's legal word, are late.[194] Yahweh's words are broader than the prophetic "word of Yahweh."[195] A theological examination of the relationship between

190.   Th. C. Vriezen, *An Outline of Old Testament Theology* (Oxford: Blackwell, 1958), 252.
191.   Ezek 5:6–7; 11:20; 18:17; 20:11, 13, 19, 21, 24.
192.   Ezek 5:6–7; 11:12, 20; 18:9, 17; 20:11, 13, 16, 19, 21, 24; 36:27; 37:24; 44:24. On two occasions (one with "my"), Yahweh "gave" them these (Ezek 20:11, 25), though I regard the second as an ironical recapitulation of 20:18.
193.   Num 15:31; Deut 5:5; 2 Sam 12:9; 1 Chr 15:15; 2 Chr 30:12; 34:21; 35:6.
194.   Gerleman, *TLOT* 1:331.
195.   Cf. Claus Westermann (*Elements*, p. 23), who, though acknowledging that his categories "only approximately and inexactly encompass the richness of God's words," divides Yahweh's words into three: the word of announcement, the directive word (*torah* understood as instruction) and the cultic word. See ibid., 17–23; also Preuss, *Old Testament Theology*, 1:196–97, for the same points.

"word" and "spirit" will entail looking at the different kinds of Yahweh's words. Precisely how Yahweh's רוח relates to these words of Yahweh, we shall examine below in Part III.

1.4. *The Book of Ezekiel Itself*

The word of Yahweh is primarily a speech event. It needs to be asked, however, to what extent the *book* of Ezekiel, as opposed to the words that the prophet received, was understood as the "word of Yahweh" by the implied author.[196] In other words, is the book of Ezekiel itself a speech event of Yahweh in its own right, or a record of a succession of speech events? Again, this is important if we are to be in a position to understand precisely at what point, if at all, and in what way, if at all, Yahweh's רוח relates to such a speech event, if it be such.

In this section, I shall look at the two main ways in which the book as a whole might be understood as Yahweh's word. First, I shall look briefly at the proposal of Ellen Davis, that the prophet communicated *in writing*. I shall argue that this approach, while recognizing the literary nature of much of the book, is ultimately not adequate. Secondly, I shall look at the significance of 1:3, and shall argue that it makes sense to see it as a superscription for the book of Ezekiel as a whole. While it does differ from the ways of marking direct discourse *within* the narrative, it makes a claim for the book as a whole—the written words of the prophet, along with the biographical information—as Yahweh's communication to the readers.

In her interesting study, *Swallowing the Scroll*, Davis puts forward the thesis that Ezekiel set out to communicate with his audience in writing. This is not to deny oral features to his oracles, but it is to say that "Ezekiel's achievement is in making narrative a vehicle of prophecy."[197] Central to her thesis is the relationship between ingestion of the scroll and Ezekiel's dumbness (2:8–3:3; 3:26): "During the period of dumbness, Ezekiel is merely the vehicle of the divinely authored text"[198] since, up to the fall of Jerusalem, his fellow exiles need no new word at all. For Davis, the move from oral to literary was not so much a response, a reaction to the past and the present, but a creative movement, one that shaped the future. By prophesying through a literary work, the focus moved from the prophet to the prophecy, from the person to the text. So she sees it as crucial that we understand "literary activity as an instrument of

---

196. Who is clearly distinct from the narrator in the book, the prophet Ezekiel himself (cf. 1:1–3).

197. Davis, *Swallowing the Scroll*, 126.

198. Ibid., 56.

social change and not merely a means of reflecting its occurrence."[199] Here, then, Yahweh's word is intimately linked with the book.

Davis' work, though, does not always account adequately for the public dimensions and oral features of the book; some features, such as the great emphasis on marking divine speech, require further explanation.[200] It is not adequate to say that these features are due to the book's being read out loud. More significantly, as Block points out, it is not obvious that the editors of the book of Ezekiel linked clearly the swallowing of the scroll and Ezekiel's dumbness.[201] Thirdly, the fact that the word came to Ezekiel "*as a text*"[202] does not mean that Ezekiel had to pass it on as text, as Davis argues. It may simply mean that the prophet is not at liberty to alter what Yahweh says, and that the prophet is to utter Yahweh's words verbatim. Davis' suggestion, then, is not compelling.

If we turn our attention to Ezek 1:3, we are faced with two questions. The first is: "In what sense is this verse a superscription?" The second, which depends on the answer to the first, is: "If it is indeed a superscription, in what way or to what extent does it signal that what follows is Yahweh's speech?"

Many of the prophetic books, as well as other books of different types, have superscriptions. Some have as their introduction a variation of the word-event formula in the third person (e.g. Hos 1:1; Joel 1:1), a formula in superscriptions that is often attributed to the circles associated with Deuteronomy.[203] Thus, these prophetic *books* could be understood as the "word of Yahweh." In Ezek 1:3, the word-event formula occurs, from the perspective of the implied author, describing Ezekiel in the third person, "the word of Yahweh came to the priest Ezekiel son of Buzi, in the land of the Chaldeans by the river Chebar; and the hand of Yahweh was on him there." Should the book of Ezekiel be understood in a similar way?

In his article examining prophetic superscriptions, Tucker excludes the book of Ezekiel.[204] There are a number of reasons why 1:3 might be excluded. First, superscriptions tend to stand at the head of the book,

---

199. Ibid., 131.
200. Cf. Meier, *Speaking of Speaking*, 241.
201. Daniel I. Block, Review of Ellen F. Davis, *Swallowing the Scroll, JBL* 110 (1991): 146.
202. Davis, *Swallowing the Scroll*, 51 (original emphasis).
203. Cf. Bergman et al., *TDOT* 3:113; Lindblom, *Prophecy*, 279–80; Gene M. Tucker, "Prophetic Superscriptions and the Growth of a Canon," in *Canon and Authority: Essays in Old Testament Religion and Theology* (ed. G. W. Coats and B. O. Long; Philadelphia: Fortress, 1977), 69.
204. Tucker, "Prophetic Superscriptions," 59.

outside the body of the work,[205] but Ezek 1:3 does not. Secondly, superscriptions are syntactically unrelated to what follows, but Ezek 1:3 is incorporated into the text (cf. the third person, "the hand of Yahweh was upon *him*").[206] Thirdly, superscriptions tend not to be clauses in their own right,[207] but Ezek 1:3 has a main verb. Fourthly, most scholars link v. 2 with v. 3, thus introducing a specificity to the "word" that came to the prophet, either to the "word" that the prophet received beginning in 2:1,[208] or to the vision as a whole.[209] Such a linking of v. 2 and v. 3 also makes this less like a superscription. Finally, v. 3 separates two standard Ezekielian elements introducing a vision—the action of the "hand of Yahweh" which precedes every vision, and the description of the vision as מראות אלהים (cf. 8:3; 40:2)—thus apparently delimiting v. 3 to the vision that follows.

There are, however, a number of strong reasons why Ezek 1:3 should be treated as a superscription for the book. First, it clearly stands apart from v. 1 and v. 4 because of the shift in person from first (vv. 1, 4) to third (v. 3); a different voice is heard—that of the implied author, not the narrator. Secondly, it is likely that v. 2 is linked more closely with v. 1 than with v. 3.[210] While it is theoretically possible that the awkward incomplete date in v. 2 was added later to specify further the time of the once clear, but now unclear, thirtieth year in v. 1,[211] it is more likely that v. 2 went with v. 1 from the beginning, given that the other dates in the book are defined with reference to Jehoiachin. This means that the form is much closer to other prophetic superscriptions. Thirdly, if v. 3 were not a superscription, the word-event formula would then introduce a vision, a unique function in the book. Fourthly, where the word-event formula is used elsewhere in Ezekiel, it is introduced differently (with ויהי not with הָיֹה הָיָה). Fifthly, Allen's observation that the singular דבר signifies only "one oracle" does not take account of the singular in

---

205. Ibid., 58.

206. Zimmerli (*Ezekiel 1*, 82), however, comments, "One has to read עלי 'upon me.'" This is based on his reconstruction of the original vision report (p. 108).

207. Tucker, "Prophetic Superscriptions," 59.

208. Greenberg, *Ezekiel 1–20*, 41.

209. Allen (*Ezekiel 1–19*, 23) comments, "It provides a superscription, not for the book, since only one oracle (דבר 'word') is in view, but strictly for the unit 1:1–3:15." Cf. Block, *Ezekiel 1–24*, 89.

210. Zimmerli, *Ezekiel 1*, 100–101; Renz, *Rhetorical Function*, 133–34.

211. Possibly in a similar fashion to the often-discerned Deuteronomistic redaction of the superscription in Amos 1:1 made necessary by the relatively short-lived specificity of the reference to the "earthquake." For this point on Amos, see Tucker, "Prophetic Superscriptions," 69–70.

Hosea, Zephaniah, Micah and Joel. Finally, its location within the text
and its different syntax are both explicable in terms of the uniqueness of
the literary setting. Not only is the narrative in the first person, but a geo-
graphical and temporal reference has already been supplied in vv. 1–2.
By giving the implied author a word that vindicates the claim of the
narrator, it advances the rhetorical purpose of the book.[212]

In conclusion, the redactional "heading" of the book is restricted to
v. 3, which serves to introduce the book as a whole.[213] It seems likely,
then, that the author of the book of Ezekiel saw the book *as a whole* as
Yahweh's word. Far from presenting an account of the prophet's ministry in any biographical sense,[214] Yahweh's word is re-presented with
fresh significance to the readers of the book.

The second question concerns the way in which or the extent to which
such a superscription indicates that what follows is Yahweh's speech.

Meier has rightly observed that these prophetic superscriptions differ
from the usual marking of direct discourse in that they summarize what
follows, rather than introduce it.[215] Further, he notes that a rubric can
become a marker of direct discourse, as in Zech 1:7, "where Zechariah's
autobiographical discourse is disconcertingly introduced as a divine
oracle."[216] For these reasons, he is reluctant to see such superscriptions as
indicating that the "entire text…is enclosed within quotation marks."[217]
To say, however, that it is not "direct discourse" in the same sense as the
original oracles does not mean that it does not "count as" Yahweh's
word. Indeed, the point in adding the superscriptions is to give authority
to the written words, with all their historical specificity, that the words
had when spoken. As Mays comments on Hosea, "The book as a whole
is 'the word of Yahweh', the message of the God of Israel. The category
of 'word' (*dābār*) is extended to include the total tradition deriving from

---

212.   So Renz, *Rhetorical Function*, 135; cf. Davis, *Swallowing the Scroll*, 77–85.
213.   So Cooke, *Ezekiel*, 5. There is no need to say that such a redactional
heading is post-exilic because of the similarities between Ezek 1:3a and Hag 1:1 and
Zech 1:1 (Zimmerli, *Ezekiel 1*, p. 110). It is more plausible that the book of Ezekiel
has influenced Haggai and Zechariah, particularly in matters of form. Cf. Steven S.
Tuell, "Haggai–Zechariah: Prophecy After the Manner of Ezekiel," *SBL Seminar
Papers, 2000* (SBLSP 39; Atlanta: Society of Biblical Literature, 2000), 263–86.
214.   The framing of the narrative of the book with reference to Yahweh's word
thus contradicts von Rad's suggestion (*Old Testament Theology*, 2:265) that "the
Book of Ezekiel is practically a long prophetic autobiography."
215.   Meier, *Speaking of Speaking*, 23: "The rubric supplies a context; the DD
[Direct Discourse] marker assumes it."
216.   Ibid., 23.
217.   Ibid., 21.

a prophet, all his oracles and the narratives which tell of his activity."[218] The book of Ezekiel confronts the readers directly with the same word that confronted the prophet, re-presented to them. Such a perspective points to an understanding of that word speaking afresh to the readers/hearers.

1.5. *The Recipients of Yahweh's Word*

The relationship between Yahweh's word and those to whom it comes is complex. The book portrays the prophetic word coming to the prophet. It envisages the prophet conveying that prophetic word to his exilic audience. Such a conveying, however, occurs through oracles addressed, apparently, to a variety of addressees, both animate (passim) and inanimate (mountains in ch. 6; the Negev in 21:3–5 [ET 20:47–49]), both present (the exiles) and absent (Jerusalemites in ch. 16).[219] It depicts Yahweh's laws and statutes, given long ago to the house of Israel's ancestors (20:11, 19), as being now Yahweh's speech both to the Jerusalemites (5:6–7; 11:12) and to the exiles (18:17; 36:27; 37:24). Further, Yahweh's words to the prophet, and the narrative framework within which they are contained, are also re-presented to the readers/hearers of the book of Ezekiel.

Such complexity renders it necessary to proffer a framework for understanding the functioning of Yahweh's word and its relationship to the different groups, as a counterpart to our discussion of the different communication actions. This is essential because we may find that Yahweh's רוח relates to Yahweh's word at particular points, or in particular communication situations.

Wolterstorff draws a number of helpful distinctions, and provides useful categorization for different recipients of a word, based on insights derived from speech act theory.[220] He notes, first, that many, not all, speech acts have an *addressee*; so, for example, "I promise *someone*." In the book of Ezekiel, Yahweh's speech acts at one level all have the prophet as the *addressee*. The book as a whole is narrated from the perspective of the prophet himself, yet the prophet is portrayed not so much as a communicator of the word of Yahweh, but as a receiver of it. At another level, however, we see how the mountains, Jerusalem and others, as well as the exiles, are also the *addressees* of the speech acts that Ezekiel is told to utter. At another level still, those to whom the book was presented are the addressees of the *book*.

---

218.   James L. Mays, *Hosea: A Commentary* (OTL; London: SCM, 1969), 20.
219.   *Pace* Brownlee, *Ezekiel 1–19*, who argues that Ezekiel did in fact deliver the oracles in person.
220.   Wolterstorff, *Divine Discourse*, 54–57.

Secondly, often persons other than the addressee will hear/read one's text. These Wolterstorff calls the *audience*. Within this audience, there is the *intended audience*. Within this *intended audience*, there are potentially two groups: the speaker or writer may have intended that particular people be in that audience (IA.1), or it may be that anyone of a certain sort would be the audience (IA.2). Where the prophet is instructed to address speech acts to addressees other than the exiles, the prophet's intended audience (IA.1) is the exiles in Babylon (3:11); indeed, the addressees are addressees in form only, since there is no indication that the prophet did indeed address his words to those whom he is apparently instructed to address. In these instances, it is not the addressees who are expected to respond to the word of Yahweh, but the intended audience, the exilic community. Where the prophet is instructed to address speech acts to the exiles, the identity of the addressees and the intended audience may well be the same.[221] It is likely, however, that where the addressees are a subgroup of the exiles (such as false prophets in exile), then the intended audience has wider scope than the addressees. With regard to the book as a whole, it is likely that the intended audience (IA.1) is the same as the addressees. We shall look at their identity below.

Thirdly, a single illocutionary act may have more than one addressee —one may address one's remarks to a number of people. In the book of Ezekiel, the prophet himself is the primary addressee of Yahweh's word. There are, though, various addressees of the prophet's words envisaged.

This, Wolterstorff says, is more obvious than the fourth point, that a single locutionary act may say different things to different addressees.[222] He gives the example of a mother at the evening family meal asserting, "Only two more days until Christmas." He observes that, to her children, the meaning is presumably something like "Isn't it exciting?," or perhaps, "Be patient!," but to her husband, she might mean "Stop going off to the golf course and get the shopping done instead!" Thus one locutionary act ("Only two more days until Christmas") may contain more than one illocutionary act. An act of imagination, of interpretation, is required on the part of the hearer or reader to discern the illocutionary force of the locutionary act. In the book of Ezekiel, the addressees of a speech act are

---

221. These include oracles that Ezekiel is to address to false prophets (13:2–16), the false prophetesses (13:17–23), the leaders ("shepherds") of Israel (34:7, 9), the exilic community as a whole (chs. 14; 18; 20; 36) and princes (45:9). In many of these oracles, it is not surprising, then, that there are direct calls to action aimed at those whom the prophet is to address (14:6; 18:30–31; 20:30, 39; 33:11b; 36:32b; 45:9).

222. Cf. Thiselton's observations about "the capacities of a single speech-act to perform a *variety* of illocutionary functions." See Anthony C. Thiselton, *New Horizons in Hermeneutics* (London: Marshall Pickering, 1992), 290.

not differentiated one from another at any point, such that the illocution-ary force could be seen to be different for different addressees. Clearly this could not be the case for Yahweh's words to the prophet, since he alone is the addressee. It could, though, be the case for Ezekiel's words he is to utter to his addressees/intended audience.

In general, the intended audience is perceived as a unity, as "the house of Israel." In that respect, Joyce is right to point to the corporate nature both of judgment and restoration.[223] There are, however, hints of a possi-ble self-differentiation within "the house of Israel" dependent on the attitudes of those hearing Ezekiel's words. One striking example is that found in 3:27. By way of modifying the apparently blanket statement about Ezekiel's dumbness, Yahweh continues in v. 27, "But when I speak with you, I will open your mouth, and you shall say to them, 'Thus says the Lord Yahweh'; let those who will hear, hear; and let those who refuse to hear, refuse; for they are a rebellious house." Here is a tacit acknowl-edgment, even anticipation, that there could be different responses to Ezekiel's words. In 11:14–20, in response to the self-centred, self-satis-fied statement of those in Jerusalem who claim that they, and not those in exile, will possess the land, Yahweh promises restoration to those in exile. In the difficult v. 21, Yahweh announces, "but as for those whose heart goes after their detestable things and their abominations, I will bring their deeds upon their own heads."[224] The most obvious reference here is to those in Jerusalem in v. 15, who are marked by "detestable things" and "abominations" (v. 18). Allen and Block, however, are right to see here a reference to those in exile who are also marked by idolatry (14:1–11; cf. 20:32), and whose heart (v. 19) needs renewing.[225] Thus in the same locutionary act at the same time to the same set of addressees, Ezekiel may be both condemning and promising, depending on the attitude and heart of those addressees.[226] An example of this is the opening vision in ch. 1. For some scholars, this vision is good news, indicating Yahweh's

223. Joyce, *Divine Initiative*, 54–55, 112–13.

224. See Allen, *Ezekiel 1–19*, 129, for a discussion of some of the textual issues.

225. Ibid., 166; Block, *Ezekiel 1–24*, 355. Other instances where there is evi-dence of (potential) distinctions in the addressees include 20:38 and 34:17–22. See further Davis, *Swallowing the Scroll*, 79–80.

226. Cf. Möller's observation on prophetic judgment oracles that "it is the addressees who 'decide' what the speech act counts as" (Karl Möller, "Words of [In-]evitable Certitude? Reflections on the Interpretation of Prophetic Oracles of Judgment," in Bartholomew, Greene and Möller, eds., *After Pentecost*, 368). There is a fine distinction between this point, and the closely related one, whereby the same *illocution* has different *perlocutionary* effects, such as hardening or contrition. This would obtain if no distinctions were recognized or envisaged within the intended audience (IA.1), but were only revealed after the locutionary act.

freedom to be active in exile.[227] For others, the throne vision is essentially bad news, speaking of Yahweh coming in judgment.[228] It makes more sense, however, to say that whether this vision is good news or bad news depends on what the addressees do with this locutionary act.[229]

Fifthly, a given text (locutionary act) can be used *on different occasions* to say different things (or to re-say the same thing) to the same or different addressees. The important distinction that Wolterstorff wants to maintain here is that saying something by *authoring* a text is different from saying something by *presenting* a text to someone, whether it is a text that one has oneself authored, or one that someone else has authored.[230] The illocutionary force may change by using someone else's speech, or by a person performing the same locutionary act in a different context. Wenk gives the example of a joke.[231] In the first setting, the force of the joke might be to entertain. The same joke, however, could be told in a different setting, whether in oral or written form, to educate, by providing an example of good, or bad, humour. Thus, though the prophet was the addressee and recipient of the word of Yahweh, its "re-presentation" within the book of Ezekiel may carry a different illocutionary force. For example, in 2:1–7, the call to Ezekiel serves as Yahweh commissioning the prophet. That is the original illocutionary force of such a statement, as the narrative presents it to us. *In* saying these words to Ezekiel in the vision, Yahweh is commissioning the prophet. The author, however, *in* re-presenting these words to his readers, authenticates the prophet. Ezekiel is a prophet who has received Yahweh's call. He also warns the readers not to be like Ezekiel's addressees but to be like the prophet.

In the same way, what Ezekiel the prophet previously said can now serve to speak to a different community by way of them being *presented* with the finished book of Ezekiel, which includes those same words.[232]

---

227.   So, e.g., Zimmerli, *Ezekiel 1*, 140; Ralph W. Klein, *Ezekiel: The Prophet and His Message* (Columbia: University of South Carolina Press, 1988), 26–27; Joyce, "Dislocation and Adaptation," 57–58. See, however, the counterarguments in Greenberg, *Ezekiel 1–20*, 58–59.

228.   So, e.g., Leslie C. Allen, "The Structure and Intention of Ezekiel 1," *VT* 43 (1993): 145–61; idem, *Ezekiel 1–19*, 44.

229.   The double-edged nature of the vision is noted particularly by Robert R. Wilson, "Prophecy in Crisis: The Call of Ezekiel," *Int* 38 (1984): 124–25, and Mein, *Ezekiel and the Ethics of Exile*, 235–36.

230.   Cf. Thiselton, *New Horizons*, 41.

231.   Matthias Wenk, "The Holy Spirit and the Ethical/Religious Life of the People of God in Luke–Acts" (Ph.D. diss., Brunel University, 1998), 106.

232.   Cf. Ronald E. Clements, "The Chronology of Redaction in Ezekiel 1–24," in Lust, ed., *Ezekiel and His Book*, 290. He comments, "The original prophetic mes-

This is true, even if the audience of the book includes some who heard the words when they were first uttered. For example, oracles initially uttered by the prophet to assert the fall of Jerusalem (a speech act Austin would probably term a "verdictive"[233]) can no longer function in that way once Jerusalem itself has fallen. By being re-presented within a larger "speech event," these same oracles *do* something different. In order to think what, it will be helpful to look at the related matter of the distinction between "direct" and "indirect" speech acts. Yule outlines this clearly.[234]

An indirect speech act is one where there is "an indirect relationship" between the "structure" of the speech act and its "function."[235] An example he gives is the utterance, "It's cold outside." When this utterance is used to make the statement, "I hereby tell you about the weather," it is functioning as a "direct" speech act. Its structure is declarative, and it functions to make a statement. When, however, this utterance is used to make a command or request, "I hereby request of you that you close the door," it is functioning as an "indirect" speech act. Though its structure is declarative, it functions not to make a statement about the weather, but as a request or command that you close the door. In the case of the oracles of judgment on Jerusalem re-presented to the book's audience, they do not function as "direct" speech acts. Though they are declarative, they do not make a statement, "I hereby tell you about the destiny of Jerusalem," *since the book's addressees already know*. Rather, as an "indirect" speech act, they surely request or command the audience to distance themselves from any allegiance to Jerusalem and from what caused such a downfall. Only this can explain adequately the ongoing life of the words. In other words, and this is critical to my reading of the book, some oracles acquire a new life, and a new illocutionary force comprehensible by seeing them as "indirect" speech acts. Through such oracles, the readers of the book are called to repentance.[236]

---

sage possessed a clear and firmly defined context dictated by the historical and political situation in which it was given. As a written prophecy, however, preserved through a period when that original context had receded into the past, it acquired a new context, partly provided by the new historical situation that had arisen, but also very substantially affected by the larger literary context in which it was now placed."

233.   Austin, *How to Do Things With Words*, 150. Austin categorizes "verdictives" as "typified by the giving of a verdict, as the name implies, by a jury, arbitrator, or umpire. But they need not be final; they may be, for example, an estimate, reckoning, or appraisal."

234.   Yule, *Pragmatics*, 54–56.

235.   Ibid., 55.

236.   See further Chapter 5 below.

This analysis means that it is not *necessary* to posit different address-ees (and an intended audience) of the book from those who had, in fact, heard the prophet himself speak. Oracles that they had heard before could have been presented again with a new illocutionary force. This observa-tion does not demonstrate that they *were* the same addressees. What it does do is show that the book of Ezekiel need not be simply a collection of the prophet's oracles, even if it be granted that the addressees had heard some (or all) of them before.

If we turn now from categorizing the addressees and seeing how Yahweh's word can be understood as coming to them, to the *identity* of the addressees, we immediately find ourselves potentially entering com-plex debates over dating, provenance and historicity. I identified four different communication situations in which Yahweh's word can be seen. The first three—Yahweh addressing the prophet, the prophet speak-ing to his intended audiences and Yahweh's statutes and ordinances being re-presented to the exiles—are all wholly intratextual, so an exami-nation of the relationship between Yahweh's רוח and Yahweh's word that comes in each one of these three situations can be conducted "within" the book itself. The fourth communication situation, however, which speaks of Yahweh's word as it comes via the book itself, *does* require us to make judgments about the identity of the addressees. Their identity is important for two reasons. First, an understanding of how the oracles or visions that came to Ezekiel function when re-presented to the addressees of the book depends on precisely to whom these words are addressed. There is, though, the problem of circularity. The identity of the addressees is determined by the content of the book. The function of the book is then determined by the identity of the addressees. Such circularity is not ultimately avoidable. The best approach is to assess the degree to which the hypothesized addressees fit with the proposed under-standing of the book and its oracles within it.

Secondly, the identity of the addressees is important within this study not so much in its own right, since we can assess the book's under-standing of the relationship between God's רוח and the word that comes to its implied readers without certain knowledge. Rather, I need to make judgments about the book as a whole, and the addressees of the book, because Part II will explore the book's portrayal of word, רוח and prophetic inspiration within the context of possible historical develop-ments. That is only possible when the book of Ezekiel itself is located within the continuum that is Israel's history.

Although a consideration of historical developments might suggest that we do need, after all, to be concerned for the historical location of the individual oracles in the book, this is diminished by the fact that the book *as a whole* points to a *terminus ad quem* of around 538 B.C.E., and not later than 516 B.C.E.,[237] and to the addressees being the exiles in Babylon. Two factors point in this direction.

First, negatively, the book does not reflect a post-exilic situation. There are a number of strands of evidence that lead to this conclusion. First, nothing in the book points to the return from exile as being an historical fact. Even the Gog oracle, which speaks of the situation where the return to the land has happened, still portrays such a return as future, and presupposes a scene never found after the exile. Secondly, the book reveals no "hint" of the Persian empire succeeding the Babylonian.[238] Thirdly, the book's assertion that the whole population of Judah was annihilated would have made little sense in view of the conflict between those who returned from exile and those who remained (and survived) in Judah.[239] Fourthly, "the book does not address any of the specific issues that arose in the post-exilic community in Jerusalem, such as dyarchic leadership, mixed marriages and the deterioration of Judah's economic conditions."[240] Fifthly, the book does not give any indication of a Diaspora setting, speaking neither of how to worship Yahweh in another

237.   This is not to say that there have not been subsequent textual glosses. It is to say that a distinction can be made between textual criticism and redaction criticism. See Allen, *Ezekiel 20–48*, 9–10. For the redactional shaping of the book, see also Terence Collins, *The Mantle of Elijah: The Redaction Criticism of the Prophetical Books* (The Biblical Seminar 20; Sheffield: JSOT Press, 1993), 88–103; and, in particular, Chapters 9, 10, 13, 14 and 15 in the collection of essays by R. E. Clements (*Old Testament Prophecy: From Oracles to Canon* [Louisville, Ky.: Westminster John Knox, 1996]). For Clements, "virtually all the substantive material in the book belongs to sixth century B.C." ("The Ezekiel Tradition: Prophecy in a Time of Crisis," in *Old Testament Prophecy*, 157; repr. from *Israel's Prophetic Traditions: Essays in Honour of Peter R. Ackroyd* [ed. Richard Coggins, Anthony Phillips and Michael Knibb; Cambridge: Cambridge University Press, 1982], 119–36). In his commentary (*Ezekiel*, 170), though, he dates the Gog oracle to "at least two centuries after Ezekiel's time." Rooker, from a linguistic perspective, concludes that the book typifies "the transitional link between pre-exilic and post-exilic BH [Biblical Hebrew]" and notes that this is "consistent with the exilic setting reflected in the book"; see Mark F. Rooker, *Biblical Hebrew in Transition: The Language of the Book of Ezekiel* (JSOTSup 90; Sheffield: JSOT Press, 1990), 186; so too A. Hurvitz, *A Linguistic Study of the Relationship Between the Priestly Source and the Book of Ezekiel: A New Approach to an Old Problem* (CahRB 20; Paris: Gabalda, 1982), and, most recently Levitt Kohn, *New Heart and a New Soul*.
238.   Allen, *Ezekiel 20–48*, xxvi.
239.   Renz, *Rhetorical Function*, 9.
240.   Ibid., 232.

land, nor how to cope with living in a foreign land with little or no expectation of a return.[241]

The second factor in arriving at an exilic date and a Babylonian provenance is the converse of the first factor. The book itself makes sense in precisely that situation because it tackles the question of "whether 'Israel' has a future or would disappear from history."[242] In other words, the book is most coherent when read from the perspective of an exilic audience located between, on the one hand, Yahweh's judgment seen in the destruction of Jerusalem and an audience unresponsive to the prophet Ezekiel's message, and, on the other hand, the return from exile. The reinstatement of the book of Ezekiel has given rise to a number of studies which in turn serve to reinforce the picture given of a book essentially complete by the end of the exile. The major exception is Tuell, who, although regarding Ezek 40–48 as having a clear shape and purpose, dates the second of the two sources he discerns in these chapters to the reign of King Darius I in the Persian era (521–486 B.C.E.).[243] It is not, however, easy to see how Tuell's view relates to the first factor above.[244] Further, the transmission of holiness envisaged in Ezek 44:19, a text dated by Tuell to the Persian era, does not sit easily with the historical understanding embodied in Hag 2:12, where it seems that holiness is *not* transmissible through contact with clothes.

In short, Kuenen's comment, originally refuting suggestions that the book of Ezekiel is pseudepigraphic, is clearly applicable to all attempts to remove the book from an exilic date and provenance:

> The book of Ezekiel…if removed from Babylonia and the exilic era to Judaea and a later century, becomes a purposeless and unintelligible piece of writing. Whoever in the future again denies its authenticity should be mindful of the duty to give at least some account of the purpose the alleged author had in mind, of the knowledge he displays, and of the expectations and ordinances he postulates.[245]

1.6. *Summary*
We have now reached the point where the lengthy survey of Yahweh's word in Ezekiel is complete.

241. Ibid.
242. Ibid.
243. Tuell, *Law of the Temple*.
244. See further Mein, *Ezekiel and the Ethics of Exile*, 252.
245. Abraham Kuenen, *Historisch-Kritische Einleitung in die Bücher des Alten Testaments* (Leipzig, 1890), I, 2, 305, as quoted in Shalom Spiegel, "Ezekiel or Pseudo-Ezekiel," *HTR* 24 (1931): 252.

The relationship between Yahweh's word, on the one hand, and the different addressees (actual or envisaged) and the different audiences, on the other, is a complex one in the book. Although it is at once apparent that everything is subsumed within Yahweh's word coming to the prophet, it is also apparent that Yahweh's word can be seen both in the words Ezekiel is commanded to utter, in the statutes and ordinances that the exiles are supposed to obey and in the contents of the book itself. Speech act theory and Wolterstorff's analysis of issues surrounding the recipients of a speech act provide a helpful framework within which to think about Yahweh's word and its relation to the different people groups to whom that word comes. In particular, the possibilities that one speech event can have a different illocutionary force for different addressees, and that the same words can have a different illocutionary force by virtue of being re-presented in a different context, perhaps as an indirect, rather than a direct speech act, provide help to explain how the *book* of Ezekiel functions as Yahweh's word. Such delineation and classification will prove essential when we look in Part II and Part III at how Yahweh's word relates to Yahweh's רוח. Finally, the addressees of the book are probably the second generation of exiles in Babylon.

2. *Yahweh's* רוח *in Ezekiel*

In the last part of this exploratory chapter, we turn our attention to Yahweh's רוח in Ezekiel. Since many occurrences will be discussed in more detail in the rest of the book, the purpose of this section is not to provide a thorough analysis, but to point to areas of scholarly agreement and disagreement, and to highlight the critical instances to which we must return in subsequent chapters. Four works will serve as the basis for our analysis: those of Albertz and Westermann,[246] Block,[247] Woodhouse[248] and Zimmerli.[249] The first is a sensitive, comprehensive dictionary article on רוח in the Old Testament. The other three are articles specifically on רוח in Ezekiel providing a wide spectrum of opinion.

Within the book of Ezekiel, רוח carries a similar breadth of meanings to that found in the rest of the Old Testament. Even within one passage (37:1–14), its meaning oscillates between the transporting "spirit of Yahweh" (v. 1), the animating "breath of life" (vv. 5–10), the "wind/points of the compass" (v. 9), and Yahweh's "life-giving spirit" (v. 14).

---

246. Albertz and Westermann, *TLOT* 3:1202–20.
247. Block, "Prophet of the Spirit."
248. Woodhouse, "'Spirit.'"
249. Zimmerli, *Ezekiel 2*, 566–68 (Excursus: רוח in the Book of Ezekiel).

2.1. *Accepted Meanings of* רוח *in Ezekiel*

2.1.1. *Meteorological.* There are six occasions in the book where it is generally agreed that רוח is used in the meteorological sense of "wind."[250] In each case רוח is the superordinate, further defined by a hyponym or qualifying noun to which it is bound. These can be categorized slightly differently, depending, for example, on the significance given to the kind of east wind mentioned (so Block speaks of the east wind in 27:26 as a "violent gale," while the east wind in 17:10 and 19:12 is "the scorching sirocco"[251]). There is general agreement that רוח סערה in 1:4 is a theophanic storm wind, as is apparent from the cloud and fire. This wind is concomitant with the divine theophany, but not in any sense to be confused with Yahweh.[252] Unlike in the other instances of רוח as "wind," it is neither a punishing nor a destructive wind,[253] though there are suggestive links to the next two occurrences to be examined: those of רוח סערות in 13:11 and 13:13. Here there is general agreement that this "wind" is a storm wind, linked with Yahweh's judgment that will come on the false prophets who whitewash fragile walls. The final three instances, רוח הקדים in 17:10, 19:12 and 27:26, all speak of an east wind, closely linked with Yahweh's judgment because of its harsh effects. Particularly striking about these is the clearly masculine gender of רוח in 19:12 and 27:26. The precise significance of the gender is debated, though the meteorological use of רוח often is masculine.[254] If a distinction is to be drawn between the winds here and the quasi-theological wind of Exod 14:21 (cf. Exod 15:8, 10), it lies in the fact that, although the winds in Ezekiel are carrying out Yahweh's (destructive) purposes, they are only agents of Yahweh in so far as the enemies of which these winds metaphorically speak are Yahweh's agents.[255]

---

250. Ezek 1:4; 13:11, 13; 17:10; 19:12; 27:26.

251. Block, "Prophet of the Spirit," 32.

252. Lys, *Rûach*, 121–22.

253. Schüngel-Straumann, *Rûaḥ bewegt die Welt*, 47.

254. Lys (*Rûach*, 123) notes that when רוח means wind, the gender is "uncertain," and suggests the masculine gender in 19:12 and 27:26 can be accounted for because its usage is metaphorical, and could be hinting at the Babylonian invader (19:12) or the enemies of Tyre (27:26). For a discussion of the masculine use of רוח, see Dreytza, *Der theologische Gebrauch von RUAḤ*, 182–88. He observes that "Das dem Wechsel zugrunde liegende Einteilungskriterium harrt noch seiner Entdeckung" (p. 186). Nonetheless, he comments that the masculine tends to be used when speaking of "wind," and in particular the east wind (p. 187). For further attempts to explain the gender, see Schüngel-Straumann, *Rûaḥ bewegt die Welt*, 66–70, and, more recently Erasmus Gass, "Genus und Semantik am Beispiel von 'theologischem' *rûḥ*," *BN* 109 (2001): 45–55.

255. Lys, *Rûach*, 123.

Secondly, there are six instances in the book where רוח has the sense "direction." This meaning is derived from "wind," as can be seen clearly in 5:2, where Ezekiel is to scatter one third of his hair "to the wind" (לרוח); this is interpreted and expanded later (5:10–12) as Yahweh scattering the people "to every wind" (לכל־רוח). This meaning can also be seen in 12:14 and 17:21, where again people are scattered "to every wind," and in 37:9, where Ezekiel is to summon הרוח to come from the four "winds" (רוחות).

Thirdly, there are five instances of רוח in 42:16–20, where the sense is that of "side." Ezekiel witnesses the man, whose appearance shone like bronze (40:3), measuring the temple area all round. The first four instances, all in the construct state, are qualified by points of the compass in the absolute. The final one describes how the man measured the four "sides" (רוחות). This meaning is the ultimate extension of רוח as "direction."

2.1.2. *Anthropological.* There are five anthropological uses where there is broad agreement about domain and referent.

In the first example, which is the second occurrence of רוח in 3:14, Ezekiel describes his internal state as he "went" after receiving his commissioning. In contrast with the רוח which lifted him up, his own רוח was somewhat depressed (מר בחמת רוחי). רוח here speaks of an emotional state or mood, describing Ezekiel's reaction to his commissioning. This is one meaning within a "rich semantic field" (i.e. anthropological uses of רוח) which describes "an entire range of human frames of mind, from the strongest emotions to the failure of all vitality."[256]

In 13:3, רוח describes the source of the false prophets' prophesying, speaking of "their mind" (רוחם) in a way parallel to לב (13:2).

A similar sense of רוח is found in 11:5. The prophet, within a vision, is instructed to say to the twenty-five men whom he has "seen" at the east gate of the temple, who are full of pride over Jerusalem, "I know the things that come into your mind (רוחכם)." Again, there is the contrast between two instances of רוח in the same verse. Here, Yahweh's רוח falls on the prophet, in an "external" fashion so that Ezekiel can know and speak of what is going on "internally," what is "going up" into the רוח of the addressees, which clearly is in contradiction with Yahweh's mind.[257]

In 20:32, רוח again speaks of the "intellect"[258] or "mind," in this case the mind of the exiles. Woodhouse translates רוח in 20:32 as "breath,"

---

256. Albertz and Westermann, *TLOT* 3:1210.
257. Cf. Lys, *Rûach*, 138; Schüngel-Straumann, *Rûaḥ bewegt die Welt*, 49.
258. Albertz and Westermann, *TLOT* 3:1212.

given the parallelism with the second half of the verse ("'What is on your breath shall never happen—that which you are saying…' "[259]), but the sense is essentially the same, since what is being spoken of is the generation of thoughts. It is impossible here not to think of the corrupt רוח that the exiles have, a רוח that needs renewing or replacing.[260]

Finally, in 21:12 (ET 21:7), Ezekiel is told what to say when the exiles ask him why he is moaning. In his reply, he is to say that, when the news of Jerusalem's fall comes, "every רוח will faint." Here רוח is the "seat of the emotions"[261] or the "psychic vigor"[262] that is to be destroyed. Rather than appearing synonymous with לב, as in the previous two instances discussed, רוח here is in parallel.

2.2. *Disagreements Over the Meaning of* רוח *in Ezekiel*

We have observed above general agreements among the four commentators on the meaning of רוח in a number of places. In this next section, I shall look at those instances where commentators disagree. There are broadly two kinds of disagreement: how רוח should be understood or rendered *within* a particular domain and the domain *in which* a particular occurrence should be placed.

2.2.1. *Anthropological.* Three almost identical uses of רוח in the book occur in 11:19; 18:31 and 36:26. In 11:19 and 36:26, Yahweh promises to give the exiles "one/a new heart and a new spirit (רוח חדשה)." In 18:31, the exiles are told to get for themselves what Yahweh elsewhere has promised, "a new heart and a new spirit." While there is agreement that the occurrences are anthropological, speaking of the human "spirit," there is disagreement about the precise significance. Here, again, רוח occurs alongside לב. Some see רוח as synonymous with לב as "will." Such a view is apparent in the expanded rendering, "new center of volition necessary for repentance and new obedience to the commandments" and the accompanying comment about the "equation" of רוח and לב.[263]

---

259.   Woodhouse, "'Spirit,'" 14.

260.   It is striking in this regard to note that only Israel ever has a רוח in Ezekiel. When the same conception, of thoughts "going up" occurs in 38:10, the word used is לבב. The owner of the heart is Gog. See Schüngel-Straumann, *Rûaḥ bewegt die Welt*, 49.

261.   Block, "Prophet of the Spirit," 46.

262.   Albertz and Westermann, *TLOT* 3:1210.

263.   Ibid., 3:1212; cf. Zimmerli (*Ezekiel 2*, 567), who observes the parallelism between the two, and notes that the only "inconsistency" is in the qualification of the "old heart" as "stone."

Block, however, while seeing רוח as "the seat of one's mental activity"[264] in 11:19 and 18:31 (thus closely paralleling לב), suggests a distinction between the two in 36:26 on the grounds of the different way לב and רוח are developed.[265] Certainly the new רוח is not a temporary gift to equip or fortify the people for a particular task. In addition, the presence of a corrupt רוח in 11:5 (albeit in those in Jerusalem) points to the need for an internal transformation and suggests essential synonymity with לב. At the same time, it is difficult to avoid the thought that רוח is not essentially human in the same way as לב is, and that רוח is somehow "complementary."[266]

2.2.2. *Theological/anthropological*. There are four instances in 37:1–10 where רוח clearly speaks of the "breath of life"[267] or the "agency of animation."[268] These occur in vv. 5, 6, 8 and 10. The dry bones lack רוח, and Ezekiel is told to prophesy to the bones, and declare to them that Yahweh will put רוח in them. In v. 10, רוח enters them. All see the sense "breath of life," too, in the call to "the breath" in v. 9 (three instances of רוח), but Zimmerli also notes the sense "wind" too, and even the link with the "world of the divine."[269] His comment is a significant one: "Here we can ascertain…the remarkable lack of clarity in some statements in the book of Ezekiel which prevents the clear differentiation of areas of meaning."[270] In somewhat similar fashion, Block, in analyzing the occurrences of רוח in Ezekiel, sees a bifurcation (meteorological, non-meteorological), rather than a trifurcation, from the meaning "wind," such that it is not always clear whether the non-meteorological uses of רוח are essentially anthropological or theological.[271] When he speaks of the "agency of animation," it does seem that he treats it as something essentially "theological," particularly since he speaks of "animating effect of the presence of the *spirit*."[272]

2.2.3. *Theological/meteorological*. There are seven occasions in the book where רוח is used in connection with the transportation of the prophet

---

264. Block, "Prophet of the Spirit," 45.
265. Ibid., 38–39, 46.
266. Cf. Knierim, *Task of Old Testament Theology*, 282; also Wolff, *Anthropology*, 38; Cooke, *Ezekiel*, 125. See further Chapter 6 below.
267. Albertz and Westermann, *TLOT* 3:1209.
268. Block, "Prophet of the Spirit," 31, 37–38.
269. Zimmerli, *Ezekiel 2*, 567.
270. Ibid.
271. Block, "Prophet of the Spirit," 29.
272. Ibid., 35 (my emphasis).

(3:12, 14; 8:3; 11:1, 24; 37:1; 43:5).[273] In six of these (not 37:1), רוח is absolute, anarthrous and marked as feminine by the finite verb(s) of which it is the subject. In each of these six, רוח "carried/picked up" (נשא) Ezekiel. In 3:14, after "picking up" Ezekiel, רוח "took" (לקח) him; in 8:3; 11:1, 24a and 43:5, after "picking up" Ezekiel, רוח "brought" (בוא Hiphil) him; in the seventh (37:1), רוח is no longer the subject, but preceded by the preposition ב. In addition, it is in the construct state, with Yahweh as the absolute (ברוח יהוה). The phrase serves to identify the agent of Yahweh's action of bringing the prophet out (יצא Hiphil) and "setting him" (נוח Hiphil) in the desert.

These are not actual transportations, but occur in visions that Ezekiel is having. In 3:12 and 3:14, Ezekiel returns at the end of his commissioning vision to the exiles among whom he has been all the time (cf. 1:1–3). In 8:3 and 11:24, visions are explicitly mentioned, while in 11:1 and 43:5, such transportation occurs in the middle of a vision. While there is no mention of vision in 37:1, it is clear that the incident with the dry bones takes place within a vision, as we saw above. Nonetheless, they are literal transportations in the sense that within the vision there is real movement, as is evident from the parallel in 8:3 between the action of what looked like a hand of the human-like figure, in taking Ezekiel by the lock of his head, and that of רוח, in lifting him up between earth and heaven. Block notes the degree of ambiguity raised by the fact that רוח is anarthrous in the six occurrences, and argues that what transports Ezekiel is Yahweh's "spirit." His chief reason is that the masculine verb forms in 8:7, 14, 16 ("he brought me to…") suggest "that the one conveying him [Ezekiel] about is the same as the person who speaks to him"[274] (the nearest masculine antecedent is "the Lord Yahweh" in v. 1). Woodhouse, on the other hand, cites Greenberg in rendering 3:12 as "wind': "as opposed to 'the wind from YHWH' that was believed to transport Elijah (I Kings 18:12; II Kings 2:16—*ruªh* [*sic*] *YHWH* is construed with masc. verbs), the 'wind' that transported Ezekiel (construed with fem. verbs) is, to be sure, supernatural in origin, but unattributed—another sign of reserve."[275] Zimmerli comments that the anarthrous usage makes רוח appear "to be an almost independently effective power" though "in its activity we are

273. Block (ibid., 34) and Albertz and Westermann (*TLOT* 3:1207, 1213) regard רוח in 11:24b as speaking also of the "agency of conveyance." The others link it with the receiving of the divine vision.

274. Block, "Prophet of the Spirit," 34; cf. Schüngel-Straumann, *Rûah bewegt die Welt*, 40: "Dabei werden die drei Subjekte *'îš*, *rwh*, und *jahwe* nicht streng unterschieden."

275. Greenberg, *Ezekiel 1–20*, 70, as cited in Woodhouse, "'Spirit,'" 14.

dealing with effects brought about by Yahweh."[276] Albertz and Westermann speak of the "intermediate position" of רוח "between the basic meaning 'wind' and the fig. meaning 'spirit.' "[277] Although the occurrence in 37:1 provides conclusive evidence, in Block's view, that what is meant is Yahweh's spirit,[278] it is possible for רוח יהוה to speak of "the wind/breath of Yahweh" (Isa 40:7).

2.2.4. *Theological/anthropological/meteorological*. In two other instances which Zimmerli sees as closely related to those mentioned above in so far as they all speak of "the רוח of the specific, prophetic experience of a call,"[279] רוח enters the prophet, prostrate before Yahweh's glory, and sets him on his feet (ותבא בי רוח, 2:2; 3:24). If the transporting רוח acts "externally" on the prophet, lifting him up almost as an object, רוח here acts internally, entering him. In 2:2, the entry of רוח is linked with Yahweh speaking to the prophet, such that Block sees hints of prophetic inspiration here,[280] as does Zimmerli, who regards רוח as making the prophet "capable of speech" after being in a "state of collapse."[281] Both, however, consider the predominant notion here as that of רוח as the "agency of animation." In this respect they are similar to Woodhouse, who regards רוח as "breath,"[282] and Albertz and Westermann, who regard these instances as examples of the "vitality" of the individual, albeit "altered theologically."[283] There is some agreement that the instances here are specifically theological. Block asks, "Is it a sudden gust of wind...? Or is it the spirit of Yahweh?" and concludes it is the latter. The scene is a royal court scene; "only the divine spirit could give him the authority or the energy to stand erect before God."[284] There is, though, some disagreement about what is meant. Thus Woodhouse agrees with Block in seeing it as a "divine רוח," but prefers to see it not as "spirit" but as Yahweh's "invigorating breath accompanying the speech of God."[285] It might seem, then, that these two occurrences ought to be categorized as "theological" disagreement. Other commentators, however, regard רוח here either as "wind" or as "breath."

276. Zimmerli, *Ezekiel 2*, 567.
277. Albertz and Westermann, *TLOT* 3:1207.
278. Block, "Prophet of the Spirit," 34.
279. Zimmerli, *Ezekiel 2*, 567.
280. Block, "Prophet of the Spirit," 41.
281. Zimmerli, *Ezekiel 2*, 566.
282. Woodhouse, "'Spirit,'" 12–13.
283. Albertz and Westermann, *TLOT* 3:1208.
284. Block, "Prophet of the Spirit," 37.
285. Woodhouse, "'Spirit,'" 14.

The second main area of disagreement within this category centres around the six occurrences of רוח linked with the movement of the living creatures and the throne in chs. 1 and 10. These will involve our close attention partly because they are the first instances in the book where there is some disagreement, and partly because I shall not be discussing them later. The first two, in 1:12 and 1:20a, explain the movement of the living creatures (v. 12) and the movement of the wheels with them (v. 20); "wherever הרוח would go, the living creatures would go too" (אל אשר יהיה־שמה הרוח ללכת ילכו, 1:12). For Zimmerli ("organ of the decision of the will"[286]) and Albertz and Westermann ("the unique inner compulsion"[287]), הרוח directs the way to be taken, and ensures that all move together. Woodhouse, however, says that this understanding has "no basis in the immediate context and seems to overlook the dominance in the whole scene of the storm wind of v. 4."[288] He prefers the meaning "wind." The sense, then, is that the living creatures are carried by the storm wind. Block, however, says that the sense "wind" is "impossible at this point."[289] He argues that הרוח here is "the vitalizing principle of life that comes from God himself."[290]

Before examining the evidence and arguments surrounding these two instances, we need to look at the other occurrences of רוח in the visions concerning movement of the living creatures and throne, in 1:20b, in 1:21 and in 10:17,[291] because Block, Zimmerli and Albertz and Westermann treat all five occurrences together, and Block, in particular, regards these three as determinative of the interpretation of the first two. Woodhouse alone detects a shift in meaning between the occurrences, from רוח as "wind" to רוח as "breath" in v. 20b and v. 21 (and in 10:17), so that it is the breath of the living creatures that moves the wheels.[292]

In each one of these latter three occurrences, רוח occurs in a construct relationship with the absolute, החיה. While some commentators take החיה as a collective noun, "living creatures"[293] or a distributive,[294] and

---

286. Zimmerli, *Ezekiel 2*, 566.
287. Albertz and Westermann, *TLOT* 3:1212.
288. Woodhouse, "'Spirit,'" 9.
289. Block, "Prophet of the Spirit," 36.
290. Ibid.
291. The second of the three occurrences of רוח in 1:20 is almost certainly due to dittography. See GKC 123d n. 2; Zimmerli, *Ezekiel 1*, 87.
292. Woodhouse, "'Spirit,'" 11.
293. E.g. Cooke, *Ezekiel*, 18, 27; cf. Zimmerli, *Ezekiel 1*, 87. So too among modern English versions of the Bible: RSV, NRSV, NIV, ESV, NASV, NJB.
294. Suggested by Cooke, *Ezekiel*, 27.

Greenberg takes the singular here as stressing "the unity of the ensemble,"[295] there are five reasons, which, taken together, point towards rendering the whole phrase "the breath/spirit of life," with החיה understood as "life." This is not simply anthropological, but the divinely given, animating, vivifying breath.[296]

First, the living creatures are until this point in the opening vision always referred to with the plural, חיות (1:5, 13, 15, 19). Although this point might seem to be negated by 1:22, where החיה clearly is a collective noun (also 10:15 and 20), such a shift to the singular is explicable. Lys explains the occurrence of the singular in 1:22 as an "error" occurring because of the three occurrences in the singular in 1:20–21, and would emend to a plural.[297] Such an emendation is not necessary for החיה to be rendered "life" in 1:20 and 21, and "living creatures" in 1:22. The "attraction" to the singular in 1:22 does not mean that the referent need be the same. Nonetheless, evidence from the LXX and Vulgate supports Lys,[298] as does the next occurrence of the word where it refers to the living creatures, 3:13; there it is plural again.

The second piece of evidence supporting the rendering "breath/spirit of life" comes from the LXX and the Vulgate. They both are careful to distinguish "living creature(s)" from "life." In 1:20–21, they render רוח החיה with πνεῦμα ζωῆς and *spiritus vitae* ("spirit of life"), while they render v. 22's על־ראשי החיה with ὑπὲρ κεφαλῆς αὐτοῖς τῶν ζῴων and *super caput animalium* ("over the head of the living creatures"). Thus they distinguish clearly between two senses of the root חיה.[299] Further, in ch. 10, where undisputed references to "living creature(s)" are always rendered in the MT by the singular, החיה (10:15, 20), LXX and the Vulgate distinguish between החיה as "living creature" (τὸ ζῷον, *animal*) in vv. 15 and 20, and החיה as "life" in the phrase "breath/spirit of life" (πνεῦμα ζωῆς, *spiritus…vitae*) in v. 17. Given the distinction between singular and plural found in ch. 10, this provides evidence for Lys' argument concerning the plural in 1:22. It also indicates, in the case of LXX, a clear understanding of the רוח החיה in 1:20c, 21 and 10:17 as "the breath/spirit of life" and not directly related to the "living creatures."

295.   Greenberg, *Ezekiel 1–20*, 48; cf. also Zimmerli, *Ezekiel 1*, 87.

296.   So Block, "Prophet of the Spirit," 36–37; Lys, *Rûach*, 127–28; Lloyd Neve, *The Spirit of God in the Old Testament* (Tokyo: Seibunsha, 1972), 95–96.

297.   Lys, *Rûach*, 127–28.

298.   See below.

299.   BDB, 312, regards the meaning "life" to be a subdivision within חיה, "a living thing, animal"; however, *HALOT*, 310, sees these two meanings as deriving from two homonyms. Neither treats the instances here as "life."

Thirdly, although the phrase here, רוח החיה, would be a unique way of designating the "spirit/breath of life" in the Old Testament,[300] and although חיה elsewhere in the book does speak of "wild animals" (e.g. 5:17; 14:15, 21) or, in 10:15, 20, explicitly of the living creatures, חיה can refer in Ezekiel to "life" (7:13).[301] Further, there are suggestive parallels in Gen 1, where נפש חיה designates "living creatures" in 1:24 (cf. LXX: ψυχὴν ζῶσαν), but "breath of life" (cf. LXX: ψυχὴν ζωῆς) in 1:30.

Fourthly, although the living creatures in ch. 1 are clearly "alive," given their movement (e.g. 1:24), there does seem to be a degree of reticence about their life, seen in the prefacing with דמות (1:5, 10, 13).[302] Further, given Ezekiel's clear reluctance throughout the book to countenance any rival to Yahweh, and to give no credence to idols or images,[303] it would be strange for Ezekiel to focus on the "breath" (רוח) of these living creatures given their subservient role with regard to the throne, their similarity to ancient Near Eastern skybearers and divine beings, and the anti-idol polemic of the prophets that the idols "have no breath in them" (e.g. ולא־רוח בם, Jer 10:14; cf. also Hab 2:19; Ps 135:17).

The final reason comes from the sense. In each of these three instances, the phrase occurs as part of an explanation for the movement of the wheels, "and when they (i.e. the living creatures) rose from the earth, the wheels rose along with them; for רוח החיה was in the wheels." It does not make sense to say that "the spirit of the living creatures was in the wheels" if this רוח is to do with "the organ of decision of the will" of these living creatures. The issue here is not the decision-making ability of the wheels, but their animation. This is not solved by arguing that "the spirit of the living creatures" speaks of the "vivifying breath of the living creatures," for as we have seen the independent life of the creatures is somewhat muted; further, nowhere in the Old Testament is anyone other than Yahweh the source of this vivifying "breath/spirit of life." It makes better sense to say that the "breath of life" (or "the spirit of life") was in the wheels, thus emphasizing the fact that everything, even the normally inanimate wheels, is animated by Yahweh's life-giving רוח. It is for this reason that they move when the whole throne-unit moves.

---

300.   Elsewhere rendered by נפש חיה (Gen 1:30), נשמת חיים (Gen 2:7), רוח חיים (Gen 6:17; 7:15), נשמת־רוח חיים (Gen 7:22). Other instances use the lexemes רוח or נשמה.

301.   It seems a late poetic form, closely related to נפש. See *HALOT*, 310.

302.   Although Lys (*Rûach*, 128) is right to point out that the living creatures turn out to be inanimate temple objects, cherubim, such an understanding is not there for Ezekiel, or for the readers, at this point in the book.

303.   See especially Kutsko, *Between Heaven and Earth*.

If it be agreed that רוח in 1:20b, 21 and 10:17 speaks of "breath/spirit of life," we are still left with the occurrences of הרוח in v. 12 and v. 20a. Some regard the referent here as determined by that of רוח in 1:20b and 1:21. However, this is not necessary, since רוח can shift its meaning within the same verse or even sentence (e.g. 11:5; 37:9), and indeed might seem unlikely, particularly since the first occurrence, in v. 12, would then lack an interpretative clue until v. 20.

In fact, to a reader or hearer, the context of v. 12 and v. 20a seems to favour the idea of רוח as "wind." Where the article is attached to רוח as here, it is either cataphoric, defined further by what follows, anaphoric, referring to a רוח that has already been introduced, or speaks of what is the most obvious referent within the context (e.g. "wind," Eccl 1:6; 8:8; Ezek 37:9; "breath," Eccl 11:5; Ezek 37:10; "spirit," Hos 9:7).[304]

In view of the fact that "wind" has already been spoken of in v. 4, the context would suggest that the article is anaphoric, referring to v. 4. In addition, the only other occurrence of רוח being the subject of הלך is in Eccl 1:6; there, רוח clearly is "wind." Although Lys argues that הרוח in v. 12 does not refer to the storm wind in 1:4,[305] none of his arguments is conclusive. That רוח in 1:4 did not "propel God's chariot" but was an "announcer" (*annonciateur*) of God's presence is not gainsaid by the references in vv. 12 and 20, since all we are told there is that the chariot goes where הרוח "would go." Further, the presence of the definite article does not serve to distinguish the two, since the indefinite "wind" of v. 4 would now be definite, and marked as such by the article. Even the shift in the gender of רוח, from feminine in v. 4 (the participle באה is feminine) to masculine in v. 12 (the verb יהיה indicates a masculine subject), is not determinative since the "living creatures" in the opening verses are sometimes regarded as feminine (e.g. the pronominal suffixes in vv. 5, 12, and the pronouns in vv. 5, 6) and sometimes as masculine (e.g. the pronominal suffixes in v. 9 and the verb forms in vv. 9, 12). It is certainly plausible that a distinction is being marked between רוח in v. 4 and in v. 12 by the shift in gender, so it is right to look for a better understanding, but Block's view that "wind" is "impossible" here is overstated.[306]

---

304. Cf. *IBHS* §13.5.

305. Lys, *Rûach*, 125.

306. Zimmerli (*Ezekiel 2*, 566) explains the masculine gender by suggesting a somewhat convoluted process, whereby the gender comes from the word to which רוח is bound (חיה), which is clearly identified in 10:15 as the masculine כרוב. The determination of gender from the absolute is appropriate, but the link to ch. 10 is not established here. Further, it also depends on the identity of referent of רוח in 1:20b with that in 1:12 and 1:20a. In discussing change in gender in Ezekiel, mention

If for the moment we grant that the use of the masculine רוּחַ, unique in Ezekiel, serves to distinguish the רוּחַ in v. 12 from that in v. 4, there is the question of referent. The use of the article can hardly be cataphoric, since the explanation is delayed until v. 20. If not anaphoric, the article must be "designating either a particular person or thing necessarily understood to be present or vividly portraying someone or something whose identity is not otherwise indicated."[307] It is theoretically possible that it could speak of the "organ of the decision of the will" (so Zimmerli) of the "living creatures." Certainly in Judg 8:3, the singular, רוּחַ, can be used distributively to refer to the רוּחַ of a group, but there the connotation is one of emotion. In Ezek 13:3, similarly, רוּחַ is used distributively. It is hardly likely, however, that רוּחַ referring to the "unique inner compulsion"[308] of the living creatures would be introduced in such a fashion, without a pronominal suffix to indicate it. It is much more likely, especially in the light of the prominence of the theological use of רוּחַ later in the book, that what is in view here is Yahweh's רוּחַ. This in turn is an unusual picture, that of Yahweh's רוּחַ "going" from place to place.

This almost independent conception of רוּחַ does have some parallels. In the book of Ezekiel itself, the prophet is to address הרוּחַ and summon it from the four winds (37:9). It is this mysterious reality that vivifies the re-formed but lifeless corpses. Certainly there is a parallel between the רוּחַ here that enlivens and directs the chariot and the רוּחַ that will enliven and direct the once-dead bones. At the same time, there are tantalizing hints of further developments. In Ps 139:7, the psalmist regards רוּחַ as Yahweh manifest in omnipresence, parallel to Yahweh's פָּנִים, "Where can I go from your spirit (מֵרוּחֶךָ)? Or where can I flee from your presence (מִפָּנֶיךָ)?" This correspondence between פָּנִים and רוּחַ can also be seen in Ps 51:13 [ET 51:15] and, in particular, in Isa 63:10–14.[309] There, רוּחַ corresponds not with "angel," but with פָּנִים.[310] רוּחַ seems to designate Yahweh's presence in the midst of the people of Israel, going with them in the wilderness. What Isa 63:14 ascribes to the action of רוּחַ, "the spirit of Yahweh gave them rest" (רוּחַ יהוה תְּנִיחֶנּוּ), Exod 33:14 ascribes to the action of פָּנִים, "My presence will go with you, and I will give you

---

should be made of the bones in Ezek 37:1–14. Here it probably is a rhetorical device linking the bones with the "whole house of Israel." The next time רוּחַ occurs, in 2:2, it is clearly feminine.

307.   *IBHS* §13.5.1e. The quotation is directed towards this chapter.
308.   Albertz and Westermann, *TLOT* 3:1212.
309.   Cf. also Ezek 39:29.
310.   See Montague, *Holy Spirit*, 57; Ma, *Until the Spirit Comes*, 125–31, 153.

rest" (פָנֶי יֵלְכוּ וַהֲנִחֹתִי לָךְ).[311] In view of the fact that in the exodus, Yahweh guided the people by means of a pillar of cloud by day, and a pillar of fire by night, there are potentially close links between רוח and this pillar. Evidence for such a link comes from the hovering (רחף Piel) of Yahweh (presumably in the pillar) over the wilderness waste (תהו, Deut 32:10–11) being paralleled to רוח hovering (רחף Piel) over the waters, with the earth being a wilderness waste (תהו, Gen 1:2). These are the only places in the Torah where the words occur.

There are clear links, then, between רוח and the theophanic pillar symbolizing the presence of Yahweh that accompanied those in the exodus. Although it is possible in 1:12 to see הרוח as the same wind as the storm wind in 1:4, it is probable that it designates Yahweh's presence, albeit in a circumscribed and mediated way. That is not to say that there are not close links to the notion of רוח as "breath of life" given by Yahweh, and coming from the four winds,[312] but there are hints towards something more—to Yahweh's presence, a presence associated with Yahweh's leading in the exodus. This means there is a subtle shift in meaning, though both are theological, between רוח in 1:12 and 20a, on the one hand, and רוח in 1:20b, 21 and 10:17, on the other. Ezekiel 1:20 should be understood as follows: "Wherever the spirit [that is, Yahweh's presence], would go, the living creatures would also go." The wheels were not left behind by this. Instead, because they were animated by Yahweh's vivifying breath, they could rise up and follow.

In view of the importance of רוח throughout the rest of the book, the significance of the references in the opening chapter should not be underestimated. Block comments:

> The precise connection among this *rûaḥ*, the stormy *rûaḥ* that had borne the apparition to the prophet (v. 4), the *rûaḥ* that would later enter and energize him (2:2; 3:24), and the *rûaḥ* that would later lift him up and carry him away (3:12, 14) is not clear. However, the reference serves as a harbinger of the role that the *rûaḥ* will play in Ezekiel's ministry…[313]

The boundaries are fluid between the different semantic domains of רוח, and ambiguity, whether deliberate or unintended, is clearly apparent.[314]

---

311. It should be noted that LXX (ὡδήγησεν) and Vulgate (*ductor eius fuit*) assume the root נחה ("he led") in Isa 63:14. See Ma, *Until the Spirit Comes*, 130: "MT takes the verb as hiphil imperfect of נוח 'he gave us rest.'"

312. Westermann dates the "almost…independent historical psalm" of Isa 63:7–14 to "not long after the fall of Jerusalem in 587"; see Claus Westermann, *Isaiah 40–66* (trans. D. M. G. Stalker; OTL; London: SCM, 1969), 386.

313. Block, *Ezekiel 1–24*, 101; cf. Kinlaw, "From Death to Life," 164–66.

314. Aelred Cody, *Ezekiel, with an Excursus on Old Testament Priesthood* (Wilmington, Del.: Glazier, 1984), 29, speaks here of "multivalent ambiguity."

2.2.5. *Theological.* The remaining five instances of רוח in the book are all explicitly theological. In 11:5, within his temple vision, Ezekiel is told to prophesy to the twenty-five men who give wicked counsel in the city. Before Yahweh tells the prophet what he is to say to them, Ezekiel relates how "the spirit of Yahweh fell upon me (ותפל עלי רוח יהוה), and he said to me…" All are agreed that this reference is theological, and most see here a reference to Yahweh's "spirit," particularly the "prophetic spirit."[315] Woodhouse, however, notes the close connection with the word coming to Ezekiel, and suggests that the phrase "makes explicit what was already implicit in 2:2 and 3:24"—רוח as Yahweh's "breath."[316]

In 11:24, there is the only occurrence of the phrase רוח אלהים in the book of Ezekiel. רוח has lifted the prophet up, and has brought him "in a vision ברוח אלהים" to Chaldea, to the exiles, mirroring his transportation to Judah at the start of the vision in 8:1–3. Block sees the reference here to רוח as the "agency of conveyance." He notes that, by analogy with the "divine visions" of 1:1, 8:3 and 40:2, it is possible that the phrase here may not mean any more than "divine wind,"[317] but prefers to see the reference being to Yahweh's "spirit" because of the determinative (for him) 37:1. Zimmerli sees ברוח אלהים as speaking of the "spirit" of God in the sense of "enveloping sphere" in which the process of transportation takes place, and links it with the pre-Israelite linguistic usage characteristic of the pre-classical prophets.[318] For Woodhouse, it is "the breath of God," which seems to be linked with the prophet's transportation, not inspiration.[319]

The other three of these five instances of the theological use of רוח are those in which Yahweh speaks of "my spirit/breath" (רוחי). In 36:26, Yahweh has promised the house of Israel "a new heart and a new spirit." In the next verse, Yahweh promises that "I will give my spirit within them" (ואת־רוחי אתן בקרבכם). In 37:14, at the end of the vision of the dry bones, in words very similar to those of 36:27, Yahweh promises that "I will put my spirit in you" (ונתתי רוחי בכם). Block regards both of these references as examples of רוח as "spirit" with "animating" effect that brings about a "radical spiritual revitalization of the nation."[320] While

315.   Block, "Prophet of the Spirit," 41.

316.   Woodhouse, "'Spirit,'" 15.

317.   Block, "Prophet of the Spirit," 34; elsewhere (*Ezekiel 1–24*, 359) Block seems to relate it more closely to the reception of the vision in his commentary.

318.   Zimmerli, *Ezekiel 2*, 567.

319.   Woodhouse, "'Spirit,'" 15–16.

320.   Block, "Prophet of the Spirit," 39. However, in the table on p. 31, both instances of רוח in ch. 36 are categorized under רוח as "mind."

the link between 36:27 and 37:14 is clear, Woodhouse prefers to see in both a reference not so much to Yahweh's "spirit" as to Yahweh's "breath." On 36:27, he notes the links with Jer 31:31–34 and comments, "there is little obvious difference between God writing his law on the heart, and placing his (speaking) breath within. Any difference seems to fade when the consequence of the latter act is seen to be obedience to the law (Ezek 36:27b)!"[321] On 37:14, Block suggests that רוח here undergoes "an extremely significant shift in meaning. The *rwḥ* that will revitalize Israel is not the ordinary, natural life-breath common to all living things; it is the spirit of God himself."[322] Woodhouse, however, does not see why such a shift is demanded.[323] While it may seem that Block and Woodhouse are very close to each other in their conceptions, since Block is conceiving of רוח at these points as the "agency of animation" while Woodhouse conceives of them as Yahweh's "breath," the substantial difference is apparent when it is seen that for Woodhouse the "breath" that is spoken of is tied closely to Yahweh's word.

In 39:29, the reference to רוח is again clearly theological. Yahweh is announcing that he will never again hide his face from the house of Israel. In this context, he speaks of pouring out "my spirit" (שפכתי את־רוחי). Although the precise relationship between such a promise and the outpouring of Yahweh's רוח will be examined in Part III, it is worth observing again the differing perspectives on רוח here. Block, noting the significance of "pouring," regards רוח here as the "sign of divine ownership,"[324] yielding a substantially different force from רוח in 36:27 and 37:14. Zimmerli regards the phrase here as a "late redactional formulation" by which the earlier statements are "transformed."[325] Albertz and Westermann, however, see no such shift, preferring to see "spirit" as the "bestowal of the spirit on the entire people of God."[326] Woodhouse again prefers to see the notion of Yahweh's "breath," though he does note that "this breath represents nothing less than the saving presence of God himself."[327]

321.   Woodhouse, "'Spirit,'" 17.
322.   Block, "Prophet of the Spirit," 38.
323.   Woodhouse, "'Spirit,'" 18.
324.   Block, "Prophet of the Spirit," 46–48.
325.   Zimmerli, *Ezekiel 2*, 567.
326.   Albertz and Westermann, *TLOT* 3:1218; cf. Lys, *Rûach*, 132, who cross-references 36:27 and 39:29 to 37:14 when commenting that what Ezek 37:9–10 expresses in a vision, 37:14 expresses in "reality" (*réalité*).
327.   Woodhouse, "'Spirit,'" 19.

2.3. *Conclusions*

There are substantial points of difference on how רוח is to be understood
and translated. Some of the disagreements are over the particular domain
in which the occurrences should be placed, whether meteorological,
anthropological or theological (e.g. on the transporting רוח). Others are
over the nuance of רוח within a particular domain (e.g. Yahweh speaking
of "my רוח"). Some of the ambiguity may be resolved by sharper exegesis. Some of the ambiguity may be explained in terms of a deliberate
ploy on the part of the author of the book. Some may be regarded as
unintended. Some may be seen as a product of our conceiving of רוח in
too sharply defined categories. As Albertz and Westermann point out, it
is possible to translate רוח as "spirit" when the "concrete meanings
'wind' and 'breath' advance to a no longer empirically perceptible realm,
without, however, becoming less real" provided that "one must be clear
that the transitions are fluid because the force mysteriously effective in
the wind and the breath points toward God from the outset."[328] They
maintain that "the specifically theological usage of *rûaḥ* as Yahweh's
spirit or the spirit of God is markedly distinct neither terminologically
nor materially from the profane usage."[329] Judgments, however, must be
made, since, if Woodhouse's conclusion is correct, that language "usually understood to refer to the 'Spirit' of God is better understood when
it is seen to be a transparent anthropomorphism to be rendered by an
English expression such as 'the breath of God,' "[330] then the connection
between Yahweh's word and Yahweh's רוח will be more in evidence.
Even meteorological uses may have a theological dimension which may
entail a relationship between word and רוח. In the following chapters, we
will explore these issues more fully.

3. *Word Not Related to* רוח?

Having looked at how the word of Yahweh and the רוח of Yahweh can
be conceived within the book, we need to pause briefly to revisit the
suggestion made by Kaufmann that "there is no biblical doctrine of the
relationship between the word and the spirit."[331] It could have been possible that, despite the prominence of both Yahweh's word and (Yahweh's)
רוח within the book, there is in fact no particular notion of a relationship
between the two. Two things can be said in response.

328. Albertz and Westermann, *TLOT* 3:1212.
329. Ibid., 3:1202–20.
330. Woodhouse, "'Spirit,'" 20.
331. Kaufmann, *Religion of Israel*, 101.

First, Kaufmann was speaking in an exaggerated fashion of one parti-cular kind of relationship—that between the prophetic "word of Yahweh" and the spirit. His purpose was to stress the uniqueness of the Israelite religion in general, and of Israelite prophecy in particular.[332] The intelli-gibility of Israelite prophecy, seen in Yahweh's "word," is set in marked contrast to pagan notions of "a specific source of mantic power" (e.g. "spirits") that characterizes "pagan prophecy."[333] Such rhetoric, and that is really what it is, conceals other statements that reveal a more nuanced position. In his discussion, for example, he comments that "the spirit is the by-product of the word,"[334] a statement that clearly implies some kind of relationship.

Secondly, even a preliminary analysis of the occurrences of Yahweh's word and רוח in the book of Ezekiel reveals possible links between the two. In 2:2, there is רוח that enters the prophet when Yahweh speaks to him (cf. 3:24). On a number of occasions in the book, the prophet, who is to be Yahweh's mouthpiece, is transported by the רוח. In 11:5, the "spirit of Yahweh" fell on the prophet and Yahweh spoke to him. In 36:27, Yahweh's רוח is linked with the house of Israel's obedience to Yahweh's word. In 37:1–14, רוח comes at the command of Yahweh's word, spoken by the prophet. In short, it is simply not correct to say that there is "no…relationship." What needs to be explored is precisely what kind of relationship the book envisages. It is to one possible domain that we now turn, to that of the inspiration of the prophet.

332.   Cf. his comment that "Israelite prophecy is in every aspect a new phe-nomenon" (ibid., 101).

333.   Ibid., 95.

334.   Ibid., 100.

Part II

WORD, SPIRIT AND INSPIRATION

Among all the wonders of the spirit the proclamation of the word of Yahweh came more and more to take the central place. That the "men of the spirit" were at the same time the mediators of the word, and that not simply in cases where a divine oracle was explicitly ascribed to the spirit, explains the profound influence both on individuals and on the nation at large which enabled them to determine decisively the pattern of religious thought.

—Walther Eichrodt[1]

---

1.   Walther Eichrodt, *Theology of the Old Testament* (trans. J. A. Baker; 2 vols.; London: SCM, 1961–67), 2:53.

Chapter 3

INSPIRATION AND EZEKIEL

In Part I, we observed how the book of Ezekiel is marked to a great degree by the presence of רוח. Many of the occurrences are either explicitly theological, or may have theological significance. Further, this emphasis sets the book of Ezekiel apart from both Jeremiah and Leviticus. There is another dimension, though, to this distinctive emphasis. Many of these theological, or theologically significant, references to רוח relate directly to the life and ministry of the prophet Ezekiel himself. רוח set Ezekiel on his feet when confronted by a vision of the glory of Yahweh (2:2; 3:24). רוח transported him from place to place, lifting him up (3:12), carrying him away to the exiles in Babylon (3:14; 11:24), to the temple in Jerusalem (8:3; 11:1), to the inner court within the "new" temple (43:5) and to a valley filled with dry bones (37:1). While it is true that all these occur within the context of visions, "that does not affect the underlying conception of the function of the spirit."[1] Further, the temple vision (8:1–11:25) came about ברוח אלהים (11:24), and, in 11:5, רוח יהוה fell on Ezekiel as Yahweh was instructing him to speak and telling him what to say. This new dimension can be seen by comparing the prophet Ezekiel's experience of רוח, "where almost every word and action of the prophet is attributed to the spirit,"[2] with that of the pre-classical and that of the classical prophets. Such a picture has attracted a good deal of scholarly attention. I shall briefly sketch the main currents before I outline my aims and direction for Part II.

First, as Zimmerli and Carley, in particular, have pointed out, the emphasis on רוח within Ezekiel's ministry serves to align the prophet closely with the pre-classical prophets.[3] Just as Yahweh's רוח is seen by popular opinion of their day as the transporting spirit, which can snatch

---

1. Schoemaker, "Use of רוח," 25.
2. Wilson, *Prophecy and Society*, 261.
3. Zimmerli, "The Special Form- and Traditio-Historical Character"; idem, *Ezekiel 1*, 42–43; Carley, *Ezekiel Among the Prophets*.

Elijah up and deposit him somewhere else (1 Kgs 18:12; 2 Kgs 2:16), so too רוח transports Ezekiel. In this way, and in other "dramatic animation[s]" such as swallowing the scroll, Zimmerli recalls "the רוח-theology of the older prophets."[4]

Secondly, the book of Ezekiel's portrayal of the influence of רוח on Ezekiel appears very different from the portrayal of the traditionally named pre-exilic classical, writing prophets.[5] In the classical prophets, there is an almost complete absence of theological uses of רוח, especially with regard to their own inspiration. This is true of Amos, Obadiah, Nahum, Habakkuk, Zephaniah and Jeremiah. There are a few disputed instances in Hosea, Micah and Isaiah. Eichrodt summarizes the distinction when he comments of Ezekiel that, "in his case the spirit plays a part unknown in the records of the other prophets."[6] Two questions animate the substantial scholarly debate about this absence in the pre-exilic classical prophets.

First, there is the question of what the Old Testament actually says. Mowinckel argues that,

4. Zimmerli, "Special Form- and Traditio-Historical Character," 520.

5. There is intense debate over the identity and self-understanding of these figures. Debates focus on whether each saw himself as a נביא, whether wider society saw each as a נביא and to what extent they are literary creations. See especially Graeme A. Auld, "Prophets Through the Looking Glass: Between the Writings and Moses," *JSOT* 27 (1983): 3–23; Robert P. Carroll, "Poets Not Prophets: A Response to 'Prophets Through the Looking Glass,' " *JSOT* 27 (1983): 25–31; H. G. M. Williamson, "A Response to A. Graeme Auld," *JSOT* 27 (1983): 33–39; Bruce Vawter, "Were the Prophets *Nābî*'s?," *Bib* 66 (1985): 206–20; Thomas W. Overholt, "Prophecy in History: The Social Reality of Intermediation," *JSOT* 48 (1990): 3–29; Robert P. Carroll, "Whose Prophet? Whose History? Whose Social Reality? Troubling the Interpretative Community Again: Notes Towards a Response to T. W. Overholt's Critique," *JSOT* 48 (1990): 33–49; Hans M. Barstad, "No Prophets? Recent Developments in Biblical Prophetic Research and Ancient Near Eastern Prophecy," *JSOT* 57 (1993): 39–60; Robert P. Gordon, "Where Have All the Prophets Gone? The 'Disappearing' Prophet Against the Background of Ancient Near Eastern Prophecy," *BBR* 5 (1995): 67–86; Philip R. Davies, "The Audiences of Prophetic Scrolls: Some Suggestions," in *Prophets and Paradigms: Essays in Honor of Gene M. Tucker* (ed. Stephen B. Reid; JSOTSup 229; Sheffield: Sheffield Academic Press, 1996), 48–62; Terry L. Fenton, "Israelite Prophecy: Characteristics of the First Protest Movement," in *The Elusive Prophet: The Prophet as a Historical Person, Literary Character and Anonymous Artist* (ed. Johannes C. de Moor; *OtSt* 45; Leiden: Brill, 2001), 129–41. In my judgment, neither prophecy nor these figures are essentially literary creations, not least because the unfolding picture that emerges would hardly be manufactured (see Fenton, "Israelite Prophecy," 140–41).

6. Eichrodt, *Theology*, 2:50. However, according to Eichrodt, it is not רוח that "endues him [Ezekiel] with the gift of prophecy."

> pre-exilic reforming prophets never in reality express a consciousness
> that their prophetic endowment and powers are due to possession by or
> any action of *the spirit of Yahweh, rûaḥ yahweh*. There is, on the contrary,
> another fundamental religious conception upon which the whole of their
> consciousness and prophetic message rest, namely *the word of Yahweh*.[7]

Many others have broadly followed him. So, for example, Albertz and
Westermann assert that the relationship between Yahweh's רוח and
his word is "completely absent in the writing prophets from Amos to
Jeremiah. Only the post-exilic period understood prophecy as the obvious work of the divine spirit."[8] In effect, they maintain that the classical
prophets do not speak explicitly of any role for רוח in their inspiration.
Such an understanding depends on eliminating any possible reference
to the divine רוח and inspiration in the prophets' self-understanding.
Important passages in this regard are Hos 9:7, Mic 3:8 (cf. 2:6–11), Jer
5:13 and Isa 30:1–2. A second view sees references to the divine רוח
within the classical prophet's self-understanding as present, but not at all
prominent.[9]

The second question relates to how this relative, or complete, absence
of רוח from the classical prophets should be interpreted: Why do the
classical prophets talk so little (or not at all) about the divine רוח when
speaking of their inspiration, especially when רוח is prominent in the
ministry of the pre-classical prophets?[10] Broadly, four lines of interpretation have been proposed.

The first interpretation is what we might call the *antithetical* view, of
which Mowinckel is the most notable proponent.[11] This view is that the
classical prophets not only saw no place for רוח in their own inspiration,
but also essentially repudiated רוח.[12] Central to Mowinckel's view is the

7. Mowinckel, "The 'Spirit' and the 'Word,'" 199 (original emphasis).
8. Albertz and Westermann, *TLOT* 3:1215. So too Wolff, *Anthropology*, 35;
Zimmerli, *Old Testament Theology in Outline*, 101; Scharbert, "Der 'Geist' und die
Schriftpropheten"; Couturier, "L'Esprit de Yahweh."
9. Arvid S. Kapelrud, "The Spirit and the Word in the Prophets," *ASTI* 11 (1977–
78): 40–47; Lindblom, *Prophecy*, 25–28.
10. The inspiration of the pre-classical prophets is sometimes carefully circumscribed, such that it does not relate to communication of words (so, e.g., Albertz and
Westermann, *TLOT* 3:1215). See further below.
11. Mowinckel, "The 'Spirit' and the 'Word.'"
12. A similar repudiation was suggested earlier by Volz in his *Der Geist Gottes*,
62–69, though in his case it was because of the demonic associations of רוח: "Man
kann daher sagen, die Propheten brauchten die Ruḥ nicht, weil sie Jahwe hatten, und
sie lehnten sie ab, weil sie ihnen und ihrem Jahwe fremd war" (p. 68). Although
Mowinckel slightly tempered his criticism of ecstasy after experience of the prophecy of the devoutly Christian and charismatic Oxford Group in the mid-1930s (see

perceived radical discontinuity between the classical prophets and the "spirit-inspired" נביא. The classical prophets not only rejected inspiration in the form of the רוח of Yahweh, since they did not like the ecstatic phenomena, but they also spoke out against the נביאים who were inspired by רוח, since they were false prophets. Couturier argues that this does not mean that רוח within prophecy always had negative connotations. He maintains that there are three quite distinct prophetic types, the ecstatic prophets, associated with Samuel (חבל נביאים) and Elijah/Elisha (בני הנביאים), the professional prophets, and the "prophètes individuels, ou de vocation."[13] The involvement of רוח in the first type, who were around until the end of the ninth century, is not criticized by the biblical authors. It is the role of רוח in the numerous professional prophets (הנביאים), who were often in groups, who plagued the individual prophets from the end of ninth century until the exile, and who, above all, peddled lies, that was instrumental in the repudiation of רוח by the individual prophets.

The second view, the *historical* view, also finds a complete absence of רוח in the classical prophets. The issue here, however, is not so much one of a repudiation of רוח found in the false prophets. Rather, it is simply a matter of history: "when this objective reality, the spirit, whose presence had to be attested by a prophet's associates, *ceased to operate*, then the prophet of the word had to rely much more on himself and on the fact that he had received a call."[14] In other words, the lack of mention of רוח points to a fundamental historical reality.

The third and fourth views, like the first, acknowledge the significant role ascribed to רוח within false prophecy, but regard the classical prophets as downplaying the role of רוח within their own inspiration, albeit for slightly different reasons. The third view argues that the absence of רוח was due to a loss of confidence in prophetism arising from false prophecy.[15] Certainly 1 Kgs 22 makes it clear that what are portrayed as "false prophets" laid claim to רוח יהוה (1 Kgs 22:24). Thus, רוח is downplayed for what might be termed *practical*, or *rhetorical*, reasons. Although רוח could "reveal" what was "true and right,"[16] inspiration by רוח was no longer determinant of true prophecy. Indeed, the classical prophets were so reticent in speaking about the action of רוח in

Mowinckel, "A Postscript to the Paper"), the article by Couturier ("L'Esprit de Yahweh") argues in support of Mowinckel's 1934 article. Further, the reprinting in 2002 of Mowinckel's 1934 article suggests "repudiation" will continue to be one way of interpreting the data.

    13. Couturier, "L'Esprit de Yahweh," 169.
    14. Von Rad, *Old Testament Theology*, 2:57 (my emphasis).
    15. Eichrodt, *Theology*, 2:56.
    16. Ibid.

their own inspiration "since it had come into disrepute through the old ecstatic and false prophets, who attributed their 'salvation prophecy' to the spirit of the Lord."[17]

The fourth view, which might be called the *theological* view, is that the prophets are "so directly constrained by the message of Yahweh that they simply do not reflect on the notion of a mediating spirit."[18] A modified version of this can be found in Jacob:

> It is clear that for all the prophets it is not the spirit but the word which qualifies them for their ministry, because only the word creates between the prophet and God a relationship of person with person. But the word presupposes the spirit, the creative breath of life, and for the prophets there was such evidence of this that they thought it unnecessary to state it explicitly.[19]

The theocentricity of these prophets thus explains the absence of רוח.[20]

For these last two views, there is not necessarily an inherent discontinuity between רוח and the prophetic word of the classical prophets, but scholars are not always clear. For some, there is in the classical prophets an implicit belief in רוח-inspiration which is hardly (or not at all) articulated.[21] For others, it is often unstated or unclear whether they think belief in רוח-inspiration was present within the self-understanding of the classical prophets.[22]

This background to the book of Ezekiel, both of the pre-classical prophets, on the one hand, and the classical prophets, on the other, has led many scholars to conclude that the book of Ezekiel recovers the notion of רוח linked with prophetic inspiration after a long absence.[23] Montague asserts that "especially does the spirit return as the instigator and the

---

17. Koch, *Geist Gottes*, 59: "weil sie durch die alten Ekstatiker und die Pseudo-propheten, die ihre 'Heilsprophetie' auf den Geist des Herrn zurückführten..., in Verruf gekommen war"; cf. Neve, *The Spirit of God*, 34–38.

18. Zimmerli, *Old Testament Theology*, 102. This is Zimmerli's tentative suggestion of "another part of the explanation" for this silence.

19. Edmond Jacob, *Theology of the Old Testament* (trans. A. W. Heathcote and P. J. Allcock; London: Hodder & Stoughton, 1958), 125. So too Kapelrud, "The Spirit and the Word"; Chevallier, *Souffle de Dieu*, 28–29; Carley, *Ezekiel Among the Prophets*, 28; Horn, "Holy Spirit," *ABD* 3:263.

20. Lindblom, *Prophecy*, 178.

21. Cf. van Imschoot, "L'action de l'esprit de Jahvé," 570–73; Lys, *Rûach*, 68; Koch, *Geist Gottes*, 55.

22. E.g. Briggs, "Use of רוח," 140; Schoemaker, "Use of רוח," 20; Zimmerli, "Special Form- and Traditio-Historical Character," 517.

23. E.g. Joachim Jeremias, 'נָבִיא *nābî'* prophet," *TLOT* 2:707; Mowinckel, "The 'Spirit' and the 'Word.'" 226; Zimmerli, *Ezekiel 1*, 42.

animator of prophecy."[24] The reason for this renewed emphasis is not often articulated.[25] Many scholars are content simply to observe the links. For Carley, however, such a picture is intimately linked with the need for the prophet to authenticate his ministry: "We have seen that he [Ezekiel] was concerned to authenticate his prophetic activities in the face of contemporary rivals. Recourse to older concepts and modes of expression would have helped establish him in the succession of earlier, and perhaps well-respected, prophets of crisis."[26]

There are three main questions that I shall endeavour to answer in this part of the book. The first is the question of whether רוח in Ezekiel is or can be understood as Yahweh's breath on which his word is carried. Naturally this will be restricted to the prophetic and the rhetorical events. The second is whether with Ezekiel there is a recovery of רוח as foundational in prophetic inspiration. Within this is the question of whether the classical prophets did indeed repudiate רוח in their own inspiration. The third is whether the emphasis on רוח within the prophet Ezekiel's ministry is best explained in terms of the authentication of the prophet.

In this chapter, I shall bring sharper definition to discussions by examining the concept of inspiration, and then shall examine the role of רוח within the ministry of Ezekiel himself, as the book portrays it. In Chapter 4, I shall turn to the picture of inspiration present both before the book of Ezekiel, within the pre-classical and the classical prophets, and in some of the biblical literature after it

Taking both chapters together, I shall argue in Part II that the link between Yahweh's רוח as "breath" and Yahweh's word is neither made nor exploited theologically in the book of Ezekiel, although there are close links between רוח and Yahweh's word; that the inspiration of Ezekiel is not qualitatively different either from that of the pre-classical prophets, or from that of the classical prophets; that the emphasis on רוח within pre-classical prophecy has been overemphasized; that the classical prophets were willing to attribute their inspiration to, or to have their inspiration attributed to, the divine רוח, despite a reluctance to speak of רוח; that the picture of inspiration after the book of Ezekiel is also not qualitatively different from that found in Ezekiel; that the prominence of

---

24. Montague, *Holy Spirit*, 45.

25. Of those that do, Volz is notable for relating it to Ezekiel's lack of sharp vision of the being of Yahweh, his closer affinity to popular belief, his greater disposition towards extraordinary trance-like experiences. See Volz, *Der Geist Gottes*, 69. Neve (*Spirit of God*, 38) relates Ezekiel's greater freedom to his being "transplanted into a new environment."

26. Carley, *Ezekiel Among the Prophets*, 73.

רוח within the prophetic ministry of Ezekiel is not explained well by the notion that the prophet recovers an emphasis that had been lost in order to authenticate his ministry.

1. *Exploring Inspiration*

First, however, if we are to evaluate the picture of word, spirit and inspiration in the book of Ezekiel and compare the relationship there with that which obtains elsewhere within Old Testament prophecy, it is essential to explore what precisely is meant by inspiration, since scholars use the word in two different senses without distinguishing between them.[27]

In the first, which we might call "word-communicating" inspiration, רוח, the divine "breath"/"spirit," effectively "breathes" or "utters" the word to the prophet, or through the prophet to the people. In other words, רוח is involved in inspiring the *words* (of Yahweh), whether such inspiration relates to the words that came to the prophet, or to the words that the prophet delivers.[28] So, for example, Neh. 9:30 is sometimes cited as a case where "the spirit is the spirit that spoke through the prophets";[29] it was ברוחך ביד־נביאיך ("by your spirit through your prophets") that Yahweh had warned the people of Israel.

In the second sense, which we might call "potentiating inspiration," "the spirit was the supernatural power that evoked the revelatory state of mind"[30] in the prophet and enabled the prophet to speak. Negatively, "potentiating" avoids giving to רוח an anachronistic personal dimension. Positively, it encompasses both the sense of creating the potential for the prophet to receive a word, or creating the situation where the prophet is ready to receive that word, and empowering the prophet for the task of delivering that word. In this sense, the spirit's work here is one aspect of that same spirit's wider work of empowering and enabling that can be

---

27. The article on רוח in *NIDOTTE* uses inspiration in both the senses I outline without distinguishing between them (M. V. Van Pelt, et al., "רוּחַ," *NIDOTTE* 3:1076).

28. Ma (*Until the Spirit Comes*, 121) uses inspiration in this sense: "The prophetic inspiration of the spirit of God throughout the Old Testament is for the preaching of Yahweh's word (e.g. Num 24.2; Mic 3.8; Ezek 11.5; Zech 7.12; Joel 3.1–2; 2 Sam 23.2; Neh 9:30; 2 Chron 15.1; 20.14)." That he is talking about רוח as the source is clear from what he says later, commenting on רוח in post-exilic times (p. 152): "the claim of the spirit of Yahweh reappears as the *source* of revelation" (my emphasis). Cf. Wilson, *Prophecy and Society*, 145.

29. Montague, *Holy Spirit*, 81. Cf. Dreytza, *Der theologische Gebrauch von RUAH*, 219: "Die Propheten haben die Worte der רוח übermittelt."

30. Lindblom, *Prophecy*, 177.

seen, for example, in the book of Judges, where the spirit "comes upon" (היה על) Othniel (3:10) and Jephthah (11:29), "clothes itself with" (לבש) Gideon (Judg 6:34), "impels" (פעם, 13:25) and "rushes upon" (צלח) Samson (14:6, 19; 15:4). Thus "inspiration" can be used as the general term to describe the "power proceeding from God" in the life of people.[31] Such a view of inspiration has been articulated clearly by Kaufmann:

> We must thus distinguish the action of the spirit of YHWH from prophecy proper. The spirit is the source of activity and creativity; it animates the ecstatic, the judge, the mighty man; it rests on the poet. It rouses the prophet to act, to speak, and endows him with the ability to harangue and poetize. The spirit of prophecy also prepares him to receive the divine word—to see visions, to hear the divine voice in dreams or ecstatic slumber. But the source of prophecy proper is other than these activities. It is in the revelation of God. In this revelation the prophet ideally is entirely passive; he but listens to what is said to him. The frenzy, the physical aberrations, even the visions are not the essence. Of visions and riddles, too, the important part is the explanation that the prophet receives passively. What makes the prophet is not any faculty of clairvoyance, or the spirit that rests on or in him; it is the word that he has heard from God or his agents.[32]

In other words, by "potentiating" inspiration I mean that רוח is involved in inspiring the *prophet*, whether to receive or deliver Yahweh's words.

Whether ultimately it is possible to distinguish "word-communicating" inspiration from "potentiating" inspiration remains to be seen, however. If the work of רוח within "potentiating" inspiration is to enable the prophet to fulfil the task to which Yahweh has called him or her, as is the case with the judges, it still raises the question of the relationship between word and spirit, since the essence of prophecy (which רוח is said to enable) is to have a word from Yahweh (cf. Jer 18:18). Thus "potentiating" inspiration may not necessarily preclude "word-communicating inspiration."

There is a second question about inspiration that needs to be addressed, too, and that is the *point* within the "life" of the "word" to which the term "inspiration" refers. We have already seen how Yahweh's word can be understood both as the word from Yahweh to the prophet (the prophetic event), and as the word which the prophet utters (the rhetorical event). Any discussion about the role of רוח and inspiration needs to explore at which point the influence of רוח can be seen. Such a distinction between the two stages of prophecy is not always preserved or highlighted in the Old Testament, whether in what has been called "ecstatic prophecy" (e.g. 1 Sam 10), or in later accounts of prophecy (e.g. Neh

---

31. Vriezen, *Outline of Old Testament Theology*, 250.
32. Kaufmann, *Religion of Israel*, 99.

9:30). This should not be surprising, since, if there was a discernible "gap" between the prophetic event and the rhetorical event, false prophecy would not have been an issue. Nonetheless, there are occasions, particularly in narrative, where a distinction is explicitly made between the two events (e.g. 1 Kgs 21:19–24). Further, there are other occasions where רוח is linked particularly with either the prophetic event (e.g. Ezek 11:5) or the rhetorical event (e.g. Isa 61:1), or simply with the prophet's ministry (e.g. 2 Kgs 2:9). Maintaining a distinction, then, between the two stages, is important.

Failure to make careful distinctions is a contributory factor in scholars reaching different conclusions. Hildebrandt seems to focus on "potentiating" inspiration when he observes the role of רוח in "commissioning, inspiring, motivating and guiding" the prophets (especially Ezekiel), and concludes that "the relationship between the word and the Spirit in the prophet's [*sic*] estimation was very intimate."[33] Kaufmann appears to focus on "word-communicating" inspiration when he concludes, on the basis of the same data, that there is no relationship between Yahweh's word and Yahweh's רוח.[34] It is with these distinctions in mind that we turn to the book of Ezekiel.

2. *The Inspiration of Ezekiel*

Our analysis of prophetic inspiration within the book of Ezekiel will focus on four areas. The first two relate to Yahweh addressing the prophet, in visions and in "word." The third relates to other instances of links between רוח and prophecy. The fourth relates to Ezekiel communicating Yahweh's word. Given every commentator's acknowledgment that רוח is strikingly prominent in the book, a degree of unanimity might be expected here, but there is in fact significant disagreement with regard to the prophet's inspiration and רוח. Koch confidently declares of Ezekiel, "At every turn, he emphasizes standing, talking and acting under the effect of *rûach Yahweh*."[35] Scharbert, on the other hand, while observing the action of רוח on the prophet in a number of respects, adds, "but nowhere is the prophetic preaching to his own fellow-believers itself characterized as a gift or even as a task of the 'spirit of God.'"[36] I shall be

33. Wilf Hildebrandt, *Spirit of God*, 167.
34. Kaufmann, *Religion of Israel*, 101.
35. Koch, *Geist Gottes*, 60: "Auf Schritt und Tritt betont er, [*sic*] unter der Einwirkung der *rûach Jahweh* zu stehen, zu reden und zu handeln."
36. Scharbert, "Der 'Geist.'" 92: "…aber nirgends wird die prophetische Verkündigung an die eigenen Glaubensgenossen selbst als eine Gabe oder auch als Auftrag des 'Geist Gottes' charakterisiert."

arguing that neither of these is accurate. There is some evidence of both "potentiating" and "word-communicating" inspiration, and such inspiration relates both to the prophetic and to the rhetorical events. Such inspiration, however, is rather less prominent than Koch states.

2.1. *Ezekiel's Visions and* רוח

We saw above, with Zimmerli, that there are five vision "units" within the book of Ezekiel.[37] Within these, both the hand of Yahweh and the spirit of Yahweh have a significant role in their reception.[38]

In 8:2–3, the prophet narrates, "A figure that looked like a human being[39]...stretched out the form of a hand, and took me by a lock of my head; and the spirit lifted me up (ותשא אתי רוח) between earth and heaven, and brought me in divine visions to Jerusalem (ותבא אתי ירושלמה במראות אלהים)" (vv. 2–3). Within the context of the book, the vision that these verses introduce extends to 11:25, where Ezekiel told the exiles all that Yahweh had shown him. With the elders sitting before the prophet (8:1), the hand of Yahweh fell upon him, and he saw the "figure" strikingly similar to the one he had seen in 1:26–27. Then the "figure" and רוח together lift him up, and this רוח transports Ezekiel in divine visions. While visions occurred within earlier prophecy (e.g. 1 Kgs 22:17, 19–22; Amos 7:1–9), and Elijah was regarded as having experienced transportation by רוח (1 Kgs 18:12; 2 Kgs 2:16), Ezekiel is unique in experiencing "visionary transportation"—that is, within the vision Ezekiel sees himself as transported by רוח.

---

37. Zimmerli, "Special Form- and Traditio-Historical Character," 516.

38. The phrase יד־יהוה (or the variant with אדני in 8:1) is always linked in Ezekiel with the prophet's ministry. Apart from the introduction to visions, it only appears at two other points in the book. In 3:14, it occurs at the close of the first vision. In 33:22, it occurs within the only narrative unit in the book, "presaging this time not an oracle...but a release from the years-long constraint on normal intercourse with his society" (Greenberg, *Ezekiel 21–37*, 681). Yahweh also speaks within the book of "my hand" (e.g. 6:14; cf. 20:33–35). Zimmerli links the origin of the use of "hand of Yahweh" with the Exodus tradition (*Ezekiel 1*, 117–18). Roberts, however, criticizes Zimmerli for ignoring non-biblical parallels, and associates it with illness and pathological behaviour; see J. J. M. Roberts, "The Hand of Yahweh," *VT* 21 (1971): 244–51. Carley notes the two strands of meaning, "power," or "alienation" of an individual's mind. He says that references speaking of Yahweh's influence on the prophet fit more easily into the second sense. For Carley (*Ezekiel Among the Prophets*, 29), רוח (anarthrous, and without the absolute, "Yahweh") speaks of conveying the prophet, while "hand" has to do with "awareness of an extraordinary state of mind."

39. Reading איש, with LXX. See Zimmerli, *Ezekiel 1*, 216.

Our concern here is not so much with the precise nature of what Ezekiel experienced,[40] but to ascertain the role of רוח with respect to the reception of the vision. At one level, the distinction between רוח and יד is clear.[41] Here, the role of רוח is to do with the *movement* of the prophet *within* the vision rather than with the reception of the vision itself. It is when the hand of Yahweh comes upon him that he receives the vision in 8:1. Thus רוח here is more properly seen as the transporting רוח, and not the prophetic or inspiring רוח. It is the "hand of Yahweh" that introduces each of the five vision reports in the book of Ezekiel. Further, it was a "hand" stretched out to Ezekiel that gave him the scroll containing the words of his message (2:8).

There are, however, three reasons why our attention should not move too quickly away from רוח and the reception of the prophet's visions. First, there is a close association in the Old Testament between Yahweh's רוח and Yahweh's יד.[42] Secondly, there is one instance in the book where Yahweh's רוח does seem to be linked explicitly with the prophet's reception of a vision (11:24). Thirdly, in one of the visions (37:1–14), the transporting רוח, usually anarthrous, is in construct relationship with, and made definite by, the absolute יהוה (37:1). The identity and function of this רוח points to a closer link between Yahweh's transporting רוח and inspiration than is sometimes recognized. We turn first to the similarity of Yahweh's רוח and Yahweh's יד.

The close association of Yahweh's רוח and Yahweh's יד can be found outside the book of Ezekiel. Prophetic inspiration is linked with music and the action of Yahweh's רוח in 1 Sam 10:6–10, but with Yahweh's יד in 2 Kgs 3:15. Divinely assisted movement is associated with Yahweh's רוח in 1 Kgs 18:12 and 2 Kgs 2:16, but with Yahweh's יד in 1 Kgs 18:46. Similarity is also found within the book, both in the transportation of the prophet and in the reception of visions. It is the form of a hand (יד) stretched out from the figure on the throne that "takes" (לקח) Ezekiel by a lock of his head, then רוח picks him up (נשא) (8:3). This is very similar

40. For a discussion of this, see Carley, *Ezekiel Among the Prophets*, 31–37.

41. Cf. Neve, *Spirit of God*, 97–98.

42. Lindblom, *Prophecy*, 58; Zimmerli, *Ezekiel 1*, 117–18; Dreytza, *Der theologische Gebrauch von RUAH*, 153–58; Koch, *Geist Gottes*, 45–46, 67; Schüngel-Straumann, *Rûah bewegt die Welt*, 54. This is not to say that they are identical. Lys (*Rûach*, 133) tentatively suggests that the difference is to be found in the nature of the action, "la main son action sur l'homme, l'esprit son action en l'homme"; Schüngel-Straumann (*Rûah bewegt die Welt*, 54–55) suggests the difference lies in the fact that Yahweh's hand designates Yahweh's power (*Macht*), while רוח is used in a more multifarious way, and is less strongly identified with Yahweh.

to 3:14, where רוח picks him up (נשא) and takes (לקח) him. In 8:1, Yahweh's יד falls (נפל) on the prophet at the start of his vision, signalling the reception of the vision. In 11:5, Yahweh's רוח falls (נפל) on Ezekiel, the only time such a collocation occurs in the Old Testament. Further, in 11:24, the divine vision attributed at the start of ch. 8 to Yahweh's יד, is attributed to רוח אלהים. Finally, the words used to describe the action of Yahweh's hand coming on the prophet (היה על[43]) is elsewhere in the Old Testament used of the coming of Yahweh's רוח.[44]

The second point linking Yahweh's רוח with divine visions is in 11:24. At the end of the vision that began in 8:1, the prophet recounts, "The spirit lifted me up and brought me in a vision by the spirit of God into Chaldea, to the exiles (ורוח נשאתני ותביאני כשדימה אל־הגולה במראה ברוח אלהים). Then the vision that I had seen left me" (11:24). Here within the same verse are two occurrences of רוח which are slightly awkward together. The significant phrase for us is במראה ברוח אלהים, but how we render it depends in part on how we are to interpret the transporting רוח which picks the prophet up. Those who favour a theological understanding of the "transporting רוח," such as the "divine energy" that transported the prophet,[45] or as Yahweh's spirit,[46] face a difficulty over the second occurrence of רוח in the verse. Neve sees the phrase ברוח אלהים as referring to the prophet being "brought," rather than to the notion that the "spirit" brought about the vision, claiming that the spirit is not "the source of the visions that Ezekiel saw."[47] Support for this might be seen to come from 37:1, where the subject of the sentence qualifies an agent in a way similar to Neve's construal of 11:24: "he (i.e. Yahweh) brought me out by the spirit of Yahweh (ברוח יהוה)." The similarity of the two instances, however, should not be overplayed. In 37:1, the agent of translocation is juxtaposed with the verb expressing the translocation, while in 11:24, if Neve's interpretation is accepted, the agent is distant from the verb. Further, this reading of 11:24 introduces substantial redundancy in the description of the agent of Ezekiel's visionary movement,

---

43. Ezek 1:3; 3:22; 8:1; 37:1; 40:1; cf. also 3:14; 33:22.

44. Num 24:2; Judg 3:10; 11:29; 1 Sam 19:20, 23; cf. 1 Sam 16:16, 23. Eichrodt (*Theology*, 2:56) suggests that the downplaying of רוח within classical prophecy is evident here, in so far as the "overwhelming effect" of Yahweh has come to be described by the "hand of Yahweh," rather than by רוח.

45. Cooke, *Book of Ezekiel*, 127.

46. Zimmerli, *Ezekiel 1*, 230; Lys, *Rûach*, 129–30; Allen, *Ezekiel 1–19*, 129; Block, *Ezekiel 1–24*, 358–59; Harold E. Hosch, "*RÛAḤ* in the Book of Ezekiel," 109, 112–13; cf. the discussion in Chapter 1 of the present study.

47. Neve, *Spirit of God*, 97–98.

a redundancy that makes ברוח אלהים seem like a gloss.[48] It is hard, however, to discern what the function of such a gloss might have been, and there is no textual evidence for a corruption, so we should endeavour to make sense of the MT. Allen captures the force of ברוח אלהים, when he says that the phrase "'by means of the spirit of God' can hardly qualify the verb of which רוח 'spirit' is subj. It seems rather to qualify the 'vision,' which virtually has a verbal force, 'that which was seen (by means of).'"[49]

Here, then, is evidence of at least a "potentiating" view of inspiration. In 11:24, the "spirit of God" is seen as responsible for giving the vision that is seen in 8:1 as due to the "hand of Yahweh." A prophetic vision is not always merely the vehicle within which the "word" comes, as Kaufmann effectively suggests, but can also be seen itself as Yahweh's "word," a divine "speech event." Thus, if the "spirit" is seen here as responsible for giving the vision, and the vision is understood not merely as a vehicle for Yahweh's word, but as Yahweh's "word" or "speech event," then it is better to see "word-communicating" inspiration articulated here.

At the same time, although it does not alter conclusions about the relationship between word and רוח, such a reading does not diminish the awkwardness of the double mention of רוח, if the first רוח is interpreted theologically. Renz, therefore, follows Greenberg[50] in rendering the transporting רוח here as "wind." He regards this verse as confirming that the רוח "operative on Ezekiel in the visions is a 'wind' rather than 'the Spirit'" because of the "differentiation made in 11:24 between this רוח and the רוח through which the vision was communicated."[51] This certainly accounts for the shift in gender and the lack of the divine name between the transporting רוח יהוה in 1 Kgs 18:12 and 2 Kgs 2:16, on the one hand, and the feminine, anarthrous, unspecified רוח in Ezekiel.[52]

The third reason why Yahweh's רוח can and should be related to Ezekiel's visions is derived from the account of the vision of dry bones

48. Cf. Cooke, *Ezekiel*, 127; Georg Fohrer, *Ezechiel, mit einem Beitrag von Kurt Galling* (2d ed.; HAT 13; Tübingen: J. C. B. Mohr [Paul Siebeck], 1955), 55; Carley, *Ezekiel Among the Prophets*, 30, 88; Eichrodt, *Ezekiel*, 112.

49. Allen, *Ezekiel 1–19*, 129. Cf. Block, *Ezekiel 1–24*, 359; Hosch, "*RÛAḤ* in the Book of Ezekiel," 112.

50. Greenberg, *Ezekiel 1–20*, 186.

51. Renz, *Rhetorical Function*, 201. Others seeing the anarthrous transporting רוח as "wind" include Brownlee, *Ezekiel 1–19*, 25; Carley, *Ezekiel Among the Prophets*, 30; Woodhouse, "'Spirit,'" 14.

52. For a different perspective, grounded in Ezekiel's monotheism, see Lys, *Rûach*, 130.

in 37:1–14. In 37:1, the reference to the transporting רוח is articulated in unique fashion. The transporting רוח is said explicitly to be Yahweh's. There must be significance in such a reference, since it was obviously possible to speak of the transporting רוח in vaguer fashion. Such a reference certainly serves to orient the reader to the other nine occurrences of רוח in the thirteen verses that follow, and in particular to highlight Yahweh's sovereign action behind these events.[53] Two questions, though, remain. One relates to the identity of רוח here. Is it a wind sent by Yahweh or Yahweh's spirit that transports the prophet in visions? The second relates to the significance of this occurrence for other instances of רוח within Ezekiel's visions. Is this instance determinative or significant for the interpretation of the other instances?

With regard to the first question, to say that רוח is Yahweh's רוח does not necessarily remove it from the principally meteorological realm, although the only other instance of the phrase רוח יהוה in Ezekiel, in 11:5, is theological. The same phrase can designate the wind at Yahweh's beck and call (Isa 40:7), and Yahweh's control over רוח *qua* meteorological phenomenon is apparent in texts such as Exod 15:8 and Num 11:31.[54] A more fruitful approach is to explore more fully the characteristics and function of רוח in v. 1 in the light of the rest of the vision. Wagner observes that רוח in v. 1 bears many of the characteristics of a storm wind, but argues that it cannot be simply a storm wind because it is not random in its action, since it takes Ezekiel to " 'the plain' (with the definite article)."[55] This is not a necessary conclusion, since we have seen Yahweh's control over רוח, and Elijah is transported to heaven in a "whirlwind" (בסערה). He argues, however, "that *rûaḥ* seems here to be the principle of revelation of prophetic experience."[56] Since Block distinguishes clearly between the transporting רוח and the רוח of prophetic revelation,[57] we need to follow Wagner's argument closely here.[58]

---

53. Cf. Renz, *Rhetorical Function*, 202.

54. Ma (*Until the Spirit Comes*, 19) notes the particular difficulty in the categorization of רוח "where the function strongly implies the 'wind' reference, but also has a strong indication that the רוח is specifically used by Yahweh."

55. Siegfried Wagner, "Geist und Leben nach Ezechiel 37,1–14," in *Ausgewählte Aufsätze zum Alten Testament* (ed. D. Mathias; Berlin: de Gruyter, 1996), 151–68 (155): ">der Ebene< (mit best. Artikel)"; repr. from *Theologische Versuche* (ed. Joachim Rogge and Gottfried Schille; Berlin: Evangelische Verlagsanstalt, 1979), 10:53–65.

56. Ibid., 154: "*rûaḥ* scheint hier das Offenbarungsprinzip prophetischer Erlebnisse zu sein."

57. Block, *Ezekiel 25–48*, 373.

58. What follows is taken from Wagner, "Geist und Leben," 151–56.

Although there is obviously a shift between vv. 1–10 and vv. 12–14, in terms of the "picture" (*Bildmaterie*), Wagner asks why we should assume unity of *Bildmaterie* as one of the criteria of authenticity. Both sections have slightly different emphases, which can explain the shift. At the same time, both sections speak of "the same reality of death."[59] In view of the fact that the exiles have experienced death (37:11) in the form of "history that has died, belief that has died, hope that has died, promises of salvation that have perished,"[60] the picture of the field of bones in vv. 1–2 is utterly appropriate. Having demonstrated the coherence and congruence of the different "pictures," Wagner then makes the crucial point that it is by Yahweh's רוח that Ezekiel is brutally confronted with the reality of death.

The significance of the storm wind motif for him is that it symbolizes Ezekiel being seized by Yahweh and torn away from his environment and his existing conditions.[61] But רוח goes beyond that, for "the *rûach* tears away all illusions and unlocks reality, making reality experienceable, comprehensible, visible. It is precisely the act which can be understood as ecstasy, as mystical experience, that leads Ezekiel into the illusion-free, present, actual, historical situation."[62] In other words, רוח brings Ezekiel to the point of greatest reality, when Ezekiel sees the situation for the exiles as it really is. For Wagner, the transporting רוח merges into the prophetic spirit of revelation.[63]

Using the categories of inspiration devised above, we can refine Wagner's conclusions. Although it is true that רוח brings Ezekiel to the place where he sees the reality of the situation for the exiles, and although what Ezekiel sees can be understood as Yahweh's speech event, רוח is not the source of what he sees. In that sense, the transporting, even the prophetic, רוח should be understood in terms of "potentiating" rather than "word-communicating" inspiration.

59. Ibid., 153: "die gleiche Todeswirklichkeit."
60. Ibid., 156: "gestorbene Geschichte, gestorbener Glaube, gestorbene Hoffnung, verstorbene Heilszusagen." For more on the image of death in 37:11, see Saul M. Olyan, "'We Are Utterly Cut Off': Some Possible Nuances of נגזרנו לנו in Ezek 37:11," *CBQ* 65 (2003): 43–51.
61. Wagner, "Geist und Leben," 155.
62. Ibid., 156: "Die *rûah* reißt aus allen Illusionen und schließt die Wirklichkeit auf, macht die Wirklichkeit erlebbar, erfaßbar, anschaubar. Gerade *der* Akt, der als Ekstase, als mystisches Erleben begriffen werden kann, führt in die illusionslose vorfindliche tatsächliche geschichtliche Situation."
63. So too Lys, *Rûach*, 130–31. Although Hosch ("*RÛAH* in the Book of Ezekiel," 114) does not specify what kind of "spirit" is in view within the semantic domain "supernatural beings," he argues for the presence of a second semantic domain, "motion" (earlier defined as "movement of air").

This perspective sheds further light on our second question, on whether 37:1 is determinative or significant for the interpretation of the transporting רוח in other visions, too.

The transporting רוח plays a significant part within the visions; indeed, the only places we encounter this רוח are in the visions. We should notice that רוח, within the visions, takes Ezekiel to (8:3; 11:1; 43:5) or from (3:12, 14; 11:24) a place where Yahweh reveals something to the prophet or speaks to him. In that sense, there is little difference in terms of *function* between the רוח יהוה in 37:1 and the anarthrous transporting רוח elsewhere. Given that in 11:24 the first occurrence of רוח most naturally seems to be that of a "wind" moving the prophet, yet functionally it acts in a way similar to the transporting-cum-potentiating spirit of 37:1, here is clear evidence of deliberate ambiguity surrounding the use of רוח. In the earlier passages where the prophet is transported, there is notable reticence to define further what is meant by this רוח. Though a meteorological sense seems most natural, we should not regard the awkwardness in 11:24 as a definitive statement that the transporting רוח is exclusively meteorological. Deliberate play on the different meanings of רוח is clearly part of the author's agenda, as is most obvious in 37:1–14, and references to "wind" do not, of course, connote a "natural cause" of Ezekiel's movement.[64] Retrospectively, we should see Yahweh's direct involvement by his "spirit," something more than hinted at earlier in the book given the close links between Yahweh's רוח and Yahweh's יד, and the near-interchangeability of איש, רוח and יהוה as agents at the start of ch. 8.[65]

The exploration of רוח-inspiration and Ezekiel's visions yields two main conclusions. First, the role of רוח within the visions, the transporting רוח, points towards the "potentiating" inspiration of the prophet, with particular reference to the prophetic event. Secondly, רוח in 11:24 demonstrates the involvement of Yahweh's רוח in the reception of the visions themselves, that is, in the prophetic event. Insofar as these visions are Yahweh's "speech event," the inspiration envisaged here is "word-communicating."

2.2. *Ezekiel Being Addressed in "Word" and* רוח
There are three instances within the book where רוח is closely linked cotextually to Yahweh addressing Ezekiel. In each of these cases, רוח clearly has an impact on Ezekiel the prophet. In each one of these three

---

64. Cf. Carley, *Ezekiel Among the Prophets*, 30.

65. Schüngel-Straumann, *Rûaḥ bewegt die Welt*, 40. Note in particular ותבא אתי (v. 3) and ויבא אתי (v. 7).

instances, there is evidence not of "word-communicating" but of "potentiating" inspiration.

2.2.1. *Ezekiel 2:2.* Within the opening vision (1:1–3:15), Ezekiel had fallen prostrate before the vision of the likeness of the glory of Yahweh (1:28). Then Yahweh spoke to him, and told him to stand on his feet. The prophet continued, "And when he spoke to me (כאשר דבר אלי),[66] a spirit entered into me (ותבא בי רוח) and set me on my feet (ותעמדני); and I heard him speaking to me."

Two questions need to be addressed if the relationship to Yahweh's word is to be discerned. The first is the identity of רוח. The second concerns the relationship between Yahweh's speaking and רוח entering. We turn first to the identity of רוח.

In the preliminary discussion in Chapter 2, we noted some degree of consensus on the theological nature of this רוח, even if some disagreement on the precise nature of it. Looking at commentators more broadly, there is some debate as to whether this רוח is theological. There are really three main views adopted: רוח as a "wind" that set the prophet on his feet, רוח as "breath of life, vigour, courage" given by Yahweh and רוח as "spirit of Yahweh."

Carley observes Ezekiel's "curious reluctance" to use the phrase "spirit of Yahweh," and thinks that people "too readily" equate "spirit" here with "the spirit of Yahweh."[67] He prefers the meaning "wind," linking it with the translating "wind" mentioned elsewhere in Ezekiel. He insists, however, that this does not attribute Ezekiel's movement to a "natural cause," since Yahweh is responsible for the wind, too. The reluctance to speak of Yahweh's own רוח until ch. 36 serves to emphasize the "spirit of Yahweh" as instrumental within Israel's revival.[68] For him, the "word-play" on רוח reveals "the prophet's intention of associating some forces with common physical phenomena."[69]

Greenberg regards רוח as "vigor or even courage...infused into the prophet by the address of God."[70] This might seem to suggest, as it does to Allen,[71] a "subjective" understanding of רוח, but language of Yahweh

---

66. LXX omits this phrase, but adds καὶ ἀνέλαβέν με καὶ ἐξῆρέν με, most of which appears in Ezek 3:14.

67. Carley, *Ezekiel Among the Prophets*, 30.

68. Carley (ibid., 30) regards the clearly theological instances in 11:5 and 11:24 as "out of character" and hence secondary (pp. 25, 88).

69. Ibid.

70. Greenberg, *Ezekiel 1–20*, 62; cf. Fohrer's "göttliche Lebenskraft" (*Ezechiel*, 15).

71. Allen, *Ezekiel 1–19*, 38.

infusing Ezekiel makes it clear that what is in view is a vigour or courage from Yahweh. In a similar vein, Woodhouse notes the links between 2:2 and 37:10, and the contiguity with Yahweh speaking, and prefers to see רוח as Yahweh's breath that enters the prophet.[72] While it should not be assumed that this "breath" that enters the prophet is necessarily related to the word that is spoken, there is support for the rendering "life-breath" from other occurrences of רוח as the subject of בוא (Qal) followed by the preposition ב. Apart from this reference, there are four others, all in Ezekiel (3:24; 37:5, 9, 10). All the instances point to רוח as life-breath.[73] Knierim, in his discussion of Old Testament spirituality, makes the important point, based on Ps 104:29–30, that ontology is not always in view when the Old Testament speaks about רוח, whether it is described as Yahweh's רוח or the human רוח. In Ps 104, whose רוח it is depends on the *location* of that רוח at a particular moment. The critical point, according to Knierim, is that "the spirit essential for human life is given and taken by God, and is not under the control of humans" (cf. נשמה in Gen 2:7).[74] Here, then, it might be that this רוח-breath that has come from Yahweh revitalizes the stunned prophet. Infused with renewed vitality and vigour, he can stand on his feet.[75]

The third view, that of רוח as Yahweh's "spirit," is derived chiefly from the fact that רוח retains its identity in setting the prophet on his feet. Thus, Ohnesorge comments that רוח here "means not only 'vitality,' but more. It has here a dynamic character, so should be understood not only anthropologically, but also theologically—in the sense of a particular working of Yahweh."[76] He goes on to observe that there are close links with 37:10, but the difference lies in the fact that "רוח in 2:2aβ (3:24aβ)

72. Woodhouse, "'Spirit,'" 12–13.
73. Other instances where רוח is the subject of בוא involve the "wind" or "air" that comes (Job 1:19; 41:8; Ezek 1:4; Jer 4:12; Hos 13:15) or that Yahweh brings (Jer 49:36) or that brought (Hiphil) Ezekiel (Ezek 8:3; 11:1, 24; 43:5). Some language of רוח being "in" (ב) a person points to רוח as "life-breath" (e.g. Gen 6:3, 17; 7:15, 22); at other points רוח clearly is God's רוח (e.g. Gen 41:38).
74. Knierim, *The Task of Old Testament Theology*, 273.
75. So Schüngel-Straumann, *Rûah bewegt die Welt*, 44. Given that elsewhere Ezekiel can respond to God's commands without reference to רוח, she sees רוח here not as replacing Ezekiel's own ability to hear and act, but as giving him *vim* where his own was lacking. The appropriate translation is then not "Spirit" but "(God's) vitality" (*[Gottes] Lebenskraft*).
76. Stefan Ohnesorge, *Jahwe gestaltet sein Volk neu: Zur Sicht der Zukunft Israels nach Ez 11,14–21; 20,1–44; 36,16–38; 37,1–14. 15–28* (Forschung zur Bibel 64; Würzburg: Echter, 1991), 303: "nicht nur 'Lebenskraft' meint, sondern mehr. Sie hat hier dynamistischen Charakter, dürfte also nicht nur anthropologisch, sondern auch theologisch—im Sinne eines besonderen Wirkens Jahwes—zu verstehen sein."

is the subject of עמד hi." while "in 37:10b the revitalized are themselves the subject of the phrase…"[77] Allen argues in similar vein that רוח is Yahweh's "spirit," and explains the lack of an article here (and in the references to רוח transporting Ezekiel) as marks of "the stereotyped style of spirit-control."[78] Block, too, sees רוח here as Yahweh's רוח, the "spirit of Yahweh": "The text notes that the raising of the prophet occurs simultaneously with the sound of the voice, which suggests that this *rûaḥ* may be the source of the word's dynamic and energizing power. This can be none other than the Spirit of God…"[79]

The second question relates to the timing of the two events of Yahweh speaking and רוח coming. In particular, it relates to the force of כאשר. On about two hundred occasions in the Old Testament, כאשר is followed by one of three verbs of speaking, אמר, צוה (Piel) or דבר (Piel); eighty of these involve דבר. The vast majority of these two hundred yield the meaning "just as," since the subordinate clause introduced by כאשר serves to confirm that a particular action has been performed "just as" has been said; new elements are not introduced. There are sixteen instances of כאשר דבר אל other than Ezek 2:2. In each of them, כאשר has this comparative sense. If כאשר is to have a comparative sense here, it is necessary that implicit in Yahweh's command to the prophet to stand on his feet is the assumption that רוח will be essential for this to happen. Prior to 2:2, however, there has been no mention within Yahweh's command of רוח entering the prophet. כאשר should therefore be understood in a temporal sense here.[80] Such a rendering, though, has been disputed. The rarity of this temporal usage, along with textual evidence, has led Zimmerli to regard the phrase as a later "clarification."[81] Allen also rejects the phrase for similar reasons, commenting in addition, "it adds little to the narrative and indeed cuts across the future aspect of v 1b."[82] The temporal use, however, *is* found in Ezekiel, despite the fact that Zimmerli, Tov, Allen and Lust all follow Cornill in denying a temporal

---

77. Ibid.: "רוח in 2,2aβ (3,24aβ) Subjekt von עמד hi. …ist" and "In 37,10b sind die Wiederbelebten selbst Subjekt des Ausdrucks…"

78. Allen, *Ezekiel 20–48*, 38.

79. Block, *Ezekiel 1–24*, 115. Others seeing the referent here as Yahweh's רוח include Lys, *Rûach*, 130–31; Hosch, "*RÛAḤ* in the Book of Ezekiel," 105–6.

80. Cf. Tov's comment: "God did not tell the prophet in so many words that Spirit would enter him, so that these words not only disturb the context, but they are also imprecise"; see Emanuel Tov, "Recensional Differences Between the MT and LXX of Ezekiel," *ETL* 62 (1986): 93.

81. Zimmerli, *Ezekiel 1*, 89. He follows Cornill in regarding the temporal usage as "unusual."

82. Allen, *Ezekiel 1–19*, 10; so too Tov, "Recensional Differences," 93.

usage of כאשר in Ezekiel.[83] In 16:50, כאשר introduces an event that preceded in time the main clause, ואסיר אתהן כאשר ראיתי ("therefore I removed them when I saw it").[84] In 35:11, כאשר introduces an event that was to happen simultaneously with that in the main clause, though both would be in the future: ונודעתי בם כאשר אשפטך ("and I will make myself known among them,[85] *when* I judge you"). More significantly, in view of the dominance of כאשר in the sense of "just as" with verbs of saying, is its occurrence with אמר in 37:18 in a clearly temporal sense: וכאשר יאמרו אליך בני עמך לאמר ("And when your people say to you…").

Textual evidence gives further pointers. It is unlikely that the phrase כאשר דבר אלי was present in the Hebrew *Vorlage* of the LXX translators, given the fact that the LXX translators were "relatively literal and consistent."[86] In addition, the absence of the phrase from the Hexapla suggests that Origen was working from a different Hebrew text and that there was a strong Hebrew text tradition other than that of the MT. The origin and dating of the plus in MT is uncertain, however, and its status and significance depends in part on the aim and the approach of the textual critic.[87] What is striking is that there is little agreement on the reason for the plus: one commentator regards the phrase as a "clarification," while another says that it effectively complicates the phrase.

With regard to the temporal relationship between the two clauses, Waltke and O'Connor observe that when two situations are contemporary, the conjunction used (if an infinitive with a preposition is not used)

83. Zimmerli, *Ezekiel 1*, 89; Allen, *Ezekiel 1–19*, 10; Tov, "Recensional Differences," 93; Johan Lust, "Notes to the Septuagint: Ezekiel 1–2," *ETL* 75 (1999): 23.

84. Some see here, as in 16:13, the presence of an archaic second feminine singular ending; there is some ancient evidence for rendering with second feminine singular, "as you saw" (see *BHS*). Zimmerli (*Ezekiel 1*, 332), however, comments, "The meaning 'when I saw it' cannot certainly be excluded."

85. In other words, "in Israel"; so Allen, *Ezekiel 20–48*, 168, as *difficilior lectio*. Zimmerli (*Ezekiel 2*, 226) deletes בם as an inadvertent repetition. LXX has σοι.

86. See Tov, "Recensional Differences," 91–92 (quotation from p. 92).

87. See Moshe Greenberg, "The Use of the Ancient Versions for Understanding the Hebrew Text," in *Congress Volume, Göttingen 1977* (ed. J. A. Emerton; VTSup 29; Leiden: Brill, 1978), 131–48, for a conservative view on the MT. In contrast, note Tov's change of mind that he documents between the first (1992) and second (2001) editions of his work on textual criticism with regard to the status he accords to the textual evidence provided principally by Greek translations. His earlier work, he writes, gave too much weight to the "canonical status" of the MT, in treating these translations as indicators of "(a) layer(s) of literary growth preceding the final composition"; see Emanuel Tov, *Textual Criticism and the Hebrew Bible* (rev. ed.; Minneapolis: Fortress, 2001), 177.

is usually כאשר.[88] כאשר, however, is also often used to describe situations when the event in the subordinate clause (introduced by כאשר) precedes that described in the main clause.[89] On syntactical grounds, it is not possible to decide whether Yahweh's speaking precedes רוח entering the prophet, such that רוח is seen as an effect of the word,[90] or whether they are simultaneous (as Block assumes[91]).

While Woodhouse is right to draw attention to the links with 37:10, Carley has also made an important point in drawing attention to the literary device of "word-play" at this point with regard to the meaning of רוח.[92] I would go further and suggest there is deliberate ambiguity. Such ambiguity is a significant feature in the book of Ezekiel, especially in Ezek 37.[93] The determining factor in understanding what is meant here needs to be the context. The context, however, points in different directions. The fact that, of the occurrences of רוח encountered so far in the book, only רוח in 1:4 has been feminine, points to a link between רוח in 2:2 and 1:4, yielding a meaning "wind." In the light of the wider literary context given by ch. 37, however, the meaning "life-breath" seems (retrospectively) preferable. This, though, should not obscure a third direction which רוח takes, that of the divine רוח as "spirit." This is suggested by the increasing role for רוח within the book, and by the fact that רוח functions as an agent acting upon the prophet.[94] Such ambiguity as is found in 2:2 serves to keep רוח at the forefront of the readers' and hearers' minds. It is also an important reminder that categories we separate readily are in fact rather fluid.[95]

---

88. *IBHS* §38.7a.

89. See BDB, 455.

90. Cf. Kaufmann's comment (*Religion of Israel*, 100) that "The word of God is not brought on by the spirit, the spirit is the by-product of the word." This is a general comment that he makes, not one specifically related to Ezek 2:2.

91. Block, *Ezekiel 1–24*, 115.

92. Carley, *Ezekiel Among the Prophets*, 30. Zimmerli (*Ezekiel 1*, 132) points out the "obscurity" as to whether it is the prophet's own "vital power" or the "divine רוח acting under the divine command."

93. See especially Michael V. Fox, "The Rhetoric of Ezekiel's Vision of the Valley of the Bones," *HUCA* 51 (1980): 1–15, and, more recently, Kinlaw, "From Death to Life."

94. That רוח is the subject and agent of both "entering" and "causing Ezekiel to stand" does not prove conclusively that it is Yahweh's "spirit" that is in view. In Job 32:18, the רוח within Elihu that acts as an independent agent to constrain him is none other than "the breath of Shaddai" (נשמת שדי) that gives a mortal understanding in 32:8.

95. Cf. Chevallier, *Souffle de Dieu*, 25.

Though, however, there is deliberate ambiguity here, and though the MT juxtaposes ותבא בי רוח and דבר אלי, it is not possible to conceive of "word-communicating" inspiration here. Such an interpretation would demand that רוח in some sense preceded Yahweh speaking, an interpretation which the syntax of the MT does not allow. Although רוח is here intimately associated with hearing Yahweh speak, the focus is not on "word-communicating" inspiration,[96] but rather on the prophet's "revival," on his being *enabled* to stand up, to hear and to respond to Yahweh's word.

2.2.2. *Ezekiel 3:24*.

This verse, closely paralleling 2:2, occurs as Ezekiel is again confronted with the divine glory, and falls on his face (3:22–23). Ezekiel recounts how "The spirit entered into me, and set me on my feet (ותבא־בי רוח ותעמדני על־רגלי); and he spoke with me (וידבר אתי) and said to me: Go, shut yourself inside your house." Similarities with 2:2 are immediately apparent. Again, רוח enters the prostrate prophet and sets him on his feet. Here, too, this experience is followed by Yahweh speaking with him, though this is subsequent to the experience of רוח. Allen considers רוח here as the divine רוח. Block agrees, commenting that "as in 2:2a, the absence of the article leaves the identity of the *rûaḥ* open. Its activity, however, resolves the issue. As before, the *rûaḥ* represents the divine power that enables and authorizes the mortal to stand in the presence of the *kābôd*, the visible sign of the One Who Is Present."[97]

While Block and Allen are right to recognize the objective side to רוח here, it is still preferable to see the same deliberate ambiguity present as in 2:2. Thus, the comments above on "inspiration" in 2:2 obtain here. Although the association between רוח and Yahweh speaking with the prophet is close, there is no hint that רוח is the source of inspiration of that word. The most that can be said here is that this רוח points to "potentiating" inspiration, insofar as the prophet is affected and influenced by its presence and action.

2.2.3 *Ezekiel 11:5*.

Within the "divine vision" from 8:1–11:25, Ezekiel is lifted up and brought to the east gate of the house of Yahweh in Jerusalem. There he sees twenty-five men devising iniquity. In 11:4, he was told to "prophesy against them." Ezekiel, as narrator, continues, "Then the spirit of Yahweh fell upon me (ותפל עלי רוח יהוה), and he said to me

---

96. *Pace* Kapelrud ("The Spirit and the Word," 42), who says that "the spirit... spoke to him."

97. Block, *Ezekiel 1–24*, 153–54.

(אלי ויאמר), "'Say, Thus says Yahweh...'" and Yahweh continues, telling him what to say.

The use of נפל with רוח is unique in the Old Testament. It is used once with Yahweh's יד in Ezek 8:1. In meaning, the phrase overlaps with the semantic domain covered by (על) צלח, used of the onrush of Yahweh's spirit, and that of (על) היה, which is used of Yahweh's spirit "coming upon" a person. Both phrases can be used with רוח for prophecy[98] or for more general empowerment.[99] Neither is used of Yahweh's רוח in Ezekiel. Instead, היה על is linked with Yahweh's hand.

Carley has seen here "word-communicating" inspiration, in that רוח "communicates a divine revelation."[100] While he is correct to see here the prophetic רוח,[101] as well as the deliberate linking with pre-classical prophecy, his observation on the relationship between the words Yahweh utters and רוח is mistaken. רוח neither explicitly inspires the words that Yahweh utters, nor the words that Ezekiel is commanded to utter. While רוח "fell" (feminine) on Ezekiel, it is Yahweh who "said" (masculine) to Ezekiel what he should say.[102] While רוח can take both feminine (passim) and masculine (1:12, 20; 19:12; 27:26) verb forms, it is unlikely that there is a shift here, since רוח characteristically in the book retains its gender when it is the subject of two verbs.[103] This verse, though, does

---

98. צלח על (1 Sam 10:6, 10; 18:10); היה על (Num 24:2; 1 Sam 19:20, 23; cf. 1 Sam 16:16, 23, of the "evil spirit" upon Saul).

99. צלח על (Judg 14:6, 19; 15:14; 1 Sam 11:6; 16:13); היה על (Judg 3:10; 11:29).

100. Carley, *Ezekiel Among the Prophets*, 70. So too Hildebrandt, *Old Testament Theology of the Spirit*, 190; Hosch, "*RÛAH* in the Book of Ezekiel," 117. This, along with this phrase's unique conception of the spirit "falling," Ezekiel's awareness of a different mode of operation of רוח in 11:1, and the lack of references elsewhere to רוח falling in connection with calls to prophesy, has led Carley (*Ezekiel Among the Prophets*, 25, 70) to see it as from a later period. So also Zimmerli, *Ezekiel 1*, 258; Ohnesorge, *Jahwe gestaltet sein Volk neu*, 51, 284. LXX (Codex Vaticanus) reads πνεῦμα.

101. Cf. Block's comment ("The Prophet of the Spirit," 41) that this is "the most explicit statement of his prophetic inspiration."

102. Cf. Neve, *Spirit of God*, 97.

103. Ezek 2:2; 3:14, 24; 8:3; 11:1, 24; 43:5. Shifts in the gender of a noun within a verse do occur in Ezekiel (e.g. 13:20; 16:58; 18:19; 20:16; 42:4, 11; 43:11; see also pp. 89–90 n. 306 above), but tend to be where the noun is feminine, and the anaphoric suffix is masculine. According to Rooker, *Biblical Hebrew in Transition*, 79–80, this is a mark of late Biblical Hebrew. It is implausible to argue, as Hosch does ("*RÛAH* in the Book of Ezekiel," 111), that "in such verbs as 'to say, to speak' introducing deity as the speaker the masculine gender is required." In 3:22, there is no possibility that it is Yahweh's hand that is "speaking," yet there is an identical surface structure grammar as in 11:5.

provide a clear instance of the inspiration of the prophet Ezekiel as a person: רוח prepares him to receive Yahweh's word.[104] It is in this sense that "the coming of the spirit leads to the prophetic word."[105] It further reveals the vital role that the divine רוח plays in the life and the ministry of the prophet.

In summary, the three instances where רוח is most closely linked with Yahweh speaking to Ezekiel do not yield a "word-communicating" view of inspiration within the book of Ezekiel. There is, however, a picture presented of a prophet who is powerfully affected by the work of the divine רוח. At the start of his commissioning, Yahweh's address to him is accompanied by the action of the divine רוח in setting Ezekiel on his feet. In the instances of Yahweh speaking that we have examined, Yahweh's רוח is associated deliberately and directly with Ezekiel's ministry, yielding a prominent, if "potentiating," view of the inspiration of the prophet by רוח.

2.3. *Other Instances of Links Between* רוח *and Prophecy*

There is one place where רוח is linked with the inspiration of prophets other than Ezekiel. In this instance, it is the inspiration of the prophets against whom Ezekiel is to inveigh that is in view. In 13:3, Ezekiel recounts what he is to say to the false prophets: "Thus says the Lord Yahweh, Alas for the senseless prophets who follow their own spirit (אשר הלכים אחר רוחם), and have seen nothing!"

This verse serves as the first part of a woe oracle against prophets, who, like Ezekiel, claimed to speak for Yahweh. If the MT is retained,[106] then the prophets against whom Ezekiel speaks prophesy "out of their own imagination" (מלבם, v. 2), and "follow their own spirit" (הלכים אחר רוחם, v. 3).

Though Ezekiel judges them on the basis of the rhetorical event (their "prophesying"), his assault on them relates to the prophetic event. He attacks the source of inspiration of these prophets. At one level, רוח can be understood effectively almost as a synonym for לב here: the messages

---

104.   Sklba ("'Until the Spirit,'" 14) confuses the prophetic event with the rhetorical when he says of this verse, "by the breath of God Ezekiel was…forced to… speak."

105.   Zimmerli, *Ezekiel 2*, 567. For Zimmerli, it is a secondary addition.

106.   So Block, *Ezekiel 1–24*, 395–96; Greenberg, *Ezekiel 1–20*, 234–35. Some other commentators follow LXX in reading πρὸς αὐτούς for לנביאי מלבם in v. 2, and τοῖς προφητεύουσιν ἀπὸ καρδίας αὐτῶν for הוי על־הנביאים הנבלים אשר הלכים אחר רוחם in v. 3; see Allen, *Ezekiel 1–19*, 188; Cooke, *Ezekiel*, 138, 142; Eichrodt, *Ezekiel*, 160; Zimmerli, *Ezekiel 1*, 285. Allen comments that the shorter reading is preferable.

that these prophets utter come from their own will.[107] By exploiting possible ambiguity in רוח here, however, Ezekiel could be making a direct assault on their claim to authority.[108] They claim to be inspired by the divine רוח, but in reality their inspiration comes from themselves and their own delusions, and not from Yahweh at all. This certainly fits well with the rest of the condemnation of these false prophets, and the condemnation found elsewhere: they have seen nothing (v. 3), they are "fools" (הנבלים; cf. Hos 9:7), they have seen lies and falsehood (v. 6; cf. Mic 2:11), they have claimed inspiration without Yahweh speaking to them (v. 7) and they have promised prosperity.[109]

This assault on the false prophets' inspiration and Ezekiel's claiming the inspiration of רוח for himself cannot be ascertained directly from ch. 13. In view of what we have already seen of the role of רוח within the ministry of Ezekiel, it is likely that Ezekiel is here contrasting the false prophets' inspiration with his own in a direct fashion. Ezekiel's pungent irony, then, serves as a claim that he has the divine רוח inspiring him, unlike the false prophets (cf. 1 Kgs 22:19–25; Mic 3:8). This is a significant observation, because here is clear evidence that a prophet who is found attacking רוח-inspiration in other prophets also acknowledged the role of רוח within his own inspiration. The two are not mutually exclusive.

With regard to the nature of inspiration in view here, it is possible that "word-communicating" inspiration should be understood. If the divine רוח is being contrasted with "their minds" by direct correspondence, then, since "their minds" are clearly the authority/source of the messages that the false prophets utter, it is apparent that the divine רוח would also be the authority/source of the messages that Ezekiel utters. Such a conclusion must remain tentative, given the difficulties over the text, over whether Ezekiel is being deliberately ambiguous and ironical in his use of רוח, and over how exact is the conception of רוח as "source" between the two different senses of רוח.

2.4. *Ezekiel Communicating the Word and* רוח

The first three ways we have examined in which רוח is linked with inspiration in the book of Ezekiel have focused more specifically on the prophetic event. Since inspiration often extends beyond the prophetic event to the rhetorical event, our final examination of the inspiration of the

---

107.   Cf. the parallels in Jer 23:16, 26. Greenberg (*Ezekiel 1–20*, 235) sees Num 16:28 as the antecedent of the phrase in Ezekiel.

108.   Cf. Block, "Prophet of the Spirit," 43.

109.   Couturier, "L'Esprit de Yahweh," 159–60.

prophet in the book looks at the communication of the word of Yahweh and the prophet's inspiration. The question that needs to be addressed is: To what extent does רוח equip Ezekiel (or, indeed, other prophets within the book) to speak, and to what extent does the divine רוח actually "speak" those words?

The work of רוח in the communication of the word can be seen in two places—the prophet's words themselves and the prophet's life.

As far as the relationship between רוח and the words that the prophet utters is concerned, there are no explicit references. It is straightforward to affirm "potentiating" inspiration, since the impact of רוח on the prophet in general is clearly apparent. It is possible to move towards "word-communicating" inspiration for the rhetorical event when two facts are put side-by-side. First, there is some evidence of "word-communicating" inspiration in the prophetic event. Secondly, the prophet is to utter verbatim what he has received. These words are not simply the past words of Yahweh (or Yahweh's רוח), but the present words. There is, however, no explicit suggestion that one of the agents is רוח in this instance of "double agency discourse."[110]

The second place where the work of רוח in the communication of the word can be deduced is from the relationship between Yahweh's word, the prophet's life, and רוח, as seen in the combination of two facts evident in the book.

First, the prophet is not required simply to speak the word, but to embody it. This can be seen from the fact that the prophet actually swallows the scroll (2:8–3:3). The word does not remain external to him, but is internalized within him so that, as Fretheim comments, "as a person the prophet *becomes* the Word of God."[111] Since God cannot be separated from the word he gives, thus he goes with that word such that in some sense he is "*absorbed into* the very life of the prophet."[112] It can also be seen from the sign-acts that Ezekiel is instructed to perform. The combination of these two, the swallowing of the scroll, and the performing of sign-acts, both point in the same direction: "it is not only what the prophet speaks but who he is that now constitute the word of God."[113]

The second fact pointing towards the role of רוח in the communication of Yahweh's word is that the prophet's movements and actions are

110.   For the phrase, and discussion of its significance, see Wolterstorff, *Divine Discourse*, 37–57 (Chapter 3).

111.   Terence E. Fretheim, *The Suffering of God: An Old Testament Perspective* (OBT 14; Philadelphia: Fortress, 1984), 153 (my emphasis).

112.   Ibid., 153 (original emphasis).

113.   Terence E. Fretheim, "Word of God," *ABD* 6:966.

constrained and directed by the divinely controlled רוח, whether as the transporting רוח (3:12, 14; 8:3; 11:1, 24; 37:1; 43:5), as the רוח that sets him on his feet (2:2; 3:24), or as the רוח that falls upon him (11:5a). Such instances, along with the emphasis on the "hand of Yahweh" and the occasions where Yahweh "brought" (הביא), "led" (הוליך), "took out" (הוציא) and "brought back" (השיב) Ezekiel point to the fact that "Ezekiel is a man seized by God."[114]

When these two facts are juxtaposed, it can be deduced that the degree to which Yahweh's רוח is involved in the movement and ministry of the prophet is also the degree to which that רוח is involved in the communication of the "incarnate," visible word. Though neither explicit nor exploited, in the book of Ezekiel there is an implicit understanding of the inspiration of רוח in the "word-communicating" sense. The prophet Ezekiel *is* that "word," which רוח directs, guides and leads.

2.5. *Summary and Conclusions*
Within the book of Ezekiel, רוח has a very significant role to play in the experience of the prophet. There is some evidence of a "word-communicating" view of inspiration in the prophetic event, both in the fact that the spirit inspired the vision of chs. 8–11 (11:24), a vision that can be understood as Yahweh's "speech event," and in the fact that Ezekiel was to inveigh against the false prophets for their auto-inspiration (13:3), whereas the source of Ezekiel's inspiration and message was not his own spirit, but Yahweh's. Further, when the focus shifts from the prophetic to the rhetorical event, "word-communicating" inspiration can also be seen to the extent that Ezekiel is portrayed as one who is constrained by the spirit and yet embodies the word, and to the extent that רוח inspires the words to Ezekiel that he, in turn, is to utter verbatim. The three instances, however, where רוח is contextually linked most closely to Yahweh speaking are precisely those which do not yield "word-communicating" but "potentiating" inspiration. In addition, the רוח which transports the prophet within visions is closely linked with Yahweh revealing a situation to the prophet, or to Yahweh speaking, but there is no suggestion of "word-communicating" inspiration. Within the book of Ezekiel, then, רוח is linked both with the prophetic event and the rhetorical event. The evidence for "potentiating" inspiration is strong in the book, but there is also evidence of "word-communicating" inspiration.

This picture shows that the *theological* explanation for the relative absence of רוח within the classical prophets is mistaken. According to this view, the silence arises from the "theocentric" thought of the

---

114. Block, *Ezekiel 1–24*, 36.

prophets. Since Ezekiel is one of the most theocentric of prophets, attributing the restoration of Israel to Yahweh acting "for the sake of his name,"[115] the theological explanation should expect Ezekiel to be silent about רוח. However, Ezekiel speaks often of רוח within his own ministry. Prophetic silence about רוח cannot be attributed to theocentricity.

---

115.   Ezek 36:22; cf. 20:9, 14, 22; 36:32. See especially Joyce, *Divine Initiative.*

Chapter 4

DIACHRONIC PERSPECTIVES
ON PROPHETIC INSPIRATION

In this chapter, as I explore the relationship between רוח and prophetic inspiration diachronically, I shall argue that Ezekiel does not "recover" the inspiration of pre-classical prophets because, on the one hand, pre-classical prophets are not depicted as being as inspired as is sometimes said (section 1), and, on the other, because classical prophets are more inspired than is sometimes allowed (section 2). In the third section, I shall argue that essentially the same picture is in evidence after the exile. In the fourth section, I shall conclude that רוח as the "breath" of Yahweh's mouth is not linked in Ezekiel with Yahweh's word. This shall enable me in the final section to revisit the question of רוח and Ezekiel's self-authentication; there, I shall argue that the relative prominence of רוח within the prophetic ministry of Ezekiel is not explained well by the notion that the prophet recovers an emphasis that had been lost in order to authenticate his ministry. I shall also argue that within the context of the *book* of Ezekiel, רוח-language may well have a secondary function of authenticating the prophet but that the focus lies elsewhere. First, we turn our attention to the pre-classical prophets.

1. *Inspiration and the Pre-Classical Prophets*

There are three points that can be made about the role of רוח and its relation to Yahweh's word in the pre-classical prophets. First, there is strong evidence of "potentiating" inspiration. Secondly, there is strong evidence of "word-communicating" inspiration. Thirdly, רוח is not especially prominent in the accounts of pre-classical prophets.

1.1. *"Potentiating" Inspiration and the Pre-classical Prophets*
There are a number of passages which point towards "potentiating" inspiration. We shall look at three in particular: that of Balaam's prophecy in Num 24, since there is an explicit link between רוח-inspiration and the

delivering of oracles; that of Saul prophesying in 1 Sam 10, since it is representative of a number of instances within the Deuteronomistic History in which רוח is linked with the Hitpael of נבא, and ecstatic prophesying seems to be in view; finally, that involving Elijah and Elisha in 2 Kgs 2, because of these prophets' links with Ezekiel.

1.1.1. *Numbers 24:2.*

> Now Balaam saw that it pleased Yahweh to bless Israel, so he did not go, as at other times, to look for omens, but set his face toward the wilderness. Balaam looked up and saw Israel camping tribe by tribe. Then the spirit of God came upon him (ותהי עליו רוח אלהים), and he uttered his oracle, saying... (Num 24:1–3)

These verses form the introduction to the third of seven oracles that the prophet Balaam utters. The first one, delivered and addressed to Balak after Yahweh has put a word in Balaam's mouth (23:5), explains how he (Balaam) cannot curse what God has not cursed (23:7–10). The second, again addressed to Balak, explains further Balaam's refusal to curse the people of Israel, for God does not change his mind. What God has blessed, Balaam cannot revoke (23:18–24). Before the third oracle, Balak, in desperation, takes Balaam to another vantage point so that Balaam might curse Israel. Numbers 24:1–3 introduces this oracle, which is addressed to Israel camping below Peor. Instead of cursing Israel, Balaam articulates the blessing that will flow to them (24:3–9). In anger, Balak dismisses Balaam. Balaam denies that he can "go beyond the word of Yahweh (את־פי יהוה)" (24:13), and declares his fourth oracle, announcing what Israel will do to Balak's people in days to come (24:15–19). The fifth, sixth and seventh (Num 24:20–24) oracles have a purview wider than the incident between Balaam and Balak.

Although the antiquity of the oracles is not disputed,[1] the question of composition of the Balaam narrative is a complex one.[2] Evidence for an early date of 24:1–2 includes the verbal phrase used to describe the arrival of רוח (היה על; cf. Judg 3:10[3]) and the archaic notion of Balaam

---

1.   Most commentators refer to W. F. Albright, "The Oracles of Balaam," *JBL* 63 (1944): 207–33. The exception is 24:21–24 (see p. 227).

2.   See Philip J. Budd, *Numbers* (WBC 5; Waco, Tex.: Word, 1984), 256–65, for a detailed discussion; also Wilson, *Prophecy and Society*, 147–50. R. Norman Whybray (*The Making of the Pentateuch: A Methodological Study* [JSOTSup 53; Sheffield: JSOT Press, 1987], 118) notes the difficulty scholars such as Noth had in handling passages such as Num 22–24 that "did not seem to yield to documentary analysis"; see also Dion, "La *rwḥ* dans l'Heptateuch," 169.

3.   The verb and preposition (היה על) point towards Balaam being possessed wholly by God's רוח when prophesying. See Lys, *Rûach*, 44–45; cf. Judg 11:29;

setting his face toward the wilderness to preserve visual contact.⁴ With regard to the role of the divine רוח here, though, there is some disagreement among scholars. Montague comments, "here for the first time in our sources, prophecy is attributed to the spirit of God."⁵ It is not clear whether Montague regards the *contents* of the prophecy as being given by the divine רוח (the "word-communicating" view) or whether it is the charismatic "gift" of prophecy.⁶ In similar a vein, Baumgärtel sees the spirit here as responsible for "prophetic or ecstatic speech,"⁷ while Noth comments that "Balaam is represented as an ecstatic prophet who utters his words under the direct influence of inspiration."⁸ Such comments do not distinguish between "word-communicating" and "potentiating" inspiration. Other scholars seem to go further, intimating "word-communicating" inspiration. Thus Davies contrasts previous divine communications, "effected by Yahweh's putting his words in Balaam's mouth (23:5, 16)" with 24:2, where he says "but now the Spirit of God came upon him."⁹ He seems to imply that the revelation which earlier came by Yahweh's word now came by Yahweh's רוח. Milgrom, too, points in this direction. He comments that "the assumption here is that instead of seeking God in a dream (22:9, 20) or having God's words 'put into his mouth' (23:5, 16), Balaam is now invested with the divine spirit and falls into an ecstatic state (vv. 3–4), the mark of a prophet (11:25–29)."¹⁰ The result is that in vv. 3–9, "Balaam introduces himself—now that he is invested with the divine spirit—as one who is privy to God's direct revelation."¹¹ Dreytza is most explicit when he speaks of רוח here "as personal speaking agent."¹²

Others, however, are more cautious about discerning "word-communicating" inspiration here. Kaufmann, commenting on this verse, says

1 Sam 16:16, 23; 19:20, 23. The occurrences in 2 Chr 15:1 and 20:14 have a very different feel. The Chronicler has adopted early forms and adapted them.

4. See Carley, *Ezekiel Among the Prophets*, 40–41. Carley notes the importance of visual contact (cf. 2 Kgs 8:11). The narrative also emphasizes Balaam seeing Israel's camp (Num 22:41; 23:13).

5. Montague, *Holy Spirit*, 12.

6. So Wolff (*Anthropology*, 35), who says that Yahweh's רוח produces "the charisma of prophecy."

7. Baumgärtel, *TDNT* 6:362.

8. Martin Noth, *Numbers: A Commentary* (trans. J. D. Martin; OTL; London: SCM, 1968), 189.

9. Eryl W. Davies, *Numbers* (NCB; Grand Rapids: Eerdmans, 1995), 266.

10. Jacob Milgrom, *Numbers* (JPS Torah Commentary; New York: The Jewish Publication Society of America, 1990), 202.

11. Ibid., 49.

12. Dreytza, *Der theologische Gebrauch von RUAH*, 216: "als personales, redendes Agens."

that "the spirit prepares a man for prophecy" and "enables him to frame parables and songs" but, he notes, they "are not properly mantic activities, nor are they peculiar to prophets."[13] Thus he denies here that the spirit is the "source" of prophecy. Rather, in view of his later comment about the spirit's role, he countenances "potentiating" inspiration.[14] Neve admits that, at first glance, v. 2 might suggest that "it is the message which has been inspired by the spirit of Yahweh."[15] However, since Yahweh is the source of the message in Num 23:5, 12, 16, 17, 26, without any indication of the spirit's work, Neve sees the spirit's activity as bringing about the ecstatic condition described in vv. 3–4. Further evidence, he says, comes from the fact that Balaam did not consult the omens, but "set his face towards the wilderness," something that he suggests is "a position preparatory to the ecstatic condition." He concludes: "thus in this chapter the spirit of God is thought of as having occasioned the condition of ecstatic sight under the influence of which Balaam sees visions of God and hears his word. In this sense, the spirit of God spoken of in v. 2 does not inspire the word...it rather causes the 'enthusiasm' which typifies this early period."[16]

It is clear from 24:10, 13, that the word of Yahweh had come three times to Balaam, yet on only two occasions is that process described explicitly (23:5, 16). The phrase "the spirit of God came upon him" (24:2) entails the reception of a word by the prophet *and* the impetus for its delivery. Precisely how the "spirit of God" relates to the word that came is not certain. Three points may be made.

First, since the "prophetic" and "rhetorical" event are merged here, the role of the spirit cannot be reduced to the prophetic event.

Secondly, while there is the possibility of "word-communicating" inspiration here, such a view is not explicitly articulated. What is certain, though, is that the prophet Balaam himself experiences the action of God's רוח, and that this action issued in prophetic words; "potentiating" inspiration, at the least, is evident in pre-classical prophecy. It is not possible to go further with certainty.

Thirdly, Balaam within the narrative is a figure who does not fit easily within categories. At points the heathen seer seems to be just that: the multiple altars are unique (23:1); he looks for omens (24:1). He, however, also seems to be the true prophet: he is the one who speaks of Yahweh in ch. 22, while the narrator speaks of Elohim; he speaks Yahweh's words,

13. Kaufmann, *Religion of Israel*, 98.
14. Ibid., 99.
15. Neve, *Spirit of God*, 15.
16. Ibid.

and Yahweh's alone (23:8; 24:13). At points, Balaam seems rather like the stereotypical picture of the pre-classical prophets, in his ecstasy (24:3–4), in his maintaining visual contact (24:2; cf. 2 Kgs 8:11), and in the role of רוח within his inspiration (24:2).[17] In his emphasis on Yahweh's word,[18] however, in the fact that he is an "individual" prophet, in his refusal to prophesy for a fee (cf. 22:7, 18), he stands closer to the classical prophets. While it may be true that "we cannot use the Balaam tradition to define the precise nature of vocation prophecy in Israel and in Judah,"[19] it is also true that the boundaries are not as sharply defined as Couturier has painted. The רוח of God *can* be linked to the coming of Yahweh's word, even in one who strongly emphasizes that word.

1.1.2. *1 Samuel 10:6, 10–11.*

> Then the spirit of Yahweh will possess you (וצלחה), and you will act like a prophet (והתנבית) along with them and be turned into a different person (לאיש אחר). (10:6)

> When they were going from there to Gibeah, a band of prophets met him; and the spirit of God possessed him (ותצלח), and he (Saul) acted like a prophet (ויתנבא) along with them. When all who knew him before saw how he prophesied (נבא) with the prophets, the people said to one another, "What has come over the son of Kish? Is Saul also among the prophets?" (10:10–11)

These references to רוח and prophecy occur within the account of the choosing and anointing of Saul as king over Israel. The first verse, 10:6, is part of Samuel's declaration of what will happen to Saul as signs to Saul to indicate that Yahweh has indeed anointed him as king (v. 7; cf. v. 1 [LXX]); vv. 10–11 are part of the narrative recounting what actually happens. In that sense, they are counterparts, although Eslinger observes the omission of the fulfilment of the first two signs, on the one hand, and the curious recounting of the third sign in v. 10 when v. 9 has already announced that the signs have been fulfilled.[20] He, like Fokkelman,[21] sees

---

17. So Couturier ("L'Esprit de Yahweh," 160–61) suggests that the oracles were inserted within the narrative because of the influence of the Elijah and Elisha cycles.

18. Compare Num 24:13 with 1 Kgs 22:14.

19. Couturier, "L'Esprit de Yahweh," 161: "nous ne pouvons pas utiliser avec certitude la tradition de Balaam pour définir la nature précise du prophétisme de vocation en Israël et en Juda."

20. Lyle M. Eslinger, *Kingship of God in Crisis: A Close Reading of 1 Samuel 1–12* (Bible and Literature Series 10; Sheffield: Almond Press, 1985), 328–30.

21. J. P. Fokkelman, *Narrative Art and Poetry in the Books of Samuel: A Full Interpretation Based on Stylistic and Structural Analyses* (4 vols.; Studia Semitica Neerlandica 20; Assen: Van Gorcum, 1981–93), 4:426.

the focus as shifting onto the nature of the reception of the "new" Saul by the people. The "rushing" of the divine רוח upon Saul will be, according to Samuel, the third of three signs that Yahweh has anointed Saul as "ruler" (10:1). The final one is to serve as confirmation to Saul that he has been indeed equipped, not just anointed, to rule. This is why he is "a different person" (v. 6), and why Samuel instructs him in v. 7 to "do whatever you see fit to do." As Klein comments, "the instruction for Saul to respond to the fulfilling of the signs by doing whatever his hand finds implies that he is to act according to the strength he has."[22] Klein sees the fulfilment of this, in the context of 1 Samuel, in the attack on the Ammonites after the spirit has again "rushed" on Saul (1 Sam 11:6). Thus, as in Num 11, the coming of the spirit is to equip, but the manifestation, in Saul's case for his own assurance, is seen in prophesying.

Questions of composition and dating are complex, but there is no reason to deny a pre-exilic date.[23] Some evidence for this is precisely the same evidence on which we must draw in order to ascertain what kind of inspiration is in view: What is meant here by the different stems of נבא? The literature on the subject is substantial.[24] Some try to associate the Hitpael of נבא with ecstatic prophetic behaviour, while the Niphal is said to relate more closely with verbal utterances, particularly those of the classical prophets.[25] By the time of the exile, they can be used synonymously. A more satisfactory analysis is given by Wilson, who rejects

22. Ralph W. Klein, *1 Samuel* (WBC 10; Waco, Tex.: Word, 1983), 92.

23. With regard to composition, Klein regards the incident in vv. 10–13 as "a proverb...explained by an etiological narrative" (ibid., 85). Fokkelman (*Narrative Art and Poetry*, 2:287), however, regards the aetiological note as an "extra" since it comes "after completion of the plot or narrative chain" and "the story is still quite independent without it." With regard to dating, Birch notes that most scholars see the pericope from 9:1 to 10:16 as from the "early source" (Bruce C. Birch, "The Development of the Tradition on the Anointing of Saul in 1 Sam. 9:1–10:16," *JBL* 90 [1971]: 55). This is not surprising given the folk-tale characteristics of the pericope, and the contrasting picture of prophecy present between the prophets in the pericope, on the one hand, and the prophet Samuel himself. See P. Kyle McCarter, Jr., *I Samuel* (AB 8; New York: Doubleday, 1980), 26–27, 182.

24. See the bibliographies in Gary V. Smith, "Prophet; Prophecy," *ISBE* 3:986–1004; Pieter A. Verhoef, "Prophecy," *NIDOTTE* 4:1067–78. See Jeremias, *TLOT* 2:697–98, for the number and distribution of occurrences.

25. E.g. Klaus Koch, *The Prophets* (trans. M. Kohl; 2 vols.; London: SCM, 1982–83), 2:26: "Out of the ecstasy (*nb'*, hitpael) there finally emerges the prophecy (*nb'*, niphal), which is directed to the people, bringing them a *dābār*, a saying of Yahweh." Cf. Couturier, "L'Esprit de Yahweh," 157–58, who links the Hitpael first of all with ecstatic group prophets and then with the "machinations" (*agissements*) of the false prophets.

such a characterization.[26] For him, the stems do not indicate *per* se particular behavioural characteristics. The Niphal is chiefly concerned with communication of oracles, while the Hitpael is concerned with manifesting stereotypical prophetic behaviour, whether ecstatic or not.

In 1 Sam 10 the Hitpael (vv. 6, 10) and the Niphal (v. 11) of נבא are effectively synonymous.[27] Further, the absence of prepositions or words suggesting comprehensible speech suggests that prophetic behaviour, rather than verbal communication, is in view.

Since the band of prophets were prophesying as they travelled down from the shrine (v. 5), it does not seem likely that the communication of words in the form of intelligible utterances for the benefit of hearers is meant.[28] Elsewhere in 1 Samuel, the Hitpael speaks clearly of prophetic behaviour that arose from the agency of an evil רוח (18:10–11), that to some degree incapacitated those "prophesying" such that they could not arrest David (1 Sam 19:20–21) and that described Saul's lying before Samuel with clothes stripped off (1 Sam 19:24).[29] Further, our analysis of the root נבא above suggests that prophetic behaviour is in view. Block suggests that נבא here is "not associated with prophetic utterance, but with prophetic action."[30] For Block, this does not mean, though, that there is no communication involved. Rather, these are "extraordinary physical expressions of Spirit possession, divinely induced non-verbal declarations. God is speaking through Saul. The witnesses and the readers of these texts are called upon to receive the communication and interpret it."[31] Although this may be possible here, in view of the fact that the function of such prophesying is to show to *Saul*, and not to the people at large, that he has been anointed ruler, it seems more accurate to say that through his prophesying God is speaking *to* Saul, not "through" him. It is the prophetic behaviour that counts as Yahweh's confirmation to Saul.

These verses clearly link the divine רוח to prophecy—it is this רוח that precipitates prophesying. If such prophesying included intelligible words, then it needs to be remembered that "no comprehensible saying

---

26. Wilson, *Prophecy and Society*, 136–38; so too Dreytza, *Der theologische Gebrauch von RUAH*, 113; David W. Baker, "Israelite Prophets and Prophecy," in *The Face of Old Testament Studies: A Survey of Contemporary Approaches* (ed. David W. Baker and Bill T. Arnold; Grand Rapids: Baker, 1999), 276.

27. Jeremias, *TLOT* 2:703. The same is true in 1 Sam 19:20.

28. *Pace* Verhoef, *NIDOTTE* 4:1073.

29. That the incapacitation is not total is evident from the fact that Saul "prophesied" as he walked along (1 Sam 19:23).

30. Block, "Empowered by the Spirit of God," 47.

31. Ibid., 48.

from them is attested."[32] This case can only be understood to support "word-communicating" inspiration if the action of Saul is understood as a prophetic word to him. If, as seems more likely, such utterances as were uttered were ecstatic and subordinate to prophetic behaviour, then "potentiating" inspiration is portrayed here.[33]

1.1.3. *Elijah and Elisha*. Some scholars have drawn attention to the parallels between Elijah and Elisha, on the one hand, and Ezekiel on the other, and, in particular, to their experience of the spirit.[34] In 1 Kgs 18:12 and 2 Kgs 2:16, the spirit of Yahweh is seen, by popular opinion, as the transporting spirit, which can snatch Elijah up, and deposit him somewhere else. Such instances are not related to inspiration, in the sense of any link with the prophetic word. In so far as this רוח is involved in the experience of Elijah, we can speak here of "potentiating" inspiration. Given, however, that when Elijah is in fact transported into heaven (2 Kgs 2:11) רוח plays no role, caution is needed when considering the transporting רוח with Elijah.[35] In 2 Kgs 2:9–15, Elisha makes a request of Elijah, "Please let me inherit a double share of your spirit" (ויהי־נא פי־שנים ברוחך אלי, v. 9). We need to explore what kind of רוח it is, and what kind of inspiration, if any, is in view.[36]

Broadly, there are three views held. Some hold that this רוח is the "human *ruach*" of Elijah.[37] Others say it is Yahweh's.[38] The third view,

---

32. Jeremias, *TLOT* 2:699.

33. Similar instances of apparent ecstatic behaviour being closely linked with (Yahweh's) רוח are those in 1 Sam 18:10 and 19:23–24. Again, there is no attested word spoken as part of Saul's prophesying. Indeed, there is even less sign there of anything intelligible being said as part of his "prophesying." There is nothing to link this רוח to a "word-communicating" view of inspiration. Rather, Saul's behaviour resembled the apparent loss of self-control that marked the prophets of Baal (1 Kgs 18:29).

34. Zimmerli, "The Special Form- and Traditio-Historical Character," 517; Carley, *Ezekiel Among the Prophets*, 23–37.

35. Cf. Lys, *Rûach*, 36; Koch, *Geist Gottes*, 44.

36. For a discussion of the dating, and a *terminus ad quem* of 721, see Carley, *Ezekiel Among the Prophets*, 8–12.

37. Neve, *Spirit of God*, 136; Lys, *Rûach*, 27, 35–37. For Lys, the action here is still God's, and *in* rather than *on* the individual. It is to avoid confusion between the human and Yahweh's "spirit" that 1 Kgs 22:24 speaks about "the spirit of Yahweh" moving from one person to another, while here the focus is on the spirit of Elijah (p. 36).

38. Cf. Block, "Empowered by the Spirit of God," 46; Mordechai Cogan and Hayim Tadmor, *II Kings* (AB 11; New York: Doubleday, 1988), 32; Koch, *Geist Gottes*, 54; Dreytza, *Der theologische Gebrauch von RUAH*, 246–47; Volkmar Fritz,

argued for by Weisman, is that this רוח, like that in Num 11:16–15, 24–25, is neither Yahweh's spirit nor the "human spirit" stirred up. Instead, it is a "personal" spirit that acts by "imparting authority," a spirit invoked by later writers because of the almost mythical status of Moses and Elijah.[39] Others comment without making their view clear.[40]

There are certainly features that require an explanation and that for Weisman set this רוח apart. Unlike the human רוח, its impact is not due to stirring up by Yahweh, but to the possession of it.[41] Unlike Yahweh's רוח, this רוח is not designated as Yahweh's, but "is defined in relation to the individual."[42] There is something both public and permanent about the transfer (cf. נוח).[43] In the case of the transfer from Elijah to Elisha, Yahweh does not seem directly involved: Elisha's request is directed to Elijah; Elijah does not make it clear that such a transfer depends on Yahweh; the sons of the prophets observe, after Elisha parts the water, that "the spirit of *Elijah* rests on Elisha."[44] Finally, the action of Yahweh's רוח in the narrative is regarded as that of an external force; similarly, the action of Yahweh's "hand" (1 Kgs 18:46; 2 Kgs 3:15), often an equivalent expression to Yahweh's רוח, is rather different from that of רוח.אליהו[45] For Weisman, these constitute a conclusive case that the רוח in 2 Kgs 2:9, 15 is not Yahweh's רוח. Given that the only other references to Yahweh's רוח in the Elijah/Elisha narratives are popular perceptions, not the judgments of the narrator, it would then mean that neither Elijah nor Elisha would have any clear relationship to Yahweh's רוח.

It is preferable, however, to regard the "spirit of Elijah" here as "a metonymic figure of speech for 'the Spirit of Yahweh which resides upon Elijah.'"[46] Block adduces as evidence Elisha's use of the mantle in

1 & 2 Kings (trans. A. Hagedorn; Continental Commentaries; Minneapolis: Fortress, 2003), 235.

39. Ze'ev Weisman, "The Personal Spirit as Imparting Authority," *ZAW* 93 (1981): 225–34.

40. Gwilym H. Jones, *1 and 2 Kings: Based on the Revised Standard Version* (2 vols.; NCB; London: Marshall, Morgan & Scott, 1984), 2:385; Gray thinks the רוח that inspired Elijah was something external, since it "equipped" him. See John Gray, *I & II Kings* (3d ed.; OTL; London: SCM, 1977), 475. Couturier ("L'Esprit de Yahweh," 153) seems to regard it as Yahweh's, given that he sees it as bringing about ecstasy.

41. Weisman, "Personal Spirit," 226.

42. Ibid.

43. Ibid., 227.

44. 2 Kgs 2:15. See ibid., 233.

45. Ibid., 233.

46. Block, "Empowered by the Spirit of God," 46.

parting the waters, the response of the people in v. 15 and the actions that Elisha subsequently performed (vv. 16–25). Further evidence comes from the fact that here Elisha is presented as the new Joshua completing what Moses had done.[47] The spirit that equipped Moses (Elijah) is now on Joshua (Elisha) (cf. Num 27:18; Deut 34:9).[48] The strongest evidence that it is Yahweh's רוח comes from the clear belief elsewhere that Yahweh's רוח can go from one person to another (1 Kgs 22:24); from the fact that Yahweh's רוח can "rest" (נוח) upon a kingly figure (Isa 11:2); and, finally, from the fact that the notion of Yahweh's רוח as constant, empowering and authorizing has already been present in the narrative of Saul's and David's kingship (Saul, 1 Sam 16:14; David, 1 Sam 16:13; 2 Sam 23:2).

Further, this רוח is intimately related to Elisha becoming a prophet. In 1 Kgs 19:16, Yahweh has instructed Elijah to anoint Elisha as a prophet in his stead (תמשח לנביא תחתיך). Elijah proceeds in v. 19 to find Elisha, throw the mantle onto him and walk off.[49] The narrative does not read, as we might expect, that Elisha became a prophet instead of Elijah.[50] Instead, after Elisha catches up with Elijah, we are told that Elisha "followed Elijah and served him" (וילך אחרי אליהו וישרתהו, v. 21). Although the location of the mantle is tantalizingly left in the air, it does seem that Elisha's actions reinstate Elijah as prophet.[51] The mantle, symbolizing prophethood, does not pass to Elisha until 2 Kgs 2, at the same time as רוח is transferred. In the meantime, Elisha is "assistant and successor-designate."[52]

This רוח, while closely resembling the leadership רוח found on Moses, Saul and David, is also the designating and empowering רוח that enables Elisha to function as a prophet. What the mantle symbolizes externally is a reality through the agency of Yahweh's רוח. Though, however, the spirit that inspired Elijah and Elisha is indeed Yahweh's רוח, and is intimately related to the prophetic task, the question of inspiration can get

47. Philip E. Satterthwaite, "The Elisha Narratives and the Coherence of 2 Kings 2–8," *TynBul* 49 (1998): 8–10.

48. Though the parallel is not exact, since in Num 27:18 Joshua already has רוח before Moses lays his hands on him.

49. There is no explicit mention of "anointing." It is apparent that Elijah walked off because Elisha had to leave his oxen and run after Elijah (v. 20). See Paul J. Kissling, *Reliable Characters in the Primary History: Profiles of Moses, Joshua, Elijah and Elisha* (JSOTSup 224; Sheffield: Sheffield Academic Press, 1996), 151.

50. A point made well by Walsh in Jerome T. Walsh, *1 Kings* (Berit Olam; Collegeville, Minn.: Liturgical Press, 1996), 279–80.

51. Kissling, *Reliable Characters*, 154.

52. Ibid., 155.

no further than this. The focus of this early narrative is more on mighty deeds than on prophetic words. At no point can a view of the inspiration of the prophet's words go any further than "potentiating" inspiration.

1.2. *"Word-communicating" Inspiration and the Pre-classical Prophets*
1.2.1. *2 Samuel 23:2*.

> The spirit of Yahweh speaks through me (רוח יהוה דבר־בי), his word is upon my tongue (ומלתו על־לשוני).

This verse starts what v. 1 terms "the last words of David," a poem cele-brating the covenant made with him, and which finishes in v. 7. In turn, the poem occurs within what is often termed the "Appendix" to the book of Samuel, chs. 21–24.

Uniquely in the Old Testament, רוח is followed directly by a verb of speaking.[53] Here, explicitly, is "word-communicating" inspiration. Given this striking fact, there are three questions that particularly concern us. The first is over the date of v. 2, and, for our purposes, whether it is pre-exilic. The second is over the nature of inspiration, whether prophetic or not. The third is over the precise point of inspiration, whether רוח יהוה speaks "through" or "to/with/in" David.

Although the oracle as a whole shows signs of antiquity,[54] the tradi-tional dating of v. 2 to the second half of the tenth century is disputed. McCarter thinks it is late because "the notion that David was a prophet has no parallel in the early literature. It arose at a later time when psalms attributed to David were being given prophetic interpretation."[55] Further possible evidence for lateness includes the apparent masculine gender of רוח,[56] the presence of the word מלה, which appears elsewhere only in

---

53. Dreytza, *Der theologische Gebrauch von RUAH*, 180.

54. So, for example, as McCarter points out, there are no traces of Deuterono-mistic language, the divine epithets are consistent with an early date, and there are close verbal links between v. 1 and the archaic Num 24:3, 15; see P. Kyle McCarter, Jr., *II Samuel* (AB 9; New York: Doubleday, 1984), 486. Simon, however, tenta-tively believes the poem to be post-exilic, because he sees the confluence of many diverse streams of thought. See László T. Simon, *Identity and Identification: An Exegetical and Theological Study of 2 Sam 21–24* (Tesi Gregoriana Serie Teologia 64; Rome: Gregorian University Press, 2000), 292–308. A survey of scholarly opinions on the date is found on p. 293.

55. McCarter, *II Samuel*, 480.

56. So, for example, Neve (*Spirit of God*, 128) says there are only 2 pre-593 passages with masculine רוח, Isa 34:16 and Ezek 1:12. Somewhat curiously, then, he dates this verse as a "transition text" from before the time of Elijah, without discuss-ing the verb form דבר (pp. 28–29).

"late" poetry,[57] and the role of רוח, "connected exclusively to the revelation of verbal announcements, and to the act of interpretation of the divine utterance."[58]

As Gordon comments, however, "there is…no reason to deny it to David himself."[59] Dating on the basis of the genesis of the prophetic interpretation of psalms attributed to David is circular. They may just as well have been given prophetic interpretation because David was considered a prophet.[60] Certainly, the linking of monarch, prophet and spirit is not alien to the book of Samuel. This is true of Saul (1 Sam 10), and there are pointers to it with David, in his reception of the spirit (1 Sam 16:13) and in his music-playing which mirrored that of the prophets.[61] The masculine gender of רוח has been explained in different ways. Anderson suggests that the "lapse in gender" with רוח "is due to the intervening word (יהוה)."[62] This is, however, unlikely, since there are six other instances in the Old Testament where a verb directly follows רוח יהוה,[63] and there is only one instance where the verb agrees with יהוה, not רוח (1 Kgs 18:12). There are, though, a number of places where רוח יהוה is the subject of a masculine verb, so it is not wholly anomalous.[64] Del Olmo Lete proposes that the masculine form of דבר can be explained by the falling away of the *mater lectionis* from the feminine form, דברה.[65] "His word" (מלתו), then, is Yahweh's word, not that of רוח יהוה. Richardson explains the present form within his framework of examining the psalm from the perspective of eleventh-century orthography.[66] Further, on literary grounds, both del Olmo Lete and Richardson argue strongly that the psalm is a unit, thus making it harder to reach McCarter's conclusion of a late date. Richardson comments, "there is

57. McCarter, *II Samuel*, 480; cf. Lys, *Rûach*, 169.

58. Simon, *Identity and Identification*, 296.

59. Robert P. Gordon, *1 & 2 Samuel: A Commentary* (Exeter: Paternoster, 1986), 309; cf. also Sklba, "'Until the Spirit from on High,'" 9.

60. Cf. Herbert H. Klement, *II Samuel 21–24: Context, Structure and Meaning in the Samuel Conclusion* (European University Studies; Frankfurt: Lang, 2000), 215. Klement distinguishes between the "specific form of the prophetic utterance" here and "the late evaluation of all David's psalms as prophetic in a general sense."

61. So ibid., 215–18.

62. Arnold A. Anderson, *2 Samuel* (WBC 11; Dallas: Word, 1989), 268.

63. Judg 6:34, 1 Sam 16:14, 1 Kgs 18:12; Isa 40:7; 59:19; 63:14.

64. 1 Kgs 18:12; 22:24; 2 Kgs 2:16; Mic 2:7.

65. G. del Olmo Lete, "David's Farewell Oracle (2 Samuel xxiii 1–7): A Literary Analysis," *VT* 34 (1984): 416–17.

66. H. Neil Richardson, "The Last Words of David: Some Notes on II Sam. 23, 1–7," *JBL* 90 (1971): 257–66.

nothing in the passage that denies such a date, while…there are some things that tend to corroborate it."[67] Particularly striking in this regard is the chiastic nature of vv. 2–3aβ (Richardson's lines 5–8), where line 5 (= v. 2a) has the "double subject first, followed by a verb and a prepositional phrase" (רח יהו דבר בי), while line 8 (= v. 3aβ) "has the prepositional phrase first, followed by the verb with the double subject last" (צר ישראל לי דבר).[68] In between, there are "two non-verbal cola in a limited stair-like parallelism" (ומלת על לשׁנ, line 6 = v. 2b) and אמר אלח יעקב (line 7 = v. 3aα).[69] Such structuring incorporates the Aramaic loan-word common in Job, מלה. Finally, the mention of רוח here is hardly problematic. The unique collocation makes it hard to date on such a basis. The conception of רוח speaking, however, is by no means necessarily late.

With regard to the second question, Neve, although noting that it is an "oracle," regards David's inspiration not as prophetic but as poetic. He has two main reasons for this: first, because the oracle is described as an "oracle of David" not an "oracle of God" (he notes the parallel with Num 24:3); secondly, because the nature of the poem is a "discourse on kingship." His conclusion is that "this text serves as the transition from the spirit as it is evidenced in this period [i.e. the early, charismatic, period] to the spirit of the prophets… [A]ctual 'enthusiasm' as related to the spirit is disappearing but prophetic inspiration is not yet present."[70] Neve's suggestion should be rejected because the parallel that he draws between "oracle of David" here and that of "oracle of Balaam" (Num 24:3) points precisely to prophetic inspiration, since Balaam was clearly an "inspired" prophet there. The elaborate introduction and the framing of the book by the only instances of נאם (1 Sam 2:30; 2 Sam 23:1) point to David as prophet.[71] As Anderson comments, "The 'spirit' in this context is not the source of ecstatic behaviour or experience…but of prophetic inspiration."[72]

If the questions of date and nature of inspiration are significant, so too is the question of the stage of inspiration. In order to ascertain whether what is envisaged here is Yahweh speaking *through* rather than *with* David, the phrase דבר ב and its cotext needs closer examination. The

67. Ibid., 257.
68. Ibid., 262. Note that the Hebrew used here follows Richardson's reconstruction.
69. Ibid., 262. He revocalizes the MT אָמַר with אֹמֵר.
70. Neve, *Spirit of God*, 29.
71. So Simon, *Identity and Identification*, 275, 289, for the first point; so Klement, *II Samuel 21–24*, 215, for the second.
72. Anderson, *2 Samuel*, 268; so also Gordon, *1 & 2 Samuel: A Commentary*, 310; McCarter, *II Samuel*, 480.

phrase itself is rare. It can mean "speak with" indicating "special inti-macy" (e.g. Num 12:2, 6, 8; Hab 2:1);[73] indeed, this is the most common meaning. There are few instances where it might mean "speak through." Although the NRSV translates ב with "through" in Hos 1:2, it is more likely to mean "with," since what follows are Yahweh's words to Hosea.[74] In 1 Kgs 22:28, the meaning "through" is possible. Usually, though, when Yahweh speaks through a prophet, the phrase used is דבר ביד;[75] it can also be דבר בפי.[76] Examination of the phrase alone might suggest "speaks with" is a better translation.[77] Here, then, would be a celebration of Yahweh's רוח involved directly in the prophetic event, "speaking" to the prophet.

The context of the phrase, however, in parallel with "his word is upon my tongue," points not so much to the spirit speaking "with" or "to" David, as to it speaking "through" him.[78] It is preferable, then, to see the spirit as speaking "through" David. If this is correct, then this is an instance of double agency discourse: what David says, the רוח of Yahweh also says. Since, however, the claim that Yahweh has spoken to or with someone is often difficult to distinguish from the claim that this person speaks for Yahweh, there is ambiguity here, as we have seen.[79] Whether the phrase refers to the prophetic event or the rhetorical event, discussion should not mask the very significant fact that here, explicitly, it is the divine רוח that "speaks."

If an early date is granted, then "word-communicating" inspiration is clearly evident in pre-classical prophecy.

1.2.2. 1 Kings 22 (= 2 Chronicles 18). A second instance of "word-communicating" inspiration can be found in the confrontation between Micaiah and Zedekiah. Israel and Aram had been without war for three years. Ahab's servants then told him that Ramoth-gilead really belonged

---

73. A meaning noted, but not adopted, by Gordon (*1 & 2 Samuel: A Commentary*, 310) and Simon (*Identity and Identification*, 275).

74. Cf. A. A. Mackintosh, *Hosea* (ICC; Edinburgh: T. & T. Clark, 1997), 7–8.

75. Josh 20:2; 1 Sam 28:17; 1 Kgs 8:53, 56; 14:18; 15:29; 16:12, 34; 17:16; 2 Kgs 9:36; 10:10; 14:25; 17:23; 24:2; Jer 37:2; 50:1; Ezek 38:17; 2 Chr 10:15.

76. Deut 23:24; 1 Kgs 8:15, 24; 2 Chr 6:4, 15; Jer 9:7; 44:25.

77. So Richardson, "Last Words," 259; Klement, *II Samuel 21–24*, 212: "in me"; "He is himself the recipient of Spirit-imparted speech" (p. 214).

78. So Simon, *Identity and Identification*, 268; McCarter, *II Samuel*, 476. Robert Alter (*The Art of Biblical Poetry* [New York: Basic Books, 1985], 10) points out that the two halves of a verse in Hebrew poetry often undergo "semantic modifications." Such a modification can be seen in v. 2bα, so need not be seen in v. 2bβ.

79. See Gordon, *1 & 2 Samuel: A Commentary*, 310.

to him, so Ahab, king of Israel, asked Jehoshaphat, king of Judah, to accompany him to war. Jehoshaphat urged Ahab first to "inquire" (דרש־נא) for the "word of Yahweh" (דבר יהוה, v. 5). Ahab then gathered four hundred prophets, who said with some ambiguity[80] that Yahweh "has given into the hand of the king" (v. 6). Jehoshaphat asked if there was any other "prophet of Yahweh" (נביא ליהוה, v. 7). In reply, Ahab mentioned Micaiah, and how he hated him because he never prophesied (לא־יתנבא) anything favourable about (על) him (v. 8).

As Micaiah was brought in, all the other prophets were "prophesying" (מתנבאים) before the two kings (v. 10). Their spokesman, Zedekiah, with a dramatic flourish of the horns of iron that he had made, announced success, and all the other prophets prophesied (נבאים) the same (v. 12). The messenger urged Micaiah to give the same message, since the other prophets were unanimous, but Micaiah insisted that "whatever Yahweh says to me, that I will speak" (את־אשר יאמר יהוה אלי אתו אדבר, v. 14). Micaiah, too, then declared success, in almost the same words as the other prophets (v. 15; cf. v. 12). After being urged to swear that he will tell nothing but the truth, however, Micaiah changed his message, and prophesied doom for Israel. King Ahab then said "I told you so" to Jehoshaphat, that Micaiah would only prophesy (יתנבא) disaster (v. 18).

In response to this, in vv. 19–23, Micaiah urged them all to "hear the word of Yahweh" and, in his reply, revealed the working of Yahweh's council. Yahweh's purpose had been, said Micaiah, trying to get through to a corrupt king, that Ahab would be enticed to his destruction (v. 20).[81] A spirit (הרוח) had eventually volunteered to be a "lying spirit (רוח שקר) in the mouth of all his prophets" (v. 21).[82] Micaiah concluded his reply by saying that Yahweh had thus put a "lying spirit" (רוח שקר) in the mouth of all these prophets (v. 22). It was Yahweh that had decreed disaster for Ahab.

In vv. 24–29, we see the reaction to Micaiah's words. Zedekiah hit Micaiah on the cheek, and said, "Which way did the spirit of Yahweh

---

80. Block, "Empowered by the Spirit of God," 49. The LXX removes the ambiguity, ascribing success to King Ahab (see Gray, *I & II Kings*, 445).

81. Moberly is perceptive and persuasive in his close reading of the text here. For him, the heavenly court is not something prior, to which Micaiah has been privy, but something concurrent with the events of Micaiah's confrontation. Thus the "deceiving" is a vehicle to help Ahab see that he is being deceived by 400 other prophets; the self-serving lying (שקר) of the prophets mirrors the lack of integrity in the king; it is God himself who is confronting the king here, trying to bring him to repentance. See R. W. L. Moberly, "Does God Lie to His Prophets? The Story of Micaiah Ben Imlah as a Test Case," *HTR* 96 (2003): 8–10.

82. For the identity of the "spirit," see below.

pass from me to speak to you?" (אֵי־זֶה עָבַר רוּחַ־יְהוָה מֵאִתִּי לְדַבֵּר אוֹתָךְ,
v. 24). Micaiah replied, "You will find out on that day when you go in to
hide in an inner chamber." Ahab then instructed Micaiah to be imprisoned
until his return, whereupon Micaiah replied confidently, "If you return in
peace, Yahweh has not spoken by me (לֹא־דִבֶּר יְהוָה בִּי)" (v. 28).

There are many complexities surrounding the composition of the
chapter, and how it relates to historical events.[83] DeVries discerns two
independent narratives about Micaiah which have been conflated. He
dates the "word-controversy narrative" (vv. 10a–14, 19–25) to the reign
of Hezekiah.[84] McKenzie, however, discerns a greater degree of rework-
ing, and suggests that the historical situation which suits 1 Kgs 22:1–38
best is the later Jehu dynasty, rather than the reign of Ahab.[85] Working
from this, McKenzie argues that "the narrative in 22:1–38..., whatever its
tradition history, is a post-Dtr addition."[86] Although he does not commit
to the dating of 22:1–38, there are no strong reasons for dating this later
than Hezekiah's reign: the nature of the role of רוּחַ, where רוּחַ is clearly
in some sense an objective agent of Yahweh inspiring the 400 prophets,
is somewhat different from the critique of Jeremiah and Ezekiel against
their opponents, who prophesy out of their own imagination;[87] further,
there is no explicit mention of their prophesying for personal gain here;[88]
finally, the issue in 1 Kings, that of true and false prophecy, is rather different from the concerns of the post-exilic Chronicler, who barely modi-
fies this chapter, yet shifts the focus towards foreign alliances with the
word "entice" (סוּת) in 2 Chr 18:2, 31.[89]

---

83. See Simon J. DeVries, *Prophet Against Prophet: The Role of the Micaiah
Narrative (1 Kings 22) in the Development of Early Prophetic Tradition* (Grand
Rapids: Eerdmans, 1978), 4–10; idem, *1 Kings* (WBC 12; Waco, Tex.: Word, 1985),
265–66; Gray, *I & II Kings*, 414–18; Jones, *1 and 2 Kings*, 2:360–2; Steven L.
McKenzie, *The Trouble With Kings: The Composition of the Book of Kings in the
Deuteronomistic History* (VTSup 42; Leiden: Brill, 1991), 88–93. For a strong
recent attempt to argue for literary integrity, while acknowledging traditio-historical
complexity, see Moberly, "Does God Lie?"

84. DeVries, *1 Kings*, 265–66.

85. McKenzie, *Trouble*, 90.

86. Ibid., 92.

87. Jer 14:14; 23:16, 26; Ezek 13:2, 3, 17. Only in Ezek 13:3 is רוּחַ used, though
see below for Jer 5:13. Cf. Mordechai Cogan, *I Kings* (AB 10; New York: Doubleday, 2001), 498.

88. Ibid., 498.

89. See William M. Schniedewind, *The Word of God in Transition: From
Prophet to Exegete in the Second Temple Period* (JSOTSup 197; Sheffield: Sheffield
Academic Press, 1995), 94–97.

Within the narrative, a number of observations can be made about the relationship between word, spirit and prophecy. First, it is clear that the Hitpael of נבא here, accompanied by a preposition and some indication of the content, involves communication of a word (vv. 8, 18); although it is used pejoratively, insofar as Ahab does not like the outcome, it cannot be reduced to mere raving. It can hardly be coincidental that the other prophets also are spoken of as "prophesying" (מתנבאים, v. 10), without there being in their case a clear word produced until v. 11. Such a usage points to the similarity, and yet difference, between Micaiah and the 400 prophets.[90]

Secondly, the Niphal is predicated of the false prophets, and relates to the communication of a word (v. 12); there is clear semantic overlap with the Hitpael of נבא in vv. 8 and 18. At the same time, there seems a distinction between the Hitpael used absolutely (v. 10) and the Niphal, used with an indication of content. In and of themselves, the stems indicate neither the truth value of what is being said, nor the precise characteristics of those prophesying.

Thirdly, Zedekiah makes it very clear that, from the perspective of these (false) prophets, it was the רוח־יהוה that *spoke* with them (v. 24).[91]

Fourthly, Zedekiah also makes it clear, from his perspective, that it was רוח־יהוה that Micaiah was effectively claiming for himself (v. 24b). Zedekiah clearly understands the work of Yahweh's רוח as actually speaking Yahweh's words—"word-communicating" inspiration.[92]

Fifthly, Micaiah, in narrating the vision that he had of the heavenly court, does not deny the role of רוח in the inspiration of prophets. He merely says that the רוח in the mouth of these prophets is not the divine רוח, but a lying one.[93]

90. See the eighth observation below.

91. Cf. Dreytza, *Der theologische Gebrauch von RUAḤ*, 218.

92. The LXX paraphrases with "What sort of spirit of/from/before the presence of Yahweh is it that spoke with you (καὶ εἶπεν ποῖον πνεῦμα κυρίου τό λαλῆσαν ἐν σοί)." Here, still, "word-communicating" inspiration is apparent, even if the meaning of Zedekiah's words is rather different from the MT.

93. Neve, *Spirit of God*, 40. Whether הרוח is Yahweh's רוח or not is disputed. Debate largely centres around the significance of the article. Jones (*1 and 2 Kings*, 368) takes the article as "generic," and translates "a spirit." Even if the article indicates that this רוח is well known, this does not, in my judgment, mean that it must be Yahweh's "prophetic spirit" of inspiration that is the lying spirit (*pace* Gray, *I & II Kings*, 452; DeVries, *1 Kings*, 268; Walsh, *1 Kings*, 351; Cogan, *I Kings*, 497). First, the idea of the divine רוח being an entity independent from Yahweh would be anachronistic (Snaith, *Distinctive Ideas*, 158). Secondly, the picture is closer to that of the angelic being in Job 1–2; thirdly, the emphasis on Yahweh's trustworthiness

Sixthly, Micaiah does not refute the validity of Zedekiah's question about the time of the transfer of רוח־יהוה from Zedekiah to himself, but merely says that Zedekiah will know the reality, that is, of Yahweh's רוח inspiring him, when his (Micaiah's) words come true and Zedekiah is in hiding.[94] That Micaiah has prophesied the truth will become evident when what he says comes to pass. Implicitly, then, Micaiah claims the inspiration of רוח־יהוה. Thus, as Neve comments, "the belief that the word is inspired by a spirit, even in the case of the 'weal' prophets, is left standing."[95] Albertz and Westermann, however, disagree.[96] They see the use of הרוח as "solely polemical" here, regarding Micaiah's reference to it as assaulting the "theological legitimization" of his opponents. Micaiah appeals to Yahweh's speech (vv. 14, 28) for his own legitimation.

There is some truth in this. Micaiah is not speaking of a past event but is using the account of the heavenly court to elicit a response from Ahab. As Moberly draws out clearly, Micaiah has already given the prophetic message in v. 17, not as an announcement of an ineluctable destruction, but as a gracious warning (cf. 2 Kgs 17:13). Ahab, however, has not heeded the warning (v. 18), so Micaiah tries again, from a different angle. The purpose of the whole vision account is rhetorical.[97] This vision account works because of some shared assumptions, one of which is the significant part played by רוח. Further, Albertz and Westermann distinguish too neatly between the inspiration of the true, classical, prophets, on the one hand, who received Yahweh's word, and the false prophets who are inspired by the spirit, on the other.[98] False prophecy was a problem because the distinction was not so neat. Rather, in the understanding

and truthfulness in the rest of 1 Kgs points to some distance between Yahweh and this spirit; even Zedekiah believed that a lying spirit could not be God's spirit (see P. J. Williams, "Lying Spirits Sent by God? The Case of Micaiah's Prophecy," in *The Trustworthiness of Scripture: Perspectives on the Nature of Scripture* [ed. P. Helm and C. R. Trueman; Grand Rapids: Eerdmans, 2002], 58–66). The point is that the false prophets believe they are inspired by Yahweh's spirit, when in fact it is a false, lying spirit. Micaiah, on the other hand, is inspired by Yahweh's spirit. There are two separate "spirits," rather than two manifestations of the same רוח: Yahweh's רוח, an extension of Yahweh's personality, and the "evil, lying spirit" inspiring false prophecy. See Evangelia G. Dafni, "רוח שקר und falsche Prophetie in 1 Reg 22," *ZAW* 112 (2000): 368–85.

94. The mention of the "inner-room" as a place of refuge is an echo of Ben-Hadad's hiding place in 20:30.

95. Neve, *Spirit of God*, 40.

96. Albertz and Westermann, "רוּחַ *Rûaḥ* Spirit," *TLOT* 3:1217. So too Couturier, "L'Esprit de Yahweh," 157–58.

97. Moberly, "Does God Lie?," 5–14.

98. See further below.

of Zedekiah and Micaiah, "it was the spirit that took hold of the prophets, and when they spoke it was the words which were given them by the spirit. The process cannot be stated more directly than is done in this narrative. The connection between the spirit and the spoken word is as close as possible."[99] "Word-communicating" inspiration is explicit here.

The seventh observation that can be drawn from this narrative is that claiming inspiration, even the inspiration of רוח, was no guarantee that what was said would happen. Not every claim to the "spirit of Yahweh" makes it a word from Yahweh, although strikingly here the lying spirit is commissioned by Yahweh. Further, majority agreement among the prophets does not materially alter the situation. This observation paves the way for the relative lack of recourse to רוח within the classical prophets.

The eighth observation concerns the points of similarity and difference between Micaiah and the other prophets. These points illuminate the picture that obtains in the following century and beyond, with Amos and the other classical prophets in their conflicts with the false prophets.[100] The false prophets attribute their inspiration to רוח; they exhibit dramatic behaviour, including sign-acts (22:10–11); they have a reputation of being willing to modify their message (v. 13);[101] they announce triumph and victory; they belong to Ahab's court ("his," v. 22);[102] they may even be willing to prophesy for any deity, since Yahweh is not mentioned in v. 6, but only after they have been present when Jehoshaphat has asked for a prophet of Yahweh (v. 7), and the name of Zedekiah and his father (כנענה) hint at the blurring of distinctions so characteristic of Ahab's reign.[103] Micaiah, on the other hand, is distinct from the other prophets (v. 8), his characteristic prophecy is one of doom (v. 8), he only speaks Yahweh's word (v. 14), he has access to the heavenly court (vv. 19–23), he appeals to the Deuteronomic test of whether a prophecy comes true as the mark of his own authentication (vv. 25, 28); all these characteristics might suggest a radical disjunction between Micaiah and the 400 prophets. Micaiah, however, accepts the notion of Yahweh's רוח speaking to him (v. 25), while making direct appeal to Yahweh's רוח for his own authentication; in addition, he acts as a prophet in a similar fashion to the others (נבא Hitpael, vv. 8, 18; cf. v. 10), and is clearly understood

---

99.   Arvid S. Kapelrud, "The Spirit and the Word," 41.
100.   J. A. Montgomery and H. S. Gehman, *A Critical and Exegetical Commentary on the Books of Kings* (ICC; Edinburgh: T. & T. Clark, 1951), 336.
101.   Walsh, *1 Kings*, 348; Cogan, *I Kings*, 497.
102.   Cogan, *I Kings*, 497.
103.   So Walsh, *1 Kings*, 347; cf. Jer 2:8; 23:13.

as another prophet like the four hundred by Jehoshaphat (v. 7).[104] Against such a background, it is hardly surprising that the classical prophets are not too keen to speak of themselves as a נביא or as רוח-inspired, for neither provides conclusive proof that such a person has spoken the truth.

1.3. *The Relative Insignificance of* רוח *Within Pre-classical Prophecy*

An examination of רוח within pre-classical prophecy with regard to "potentiating" inspiration and "word-communicating" inspiration has demonstrated that both understandings are clearly present. By focusing our attention here, though, there is a danger of obscuring two facts. First, as Kaufmann notes, the work of the spirit is not always related to the communication of a word from Yahweh.[105] When the "spirit" "clothes itself" (לבש) with Gideon (Judg 6:34) and animates (פעם) Samson (Judg 13:25; cf. 14:6, 19; 15:14), the effect is that they have strength—but no word of Yahweh is involved. The agency of Yahweh's רוח is in no way restricted to the prophetic רוח. Secondly, and conversely, words could come from Yahweh without any mention of רוח. This is true for Abraham, Jacob, Joshua, Gideon and Samuel. Even within the books of Samuel and Kings, there are no claims for רוח-possession for many of the prophets, such as Nathan and Ahijah (1 Kgs 11; 14), for the prophets of Judah or Bethel (1 Kgs 13) or for Jehu (1 Kgs 16). In other words, the place and significance of רוח within pre-classical prophecy should not be overstated or overemphasized.

2. *Inspiration and the Classical Prophets*

At the start of Part II, we observed how the classical prophets are relatively (or totally) silent on the role of רוח within their ministries, and we saw the four main views of how scholars have interpreted this silence (*antithetical, historical, rhetorical, theological*). In particular, many scholars have seen in the book of Ezekiel a recovery of the role of רוח within Ezekiel's ministry after an absence within the classical prophets. If we are going to evaluate the significance of the book of Ezekiel, we must examine the significant points within the classical prophets where רוח-inspiration has been observed or denied. I shall argue that, while it is certainly true that רוח-inspiration is not prominent, both "potentiating" inspiration and "word-communicating" inspiration as concepts may be found.

---

104.   Notice particularly עוד, which highlights the similarity. Cf. Moberly, "Does God Lie?," 5.

105.   Kaufmann, *Religion of Israel*, 97–98.

2.1. *"Potentiating" Inspiration and the Classical Prophets*
2.1.1. *Hosea 9:7.*

> The days of punishment have come, the days of recompense have come;
> Israel cries[106] "The prophet is a fool (אֱוִיל הַנָּבִיא), the man of the spirit is
> mad (מְשֻׁגָּע אִישׁ הָרוּחַ)!" Because of your great iniquity, your hostility is
> great.

This verse occurs as part of a tightly structured unit from vv. 7–9.[107] This
is in turn part of the section from vv. 1–9 which outlines the conflict
between Hosea and his addressees about the value of their festivals and
their consequent disapproval of his ministry. There are two main questions
that concern us. First, who is uttering these words about "the prophet"?
Secondly, if it is not Hosea himself, how much of this pejorative carica-
ture can confidently be said to be part of Hosea's self-understanding,
especially given the fact that the phrase א אִישׁ הָרוּחַ only occurs here?

With regard to the first question, Mowinckel argues that the prophet
here is inveighing against "the *nebhiʾim*," on the grounds that the prophet
would hardly accept such a description of himself, given the strong
expressions contained in the words "fool" and "mad."[108] Mowinckel, however, does not pay sufficient attention to the context, which is of Israel
insulting the prophet, thereby showing how guilty Israel truly is.[109]

---

106. On the basis of context, most commentators amend the MT (יָדְעוּ/) to יָרֻעוּ
("cry"/"shout," Hiphil imperative of רוּעַ); cf. the LXX's καὶ κακωθήσεται Ισραηλ (=
יֵרַע, Hiphil imperative of רָעַע). See Hans W. Wolff, *A Commentary on the Book of
the Prophet Hosea* (trans. Gary Stansell; Hermeneia; Philadelphia: Fortress,
1974), 150. Although Mackintosh (*Hosea*, 351–52) thinks the suggestion "dubious"
because רוּעַ usually speaks of raising a shout, in joy or in battle, Couturier ("L'Esprit
de Yahweh," 134) points out that the parallel between Ephraim as a hunter spying on
game (v. 9) and Israel's activity in v. 7 makes a "declaration of war against Hosea"
more likely than knowledge about Hosea.

107. Couturier ("L'Esprit de Yahweh," 133–34) notes the close structure of
vv. 7–9 here, which I have summarized in the following table:

> 7a: declaration of judgment; יְמֵי ;פָּקַד
> 7b: attack of people against Hosea; verbal threat; Israel; hostility
>   vs. God (מַשְׂטֵמָה)
>   7c: recollection of guilt: reason
>   8: attack of people against Hosea; physical threat; Ephraim;
>   hostility vs. prophet (מַשְׂטֵמָה)
> 9: declaration of judgment; יְמֵי ;פָּקַד

108. Mowinckel, "The 'Spirit' and the 'Word,'" 204–5; so too Schoemaker,
"Use of רוּחַ," 16.

109. So Volz, *Der Geist Gottes*, 64; Wolff, *Hosea*, 156–57; Douglas Stuart,
Hosea–Jonah (WBC 31; Waco, Tex.: Word, 1987), 145; Couturier, "L'Esprit de

With regard to the second question, Wolff points out that these words are on the lips of the people, and that, therefore, "Hosea does not speak of himself as a person filled with the 'spirit.'"[110] Many commentators argue from this fact that Hosea cannot and should not be understood as claiming the inspiration of רוח for himself.[111] In particular, Couturier looks closely at the adjectives predicated of "the prophet" and "the man of the spirit," and, in addition to noticing the obvious pejorative nature of them, also observes, correctly, that the word "mad" (משׁגע) only occurs in carefully circumscribed contexts (1 Sam 21:11–16; 2 Kgs 9:11; Jer 29:24–32). Within the prophetic context, it is associated with the Hitpael of נבא, and, for Couturier, is essentially related to ecstasy within prophecy. From the rarity of the term, and its precise usage, Couturier argues that the people's accusation is not simply that Hosea is "mad," but that he is part of a band of prophets who go around under the influence of רוח. The people's charge, then, "goes beyond the simple accusation of madness; it refers to a precise tradition in the history of prophecy, whose characteristic is ecstasy accompanied by trances."[112] Given that for Couturier there is a clear distinction between the three different prophetic groups, it is wholly inconceivable that Hosea, as an individual prophet, would have identified in any sense with the charge that he was one of the ecstatic group.

Such a sharp distinction, however, is neither the only nor the best interpretation. While it is, of course, true that he does not *explicitly* claim to be "a man of the spirit," the point also needs to be made that Hosea does not distance himself from these titles.[113] More significantly, elsewhere he identifies himself as a prophet, one of the titles with which, on this analysis, he was being lampooned (9:8; cf. 6:5; 12:11 [ET 12:10], 14, where he has a positive view of the נביא).[114] Though it is possible that Hosea accepts the first title ("prophet") but denies the second ("man of the spirit"), such that it is the entire mischaracterization ("the man of the spirit is mad") that serves to demonstrate Israel's guilt, it is preferable to

Yahweh," 133; G. I. Davies, *Hosea* (NCB; London: Marshall Pickering, 1992), 220; Mackintosh, *Hosea*, 336, 351–53.

110.   Wolff, *Hosea*, 157.

111.   E.g. Mays, *Hosea*, 129–30; Scharbert, "Der 'Geist' und die Schriftprophe-ten," 89; Couturier, "L'Esprit de Yahweh," 132–36; Schüngel-Straumann, *Rûah bewegt die Welt*, 32–33.

112.   Couturier, "L'Esprit de Yahweh," 136: "dépasse la simple accusation de démence; il fait référence à une tradition précise dans l'histoire du prophétisme, dont la caractéristique est l'extatisme accompagné de transes."

113.   Cf. Jacob, *Theology*, 125.

114.   Verhoef, *NIDOTTE* 4:1074. It is of course true that Hosea, like the other prophets, fulminates against false prophets (4:4–5).

see that he is willing to identify himself as a "man of the spirit."[115] This is partly because of the synonymy, as Couturier himself notes,[116] between "prophet" and "man of the spirit" and partly because there is not the contrast between the "individual" Hosea, on the one hand, and the "plural" נביאים (6:5; 12:11) in Hosea that Couturier regards as determinative elsewhere.[117]

The insult of the people comes not in the title given to Hosea (נביא, איש הרוח), but in the way such titles are predicated. It is presumptuous to argue that Hosea's silence on ascribing רוח to himself is tantamount to rejection or repudiation. The verse needs to be understood like this: though Hosea is a נביא and a "man of the spirit," like Elijah (1 Kgs 18:12), Micaiah ben Imlah (1 Kgs 22) and Elisha (2 Kgs 2:9), he cannot be dismissed as a "raving ecstatic" like others who claim to be also נביאים and "men of the spirit." The difference between the true and the false is precisely that: one is a true prophet, the other is false. The distinction should not be found in "ecstasy/strange behaviour" or in the presence of רוח.[118]

The picture that emerges here is of a people who recognize the work of the divine רוח in a prophet and are scornful, and of a prophet who, while not using the term of his own ministry, does not repudiate such a reference. Nonetheless, the work of the spirit evident here is not necessarily that of "word-communicating" inspiration. Here, again, it is the prophet who is inspired by the divine רוח; how that רוח-inspiration relates to the words the prophet utters is not articulated here.[119]

2.1.2. *Micah 3:8.*

> But as for me, I am filled with power, with the spirit of Yahweh (את־רוח יהוה), and with justice and might, to declare to Jacob his transgression and to Israel his sin.

This verse concludes Micah's oracle, begun in v. 5, against "the prophets who lead astray" God's people by declaring "peace" when their stomachs

---

115. Montague (*Holy Spirit*, 34) sees this as an "exception" to cases where classical prophets wanted to distance themselves from the spirit. Wolff (*Hosea*, 157), van Imschoot ("L'action de l'esprit de Jahvé," 571), Carley (*Ezekiel Among the Prophets*, 27) and Mackintosh (*Hosea*, 353) see Hosea as accepting this title, "man of the spirit."

116. Couturier, "L'Esprit de Yahweh," 134.

117. Cf. Jeremias, *TLOT* 2:702.

118. See James L. Crenshaw, *Prophetic Conflict: Its Effect Upon Israelite Religion* (BZAW 124; New York: de Gruyter, 1971), 54–55.

119. Cf. Koch, *Geist Gottes*, 56.

have been fed by those who have come to them, but who "declare war" on those who have not fed them. Having spelled out his charge against them (v. 5), and the judgment that shall come to them (vv. 6–7), Micah now states his own authority (v. 8).[120] There are two significant issues here. The first is the authenticity of the phrase "with the spirit of Yahweh." The second is, if it is authentic, the implications of such a claim in the ministry of Micah.

With regard to authenticity, many commentators regard it as a gloss. They do so on five main grounds: first, metre, that "it interrupts the three-stress colon"[121] and "overloads" it,[122] making the first colon much too long in what is otherwise a well-structured chapter;[123] secondly, grammar, that there is a "superfluous אֵת (without a copula!)";[124] thirdly, sense, that it confuses the source of the endowment of charismatic gifts (the spirit) with the gifts themselves,[125] and spoils the "matching triad";[126] fourthly, chronology, that the linking of רוּחַ with "filling" is only found in (the later) P,[127] or that it is an explanatory gloss for "power" (כֹּחַ) at a time when prophets were held as inspired by Yahweh;[128] fifthly, sense, for, according to Mowinckel, רוּחַ is linked with "lying" (שֶׁקֶר) and "deceit" (כָּזָב) in 2:11, and so Micah is contrasting his own authority ("power," "might" and "judgment," 3:8) with the רוּחַ of the נְבִיאִים.[129] A claim to רוּחַ "in the mouth of Micah" is "suspicious," "since it is associated too clearly with the claims of the false prophets whom he excoriates and the terminology they used."[130] The conclusion, then, is that "the words are

120.   Leslie C. Allen, *The Books of Joel, Obadiah, Jonah and Micah* (NICOT; Grand Rapids: Eerdmans, 1976), 310.

121.   Hans W. Wolff, *Micah: A Commentary* (trans. Gary Stansell; Minneapolis: Augsburg, 1990), 91–92.

122.   James L. Mays, *Micah* (OTL; London: SCM, 1976), 81; Wolff, *Micah*, 91–92.

123.   Couturier, "L'Esprit de Yahweh," 144.

124.   Hans W. Wolff, *Joel and Amos: A Commentary on the Books of the Prophets Joel and Amos* (trans. W. Janzen, S. D. McBride Jr. and C. A. Muenchow; Hermeneia; Philadelphia: Fortress, 1977), 91–92; Couturier, "L'Esprit de Yahweh," 144–45.

125.   Mays, *Micah*, 85–86; Couturier, "L'Esprit de Yahweh," 145.

126.   Volz, *Der Geist Gottes*, 65: "passenden Dreiklang."

127.   Ibid., 65; Albertz and Westermann, *TLOT* 3:1216.

128.   Scharbert, "Der 'Geist' und die Schriftpropheten," 90; cf. Joseph Blenkinsopp, *A History of Prophecy in Israel* (rev. and enl. ed.; Louisville, Ky.: Westminster John Knox, 1996), 261.

129.   Mowinckel, "The 'Spirit' and the 'Word,'" 205–6.

130.   William McKane, *The Book of Micah: Introduction and Commentary* (ICC; Edinburgh: T. & T. Clark, 1998), 109.

surely an addendum, from the time when it was usual to associate ruach and prophecy."[131]

The authenticity of the phrase has been defended by Hillers[132] and others, however.[133] Hillers maintains that the verse is metrically adequate,[134] that none of the terms supposed to be "glossed" are obscure (though there may be reasons for a gloss other than obscurity); that the prophet as man of the spirit can be seen elsewhere (2:11),[135] and that the expression is not anachronistic (he cites 2 Sam 23:2). Further to his arguments, רוח as a liquid metaphor, as in the phrase "I am filled with…the spirit of Yahweh," is quite common,[136] and need not be late (e.g. Isa 30:28); the other instances of an individual being "filled with the spirit" (Exod 31:3; 35:31; Deut 34:9) do not use את, so the unique syntax here guards against a too ready equation of the phrase in Mic 3:8 with occurrences assigned to P; also, את is not necessarily awkward, for it could indicate that Micah is filled with power through the assistance of Yahweh's רוח (cf. את in Gen 4:1);[137] finally, excising it as a theological interpretation from a later date is a convenient way of dealing with an otherwise potentially problematic piece of evidence—it assumes what is

131.   Volz, *Der Geist Gottes*, 65: "Die Worte sind sicherlich Nachtrag, aus der Zeit, in der man gewohnt war, Ruh [*sic*] und Prophetie zusammenzudenken."

132.   Delbert R. Hillers, *A Commentary on the Book of the Prophet Micah* (Hermeneia; Philadelphia: Fortress, 1984), 44–45.

133.   Allen, *Books of Joel, Obadiah, Jonah and Micah*, 314; Lindblom, *Prophecy*, 175; John Breck, *Spirit of Truth: The Holy Spirit in Johannine Tradition*. Vol. 1, *The Origins of Johannine Pneumatology* (Crestwood, N.Y.: St. Vladimir's Seminary Press, 1991), 37–38; Charles S. Shaw, *The Speeches of Micah: A Rhetorical-Historical Analysis* (JSOTSup 145; Sheffield: JSOT Press, 1993), 103–4.

134.   So too Allen, *Books of Joel, Obadiah, Jonah and Micah*, 314; Lindblom, *Prophecy*, 175; Shaw, *Speeches of Micah*, 103.

135.   רוח is not used in a positive sense in Mic 2:11, but it is further defined by שקר. Hillers suggests that the phrase רוח ושקר is a hendiadys (cf. Isa 41:29); alternatively, he suggests emending to רוח שקר, noting the parallel in 1 Kgs 22:22; see Hillers, *Micah*, 36. Mowinckel ("The 'Spirit' and the 'Word,'" 206), Mays (*Micah*, 73), followed by Shaw (*Speeches of Micah*, 71), and Couturier ("L'Esprit de Yahweh," 136–41), however, see it as a description of רוח as the windy inspirer of the false prophets' lying oracles, though Mays does admit of the possibility of hendiadys here.

136.   See further Chapter 6 below.

137.   Carl F. Keil, *Commentary on the Old Testament*. Vol. 10, *The Minor Prophets* (trans. James Martin; repr., Peabody, Mass.: Hendrickson, 1996 [1861–99]), 307; van Imschoot, "L'action de l'esprit de Jahvé," 568; Allen, *Books of Joel, Obadiah, Jonah and Micah*, 314; Shaw, *Speeches of Micah*, 104. Jacob (*Theology*, 125) suggests that "instead of suppressing *ruach* we could just as well take *koach* as a gloss uselessly repeating *geburah*"; so too Lys, *Rûach*, 91.

being debated and forecloses debate. Carley comments that "there are no generally accepted grounds for such an emendation."[138] In view of this, he says that "to retain the phrase is to treat the text more fairly."[139] Mowinckel's question regarding the sense of the passage and its relation to 2:11 is best answered by looking at how the phrase functions within the verse, and at the significance of the verse.

With regard to the function of this verse, nowhere else in the book of Micah is there a call report that functions to authenticate the prophet and his unpopular message;[140] here, v. 8 serves to communicate Micah's credentials.[141] Were Mowinckel correct in his analysis of the pre-exilic reforming prophets, we would expect here a reference to the word of Yahweh as well as the supposed repudiation of רוח that he says is found in 2:11. It is likely, however, that Micah is here purposefully using irony, when set alongside 2:11. Men "walking after the wind"[142] (הלך רוח) and uttering falsehoods do not do so with the divine רוח, but with emptiness (רוח) and lies (שקר)—in contrast to Micah, who has the divine רוח.[143] In other words, Micah here is conducting an assault on the very heart of their inspiration by appealing to his own.[144] It is too simplistic an analysis to speak of "true prophets appeal to the word of Yahweh," while "false prophets appeal to the רוח," since in 1 Kgs 22, we see a true prophet appeal to the divine רוח, and in Ezekiel we see the false prophets appeal to the "word of Yahweh."[145] As we have seen, false prophecy was such a problem *precisely because* there was no foolproof method of distinguishing between true and false.

In summary, this verse cannot be discounted as evidence in the case that the classical prophets spoke of רוח for their own inspiration. The phrase makes sense in its context, and other arguments against its authenticity are inconclusive. The picture that this verse gives, then, is of Yahweh's רוח being intimately involved with prophecy, and, in particular, with the rhetorical event. Micah is "full of the spirit of Yahweh…to

---

138.   Carley, *Ezekiel Among the Prophets*, 27.

139.   Ibid., 88.

140.   E.g. Amos 7:14–15; Isa 6; Jer 1:4–10; Ezek 1–3.

141.   Mays, *Micah*, 84–86; Ralph L. Smith, *Micah–Malachi* (WBC 32; Waco, Tex.: Word, 1984), 33–34.

142.   Keil, *Commentary*, 302.

143.   Hehn (Hehn, "Zum Problem des Geistes," 222–23) observes that "in a neo-Babylonian letter, it says, 'I know that all you say about me is a lie and wind'" ("In einem neubabylonischen Briefe heißt es: 'Ich weiß, daß alles, was du über mich sagst, Lüge und Wind ist").

144.   *Pace* Couturier, "L'Esprit de Yahweh," 136–41.

145.   Ezek 13:6, 7; 22:28.

declare…"[146] This inspiration, while explicitly stated here, cannot, however, be said necessarily to be "word-communicating." Micah's credentials, which include "power," "justice" and "might," given by the divine
רוח, all imply the empowering of him as a prophet, rather than his words.

2.1.3. *Jeremiah 5:13.*

The prophets are nothing but wind (והנביאים יהיו לרוח), for the word is
not in them (והדבר אין בהם).[147] Thus shall it be done to them!

Theological uses of רוח are remarkably absent from the book of
Jeremiah. There is only one place where there is a possibility of a theological nuance to רוח in the book, and it occurs within "a collection of
poetic fragments"[148] which are somewhat awkward because of the change
in speaker and addressee. The literary context is of an impending inva-
sion from the north, declared by Jeremiah (4:5–6:30), and of the complete
absence of any righteous person in Jerusalem, whose presence would
avert Yahweh's judgment (5:1–9). The next two verses, 5:10–11, seem to
be addressed to the impending invaders, urging them to begin their
destructive work, though not to make a "full end" (5:10; cf. 4:27; 5:18).
In 5:12, there is a shift in speaker. Jeremiah gives his verdict on those
who have spoken falsely of Yahweh.[149] In the verses following v. 13,
5:14–17, Yahweh declares judgment on those who have spoken falsely;
such false speaking is revealed as a prime cause of the consumption of
the people by the invading nation.[150] There are two critical questions
concerning v. 13: first, "Of whom are these words predicated?" and, secondly, "What is the force of רוח here?"

---

146.   I do not see how the "dependent clause" ("in order to proclaim…") "only
distantly refers to prophecy" as claimed in Albertz and Westermann, *TLOT* 3:1216.

147.   I translate with most commentators, who follow the LXX here (καὶ λόγος
κυρίου) and emend to הַדָּבָר. Holladay prefers the MT as the *lectio difficilior*, with the
"postbiblical Hebrew" meaning "revelation"; see William L. Holladay, *Jeremiah 1:
A Commentary on the Book of the Prophet Jeremiah* (Hermeneia; Minneapolis:
Fortress, 1986), 183, 187. If, however, דִּבֵּר is "postbiblical," this explains the MT,
but suggests an original הַדָּבָר.

148.   Peter C. Craigie, Page H. Kelley and Joel F. Drinkard, Jr., *Jeremiah 1–25*
(WBC 26; Dallas: Word, 1991), 90; so too Robert P. Carroll, *Jeremiah* (OTL; London: SCM, 1986), 182; John Bright, *Jeremiah* (AB 21; Garden City, N.Y.: Doubleday, 1965), 42. McKane tentatively regards Jeremiah as the speaker throughout
vv. 12–14. See William McKane, *Jeremiah* (2 vols.; ICC; Edinburgh: T. & T. Clark,
1986–96), 1:120–22.

149.   Holladay, *Jeremiah 1*, 186; McKane, *Jeremiah*, 1:121.

150.   Couturier, "L'Esprit de Yahweh," 149–50.

Those who see this verse as revealing Jeremiah's view of רוח and רוח-inspiration as totally negative see v. 13 as being a quotation of Jeremiah himself, expressing Yahweh's verdict on the false salvation prophets. רוח is what inspires (probably by their own admission) the false prophets of hope, who say that Yahweh will do nothing, and that no harm will come (v. 12). Jeremiah here, with a pungent word-play on רוח, says the prophets are "nothing but spirit/wind," because, in contrast to Jeremiah, they do not have the "word" in them (cf. Jer 18:18). Couturier comments, "One cannot avoid, therefore, seeing here not only a strong opposition between two types of prophets, but again between the 'spirit' (wind) and the 'word.'"[151] Such a conclusion, however, is by no means unavoidable.

One way in which such a conclusion has been avoided is to answer the first question, "Of whom are these words predicated?" with "Jeremiah and other prophets of doom." This is the approach of many modern English versions, which treat v. 13, until בהם, as a continuation of the culpably false words of those cited by Jeremiah in v. 12.[152] With this approach, Jeremiah and the other prophets declaring doom are denounced by the false prophets, in v. 13, as uttering empty words.[153] Given that Jeremiah himself can speak of "the prophets" in either positive or negative terms,[154] it is possible that his opponents can do the same. The false prophets, then, declare that הנביאים (i.e. Jeremiah and other doom prophets) are nothing but wind, and the word is not in them (v. 13). This interpretation has rightly been criticized, though not always effectively.

Holladay argues that הנביאים preceding the verb signals a "contrast" with what has come before. This, however, is not an adequate refutation.[155] The fronting of הנביאים does not necessarily serve to mark a change in speaker; it could simply mark a change in the topic of the false prophets' speech, from their denial of the gloomy words, to the fate of

151. Ibid., 149: "On ne peut donc pas éviter de voir ici une forte opposition non seulement entre deux types de prophètes, mais encore entre l'esprit' (vent) et la 'parole.'"

152. So NRSV, NIV, ESV, NASB; also Vulgate and, according to McKane (*Jeremiah*, 1:121), the commentaries of Duhm, Rudolph and Weiser.

153. That false prophets (or the people citing the words of the false prophets) are in view in v. 12 is apparent from the similarity between their words here and those of the false prophets elsewhere (e.g. Jer 14:13; 23:17).

154. That Jeremiah can speak positively of the plural נביאים is apparent from 2:30, where Judah's guilt is apparent from its treatment of its prophets (cf. McKane, *Jeremiah*, 1:51); that he can also speak of them negatively is apparent from 5:31, where they are said to prophesy falsely (cf. 14:13–22; 23:9–40).

155. Holladay, *Jeremiah 1*, 187.

the gloomy prophets. A stronger reason for linking v. 13 with the words
of Jeremiah is that the indictment of הנביאים here sounds rather similar
to his indictment of them elsewhere. The mention of רוח in 5:13 and of
the prophets prophesying בשקר in 5:31 (cf. 14:14; 23:14) is strongly
reminiscent of Mic 2:11; further, the assertion that Yahweh's word is
"not in them" is similar to Jeremiah's accusations elsewhere (e.g. 14:14;
23:18–22). On this reading, given the lexicalization of "prophets" in
v. 13, the subject of כחשו and ויאמרו in v. 12 needs to be a group other
than the prophets, presumably the people of Judah who regurgitate the
words of the false prophets.

Given, then, that these words *are* the words of Jeremiah against the
false prophets, there is still the question of the force of רוח here. The
relevant phrase is והנביאים יהיו לרוח. The preposition ל indicates what
the prophets will become, that is, "nothing" (cf. Jer 2:14),[156] or perhaps
what they belong to,[157] rather than what they possess (given the lack of ל
with הנביאים). Certainly, the primary sense of רוח is of "wind" or "noth-
ingness." As I noted above, however, many see here a word-play on רוח,
linking this primary sense with רוח as the source of the (false) prophets'
inspiration. *Even* if this were true, and it seems plausible, this does not
necessarily mean that Jeremiah is hostile to רוח-inspiration. Jeremiah
could just as easily be denying the legitimacy of their claim to the divine
רוח here, and confronting them directly in their claim to the spirit's
inspiration (cf. Ezek 13:3). Just as he inveighs against prophets, while he
himself is one (1:5),[158] so too he can inveigh against claims to the divine
רוח while regarding himself as having that same divine רוח (cf. Micaiah).
His silence on the question of his own "inspiration" and the divine רוח
should not necessarily be interpreted as antipathy towards רוח.[159]

Such a conclusion is further supported by the fact that Jeremiah does
not confront the other prophets on the grounds of the style of their prophecy, repudiating the more ecstatic manifestations, but on the grounds of
whether Yahweh is the source of their message. Indeed, he himself has
visions (1:11–13); he experiences the powerful "hand of Yahweh" on him
which overwhelms him, probably with external manifestations (15:17;
cf. 1:9);[160] he was "enticed" and "overpowered" by Yahweh (20:7); he

156.   The prophets "will be shown to be the windbags that they are," according
to Bright, *Jeremiah*, 40.
157.   Cf. Couturier, "L'Esprit de Yahweh," 148.
158.   Jeremias, *TLOT* 2:702.
159.   Cf. Chevallier, *Souffle de Dieu*, 29; Craigie, Kelley and Drinkard, *Jeremiah
1–25*, 92; Kapelrud, "The Spirit and the Word," 43; Koch, *Geist Gottes*, 59–60.
160.   Cf. Roberts, "The Hand of Yahweh."

experienced crushing emotions (4:17); he performed elaborate sign-acts (27:1–28:17) and, finally, both true and false prophecy in the book of Jeremiah are marked by the Niphal of נבא (e.g. true: 19:14; 25:13; 26:11, 12; false: 2:8; 5:31; 11:21) *and* by the Hitpael (true: 26:20; false: 14:14; 23:13).[161] It is therefore no surprise that Jeremiah, like Hosea, was regarded as "mad" (משגע, Jer 29:26–27; cf. Deut 28:34; 2 Kgs 9:11; 1 Sam 21:15–16 [ET 21:14–15]); there was some evidence pointing in that direction within his ministry.[162]

This picture makes it unlikely that Jeremiah actually repudiated רוח in his own inspiration. It is, however, impossible to argue that he explicitly endorsed it. If a word-play is intended in 5:13, what is clear is that certain prophets in Jeremiah's day *did* lay claim to the divine רוח (even if we have no record of Jeremiah doing so explicitly).[163] As Koch comments, "So an indirect witness for the *rûach Yahweh* as source of prophetic inspiration may lie in this word of mockery."[164] Precisely what kind of "prophetic inspiration" is in view cannot be determined. It is not possible to decide whether such a view of inspiration, as evinced in the late pre-exilic period, was "potentiating" or "word-communicating."

2.2. *"Word-communicating" Inspiration and the Classical Prophets*
2.2.1. *Isaiah 30:1–2.*

> Oh, rebellious children, says Yahweh, who carry out a plan, but not mine (ולא מני); who make an alliance,[165] but against my will (לא רוחי), adding sin to sin; who set out to go down to Egypt without asking for my counsel (ופי לא שאלו).

The only possible linking of רוח to "word-communicating" inspiration in texts generally accepted as pre-exilic within the classical prophets occurs

---

161.   Cf. van Imschoot, "L'action de l'esprit de Jahvé," 572–73; Koch, *Geist Gottes*, 60.

162.   This point is acknowledged by Fenton ("Israelite Prophecy," 132), though his correct observation that society "*expected*" the prophet "to behave abnormally" and that the behaviour of the "new prophets" was somewhat distinct from the frenzy found in 1 Kgs 18, for example, leads to the implausible suggestion that the strange behaviour of these "new prophets" should be interpreted wholly as an attempt "to feign at least a degree of eccentricity in order to inspire any confidence in their audience." See ibid., 132–33.

163.   So Holladay, *Jeremiah 1*, 187; Douglas R. Jones, *Jeremiah* (NCB; London: Marshall Pickering, 1992), 123–24.

164.   Koch, *Geist Gottes*, 60: "So dürfte in diesem Spottwort ein indirektes Zeugnis für die *rûach Jahweh* als Quelle der prophetischen Inspiration vorliegen."

165.   The phrase is ולנסך מסכה, which can be rendered more literally "pour out a libation" or "cast an idol" (cf. 30:22).

in Isa 30:1–2.[166] These verses come within the larger unit of vv. 1–11, which form an "oracular report concerning YHWH's dissatisfaction with the people's embassy to Egypt."[167] Within this, there are three sub-units. The first, vv. 1–5, is "the oracular report of YHWH's woe oracle."[168] Verse 1a reports the woe statement, and vv. 1b–2 spell out the offence. Isaiah's addressees carry out a plan (עצה) that does not come from Yahweh, in sending to Egypt for protection. Essential to any conclusion on spirit, prophecy and inspiration is an analysis of how, in v. 1, רוחי relates to מני, to which it clearly corresponds. רוחי has been understood in four main ways.

First, it has been understood as "the inner nature of God."[169] Such a view is based upon the parallel between "from me" and "[by] my spirit." As Albertz and Westermann point out, however, this "involves an abstract concept foreign to the Old Testament."[170]

Secondly, it has been understood as the power of Yahweh, or as the "effect of Yahweh's might."[171] Although, however, the notion of Yahweh's power is elsewhere contrasted with Egypt's weakness, it is not found in the immediate context here.[172]

Thirdly, it has been understood as the "mind of Yahweh." Isaiah's point is not so much that their plan to send an embassy to Egypt is not empowered by Yahweh, but that this plan is not Yahweh's will.[173] This view has the strength of taking seriously the parallel between "by me" and "by my spirit." Neve concedes, though, that this meaning, "the center of volition in Yahweh himself,"[174] is only found at one other point in the Old Testament,[175] and never elsewhere in First Isaiah.

166.   With regard to dating, Ma (*Until the Spirit Comes*, 46) notes that "the authenticity of the passage has not been seriously questioned."

167.   Sweeney, *Isaiah 1–39*, 389.

168.   Ibid.

169.   Baumgärtel, *TDNT* 6:364.

170.   Albertz and Westermann, *TLOT* 3:1216; Koch, *Geist Gottes*, 58. In Isa 31:3, ontology is not in view; rather, there is a contrast between Yahweh's power and animal/human frailty.

171.   Albertz and Westermann, *TLOT* 3:1216.

172.   Neve, *Spirit of God*, 54.

173.   Ibid., 54. So also Mowinckel, "The 'Spirit' and the 'Word,'" 201; Tengström, *ThWAT* 7:397–98; cf. Otto Kaiser, *Isaiah 13–39* (trans. R. A. Wilson; OTL; London: SCM, 1974), 285: "In a few intense words Isaiah states that the plan has not come from Yahweh, and the treaty is neither in accordance with his will nor derives from him."

174.   Neve, *Spirit of God*, 54.

175.   Isa 40:13; see ibid., 98.

The fourth way of understanding רוח is to see it as the "prophetic spirit."[176] This view interprets v. 2a as expanding further on v. 1b. Thus not asking for Yahweh's counsel, "an ancient technical term for seeking an oracle from Yahweh" now in the form of "an utterance by a prophet,"[177] explains "not by my spirit." Implicit is the assumption that the spirit inspires the prophet's message. Not to ask for Yahweh's counsel from his prophet is not to go with what the spirit says (v. 1b). While this would be a unique usage in First Isaiah, its chief virtue, as Ma points out, is that it makes good sense in the context, for the passage speaks of the "conflict between the prophet and the court politicians."[178] The wider context of 30:9–10 and 31:1 also supports this conclusion, where the issue is acting without reference to a prophet or consulting Yahweh. The criticism of Volz that it is unlike Isaiah to put himself in the middle as a kind of mediator, because elsewhere all the people need to do is look to the Holy One of Israel (e.g. 5:12; 31:1), is invalid.[179] Indeed, the "consulting" (דרש) of Yahweh that is found in 31:1 is elsewhere seen to be through the agency of a prophet (e.g. 1 Kgs 22; 2 Kgs 1:3; Ezek 14:10). If Isaiah is referring to the "prophetic spirit" here, then what is pictured is a "word-communicating" inspiration. The spirit is not merely the one who equips Isaiah to speak, but is responsible for the message that Isaiah gives.

Both the third and the fourth views have much to commend them. It is difficult to be certain, but it would be unwise to dismiss the possibility that Isaiah is here speaking about the "prophetic spirit," either on dogmatic grounds (not least because both usages are unique), or because it is "impossible exegesis,"[180] which it is not.

2.2.2. *Summary and conclusions.* First, though Jer 18:18 makes it clear that the people expected a prophet to bring a "word" from Yahweh, it is also clear that people in general linked prophecy to the divine רוח (Hos 9:7). This common perception was not restricted to a particular group. Such a linkage involved a belief that the prophets behaved in strange ways, which bore at least some resemblance to madness (משגע, Hos 9:7; Jer 29:26–27). Although this was a popular opinion, and in its context

---

176.   Van Imschoot, "L'action de l'esprit de Jahvé," 568, 571–72; Jacob, *Theology*, 126; Ma, *Until the Spirit Comes*, 49; John N. Oswalt, *The Book of Isaiah Chapters 1–39* (NICOT; Grand Rapids: Eerdmans, 1986), 545.
177.   Kaiser, *Isaiah 13–39*, 285.
178.   Ma, *Until the Spirit Comes*, 49.
179.   Volz, *Der Geist Gottes*, 66.
180.   Mowinckel, "The 'Spirit' and the 'Word,'" 201.

both references are derogatory words in the mouth of opponents, there is evidence that the classical prophets were not as "rational" as Mowinckel maintains. Neither Jeremiah nor Hosea distanced themselves from such comments.[181] Indeed, I have shown above how such abuse cannot be dismissed as pure hyperbole, since Hosea willingly, if implicitly, identified himself as a prophet, and ascribed a significant function to such prophets (9:8). Further evidence of the "unusual" behaviour of the classical prophets comes from the involvement of the "hand of Yahweh" in their experience (e.g. Isa 8:11; Jer 15:17; cf. Jer 20:7).[182] These instances of the prophets being caricatured as "mad" and of the influence of the "hand of Yahweh" put the classical prophets nearer to the pre-classical ones than is often recognized.

Secondly, Volz, Mowinckel and Couturier are not correct to say that the pre-exilic writing prophets repudiated the inspiration of רוח.[183] There is not a single text supporting such a view. While they were antithetical to false prophets, they were not antithetical to the רוח that the false prophets claimed for themselves. Hosea (Hos 9:7), implicitly, and both Micah (Mic 3:8) and Isaiah (Isa 30:1), explicitly, make clear that they regard the divine רוח as having a place within their inspiration as prophets. This ought not be surprising, in view of some of the similarities we have observed between the classical prophets and prophets in general. This also means that the *historical* view on the absence of רוח in prophecy is, like the *antithetical* view, mistaken. It was not the case that "the spirit…ceased to operate."[184]

Thirdly, it is true to say that רוח is relatively absent from the pre-exilic writing prophets. In view of what we have just said, the relative absence of the prophets attributing their ministry to the divine רוח cannot be explained by recourse to a radical disjunction between the "rational" classical prophets and the "ecstatic *nebhi'im*." Further, it is not likely that such reticence was due to the influence of רוח within "false prophecy," if what is meant by this is that the "true prophets" did not want to be associated with the רוח found in false prophets. Micah assaults directly

---

181.   It is not likely that they were called "mad" simply because of their advice, since that overplays the distinction between mental states and external behaviour. "Madness" was clearly visible in 1 Sam 21:15–16 and 2 Kgs 9:11. It should be noted, however, that manifestations of either "trance" or "possession" could vary. See Hildebrandt, *Spirit of God*, 160. For the distinction between "trance" ("ecstasy") and "possession," see Wilson, *Prophecy and Society*, 34.

182.   A. S. van der Woude, "יָד *yād* hand," *TLOT* 2:502.

183.   Volz, *Der Geist Gottes*, 62–69; Mowinckel, "The 'Spirit' and the 'Word' "; Couturier, "L'Esprit de Yahweh."

184.   As von Rad (*Old Testament Theology*, 2:57) maintains.

the prophetic inspiration claimed by those with whom he does not agree, but in so doing he does not renounce the divine רוח for himself. Two points come to the fore. First, mention of רוח may well have entailed connotations more usually associated with false prophets, connotations that the classical prophets tried to avoid. Secondly, appeals to the influence of רוח did not foreclose any dispute about the truth of the prophecy, nor did they *a priori* authenticate a prophet's ministry. While earlier it may have been true that physical manifestations were regarded as proof of divine endorsement, clearly such a perspective did not last, not least because it was not a reliable indicator of the truth (cf. 1 Kgs 22). Asserting the fact of inspiration by means of particular external behaviours gave way to speaking the inspired message. Since such appeals would not have furthered any claims to authenticity, the relative silence with regard to רוח in the prophet's ministry is due to the prophet's desire to emphasize another side of his task, "that it was the decision of Yahweh he was preaching. So the word had to come into the foreground."[185] In other words, the relative silence is a *rhetorical* strategy.

Fourthly, the view of inspiration that obtains in the prophets cannot be characterized by evolutionary development. There is some evidence that early within classical prophecy, רוח is linked to the communication of the words of the prophet (Isa 30:1) and therefore, to what we have termed "word-communicating" inspiration. There is also, as we have seen, pre-exilic evidence of "potentiating" inspiration, whereby the spirit is seen as the one which "rouses the prophet to act, to speak, and endows him with the ability to harangue and poetize" and "prepares" the prophet "to receive the divine word—to see visions, to hear the divine voice in dreams or ecstatic slumber"[186] (Hos 9:7; Mic 3:8). It is erroneous to say that "only the post-exilic period understood prophecy as the obvious work of the divine spirit."[187]

Fifthly, the influence of רוח on the classical prophets is not restricted to either the "prophetic" or the "rhetorical" event. The reference in Hos 9:7 does not make it clear precisely at which point the inspiration of רוח is to be seen. Micah 3:8 links the operation of רוח more closely to the proclamation of his message than to its reception. Isaiah 30:1, on the other hand, traces the source of Isaiah's message to Yahweh's רוח. There is not a particular point in the life of Yahweh's word where Yahweh's רוח is more evident.

---

185.   Kapelrud, "The Spirit and the Word," 46.
186.   Kaufmann, *Religion of Israel*, 99.
187.   Albertz and Westermann, *TLOT* 3:1215.

3. *Inspiration After the Exile*

The final place we shall look for the Old Testament's understanding of prophetic inspiration and the role of רוח within that is the post-exilic literature. This will be illustrative rather than exhaustive, since my aim is to assess the book of Ezekiel's place within the general trend, rather than to give an account of every instance.[188] Here, too, in the post-exilic literature, both "potentiating" and "word-communicating" inspiration are evident.

3.1. *"Potentiating" Inspiration After the Exile*

3.1.1. *Chronicles.* In this post-exilic, post-Ezekielian work, there are a number of instances of the spirit being linked to the utterance of people which recall earlier terms. Thus, in 1 Chr 12:19 (ET 12:18), the spirit "put on" (לבשה) the soldier Amasai before he uttered a pronouncement of loyalty to David.[189] The same verb is used in 2 Chr 24:20, alerting readers to the significance of the priest Zechariah's words as he upbraids the people for their disobedience and explains Yahweh's absence on these grounds.[190] In 2 Chr 15:1 and 20:14, the spirit "came upon" (היתה עליו) Azariah and the Levite Jahaziel, who then go on to speak.[191] In these latter two references, such speaking is explicitly linked to prophecy. In 15:8, the words of Azariah, addressed to Asa, all Judah and Benjamin are described as "prophecy" (הנבואה). In these words, Azariah reminds them of how Yahweh is with those who are with him, and abandons those who abandon him. This, in turn, gives rise to a call for them, fresh from victory over the Ethiopians, to take courage (v. 7). In ch. 20, Jahaziel addresses Jehoshaphat, all Judah and the inhabitants of Jerusalem, and urges them not to be afraid of the Ammonites and Moabites, for the battle is Yahweh's, not theirs (v. 15). Jehoshaphat responds the next day by urging the people on, telling them to believe in Yahweh their God and to "believe his prophets" (האמינו בנביאיו, v. 20). Four points in particular are important.[192]

188. Other instances of רוח (possibly) linked with prophecy which most scholars associate with the exilic and post-exilic period, and which I shall not be discussing, are Num 11:26–29; Isa 42:1–4; 48:16; 59:21; 61:1–3; Joel 3 (ET 2:28–32); Zech 13:2–6. For those in Isaiah, see especially Ma, *Until the Spirit Comes*.

189. Cf. Judg 6:34, and Gideon.

190. So H. G. M. Williamson, *1 and 2 Chronicles* (NCB; London: Marshall, Morgan & Scott, 1982), 108, commenting on 1 Chr 12:18.

191. Cf. Num 24:2; Judg 3:10; 11:29; 1 Sam 19:20, 23.

192. For further discussion, see especially Schniedewind, *Word of God in Transition*; idem, "Prophets and Prophecy in the Book of Chronicles," in *The Chronicler*

First, the theological use of רוח in Chronicles is limited to revelation (1 Chr 28:12,[193] where King David learns of the dimensions of the new temple by means of רוח[194]) or authorization of someone's words.[195] At the same time, רוח plays a part not found in Samuel or Kings.[196] The incident reported in 1 Chr 12:19 in which רוח clothes Amasai, chief of the thirty, before he utters words declaring his allegiance to David is not present in 1 Sam 30. The same picture is found with the incidents in 2 Chr 15:1, 20:14 and 24:20, absent from 1 Kgs 15, 22 and 2 Kgs 12, respectively.

Secondly, רוח-inspiration is not linked with those spoken of by the Chronicler as prophets, using one of the prophetic role labels.[197] This is reinforced by the fact that the verbs used to describe the action of רוח are found in the equipping not of the pre-exilic prophets, but of the judges.[198]

---

as Historian (ed. M. Patrick Graham, Kenneth G. Hoglund and Steven L. McKenzie; JSOTSup 238; Sheffield: Sheffield Academic Press, 1997), 204–24.

193.   1 Chr 28:12: ‏ותבנית כל אשר היה ברוח עמו‎.

194.   See Schniedewind, *Word of God in Transition*, 202–3, for רוח as "spirit" rather than "mind."

195.   1 Chr 12:19 (ET 12:18); 2 Chr 15:1; 20:14; 24:20. The four references in 2 Chr 18:20–23 are taken over from 1 Kgs 22; they also speak of revelation.

196.   See Sklba, "'Until the Spirit from on High,'" 16.

197.   Schniedewind, *Word of God in Transition*, 70. In a different work ("Prophets and Prophecy," 217–18), Schniedewind sees in these "possession formulas" (i.e. those that speak of the action of רוח) a conscious and clear distinction being maintained between the classical prophets, for whom רוח plays no part, and "inspired messengers." The inspired messengers utter "a different type of prophecy" directed not to the king, but to the people as a whole; the function too is different: "they do not explain how God acts [this is what the prophets do] but exhort the people, telling them how they should act" (p. 221). In other words, there is for him "both a *distinction* between prophecy in pre-exilic and post-exilic periods and a *continuity* in the prophetic voice" (pp. 207–8). The apparent exception to this, where the Levite Jahaziel seems to be spoken of by Jehoshaphat as one of the "prophets" (2 Chr 20:20), Schniedewind explains differently. He argues persuasively that Jehoshaphat's appeal in v. 20 to "believe in his prophets" (‏בנביאיו‎) is in fact an appeal to believe in what God had said *in the past* through the prophets. There are two main pieces of evidence. First, Jahaziel's exhortation is closely dependent on older (prophetic) texts (e.g. Exod 14:13–14; Isa 7:9b). Secondly, Jehoshaphat urges for trust "in his prophets" in the plural when only Jahaziel has spoken. See ibid., 115–18, 182–84.

198.   Schniedewind (*Word of God in Transition*, 72–73, 116) follows Mowinckel closely in his discussion of רוח-inspiration. We have seen, however, that silence does not mean they thought "possession by the spirit as something undesirable" (Mowinckel, "The 'Spirit' and the 'Word,'" 200; cited in Schniedewind, *Word of God in Transition*, 116). Schniedewind does not address the question of why Neh 9:30 and Zech 7:12 link רוח to pre-exilic prophecy.

The prophetic voice continues to be heard through different channels as a word of encouragement or exhortation chiefly to the people.[199]

Thirdly, רוח can relate both to the prophetic event (1 Chr 28:12) and to the rhetorical event (e.g. 1 Chr 12:19).

Fourthly, references to the work of רוח in inspiration serve to draw attention to what follows, and appear to give divine accreditation to what follows, but at no point in the linking of רוח with the rhetorical event is it said explicitly that the רוח has inspired the words, as opposed to the person who has uttered the words. The picture that is gained from these references to רוח cannot conclusively be said to be "word-communicating" inspiration.[200] Certainly, though, "potentiating" inspiration is in view. The closest to "word-communicating" inspiration that Chronicles gets is in 1 Chr 28:12, where רוח does seem to be the medium by which David has received the temple plans. It is to clear instances of "word-communicating" inspiration we now turn.

3.2. *"Word-communicating" Inspiration After the Exile*
3.2.1. *Nehemiah 9:30*.

> Many years you were patient with them, and warned them by your spirit
> through your prophets (בְּרוּחֲךָ בְּיַד־נְבִיאֶיךָ)…

As Ezra looks back at entry into the land, and life in the land (vv. 22–31), he catalogues again Yahweh's mercy and patience. One manifestation of Yahweh's patience was his sending prophets to warn them. Many commentators do not mention the spirit's work in inspiration here, so evident is it.[201]

It is possible that בְּרוּחֲךָ does not refer to the origin of the warning, but refers to the "potentiating" inspiration of the prophet.[202] It was "through" in the sense of "with the help of" Yahweh's רוח that the prophets warned their ancestors. The alternative is that the warning that came to the people

---

199. Lys, *Rûach*, 185; Schniedewind, "Prophets and Prophecy," 221. For Schniedewind, the book of Chronicles as a whole functions rather like the words of spirit-inspired messengers. It is a word of *"exhortation"* rather than *"interpretation"* (ibid., 224 [my emphasis]; see also idem, *Word of God in Transition*, 231–52).

200. *Pace* Schoemaker, "Use of רוּחַ," 33; Dreytza, *Der theologische Gebrauch von RUAH*, 220.

201. F. Charles Fensham, *The Books of Ezra and Nehemiah* (NICOT; Grand Rapids: Eerdmans, 1982), 223–34; Carl F. Keil, *The Books of Ezra, Nehemiah, and Esther* (trans. S. Taylor; Edinburgh: T. & T. Clark, 1873), 245–47; Jacob M. Myers, *Ezra–Nehemiah* (AB 14; New York: Doubleday, 1965), 158–70; Mark A. Throntveit, *Ezra–Nehemiah* (Interpretation; Louisville, Ky.: John Knox, 1989), 92–111; H. G. M. Williamson, *Ezra, Nehemiah* (WBC 16; Waco, Tex.: Word, 1985), 300–19.

202. For different uses of בְּ, see *IBHS* §11.2.5.

was brought by double agency: it was both the spirit and the prophets who spoke.[203] The latter seems preferable in view of the close parallel with Zech 7:12, where the spirit's links with the words of Yahweh are made clear.[204] Further, the fact that the prophets, who are clearly an agent, are separated from the verb עוד (Hiphil) by "by your spirit," suggests another agent is in view (cf. 2 Kgs 17:13); accordingly, the second prepositional phrase functions epexegetically: "He warned them through his Spirit; the prophets have conveyed the words of the רוח."[205] Here, explicitly, is the "word-communicating" view of inspiration whereby it is the divine רוח who is seen as "speaking."[206]

3.2.2. *Zechariah 7:12*.

> They made their hearts adamant in order not to hear the law (התורה) and the words that Yahweh of hosts had sent by his spirit through the former prophets (ברוחו ביד הנביאים). Therefore great wrath came from Yahweh of hosts.

In its literary context, this verse forms part of Zechariah's answer to the question from the people of Bethel, brought by Sharezer and Regemmelech (7:2), though the answer is to "all the people of the land" (7:5). The material included here about their fathers' unwillingness to listen to what Yahweh has said (v. 12), and Yahweh's subsequent punishment

---

203.   So Dreytza, *Der theologische Gebrauch von RUAH*, 219; Block, "Empowered by the Spirit of God," 46.

204.   The parallel with Zech 7:12 is closer than that with Neh 9:20. In Neh 9:20, רוח is linked with the teaching of the law and the giving of the commandments. This is clear from the close parallels between vv. 12–15 and vv. 19–25. Within the section from v. 12 to v. 21, there are the themes of God's gracious provision (vv. 12–15), the people's ungrateful rebellion (vv. 16–18) and God's continuing mercy (vv. 19–21). Within this schema, v. 20a is parallel to vv. 13–14, just as v. 19 parallels v. 12, and v. 20b–21 parallels v. 15; vv. 22–25 parallel v. 15b (note the repetition of ירש). Thus "you gave your good spirit to instruct them" parallels Yahweh speaking to Moses and giving them "right ordinances and true laws, good statutes and commandments"; see Williamson, *Ezra, Nehemiah*, 313–14.

205.   Dreytza, *Der theologische Gebrauch von RUAH*, 219: "Er warnte sie durch seinen Geist; die Propheten haben die Worte der רוח übermittelt." So too Lys, *Rûach*, 197. Lys wonders whether "by the hand of the prophets" is in fact a gloss, serving to illuminate further the mode of the action of רוח. Consonant with his emphasis on the interior operation of רוח, he observes how the parallel to רוח is not now Yahweh's hand, but the *prophets'* hand.

206.   Cf. van Imschoot's comment (*Theology*, 175) that "the spirit appears as a permanent medium who by way of the prophets conveys Yahweh's orders to His people."

(v. 14), serves to justify Yahweh's anger which has lasted for seventy years (1:12; 7:5).[207] In v. 7, Zechariah refers to words proclaimed "by the hand of the former prophets" (ביד הנביאים הראשנים). In v. 12, the picture is expanded to include the law (התורה) as part of what they had rejected,[208] and to include רוח within the process of Yahweh's sending the words. The picture of inspiration here is very close to that of Neh 9:30. Here, most probably, is "word-communicating" inspiration. The prophets were "agents inspired by Yahweh's words to the people,"[209] or, as Carol and Eric Meyers put it, "the prophetic word is said to have been sent by Yahweh's spirit."[210] This perspective, though post-exilic in date, is based on the experience of Israel *in the past*, not in the present. The inspiration of the prophets by the divine רוח is not conceived of as a quality present in this verse. Zechariah, though identified as a prophet in the book (1:1, 7), nowhere has his ministry linked to Yahweh's spirit.

4. *Preliminary Conclusions*

The start of Part II raised three questions. The first was whether רוח is or can be understood as Yahweh's breath on which his word is carried. The second was whether Ezekiel recovers רוח as foundational in prophetic inspiration. Within this was the question of whether the classical prophets did indeed repudiate רוח in their own inspiration. The third was whether the emphasis on רוח within the prophet Ezekiel's ministry is best explained in terms of his attempts at self-authentication.

There are a number of conclusions that can be drawn from the discussion.

First, while there is a conceptual link between Yahweh's רוח as "breath" and Yahweh's word, that link is neither made nor exploited theologically in the book of Ezekiel. רוח as the "breath" of Yahweh's mouth is not linked with Yahweh's word. This, however, does not mean that there are not close links between Yahweh's word and Yahweh's רוח when speaking of the inspiration of Ezekiel (or other prophets). Such links relate to the prophetic event, in so far as Yahweh's רוח transports

207.   Edgar W. Conrad, *Zechariah* (Readings: A New Biblical Commentary; Sheffield: Sheffield Academic Press, 1999), 139–40.
208.   For the unique pairing of "Torah" and "words," see Carol L. Meyers and Eric M. Meyers, *Haggai, Zechariah 1–8* (AB 25B; New York: Doubleday, 1987), 402.
209.   David L. Petersen, *Haggai & Zechariah 1–8* (OTL; London: SCM, 1984), 293.
210.   Meyers and Meyers, *Haggai, Zechariah 1–8*, 403; so too Eichrodt, *Theology*, 2:64; Dreytza, *Der theologische Gebrauch von RUAH*, 219.

the prophet to the place where Yahweh speaks to him ("potentiating" inspiration), and gives him the vision that can be understood as Yahweh's "speech event" (11:24—"word-communicating" inspiration). These links are not simply related to the prophetic event, but are also linked to the rhetorical event, in so far as the רוח-constrained Ezekiel embodies the word that Yahweh has given him (cf. also Mic 3:8). Further, such links, while more usually conceived in terms close to that of Kaufmann's analysis of inspiration, also extend to a more direct form of inspiration, which we have termed "word-communicating" inspiration.

Secondly, although both "word-communicating" inspiration and "potentiating" inspiration as distinguishable categories are clearly evident in the Old Testament, there is not clear evidence of an interest in distinguishing between the two. Thus there are some indisputable instances of רוח speaking Yahweh's words (most notably 2 Sam 23:2; 1 Kgs 22; Neh 9:30; Zech 7:12), both *to* and *through* the prophet. There are other instances where Yahweh's רוח inspires the prophet, while the narrative makes it clear that such an inspiration is preparatory to, but does not entail the receiving of, Yahweh's word (e.g. Ezek 2:2; 3:24; 11:5). This does not mean that Yahweh's רוח cannot be conceived as responsible for "speaking" or "breathing" that word, but it does mean that at these points the authors did not articulate or demonstrate that conception. Further, there are a number of points at which the inspiration of Yahweh's רוח serves as a shorthand way of describing the entire process from the prophetic to the rhetorical event, and embraces both "potentiating" inspiration and "word-communicating" inspiration (e.g. Num 24:2). Here, too, while "word-communicating" inspiration is not explicitly articulated, it is also not expressly precluded.

Thirdly, the book of Ezekiel gives a greater prominence to the role of the divine רוח within the inspiration of the prophet than any of the other Old Testament books, both before and after the exile. It is an exaggeration, however, to say, as Montague does, that with Ezekiel, there is "an entirely new 'wind'...blowing."[211] The perspective that the book gives on inspiration, while having a different degree of *emphasis* on the work of רוח within prophecy, does not provide anything different in *kind* from what precedes the book of Ezekiel. While there is evidence of "word-communicating" inspiration—that of the spirit inspiring the prophet's words (11:24 [Ezekiel's visions]; 13:3; and Ezekiel's sign-acts), such a perspective was present before the exile (2 Sam 23:2; 1 Kgs 22; Isa 30:1). In the same way, while "potentiating" inspiration by רוח is clearly apparent in Ezekiel (רוח falling on him—11:5a; רוח entering him—2:2;

211. Montague, *Holy Spirit*, 45.

3:24), and transporting him (3:12, 14; 8:3; 11:1, 24; 37:1; 43:5), such inspiration can be seen not just in the pre-classical prophets, but also, though in a muted fashion, within the classical prophets (Hos 9:7; Mic 3:8; possibly in Jer 5:13). The view that Ezekiel revives רוּחַ-inspiration fails to recognize the relative infrequency of references to the divine רוּחַ in inspiration throughout the Old Testament, including the pre-classical times. Even in pre-classical times, prophetic activity could take place with no mention of the divine רוּחַ. It also fails to account for the presence of some (albeit a few) references within classical prophecy to the inspiration of the prophet by רוּחַ. Finally, it does not acknowledge that Ezekiel himself says nothing new or different with regard to inspiration.

Fourthly, the relative silence of the classical prophets concerning their own inspiration by רוּחַ should be understood *rhetorically*. We have seen that there is no text where they repudiated רוּחַ, so the *antithetical* view is clearly wrong. We have also seen that there are some instances where they do claim רוּחַ-inspiration, so the *historical* view, where רוּחַ stopped operating, is also wrong. Finally, we have also seen that a *theological* interpretation that appeals to the prophets' theocentricity for the silence, fails to account for the prominence of רוּחַ in the radically theocentric Ezekiel. This *rhetorically* motivated silence came from the claims to רוּחַ among false prophets. Appeals to רוּחַ would not have foreclosed questions of authenticity and would have potentially risked association with the false prophets and their claims.

5. *The Authentication of Ezekiel?*

We have seen that the book of Ezekiel does not portray something fundamentally new or different about inspiration, so it is not possible to explain the book's emphasis by saying that the book's author was doing something new in this area. The theological perspective before the book of Ezekiel does not give in essence a very different picture, nor, indeed, does what follows. In the post-exilic writings there can still be found both "word-communicating" and "potentiating" inspiration. Such a view is not merely retrospective. If Zechariah and Nehemiah seem to look on spirit-inspiration as something that is past, Chronicles looks on it as something that is present, by prefacing exhortations to the people with ancient רוּחַ-possession formulae, reapplied to the (non-prophetic) speakers of these exhortations.

The explanation most commonly suggested for the prominence of רוּחַ-language concerning Ezekiel's inspiration is that it serves to authenticate the prophet, aligning him with the pre-classical prophets. We need to distinguish between two versions of this explanation. The first version is not simply that the *book* authenticates the prophet by means of רוּחַ-language, but that the *prophet* himself did so.[212]

There are a number of arguments that can be, or have been, put forward in its favour.

First, there are many links with pre-classical prophecy within the book of Ezekiel, such as Ezekiel setting his face towards the subject of his prophecy,[213] translocation by רוּחַ (cf. 2 Kgs 2:16), the action of the hand of Yahweh (cf. 1 Kgs 18:46; 2 Kgs 3:15), and a prophet being consulted by the elders.[214] These are "all found in the autobiographical narrative."[215]

Secondly, the fact that there is some adaptation in Ezekiel's use points against their merely being "literary conventions or devices." An example of adaptation is that in the book of Kings, the hand of Yahweh transports Elijah (1 Kgs 18:46); in Ezekiel, it is רוּחַ that transports him. The hand of Yahweh is associated particularly with the reception of Ezekiel's visions.[216]

Thirdly, it is sociologically plausible. Porter proposes that one way a society recognizes a "divinely possessed person" is to look at the characteristics of a person recognized as such in the past, and to compare those with the person in the present. It would be expected that a person claiming to be in a particular tradition will adopt something of the stereotypical behaviour expected.[217]

Fourthly, the fact that the classical prophets were not *antithetical* towards רוּחַ-inspiration makes it more plausible.

Finally, the action of רוּחַ can serve to authenticate people (cf. 1 Sam 10; Num 11). It is also true, more significantly, that רוּחַ within the authentication of prophetic ministry is found in Isa 42:1–4 and 61:1–3.[218]

---

212. See especially Carley, *Ezekiel Among the Prophets*, 69–73; also Sklba, "'Until the Spirit from on High,'" 14.

213. Cf. Balaam in Num 22–24 and Elisha (2 Kgs 8:11).

214. Cf. 2 Kgs 6:32, paralleled by the scenes in Ezek 8; 14; 20. Other examples include the word-event formula and the prophetic proof-saying, "you shall know that I am Yahweh" (cf. 1 Kgs 20:13, 28). See Walther Zimmerli, "The Word of Divine Self-Manifestation (Proof-Saying): A Prophetic Genre," in *I Am Yahweh* (ed. W. Brueggemann; trans. D. W. Stott; Atlanta: John Knox, 1982), 99–110.

215. Carley, *Ezekiel Among the Prophets*, 70.

216. Ibid.

217. See J. R. Porter, "The Origins of Prophecy in Israel," in *Israel's Prophetic Tradition: Essays in Honour of Peter R. Ackroyd* (ed. Richard Coggins, Anthony Phillips and Michael Knibb; Cambridge: Cambridge University Press, 1982), 12–31 (24).

218. For a detailed discussion of these passages and the place of רוּחַ, see Ma, *Until the Spirit Comes*, 88–96, 120–25. He notes the prophetic dimension to the

Although, however, in a sense I have made it harder to argue against such a view by supporting a continuum in רוח-inspiration from the pre-classical prophets through to Ezekiel, there is a critical difficulty with such an explanation. In view of the relative silence on prophetic inspiration and its links with רוח in the classical prophets, it is hard to see why appeals to the divine רוח, in particular, should be seen to authenticate Ezekiel's ministry, when such appeals had not been used for at least one hundred years before Ezekiel prophesied by the prophets to whom Ezekiel was in other respects closest, precisely for rhetorical reasons: because they did *not* serve to distinguish the true prophet from the false one, and did *not* authenticate a prophet. This is not to say that Ezekiel did not speak of רוח in his own ministry, but it is to question whether he did so merely or chiefly to authenticate his own ministry.

The second version of the "authentication" explanation of Ezekiel's רוח-inspiration relates it more explicitly to the *book* of Ezekiel. Collins remarks that "the image of Ezekiel...has a certain contrived artificiality about it... Ezekiel is robed in the mantle of Elijah and Elisha, and this seems to be done expressly in order to make the point that 'a prophet has been among them' (Ezek. 33.33)."[219]

This version is supported by many of the arguments noted above, and, in addition, is further supported by the fact that, once Jerusalem had in fact fallen, there was *prima facie* evidence that Ezekiel was indeed, after all, a prophet.[220] This analysis provides an explanation for appeals to רוח for authentication found elsewhere (e.g. Isa 42:1–5; 61:1–3). These make sense only because Ezekiel has served to reinstate talk of רוח within inspiration *having already been* demonstrated to be a true prophet by the fall of Jerusalem. In that sense, it is surely right to see, in the רוח-inspiration of Ezekiel in the book, a dimension of authentication of the prophet.

This, however, should not be thought to be an exhaustive explanation. First, the book argues that the people will recognize Ezekiel as a prophet not so much through external credentials, but through the chief criterion of discerning a true prophet (Deut 18:21–22): the unfolding of history

---

figure at the centre of both passages, while also rightly acknowledging that the figure does not *only* fit there.

219.   Collins, *The Mantle of Elijah*, 100–101; in similar vein, Wilson (*Prophecy and Society*, 285) suggests that Ezekiel was a peripheral figure in the exilic community, and that, in addition to a number of other ways of trying to establish his authority, "the role of the spirit in the book may also reflect attempts to enhance Ezekiel's authority."

220.   Cf. Katheryn Pfisterer Darr, "The Book of Ezekiel: Introduction, Commentary and Reflections," *NIB* 6:1087–88.

according to Ezekiel's words (2:5; 12:21–28). While there is some sar-
casm or "pretended religion" on the part of the exiles in urging one
another to "come and hear what the word is that comes from Yahweh"
(33:30), it is hard to avoid the picture that the evidence already lay before
them that Ezekiel was, in fact, a prophet. After news of the fall of Jerusalem had come, what the exiles (and the addressees of the book) needed
was not further authentication (though that, in turn, would happen "when
it comes" (ובבאה, 33:33),[221] but rather for *themselves* to *act* upon what
Yahweh was saying through his servant, and treat a prophet as a prophet,
rather than as an entertainer (cf. 33:30–33). The book of Ezekiel presents
to its addressees the exiles' failure to do that.

Secondly, *any* claim to Yahweh's involvement within a prophet's call,
or within the prophetic or rhetorical events, can be seen at one level as a
means of giving authority to the prophet when there is no objective proof
that they are indeed Yahweh's agent. These claims of involvement,
however, are hardly *merely* means of authentication within a prophetic
book. For example, the word-event formula could simply be a claim to
authenticity: "Yahweh has spoken to me." Within the book, however, it
also functions to structure the book, to portray the prophet not simply as
a speaker but as a hearer of Yahweh's words, and to confront the readers/
hearers of the book with the same words that confronted the prophet's
addressees.

Thirdly, the use of רוח within the prophet's own ministry should not
be isolated from other occurrences of רוח. Some of the occurrences, such
as those in 2:2 and 3:24 where רוח enters the prophet, have no parallel
with the pre-classical prophets, but function within the book as whole.
Even occurrences speaking of the transportation of the prophet acquire
significance when placed in the book of Ezekiel.

In other words, although the language of רוח-inspiration of Ezekiel
does have an authenticating function within the book of Ezekiel, there is
more to it than that. As these three points intimate, the book of Ezekiel is
less concerned with authenticating the prophet than with the transformation of its readers. It is with this in mind that we must turn now to an
examination of a second area in which Yahweh's רוח is related to Yahweh's word—transformation.

---

221.   For the prophet, such words were reassuring. For his addressees, and for
the addressees of the book, there is an implicit threat, allied to a promise if they treat
his words as they ought to be treated. Cf. Allen, *Ezekiel 20–48*, 154; Greenberg,
Ezekiel 21–37, 692; Block, *Ezekiel 25–48*, 267.

Part III

WORD, SPIRIT AND TRANSFORMATION

[T]he prophets...were totally dedicated to the words of the covenant because they were "men of the spirit."

—George T. Montague[1]

---

1. George T. Montague, *Holy Spirit: Growth of a Biblical Tradition* (New York: Paulist Press, 1976), 60.

Chapter 5

RESPONDING TO YAHWEH'S WORD:
DISOBEDIENCE AND OBEDIENCE

The book of Ezekiel has been carefully crafted and structured. A preliminary study reveals a macrostructure consisting of oracles of judgment in
chs. 1–32 (oracles against Judah in chs. 1–24, OAN in chs. 25–32), and
promises of a new future in chs. 34–48, with the news of Jerusalem's fall
in ch. 33 as "the turning-point."[1] Within this schema, several scholars
have observed the notion of "reversal"—that the judgments announced
or experienced in the first part of the book are reversed in the third part.[2]
Three examples illustrate this. First, in connection with leadership,
Duguid has argued cogently that "there is a coherent and connected attitude taken toward…leadership groups throughout the book: those singled
out for the most reproach in Ezekiel's critique of the past are marginal-
ized in his plan for the future, while those who escape blame are assigned
positions of honour."[3] Secondly, moving from theme to motif, there is
the motif of Yahweh's glory. In judgment, Yahweh's glory leaves the

1. Renz, *Rhetorical Function*, 102; so too R. Rendtorff, "Ezekiel 20 and 36:16ff.
in the Framework of the Composition of the Book," in his *Canon and Theology:
Overtures to an Old Testament Theology* (trans. and ed. M. Kohl; Edinburgh: T. &
T. Clark, 1993), 191; Collins, *Mantle of Elijah*, 89; cf. Ernst R. Wendland, "'Can
These Bones Live Again?': A Rhetoric of the Gospel in Ezekiel 33–37, Part I,"
AUSS 39 (2001): 91.

2. E.g. Block, *Ezekiel 1–24*, 14–15; idem, *Ezekiel 25–48*, 271; Lawrence Boadt,
"The Function of the Salvation Oracles in Ezekiel 33 to 37," *Harvard Annual Review*
12 (1990): 13; Davis, *Swallowing the Scroll*, 119; Paul M. Joyce, "Ezekiel and
Individual Responsibility," in Lust, ed., *Ezekiel and His Book*, 115, 162–63; Mein,
Ezekiel and the Ethics of Exile, 220; Ernst R. Wendland, "'Can These Bones Live
Again?': A Rhetoric of the Gospel in Ezekiel 33–37, Part II," *AUSS* 39 (2001): 263.
For "reversal" in another prophetic book, Isaiah, see K. T. Aitken, "Hearing and
Seeing: Metamorphoses of a Motif in Isaiah 1–39," in *Among the Prophets: Lang-
uage, Image and Structure in the Prophetic Writings* (ed. P. R. Davies and D. J. A.
Clines; JSOTSup 144; Sheffield: JSOT Press, 1993), 12–41.

3. Iain M. Duguid, *Ezekiel and the Leaders of Israel* (VTSup 56; Leiden: Brill,
1994), 1.

temple, the journey of its departure portrayed in Ezekiel's vision of the abominations in the temple (9:3; 10:4, 18, 19; 11:22–23; cf. chs. 1–3). In the vision of restoration, Yahweh's glory returns to the new temple via the east gate by which it had left (43:2–4). Thirdly, moving from motif to word, there is Yahweh's attitude to being consulted. When elders come to Ezekiel in exile, before news of the fall has come, Yahweh instructs the prophet to declare that he will not be consulted (דרש) by them (20:3, 31; cf. 14:3). In the future, however, Yahweh will "let the house of Israel ask (דרש)" him "to do this for them: to increase their population like a flock" (36:37). Hals puts it succinctly when he says that "the major technique employed to formulate messages of hope in Ezekiel is to express them as the undoing of past evil situations."[4]

The notion of "reversal" is not restricted, however, to the nature of Yahweh's judgment and restoration. It is also evident in the house of Israel's response to Yahweh's word, whether the prophetic word of Ezekiel to his intended audience, or Yahweh's statutes and ordinances: disobedience and rejection will give way to obedience and trust. The house of Israel will be transformed.

This chapter will explore the disobedience to Yahweh's word exhibited by the house of Israel and how the book portrays the move from disobedience to obedience. I shall argue that these two encounters with Yahweh's word are re-presented to the addressees of the book of Ezekiel to illustrate the move that they need to make/be part of, if they are to participate in the envisaged restoration. In particular, I shall argue that the book of Ezekiel presents the prophet as a paradigm, or model, of the obedience they should exhibit.

In Chapter 6, I shall explore the role of רוח in the obedience of Ezekiel and of the exiles. I shall argue that, within Ezekiel's paradigmatic role, Yahweh's רוח is essential for his and for the exiles' obedience. Yahweh's רוח is intimately related, then, to his word, in so far as that רוח is essential for the right response to Yahweh's word. Yahweh's רוח is intimately linked with transformation.

1. *The Exiles' Disobedience*

1.1. *The Exiles' Disobedience to Yahweh's Word Through Ezekiel*
As we look first at the disobedience of Ezekiel's intended audience to Yahweh's word uttered through him, it is at once apparent that analysis is made more complex by the variety of rhetorical situations in the book. There are three different "levels."

---

4. Hals, *Ezekiel*, 288.

At the "top" level, there is the author of the book and his own address-ees. At no point in the book does the author step outside recounting his narrative to confront his own addressees directly. His addressees need to infer what they are to do from within the narrative itself.

At the second level is the prophet and his intended audience. Almost never in the book of Ezekiel is the prophet recorded as confronting directly the exilic addressees, his intended audience (the only instance is 24:20–27).

At the third level is Yahweh instructing and commanding the prophet. In analyzing the response that Yahweh called for, the response that the beginning of the book anticipates, and the response that the rest of the book portrays, it is almost exclusively the word of Yahweh addressed to the prophet (i.e. this "third" level of interaction) that must be examined, since everything is subsumed within this prophetic event. In other words, the book comprises many indirect speech acts, whose illocutionary force needs to be discerned.[5]

1.1.1. *Discerning the response called for.* If the disobedience of the exiles is to be demonstrated, what must be identified first is the book's portrayal of the response that the prophet demanded. There are three different ways in which the book illustrates this. Central here to my interpretation is the distinction between the *locutionary* act (what the prophet or author said) and the *illocutionary* act (what the prophet or author was *doing* in saying that). To put it more succinctly, the *form* of words is not necessarily a guide to the *force* of those words.[6]

1.1.1.1. *Oblique calls.* These require the exiles to do three things: to see how Yahweh has acted, or will act, towards a third party; to understand the reasons why Yahweh has acted, or will act, this way; and to see themselves as potentially, or actually, in the same situation.

For example, in ch. 16, the prophet is instructed to make known to the city of Jerusalem her abominations (v. 2). The prophet is then to recount the history of Jerusalem, with the depths to which she had plunged apparent in v. 48, where her behaviour is portrayed as worse even than Sodom.

5. See especially Chapter 2, above.
6. For recent treatments that focus on different dimensions of repentance, see Lapsley, *Can These Bones Live?*, 67–77, and Mein, *Ezekiel and the Ethics of Exile*, 202–13. Lapsley examines the subject with a view to discerning the underlying anthropological assumptions implicit in such language. For her, such language "indi-cates that the predominant view of the virtuous moral self informs this prophet's view of human nature as well" (p. 68). Mein discusses the *function* of calls to repentance and the *value* of repentance in the light of apparently unconditional promises of salvation.

Though the formal addressee is Jerusalem, these oracles have the exiles as their intended audience. Nonetheless, the exiles are not in view on the surface of the oracle. They need to see themselves in the history of Jerusalem (indeed, they were, of course, part of that history; they too were "the house of Israel," a phrase that "intentionally expresses the nation's family solidarity"[7]), and distance themselves from what Jerusalem had done. The oracle was not only "a vehement ploy to communicate the necessity of the fall of Jerusalem, dragging Judah down with it";[8] it also served to illustrate the kind of behaviour that Yahweh found unacceptable. By implication, continued acceptance of such behaviour merited the same judgment that Jerusalem was facing.

The oracle against Tyre in ch. 27 is another example of this. Tyre "symbolized supreme self-confidence and permanence,"[9] saying "I am perfect in beauty" (27:4); she was in the heart of the seas, laden with wares (27:4, 25). But in her pride, Tyre would end up in the "heart (depths) of the seas" (27:26, 27). As Miller comments, "the means of her pride becomes the means of her destruction."[10] The destruction of Tyre mirrored that of another city, Jerusalem, whom Yahweh had set in the "centre of the nations" (5:5) and who saw herself as "perfect in beauty" (Lam 2:15; cf. Ezek 16:14). The oracle against Tyre shows that Yahweh is against self-sufficiency, expressed in self-righteousness, wherever it may be found. The exiles had no grounds for pride, but they too needed to take heed of this call (cf. 18:2). A continued attitude of pride risked the same judgment that struck both Tyre and Jerusalem.

That such declarations by Yahweh of his judgment against a third party can function didactically, as a call for a particular kind of behaviour, is clear from ch. 14. In vv. 7–8a, Yahweh's announcement of judgment towards a third party—those who are marked by idolatry and iniquity and yet come to inquire of a prophet—occurs alongside the declaration that this party will be a "sign and a byword" (לאות ולמשלים). Further, it also occurs alongside an *explicit* call to repentance (v. 6).

1.1.1.2. *Indirect calls.* Secondly, within oracles addressed to others, there are occasions when the desired response is spelled out specifically, but in the third person. The prophet is not told to confront the exiles directly with these; nonetheless, the response demanded by the prophet is clear. We might call these *indirect calls*. So in 6:8–10, in the context of

---

7. Block, *Ezekiel 1–24*, 32.

8. Allen, *Ezekiel 1–19*, 247.

9. Joseph Blenkinsopp, *Ezekiel* (Interpretation; Louisville, Ky.: Westminster John Knox, 1990), 121.

10. Patrick D. Miller, *Sin and Judgment in the Prophets* (SBLMS 27; Chico, Calif.: Scholars Press, 1982), 72.

an oracle that Ezekiel is to utter to the mountains of Israel, Yahweh instructs the prophet to tell the mountains that he will spare some, who will "remember me among the nations where they are carried captive... then they will be loathsome in their own sight for the evils that they have committed, for all their abominations." The oracle serves to make the exiles aware that the response they should have in exile is one of self-loathing.[11]

A call that is more explicit still, though not to be addressed by the prophet to the exiles, can be found in 43:9–10 (cf. also 44:6). As Ezekiel is being shown the new temple, he hears someone speaking to him from the temple (43:6). The voice is Yahweh's, since it speaks of "my throne" (v. 7). The call is clear: though there is a promised future (vv. 7–8), there is something for the exiles to do in the present, "Now let them put away their idolatry and the corpses of their kings far from me" (v. 9). In v. 10, there is a second communication, where the prophet is told to describe the temple to the house of Israel. In the same breath as Ezekiel is to say to them, "let them measure the pattern," he is also to utter, "let them be ashamed of their iniquities." Allen comments appropriately, "If such wrong practices had resulted in exile...a prerequisite for return from exile was a change of heart that took seriously their shamefulness. Proclamation of Yahweh's new work of salvation was to stimulate a realization of how far the people stood from God and from his will."[12]

1.1.1.3. *Explicit calls*. The third way in which the call to the exiles can be seen is the presence of direct commands to the exiles which Ezekiel is instructed to utter. There are six such instances of what we might term *explicit calls*.

In ch. 14, in response to the elders coming to consult Ezekiel, he is to reply by addressing the exiles directly with a call to repentance: "Repent

---

11. The phrase אֲשֶׁר נִשְׁבַּרְתִּי in v. 9 is awkward. Lapsley (*Can These Bones Live?*, 140; cf. p. 129) emends to שָׁבַרְתִּי (presumably וְשָׁבַרְתִּי, since she refers to *BHS*) and treats the phrase temporally: "they will remember me...when I have broken their whoring heart." So also, tentatively, Zimmerli, *Ezekiel 1*, 180; he notes that the LXX "does not presuppose אשר." Textual evidence in favour of אֲשֶׁר שָׁבַרְתִּי includes Aquila, Symmachus, Theodotion, Targums and Vulgate; this then makes the exiles' self-loathing consequent on Yahweh's action. Greenberg (*Ezekiel 1–20*, 230) and Allen (*Ezekiel 1–19*, 82–83), however, prefer the MT, and translate similarly, with variations on "how stricken I was by..." The LXX (ὀμώμοκα) suggests a Vorlage נשבעתי, with consonants similar to the MT, including an initial נ. The main objection against Lapsley's reading, as Allen points out, is the notion of Yahweh breaking not just "their heart" but also "their eyes." I prefer to see here an expectation of what those carried off *ought* to do, without specifying whether it has required Yahweh's prior action.

12. Allen, *Ezekiel 20–48*, 257; cf. Davis, *Swallowing the Scroll*, 121–22.

and turn away from your idols; and turn away your faces from all your abominations" (v. 6).

In ch. 18, Ezekiel receives a word from Yahweh explaining how the destruction that is falling on Jerusalem is their own fault. The question of individual responsibility is not in view here; rather, the question is "Why is this inevitably communal, national crisis happening?"[13] At the end of the chapter, picking up promises made to the exiles in 11:14–21, there is an explicit call to repentance,

> Therefore I will judge you, O house of Israel, all of you according to your ways, says the Lord Yahweh. Repent and turn from all your transgressions; otherwise iniquity will be your ruin. Cast away from you all the transgressions that you have committed against me, and get yourselves a new heart and a new spirit! Why will you die, O house of Israel? (Ezek 18:30–31)[14]

The third instance can be found in 20:30, 39. After recounting in revisionist fashion the history of Israel in such a way as to focus at great length on the exodus, a situation parallel to those in exile, Ezekiel is to confront them. In v. 30, he is to ask them whether they will go the same way as their ancestors after "detestable things," and then in v. 39, he is to assail them with bitter irony, "Go serve your idols…if you will not listen to me."

The fourth instance occurs in 33:11. Ezekiel, as the watchman (33:1–9), is to respond to the exiles' despairing cry ("Our transgressions and our sins weigh upon us, and we waste away because of them; how then can we live?," 33:10) with an assurance of Yahweh's desire that none should perish, and a call to those in exile, "Turn back, turn back from your evil ways; for why will you die, O house of Israel?"

Fifthly, in 36:32, after spelling out Yahweh's plan to restore and cleanse them and the land for the sake of his name (vv. 24–31a), Ezekiel is to call on them, "Be ashamed and dismayed for your ways, O house of Israel."[15]

---

13. Joyce, *Divine Initiative*, 46.

14. Mein examines the calls to repentance in chs. 14 and 18 carefully, and argues persuasively that the narrowing of the focus of ethical demands to a more domestic and individual sphere reflects an exilic context. The strongest evidence comes from a comparison of the sin lists in ch. 18 and 22:6–13. See Mein, *Ezekiel and the Ethics of Exile*, 198–202. His approach is different from mine in two respects. First, he focuses on Ezekiel's message through historical rather than literary lenses. Secondly, and related to this, he identifies calls to respond on the basis of form alone.

15. Lapsley (*Can These Bones Live?*, 143) regards this call as wholly future, after the restoration, because "the pre-deliverance people are apparently unable to feel shame." The call for the exiles to do something that Yahweh will do for them,

The sixth and final instance of an explicit call within the book is in 45:9, where, in an "abrupt change from statistical legislation to accusation and appeal,"[16] Yahweh confronts the princes of Israel, and says to them, "Put away violence and oppression, and do what is just and right. Cease your evictions of my people." Although the call is directed towards princes (משיאי ישראל) in the restored community, it has a contemporary edge, given past failures (cf. 22:6).

1.1.1.4. *Summary*. The picture generated from these three kinds of call is a clear one. The exilic community, according to the book's portrayal of Ezekiel's preaching, is to be marked by self-loathing for the past, and repentance in the present from all that was causing/had caused Yahweh's judgment to fall on Jerusalem. They were to see themselves as no different. Only then could there be a hope for the future. In short, they were to accept Ezekiel's verdict, and look to his words for any hope.

Our concern, then, is with the *book's* portrayal of Ezekiel's message, in particular as it is re-presented to its exilic addressees. Thus it differs from the approach taken by Raitt, who focuses on Ezekiel's message itself. Concentrating on the judgment and salvation oracles from a form-critical perspective, Raitt discerns, as "one of the most basic hypotheses" in his book, a development in the preaching of Ezekiel (and of Jeremiah) from the preaching of repentance to inevitable annihilation to unconditional salvation. He argues that, because the salvation oracles lack qualifications and preconditions, the exiles' salvation did not depend on people's repentance, nor did it assume their moral capacity had improved. For him, their salvation was "*unconditional*."[17] Though it is possible to challenge Raitt's developmental hypothesis on its own terms,[18] our concern with

however, is also found in 18:31 (cf. 36:26). Greenberg, like Lapsley, points out that "restoration precedes contrition," but regards the call as a reflection of the fact that "the prophet cannot stifle his vocation to censure"; see Moshe Greenberg, "Salvation of the impenitent *ad Majorem Dei Gloriam*: Ezek 36:16–32," in *Transformations of the Inner Self in Ancient Religion* (ed. Jan Assmann and Guy G. Stroumsa; Studies in the History of Religions 83; Leiden: Brill, 1999), 267.

16. Block, *Ezekiel 25–48*, 655.

17. Thomas M. Raitt, *A Theology of Exile: Judgment/Deliverance in Jeremiah and Ezekiel* (Philadelphia: Fortress, 1977), 108 (original emphasis); cf. also Greenberg, *Ezekiel 21–37*, 691–92.

18. For example, oracles of judgment do not *necessarily* preclude the possibility of repentance. See Walter Houston, "What Did the Prophets Think They Were Doing? Speech Acts and Prophetic Discourse in the Old Testament," *Biblical Interpretation* 1 (1993): 167–88; Möller, "Words of (In-)evitable Certitude?"; idem, *A Prophet in Debate: The Rhetoric of Persuasion in the Book of Amos* (JSOTSup 372; London: Sheffield Academic Press, 2003), 141–44. Scholarly debate on the intention

the book as a whole, rather than with the prophet's message, brings a different perspective. Renz comments that "the call to repentance is addressed to the exiles and never revoked in the book."[19] Certainly the *book* does not hint that the call to repentance is something in the past.

1.1.2. The response anticipated, as set out at the beginning of the book. If that was the response that Ezekiel called for, what response to the word of Yahweh does the opening of the book anticipate?

The commissioning scene makes it very clear that there was an expectation from the outset of the prophet's ministry that the people to whom he was going to preach would not listen. There are a number of ways in which this is emphasized.

First, there is the repetition of the phrase, "whether they hear or refuse to hear" (2:5, 7; 3:11, 27). Although the stress here is on the task of Ezekiel delivering his message, whatever the response, there is a sense of foreboding that the latter, rather than the former, will be the case.

Secondly, there is the repeated emphasis on the prophet's addressees as a "rebellious house" (2:5, 6, 7, 8; 3:9, 26, 27). Here again, the recurring phrase anticipates an unwillingness to listen to the prophet, an unwillingness that has marked Israel's history from the beginning, and still does so.[20]

Thirdly, there are other references to the addressees which illustrate the anticipated rejection of the prophet and his message. They are described as "nations of rebels"[21] (2:3), as those "who have rebelled against me" (2:3), as those who are like their ancestors in "transgressing against me to this very day" (2:3), as "impudent and stubborn" (2:4), as ones who will oppose Ezekiel, possibly causing him to be afraid (2:6; cf. 3:25), as less willing to listen even than those of "obscure speech and difficult language" (3:6). In 3:7, the anticipated unresponsiveness to the word of the prophet is articulated most explicitly: "But the house of Israel will

of such oracles, particularly in the pre-exilic prophets, tends to polarise between those who regard them as chiefly concerned with bringing about repentance, and those who regard them as an attempt to persuade hearers to accept the inevitable acts of divine judgment. For a bibliography of exponents of both views, see Möller, *A Prophet in Debate*, 141–42.

19. Renz, *Rhetorical Function*, 112–13; cf. Matties, *Ezekiel 18*, 224: "The call for decision in chap. 18 is not nullified by other assertions of divine enablement."

20. So Zimmerli, *Ezekiel 1*, 132–33.

21. MT. Without the co-ordinating ו, the phrase clearly is in apposition to, and thus refers to, "the sons of Israel." For a discussion of the authenticity of אֶל־גּוֹיִם and whether גּוֹיִם or גּוֹי should be read, see Block, *Ezekiel 1–24*, 115; Allen, *Ezekiel 1–19*, 10.

not listen to you, for they are not willing to listen to me; because all the house of Israel have a hard forehead and a stubborn heart." This pessimistic tone is not negated by the assertion in 2:5 that "they shall know there has been a prophet among them" (cf. 33:33). This is not something positive for them, since the hardness of their hearts is complete. The tone is ominous, rather than encouraging in both contexts. Finally, the absence of the wicked repenting in the watchman paragraph in 3:16–21 points towards a negative response to Ezekiel's preaching.

The overall picture, then, is clear. The book portrays Ezekiel's exilic audience as unwilling to listen to him, even at the outset of his ministry.

1.1.3. *The actual response, as worked out through the book.* We have seen how the response that is anticipated in the context of Ezekiel's commissioning is one of rebelliousness and hard-heartedness. That anticipated response proves to be the actual one throughout the book's account of the prophet's ministry.[22]

Before news of the fall had reached the exiles, their rebelliousness is evident. In 12:2, Yahweh articulates to the prophet that he "is living in the midst of a rebellious house" (cf. v. 3); the exiles "have eyes to see but do not see" and "have ears to hear, but do not hear." Ezekiel has spoken, he has uttered the words Yahweh has instructed him to, but they are rebellious (12:25). They are sceptical of whether the prophet's words will be fulfilled (12:22); they are cynical over the delay between the prophet's words and their fulfilment (12:27). In 17:12, they are still spoken of as a "rebellious house"; in 18:2 and 18:25, they are blaming Yahweh, claiming that his actions are unfair, despite the portrait of Jerusalem as being utterly worthy of judgment. In 21:5 (ET 20:49), the same scepticism is evident again, when Ezekiel, in a rare address to Yahweh, confides with Yahweh how the exiles are responding. Instead of taking him seriously, the exiles speak of him as "a maker of allegories" (ממשל משלים). As Allen comments, "his protest is born of painful experience ('alas') of contemptuous dismissal of his oracles among his contemporaries."[23] In 24:3, just before the fall of Jerusalem, they are still rebellious. With great irony, Yahweh instructs Ezekiel to do just the thing for which they have ridiculed him, and "utter an allegory" (ומשל...משל). It is

---

22. Applegate has recently highlighted the importance of the recording of audience response within prophetic narratives; see John Applegate, "Narrative Patterns for the Communication of Commissioned Speech in the Prophets: A Three-Scene Model," in *Narrativity in Biblical and Related Texts* (ed. G. J. Brooke and J.-D. Kaestli; BETL 149; Leuven: Leuven University Press, 2000), 69–88.

23. Allen, *Ezekiel 20–48*, 25.

Yahweh himself, and not simply Ezekiel, who is the "maker of allegories." Their quarrel is thus not so much with Ezekiel, but with Yahweh.
For the addressees of the book, the scorn of 21:5 (ET 20:49) is exposed
for the folly that it is.

As the first half of the book draws to a close, for the only time in the
book a statement that the exiles make is recorded as part of the narrative
(24:19). This statement is unusual in another respect, too, for it is not
criticized.[24] Perhaps at last, with the fall of Jerusalem about to happen,
the exiles will get the message, and respond appropriately to the word of
Yahweh? After the tension-building oracles against the nations in chs.
25–32, there is a further hint that Ezekiel's words were in fact getting
through. In 33:10, the exiles have clearly come to the prophet with an
awareness of their failings: "Our transgressions and our sins weigh upon
us, and we waste away because of them; how then can we live?" Perhaps
the groaning and pining for their sins (24:23) that was to mark their
behaviour on hearing the news of the fall could already be discerned?

When news of the fall of Jerusalem reaches the prophet in 33:21–22,
however, the reality is very different. The exiles' response to this new
phase in the prophet's ministry is illustrated in 33:30–33. Since the
prophet has not uttered an oracle subsequent to news of the fall, these
verses are not put here because of chronological sequence, but serve to
illustrate the *continued* response of the exilic addressees of the prophet
after news of the fall arrived, and to orient the addressees of the book to
that response. Since Block disagrees and regards this unit as functioning
retrospectively, creating an "effective *inclusio* with his call and commission (2:1–3:15),"[25] we need to look more closely at these verses.

Though it is true that the notion of Ezekiel as a singer of "lust songs"
(עגבים, 33:32) is reminiscent of ch. 23,[26] rather than any of the oracles
that follow, there are three reasons why it is not likely that 33:30–33
speaks retrospectively of pre-fall oracles such as ch. 23, but prospec-
tively, of chs. 34–48. First, though the book portrays the elders coming
to consult Ezekiel before news of the fall of Jerusalem has come (8:1;
14:1; 20:1), the book also makes it clear that Ezekiel's pre-fall oracles
were *not* popular (3:9, 25; 21:5 [ET 20:49]); while earlier in the book, it
was not the people as a whole who came, here the situation is "much

---

24. For more on criticism of the people's speaking, see Kelvin G. Friebel,
Jeremiah's and Ezekiel's Sign-Acts (JSOTSup 283; Sheffield: Sheffield Academic
Press, 1999), 188.

25. Block, *Ezekiel 25–48*, 265.

26. The noun is used in 23:11; the cognate verb appears in 23:5, 7, 9, 12, 16, 20.
Neither occurs elsewhere in Ezekiel (other than 33:30–33).

more open."[27] Secondly, the eagerness of the people to listen points to the "soothing" as well as "demanding" nature of the message.[28] Thirdly, the literary position links this report with what follows, coming as it does *after* news of the fall has reached those in exile (vv. 21–22), and after the oracle in vv. 23–29 which presupposes the destruction of Jerusalem and indeed some regrouping in Judah after the "initial shock."[29] If this oracle were speaking of a situation pre-587, it is hard to say why it is here, or what has changed. It is more likely that people flocked to Ezekiel because of his vindicated reputation now that Jerusalem had fallen, and because of their own preoccupation (כי־עגבים בפיהם, 33:31).

Further, the lack of obedience (33:31) in the rest of the book demonstrates that these verses serve to illustrate the *continued* response of the prophet's exilic addressees. Such disobedience can be seen both in the presence of the continued call to "be ashamed" (36:32) and in the unresponsiveness to Yahweh's word that remains a trait of Ezekiel's exilic audience. Even to the end of the book itself, the addressees are still "the rebellious house" (44:6).

Thus, in the programmatic 33:30–33, the exiles have all the appearance of being interested in hearing what the prophet has to say. Not only do they apparently recognize it as "the word that comes from Yahweh" (v. 30), so ostensibly discerning that there has been a prophet among them (cf. 2:5), but their call to "Come and hear" echoes Ezekiel's own (cf. 6:3; 13:2; 16:35 et al.). They have all the appearance of Yahweh's covenant people ("my people," v. 31).[30] Appearances, though, can be deceptive. Yahweh tells Ezekiel that his popularity is superficial; for all the exiles' enthusiastic words and actions in coming to hear Ezekiel's words, they do not obey them; "the organs of obedience, their mouths and hearts, are otherwise occupied."[31] The prophet is an entertainer to them, not one whose words, being the words of Yahweh, should be obeyed (v. 32).

27. Zimmerli, *Ezekiel 2*, 201.

28. Greenberg, *Ezekiel 21–37*, 691. Greenberg sees that the element of demand envisaged in ch. 33 points to it being "the last gasp of Ezekiel's pre-fall theology" (p. 692). As we have seen, the book of Ezekiel retains that element of demand right to the end.

29. So Allen, *Ezekiel 20–48*, 151; Zimmerli, *Ezekiel 2*, 200–202.

30. So Greenberg, *Ezekiel 21–37*, 686, who regards it as "ironical: acting as though they were devoted to me." Block (*Ezekiel 25–48*, 264) sees its omission from LXX and Syriac as due to the awkwardness of its position as the delayed subject. Allen (*Ezekiel 20–48*, 150) emends the MT, thinking it is a "marginal gloss on עם 'people' earlier"; so too Cooke, *Ezekiel*, 369.

31. Greenberg, *Ezekiel 21–37*, 690.

The picture, then, of the exiles' response to the word of Yahweh throughout the book tallies exactly the expectation and the anticipated response that was seen in Ezekiel's commissioning. They remain a rebellious house, rejecting the ministry of the prophet as a prophet who needs to be obeyed, even after the news of the fall of Jerusalem has reached them and Ezekiel's earlier oracles have been proved right. The exilic audience of Ezekiel are portrayed as rebellious from first to last.

1.1.4. *The destiny of those not responding.* The book of Ezekiel not only portrays the anticipated response of Ezekiel's addressees and their response in reality, it also portrays the destiny of those who reject his message. Judgment is not simply inevitable (for Jerusalem), re-presented to the book's addressees as a past event; it is also a future event.

In 3:16–21, those who reject the watchman's message will die, for they are wicked (cf. 33:1–20). In 13:22, Yahweh gives the reason for his announcement of judgment on "the daughters of your people, who prophesy out of their own imagination" (13:17). Their guilt lies in part in that fact that they "have encouraged the wicked not to turn from their wicked way and save their lives." In 18:23, the same fate is envisaged for those who do not "turn from their ways and live." In that context, the judgment according to their ways, as envisaged in 18:30 (and in 33:20), holds out little hope for those who have not obeyed the word of Yahweh. In 20:33–38, Yahweh's response to the exiles, insofar as they continue in rebellion and idolatry, is spelled out. Yahweh will bring the exiles out in a new exodus, and will "enter into judgement" (vv. 35, 37) with them. There will be a sifting process, whereby some will not enter the land (v. 38), for they will have failed to meet the covenant obligations. "This announcement of a partial judgment was meant as a powerful warning to the exiles not to exclude themselves from restoration to the land."[32] In 34:17–22, Yahweh will "judge between sheep and sheep" as part of his purpose to save his flock (v. 22). The destiny of those in exile who fail to respond to Yahweh's message is little different from the death that is envisaged for Jerusalem (e.g. 5:2–4). The choice is between life and death for the exiles, depending on the response they make to the words of the prophet. To continue in disobedience and rejection is to experience the "death" that is already their state (18:23; 37:1–10).[33]

32. Allen, *Ezekiel 20–48*, 14.

33. For metaphorical "death," see Lloyd R. Bailey, *Biblical Perspectives on Death* (OBT 5; Philadelphia: Fortress, 1979), 39–41. See also Walther Zimmerli, "'Leben' und 'Tod' im Buche des Propheten Ezechiel," *TZ* 13 (1957): 494–508.

1.1.5. *Summary.* We have seen, then, how the book portrays Ezekiel's calls, whether oblique, indirect or explicit, as calls to repentance. Only then could there be a future. We have also seen how the book portrays his audience's response as one of disobedience, a response anticipated at the outset of the book, and proved to be just that in the rest of the book. Finally, we have seen how the book declares "death" to be both their present state, and the end for those who do not repent in the face of Ezekiel's calls. Such a grim portrayal is not restricted to the exiles' response to Yahweh's word spoken through the prophet. It is also apparent in their disobedient response to Yahweh's ordinances and statutes.

1.2. *The Exiles' Disobedience to Yahweh's Ordinances and Statutes*
The juxtaposition of three facts points clearly to the exiles' disobedience to Yahweh's word as expressed in Yahweh's ordinances and statutes, and their destiny of death if such disobedience persists. First, there is the portrayal of such disobedience to Yahweh's ordinances and statutes as the cause of the destruction of Jerusalem. Secondly, there is the solidarity, or common guilt, between those in Jerusalem and those in exile. Thirdly, the prophetic calls to repentance point explicitly to the exiles' own disobedience.

1.2.1. *The disobedience that precipitated Yahweh's judgment.* As Klein notes, there are many words occurring in Ezekiel that spell out the problems that precipitated Yahweh's judgment: "abominations" (תועבות, 41×), "detestable things" (שקוצים, 8×), "idols" (גלולים, 36×), and "harlotries" (תזנותים, 19×).[34] These words described cultic and moral sins, though such a distinction should not be pressed too far, nor should Ezekiel be thought apolitical. All of life was lived before Yahweh; the clearly political agenda of Ezekiel (e.g. chs. 16; 17; 19; 23) is framed in moral or cultic terms.[35]

Cultic sins included altars, incense and idolatry on the mountains (6:1–9), summarized in the poignant phrase in 6:9, where Yahweh says that he was "shattered" (נשברתי)[36] because of their "prostituting heart" (לבם הזונה). Further, ch. 8 catalogues four abominations: having an altar outside the temple itself, thus violating Deuteronomy's law of centraliza-

---

34. Ralph W. Klein, *Israel in Exile: A Theological Interpretation* (OBT; Philadelphia: Fortress, 1979), 77; cf. also John F. Kutsko, "Ezekiel's Anthropology and Its Ethical Implications," in Odell and Strong, eds., *The Book of Ezekiel*, 120–25.

35. For more on Ezekiel's political agenda, see Mein, *Ezekiel and the Ethics of Exile*, 76–136.

36. For a discussion of the MT reading, see n. 11 on p. 177 above.

tion; holding a secret rite in a dark room (8:7–13), which may be linked with cult of the dead or Osiris; women weeping for the Sumero-Babylonian vegetation deity Tammuz or Dumuzi (8:14–15); and 25 men worshipping the sun at the temple door. Chapters 16 and 23 portray the history of Israel as one loose woman (two in ch. 23), consorting, even cavorting with other nations and their gods. Other cultic sins included despising Yahweh's holy things and profaning his sabbaths (22:8) and child sacrifice (23:37, 39). Priests aided and abetted in this (22:26). Although the leaders are conspicuously excluded from involvement in cultic abuses, apart from 43:7–9, where the kings' condemnation is "parenthetical,"[37] Zedekiah is condemned for breaking his ברית with Nebuchadnezzar (17:12–21).[38] Because "this oath was sworn before Yahweh," he had not only broken his agreement with the Babylonians, "he had broken Yahweh's oath and covenant."[39]

Moral sins included failure to help the poor and needy in a way far worse even than Sodom (16:47–50; cf. 18:7–9; 22:7, 29),[40] sexual immorality (18:6), bloodshed (7:23; 9:9; 16:38; 18:10; 22:2–3), greed and extortion (22:12). Instead of speaking out against this, the prophets have "smeared whitewash" (22:28). Not one group is innocent. The kings are guilty of devouring the people (19:6–7;[41] cf. 34:1–9;[42] 45:8–9) and of bloodshed (22:6, 25[43]).[44] The עם הארץ are guilty, too, of extortion,

37. So Duguid, *Ezekiel and the Leaders*, 42.

38. Cf. also 21:30–32 (ET 21:25–27), where a curse oracle against Zedekiah spells out his fate, more than his sins, but his wickedness is highlighted in the address "vile, wicked prince of Israel" (חלל רשע נשיא ישראל).

39. Koch, *Prophets*, 2:95.

40. Cf. Blenkinsopp, *Ezekiel*, 79; Block, *Ezekiel 1–24*, 509.

41. Such language of "devouring" is not just normal behaviour within metaphor (*pace* Zimmerli, *Ezekiel 1*, 395, who comments, "the proud walking about among the lions, the lust for prey, and the destruction of cities and lands should not be interpreted historically and concretely of Jehoiachin's actions, but simply serve to elaborate pictorially his awesome royal majesty"), given the parallel in Ezek 22:25; rather, the phrasing exploits ambiguity in the metaphor here. See Hals, *Ezekiel*, 129; Duguid, *Ezekiel and the Leaders*, 35–36.

42. That this passage refers to kings, rather than to leaders in general, is likely both from the fact that other leaders are condemned in 34:17–21, and that the remedy for these wicked shepherds is one shepherd, Yahweh. See Duguid, *Ezekiel and the Leaders*, 39–40, 121–22.

43. Reading אשר משיאה with LXX, rather than MT's קשר נביאיה ("the band of the prophets"), for the prophets are indicted in v. 28. See Zimmerli, *Ezekiel 1*, 465.

44. Though Ezekiel can use נשיאים of leaders in general (7:27; 32:29), it is likely that kings (Zedekiah and his predecessors) are in view here because of parallels with 19:1, 6–7. See Duguid, *Ezekiel and the Leaders*, 38.

robbery, oppression and bloodshed (22:12, 29), and none would "stand in the breach" to oppose it (22:29–30). Ezekiel was not simply concerned with private morals, but with social justice.

In short, they had not "walked" (הלך) in Yahweh's "statutes" (חקות/חקים) and had not "done" (עשה) or "kept" (שמר) his "just ordinances" (משפטים). Indeed, they had "rebelled" (מאס) against them, and thus had broken the covenant.[45] By observing these, they would have lived (18:17, 19, 21; 20:11). The ultimate indictment against Jerusalem is expressed in ch. 5. In rebelling against Yahweh's "statutes and ordinances," Jerusalem had become "more wicked than the nations and countries all around her" (5:5–6). The outcome of such a rejection of Yahweh's statutes and ordinances, indeed the direct result, was Yahweh's judgment, as seen in the destruction of Jerusalem.[46]

1.2.2. *The solidarity of the exiles with those in Jerusalem.* This judgment on those in Jerusalem could have led the exiles to a sense of moral superiority. Throughout the book, however, there is no hint that the exiles are somehow a righteous remnant, preserved by Yahweh. Instead, their guilty solidarity with those in Jerusalem is portrayed starkly.

First, they too share in the guilt of their ancestors. The phrase "the house of Israel" expresses that solidarity. Such solidarity between those in exile and previous generations is particularly evident in ch. 20. The chapter charts the failures not of Israel as one woman (ch. 16) or two (ch. 23), but of Israel, generation by generation, from the earliest days in Egypt (20:7) right up to the present generation in exile in Babylon (20:30–31). Throughout, Israel's history has been one of constant failure in every generation. Those in the wilderness rejected Yahweh's "ordinances and statutes" (20:13, 16). Their children were instructed to "walk" in the "statutes" and "keep" and "do" the ordinances (20:19), but they too rebelled against them (20:21). Such a failure had dogged them not merely to the events of 597 B.C.E., but beyond—the exiles, too, were guilty.[47]

<hr/>

45. Cf. Lev 26:3, where these same words occur (though מצותי, not משפטי) as the prelude to covenant blessings, and Lev 26:14–15, where they occur as the prelude to covenant curses.

46. The organic link between behaviour and judgment can be seen in 5:7–8, 11; 15:8; 16:43; 20:16, 24; 22:19; 23:30, 35; 34:21. This judgment is not simply mechanical, though. See Ka Leung Wong, *The Idea of Retribution in the Book of Ezekiel* (VTSup 87; Leiden: Brill, 2001).

47. Compare 20:23–26 with 20:30–31 and 23:37; cf. 2:3–4. Notice also the language of eating upon the mountains (18:6, 11, 15; 22:9); the solidarity is not to deny that there are some changes made in the scale of sin because of the move to exile,

Secondly, there is the clear denial of righteousness to those who escaped from the destruction of Jerusalem. Though they themselves were not the addressees of Ezekiel's oracles to be delivered before that destruction, the book allows them no scope for maintaining their innocence. Their survival and arrival in exile would serve not as a contradiction of the prophet's assertions that all would be destroyed,[48] but as a proof to those already in exile that Yahweh had been just in obliterating Jerusalem (14:22–23; cf. 11:16).[49]

Thirdly, in oracles of restoration, the restored house of Israel is to be marked by shame and self-loathing, clear pointers to their own guilt (16:59–63; 20:42–43; 36:31).[50]

In other words, everyone in exile, whether those who arrived in the deportation of 597 B.C.E., or after the fall of Jerusalem in 587 B.C.E., is as guilty as those who perished in Jerusalem.

1.2.3. *Explicit disobedience of the exiles.* The very existence of calls to repentance by the prophet reveals clearly the book's portrayal of the disobedience of the exiles to Yahweh's statutes and ordinances. Such disobedience entailed injustice, self-sufficiency expressed in self-righteousness, transgressions and, in particular, idolatry. Thus in 14:6, the exiles are to turn away from their idols, and to turn their faces away from all their abominations, and in ch. 20, the idolatry mentioned is explicitly not that of their ancestors, but the exiles' own, for it is emphasized by the dramatic "to this day" (עד־היום, v. 31).[51]

---

but "there is still a great deal of common ground between the two"; see Mein, *Ezekiel and the Ethics of Exile*, 191–94, 198 (quotation).

48. John W. Wevers, *Ezekiel* (NCB; London: Nelson, 1969), 114.

49. Cf. Klein, *Ezekiel*, 103; Joyce, *Divine Initiative*, 74–75.

50. Cf. Margaret S. Odell, "The Inversion of Shame and Forgiveness in Ezekiel 16:59–63," *JSOT* 56 (1992): 101–12; Jacqueline E. Lapsley, "Shame and Self-Knowledge: The Positive Role of Shame in Ezekiel's View of the Moral Self," in Odell and Strong, eds., *The Book of Ezekiel*, 143–73; idem, *Can These Bones Live?*, 141–45.

51. Cf. Peter R. Ackroyd, *Exile and Restoration* (OTL; London: SCM, 1968), 42; Block, *Ezekiel 1–24*, 646. Eichrodt (*Ezekiel*, 274–75), however, is convinced that these verses are out of place here, regarding the charge of idolatry as "strange and suspicious" (p. 275) and the mention of child sacrifice and idolatry as depriving Ezekiel's "proofs of all force" (p. 274). Zimmerli (*Ezekiel 1*, 412), too, thinks the mention of idolatry is "a piece of later exaggerated elaboration," and that the mention of child sacrifices has been added "clumsily" by a "still later hand." Others see it as a reference to child sacrifice going on in Jerusalem (e.g. Mein, *Ezekiel and the Ethics of Exile*, 118; George C. Heider, "A Further Turn on Ezekiel's Baroque Twist in Ezek 20:25–26," *JBL* 107 [1988]: 722). Although there is no knowledge of child

1.3. *Summary/Conclusions*

The book's portrait of the exiles' "current" response to Yahweh's word is universally negative, whether it is Yahweh's word as expressed in Ezekiel's word to them, or Yahweh's word as found in his statutes and ordinances. These two responses tend to merge into one another, since to listen and respond to Ezekiel's word *is* to turn away from idolatry and disobedience to Yahweh's ordinances and statutes. In the same way, the destinies for disobedience merge. We have seen how the destiny for not obeying Ezekiel's calls to repentance is death. The same is also true of those who persistently indulge in idolatry, as is evident both from the fate of Jerusalem and from Ezek 20:38, where Yahweh will purge out all the rebels as part of his initiative in restoration.

Such a negative perspective, however, is not the only response to Yahweh's word to be found in the book. The book envisages a time when the exilic community ("the house of Israel") will be marked by obedience, not by disobedience. Unsurprisingly, the response to both kinds of Yahweh's words merges into a unitary notion of obedience.

2. *The Portrayal of the Future Obedience of the Exiles*

2.1. *Renewed Cultic Obedience*

We can see renewed cultic obedience illustrated in the following three examples. First, in 11:17–21, restoration to the land (v. 17) will be accompanied by an internal renewal which will lead to obedience, including the removal of the land's שִׁקּוּצִים and תּוֹעֵבוֹת (vv. 18–20).

Secondly, in 20:40–44, the prophet is to assert how all the house of Israel will serve Yahweh in the land, on his holy mountain. When Yahweh has gathered them into the land, "there you shall remember your ways and all the deeds by which you have polluted yourselves; and you shall loathe yourselves for all the evils that you have committed" (v. 43).

---

sacrifices among the exilic community beyond this reference, such practices cannot be ruled out. In view of the connections with 20:23–26, however, it may be a misunderstanding of prophetic metaphor and rhetoric to take such actions necessarily as a reflection of exilic practices. The prophet here is expressing the *guilt* of the generation in exile, that they are no better than their ancestors. Ezekiel announces that their practices, whether literally involving child sacrifice or not, are no different in Yahweh's eyes. Cf. Greenberg's comment (*Ezekiel 1–20*, 253) on 14:1–11 that "The 'idols' in the people's thoughts and 'before their faces' must be a rubric for an unregenerate state of mind." For similar reflections about the "pedagogical and hortatory function" of the lists of sins in chs. 18 and 22, as opposed to their providing "specific evidence of the times," see Michael Fishbane, "Sin and Judgment in the Prophecies of Ezekiel," *Int* 38 (1984): 146–47.

The self-loathing which was to have marked them will one day be a mark of them.[52] They will renounce their idolatry (cf. 20:43) and be characterized instead by offerings that are acceptable to Yahweh (20:40).

Thirdly, this obedience is illustrated further in chs. 40–48. This vision, which functions as "a proleptic corroboration" of the promises found in 37:24b–28,[53] emphasizes the reversal of cultic failures of the past. Thus, for example, the priests who did not make the distinction between holy and common (22:26) will now teach of the differences (44:23); the idolatry of the temple seen in chs. 8–11 (see esp. 8:10) will be a thing of the past (43:9; 44:10, 12); the presence of uncircumcised aliens within the temple area will not happen again (44:6–8). Yahweh's presence is confirmed as permanent (43:7, 9; cf. 48:35), a permanence possible only through renewed obedience ensuring a renewed purity. Further, in view of the fact that the people were vomited out of the land because they had defiled the land through their disobedience (36:17; cf. Lev 18:24–30), other references that do not explicitly mention the obedience of the people to the word of Yahweh, but do speak of the people back in the land (such as chs. 38–39), presuppose the obedience of the people.

2.2. *Renewed Moral Obedience*

Moral sins, too, will be reversed. At the level of leadership, the wicked shepherds of 34:1–9 will be replaced by a new shepherd, Yahweh's servant (34:23–24), who will not oppress the people (45:8, 9; 46:18), but will reflect Yahweh as shepherd (cf. 34:11–16). Instead of devouring the people (19:6; 22:25), he will feed them (34:23); instead of letting them be scattered, becoming food for the animals (34:4–6), he will be their shepherd.[54] The resident alien, instead of being treated with contempt (22:7, 29), will have an inheritance (47:22–23). Instead of injustice for the people (8:17; 9:9), there will be honest scales (45:10–12) and equitable land distribution (46:18; 48). Instead of the weak being "butted" (34:21), they will no longer be ravaged (34:22). The picture of security,

52. Cf. Lapsley, *Can These Bones Live?*, 141–42; idem, "Shame and Self-Knowledge."

53. Moshe Greenberg, "The Design and Themes of Ezekiel's Program of Restoration," *Int* 38 (1984): 182.

54. Levenson (*Theology of the Program*, 86–87) comments that "in each case, the restoration of the relationship with Israel is presented as God's compensating for the defects of Israel's rulers, almost point-by-point. He does what they failed to do. The coming divine regime is a mirror image of the past human regime in which each standing failure is corrected." In similar fashion, Duguid (*Ezekiel and the Leaders*, 49) comments, "once again the promise of restoration represents a conscious repairing of the flaws of the past."

contentment and justice is reflected in the portrayal of the restored community before the onslaught of Gog and his hordes. Where the people of Judah had once been complacent in their "quietness" (שקט) (16:49), now they will be "quiet" (שקט) with no need for "walls," "bars" or "gates" (38:11). Since all have sufficient, there is no jealousy, violence, theft or external threat.

2.3. *Summary*

Both cultic and moral obedience will be renewed in the future, an obedience that is encapsulated in the contrast between the summary statement of the house of Israel's failure, and the summary statement of their future obedience. Corresponding to Israel's rebellion, seen in their failure to "walk" (הלך) in his "statutes" (חקים/חקות) and to "keep" (שמר) and "do" (עשה) his ordinances (משפטים), the restoration promised by Yahweh involves them doing *precisely* what Yahweh has called them to do: "I will cause you to follow my statutes and be careful to observe my ordinances" (36:27; cf. 11:20; 37:24). As Raitt puts it, "the same law *by which* the people were judged becomes the law *to which* they are saved."[55] Within the flow of the narrative, these instances occur with great prominence, overarching, interpreted by and evident in all that follows. The reference in 11:20 occurs within the first oracle to speak of hope for the future within the book; the trajectory of hope for the future for the readers of the book is defined by this initial occurrence. The reference in 36:27 receives its prominence from its proximity to the distinctively Ezekielian theme of Yahweh's רוח. The reference to renewed obedience in 37:24b serves as part of a "climactic summary of future blessing."[56] Its climactic nature is apparent from the shift in perspective at the start of ch. 38 to a projected scene where the future restoration is now a reality. Together, they embody the future obedience that will one day mark the house of Israel.

3. *The Purpose of the Dichotomy Between Disobedience and Obedience*

The response to the word of Yahweh is a mixed one in the book of Ezekiel. The exilic addressees/intended audience of the prophet are clearly envisaged as being, and remaining, disobedient and hard-hearted. Such disobedience relates both to Yahweh's word through the prophet, and to Yahweh's word through his ordinances and statutes. There is, however,

---

55. Raitt, *Theology of Exile*, 182 (original emphasis).
56. Greenberg, *Ezekiel 21–37*, 760.

an expectation that one day Yahweh will intervene to gather, restore and renew the people, such that they will obey him and remain for ever in the renewed and restored land. Unlike their ancestors and unlike Ezekiel's exilic addressees, those who are part of Yahweh's future will "walk" in the "statutes" and "keep" and "do" the ordinances (36:27). The function of this dichotomy, as portrayed in the book, and re-presented to the book's exilic addressees, is twofold.

First, it serves to demonstrate that neither Yahweh's word nor Yahweh's prophet were failures. It was not unexpected or surprising that Ezekiel's exilic addressees did not respond. Even at the outset of his ministry, rebelliousness was anticipated. The subsequent portrayal of unresponsiveness, a portrayal that the addressees of the book would presumably have known was only too accurate, is merely the outworking of what was anticipated in the commissioning, and a confirmation of Yahweh's word, not a refutation of it.

Secondly, the re-presented oracles serve to provide a profound call to the exilic addressees of the book, both negatively and positively. Negatively, the disobedience of the exiles functions in exactly the same way as Ezekiel's oracles of judgment against Jerusalem. Ezekiel's oracles of judgment against Jerusalem were to persuade his intended audience to sever their allegiance to Jerusalem.[57] In just the same way, the re-presentation of the disobedience of Ezekiel's intended audience serves to persuade the book's addressees to sever *their* links with the disobedient behaviour that characterized Ezekiel's audience.[58] In that sense, the prophet Ezekiel's audience is anti-paradigmatic. On the other hand, the positive anticipated response, not restricted to a particular point in time, serves to move the audience to take seriously the prophet's ministry, and the calls that he made. The exilic addressees of the book should not give up on the prophet's message because their predecessors (or, conceivably, they, when they were much younger) had not responded positively to his words. Instead they need to respond appropriately to the word of Yahweh in the book, since they are in precisely the same position as the prophet's exilic addressees, confronted with the same words (hence the emphasis on the prophetic event). Discerning the response requires an act of imagination, of interpretation, because there are no calls to repentance directed

57. Odell ("Genre and Persona," 201) interprets the proscription against mourning in ch. 24 in similar fashion: "the actions of Ezekiel and the exiles define their relationship to Jerusalem. They are to sever completely any remaining ties."

58. Renz (*Rhetorical Function*, 138) puts it succinctly, "For the book to function properly, the audience *of* the book (the readership) needs to distance itself from the audience *in* the book (the original audience of the prophet)" (original emphasis).

explicitly at them by the author of the book, and there is not a straightforward one-to-one mapping between locutionary and illocutionary act. At its heart, the required response is this: the exiles too must respond to the call of the prophet, as set out in the book, if they are to avoid being sifted out (20:33–39), if they are to live, and not die (18:31; 33:11).[59]

The book, however, does not simply present a negative example, of disobedience to Yahweh's word, and a future obedience which may well have seemed unreal in view of the failures of the prophet's addressees to respond. It also presents the prophet Ezekiel as a paradigm of the obedience to Yahweh's word that is required.[60] In the prophet, the future (obedience) has become a present reality. In the prophet's experience lies the bridge for the exiles between the present and the future.

4. *The Prophet as a Model of Obedience*

If the prophet Ezekiel is a model of obedience, we need to demonstrate conclusively the prophet's obedience. Secondly, we need to establish that the book of Ezekiel clearly portrays the prophet as a model or paradigm, since it is quite possible that the dichotomy between the exiles' disobedience and the prophet's obedience is a felicitous by-product of any book which charts a prophet's lonely call to a rebellious people.

4.1. *The Obedience of the Prophet*
In view of the fact that the prophet is seen much more as object than subject within the book, as evinced by the dominance of the word of Yahweh coming to Ezekiel, it might be expected that the obedience of the prophet be a minor theme. Within the commissioning of the prophet in chs. 1–3, in particular, and elsewhere in the book, however, the theme of the prophet's obedience is a significant one.

The portrayal of Ezekiel's obedience in the opening chapters is complicated by the fact that, as Habel observed,[61] in the typical prophetic call narrative there is also an objection to the commissioning by the prophet. Glazov has recently produced a thorough analysis of the call narratives

59. This helps explain the "characteristic" of the book noted by Block (*Ezekiel 1–24*, 580) that often the words of "the prophet's interlocutors" are heard. He lists 8:12; 9:9; 11:15; 12:22, 27; 18:2, 25; 20:32; 33:10; 37:11. To these may be added some examples he has missed and the words of others who form dialogical partners: 12:9; 24:19; 26:2; 27:3; 28:2, 9; 29:9b; 33:17, 20, 24; 35:10; 36:2, 20; 38:11. See further Applegate, "Narrative Patterns."
60. Cf. Davis, *Swallowing the Scroll*, 83–84; Renz, *Rhetorical Function*, 140–41.
61. Norman C. Habel, "The Form and Significance of the Call Narratives," *ZAW* 77 (1965): 298.

of Moses, Isaiah, Jeremiah and Ezekiel, and has refined the analysis of these objections.[62] He defines "a prophet as a divine messenger character-ized by two 'identifications': with Yhwh and with his people."[63] These in turn give rise to two kinds of objection to the prophetic call. What he terms the "first objection" arises from the "senses of personal inadequacy, guilt and fear of one's own identity before the *mysterium tremendum*."[64] In other words, it arises from the prophet's identification with Yahweh. It is evident, for example, in Isaiah's cry "Woe is me" (Isa 6:5). The second arises from the identification of the prophet with the people, and is par-ticularly associated with the call to proclaim Yahweh's words of doom and judgment. The prophetic resistance to the message he is to utter is apparent in either "intercessory objection" or "lament"[65] on behalf of the people. It is evident, for example, in Isaiah's question, "How long, O Lord?" (Isa 6:11).

Given the customary presence of an objection, it is striking that in the call of Ezekiel there is no objection of either kind vocalized by the prophet. Glazov suggests that the first kind of objection, based on pro-phetic inadequacy, might be found in Ezekiel falling on his face before "the appearance of the likeness of the glory of Yahweh" (Ezek 1:28).[66] For the second kind of objection, Glazov follows Zimmerli, Habel and others in finding it in the call to Ezekiel not to be rebellious but to open his mouth (2:8).[67] Certainly Ezekiel's struggle with the task he has been given is unmistakable in some of the occasions when his voice is heard addressing Yahweh (e.g. 9:8; 11:13).[68] The lack, however, of a voiced objection here does require an explanation. A plausible one is that, while there *may* be hints of reluctance, it is because Ezekiel's obedience is

62. Glazov, *Bridling of the Tongue*.
63. Ibid., 317.
64. Ibid., 317–18.
65. Ibid., 318.
66. Ibid., 266, 320; in contrast, see p. 233, where he says, "there is no time or room for any first objection." A sense of personal inadequacy can be seen, according to Habel ("Form and Significance," 313), in Yahweh's command to Ezekiel not to be afraid of his addressees (2:6; cf. 3:9) and in the words of reassurance. This kind of personal inadequacy is rather different from Glazov's, because it does not arise from the prophet's identification with Yahweh.
67. Habel, "Form and Significance," 313; Glazov, *Bridling of the Tongue*, 229, 320; Block, *Ezekiel 1–24*, 12, 123. Zimmerli (*Ezekiel 1*, 135) asks, "Can we see in this…a surreptitious side glance at the possibility of a personal resistance such as appears in Jer 1:6?" He answers his own question in the affirmative, because he can see no other reason for such a summons to obedience, particularly made so sharply. Allen (*Ezekiel 1–19*, 14), however, doubts whether an objection is present here.
68. Cf. Meier, *Speaking of Speaking*, 230–31.

highlighted in these chapters. Ezekiel is obedient while knowing fully the painful path that obedience would entail. His obedience confronts personal reluctance and prevails.[69]

At the end of ch. 1, the author recounts how Ezekiel was confronted by a vision of the glory of Yahweh himself (1:27–28). In response, Ezekiel fell on his face. Then he heard the voice of Yahweh speaking to him, instructing him to stand up, so that Yahweh could speak with him. As Yahweh spoke with him, רוח entered into Ezekiel and caused him to stand. He did as he was commanded.

In 2:8, Ezekiel is instructed not to be rebellious; he is to be different from the rebellious house he is to confront. Rebellion was a real possibility for the prophet, but Ezekiel was obedient.[70] Some commentators see in the narrative of the swallowing of the scroll a reluctance on the prophet's part. Block questions why the prophet needs to be told three times to eat the scroll, and asks why it is that Yahweh needs to feed the scroll to Ezekiel.[71] Greenberg sees the third command, "whatever you find there, eat!" as Yahweh insisting on "unqualified submission" and implying "hesitation" on the part of the prophet to carry out the command of 2:8b.[72] The narrative, however, functions to increase the tension. As Greenberg notes, when the prophet is told in 2:8b to "eat what I give you," there is expectation of food. Verses 9–10 do not serve to show the prophet's disobedience so much as to show the extraordinary, unenviable task that is before him. By allowing the addressees of the book to experience what he experienced, the possibility of disobedience is brought to the fore, but is decisively rejected. The command that Yahweh uttered is repeated in 3:1, in resumptive fashion, not because the prophet will not eat, but because the readers have now shared in his vision. This heightened tension, resulting in the prophet's obedience, can be seen in the correspondence between Yahweh's command to the prophet in 2:8, which is obeyed explicitly in 3:2–3. In 2:8, Yahweh told the prophet to open his mouth and eat the scroll. In 3:2, the prophet opens his mouth; then, in

---

69. Glazov (*Bridling of the Tongue*, 233) accounts for Ezekiel's silence by drawing analogies with Jeremiah and the forbidding of intercession. It still seems to be related to the prophet's obedience, but his reasoning is rather unclear.

70. For the idea of this command as a test of obedience, see Greenberg, *Ezekiel 1–20*, 73, 77–78, and especially Odell, "Inversion of Shame." This does not, however, exclude the notion that the scroll contains the message Ezekiel is to utter (*pace* Odell). See Chapter 2, above, and Glazov, *Bridling of the Tongue*, 228–38.

71. Block, *Ezekiel 1–24*, 12.

72. Greenberg, *Ezekiel 1–20*, 67. The phrase is missing from LXX. Eichrodt (*Ezekiel*, 60) and Zimmerli (*Ezekiel 1*, 92) regard it as a gloss, making connections with Jer 15:16. Greenberg ("Use of the Ancient Versions,", 138–40) defends the MT.

3:3, he eats it. Yahweh feeding the prophet (3:2), then, should be seen not as a sign of the deity's overcoming of the prophet's reluctance, but of the divine initiative at every stage in the process. Once the prophet has put the scroll in his mouth, it tastes as sweet as honey. Since the message itself was one of "lamentation, mourning and woe," the sweetness cannot be derived from the content of the divine words he has been told to utter. Further, in view of the prophet's reactions in vv. 14–15, it cannot be the sweetness of being commissioned *per se*. The sweetness must lie either in the mere fact that God's word is sweet to taste (cf. Ps 19:11), or, more probably, in the act of obedience, the sweetness of being addressed by Yahweh and of responding appropriately to the divine word.[73]

In 3:4–11, there are so many parallels with 2:3–7 that Block sees this "need for a second commissioning speech" as reflecting "Ezekiel's continued hesitation to accept Yahweh's prophetic charge."[74] This second commissioning speech should be interpreted differently. It is true that this unit corresponds closely to 2:3–7, but the concentric arrangement militates against seeing it as mere repetition: 3:10–11 mirrors 2:3–5, speaking of the charge to Ezekiel; 3:4–9 speaks of the encouragement to the prophet to carry out the charge, mirroring 2:6–7.[75] Further, within the encouragement sections, the three elements (the call not to fear, the reason introduced by כִּי, and the concluding instruction to speak) are "structurally inversely parallel to each other."[76] Such structuring highlights the obedient action of swallowing the scroll. In addition, throughout these opening scenes, the twin themes of anticipated opposition and the prophet's requirement to obey are both highlighted and steadily built up. The dichotomy between the anticipated response of the exiles, as envisioned in vv. 5–9, and the call to the prophet in vv. 10–11 is again emphasized. The paradigmatic response to the word of Yahweh is set out again. In 2:8, the prophet was to open his mouth and eat what Yahweh gave him—he was to fill his very self with the word of Yahweh (cf.

---

73. Cf. Joel Rosenberg, "Jeremiah and Ezekiel," in *The Literary Guide to the Bible* (ed. Robert Alter and Frank Kermode; London: Fontana, 1987), 197: "The taste of honey…signifies not a sensation of the prophet's tastebuds, still less his reaction to the inscribed woes—only a typically emblematic and allegorical affirmation of the objective 'sweetness' of that most precious commodity, obedience to divine imperative." Thomson comments (on the similar notion in Jer 15:16), "To eat God's Word is to make it one's own, by admitting it into the mind, by submitting to it and assimilating it"; see J. G. S. S. Thomson, *The Word of the Lord in Jeremiah* (London: Tyndale Press, 1959), 12.

74. Block, *Ezekiel 1–24*, 128.

75. Schwartz, "Concentric Structure," 111–13.

76. Ibid., 111.

Ps 40:9 [ET 40:8]). Here, he has to receive all the words Yahweh speaks to him in his heart, hear them with his ears, then go. Ezekiel's obedience to this commission, ולך בא אל־הגולה (3:11), is apparent in vv. 14–15: ואלך...ואבוא אל־הגולה.

It might seem that the theme of the prophet's obedience is falsified by his behaviour outlined in 3:14–15. After receiving his call, רוח lifted him up and bore him away. We are told that Ezekiel went "bitter in the heat of my spirit" (מר בחמת רוחי). Then, in v. 15, the prophet sits among the exiles, "stunned" (משמים), for seven days. Greenberg comments, "Perhaps the greatest inconsistency is that between the behavior of the prophet subsequent to his commissioning and the task he was called to perform."[77] This, however, is overstating the case.

With regard to the phrase מר בחמת רוחי, questions of interpretation revolve around three issues, though at points they interact. The first is the place and meaning of מר. Both Allen[78] and Zimmerli[79] see it as a later addition, in view of the fact that there is no corresponding word in either the LXX or the Syriac. While Zimmerli treats it as an explanatory gloss, Allen regards the meaning as having been changed by its addition. He notes the (semantic) relationship to "sweet" (v. 3), and conjectures that "bitter" was perhaps a marginal gloss on 2:8bβ, with the contrast between something that is naturally bitter, but turns out to be sweet; he also suggests there may be a "clever interplay" on "rebellious" (מרי); "bitter" became displaced by someone thinking "passion" (חמה) in v. 14 is really "anger."[80] This he sees as contrasting with the LXX's "in the 'vehemence' (= surging) of my spirit" (ἐν ὁρμῇ τοῦ πνεύματός μου).[81]

Attractive as Allen's suggestion is, it is not possible to be certain here. If מר is retained, there is still the issue of its meaning. Some scholars have related it to the Ugaritic *mrr*, "to strengthen, empower," rendering it "empowered" (cf. Judg 18:25),[82] but this link has been disputed.[83] In his commentary on Ezekiel, Block retains מר but changes his mind on the

---

77. Greenberg, *Ezekiel 1–20*, 79. He notes the close parallels with Jer 15:17.

78. Allen, *Ezekiel 1–19*, 13.

79. Zimmerli, *Ezekiel 1*, 94, 139.

80. As elsewhere in the book of Ezekiel, though according to Block (*Ezekiel 1–24*, 137), it is always used of divine anger, except in 23:25.

81. The noun ὁρμή occurs seven times in the LXX: Num 11:11, 17; Prov 3:25; 21:1; Jer 29:3; Ezek 3:14, 27:11. None have the meaning "anger." The closest instances are those in Num 11, where it means something like "burden" or "pressure," which rises up against Moses. The people are distressed. It is Yahweh who is angry.

82. E.g. Lys, *Rûach*, 136–37; Block, "Prophet of the Spirit," 44–45.

83. See Block, *Ezekiel 1–24*, 136 for bibliography.

meaning from his earlier article,[84] preferring the "normal meaning" ("bitter"): "Ezekiel is infuriated by the divine imposition on his life and the implications of Yahweh's commission for him."[85] מר, however, can also speak of "bitter," not in the sense of "resentful" towards someone, but in the sense of "bitterly distressed," in the sense of suffering a bitter blow (e.g. Ezek 27:31; Isa 33:7).

The second issue is the meaning of the word חמה. Elsewhere in the book of Ezekiel, חמה occurs thirty-two times. Always the meaning is "anger," "wrath," with every instance except 23:25 speaking of Yahweh's anger.[86] In 3:14, however, it is clearly Ezekiel's emotional state that is in view, so the other instances are not determinative. There are different possibilities here, other than "anger." We have already seen Allen's rendering, supported by the LXX, of "vehemence." Another related meaning is "heat,"[87] or "excitement," given the root יחם (וחם), "to be on heat," from which the noun is derived.[88]

The third issue is whether the emotion encapsulated in the phrase is Ezekiel's attitude to Yahweh in response to his commissioning,[89] Ezekiel's reflecting and embodying Yahweh's response to a rebellious people[90] or Ezekiel experiencing the effects that the message of the scroll will have on the people.[91]

If Allen's suggestion concerning מר is taken up, the phrase means something like, "I was passionately moved." If Allen's suggestion is not taken up, the bitterness should be associated not with the prophet's attitude to Yahweh, but with the bitterness of the word, now it is in his stomach. It was sweet to taste in his mouth, but now he is being carried

---

84. Block, "Prophet of the Spirit."

85. Block, *Ezekiel 1–24*, 137.

86. In 23:25, it is closely associated with Yahweh's jealous actions and speaks of the nations, Oholibah's lovers, acting against her "in fury."

87. So *HALOT*, 326.

88. See G. Sauer, "חֵמָה *hēmâ* excitement," *TLOT* 1:435–36.

89. Block, *Ezekiel 1–24*, 136–38; Douglas Stuart, *Ezekiel* (MOT; Dallas: Word, 1988), 45.

90. E. W. Hengstenberg, *The Prophecies of Ezekiel Elucidated* (trans. A. C. Murphy and J. G. Murphy; Edinburgh: T. & T. Clark, 1869), 37; Iain M. Duguid, *Ezekiel* (NIVAC; Grand Rapids: Zondervan, 1999), 70. Cf. Greenberg's comment (*Ezekiel 1–20*, 71) that, "It is not clear whether his bitterness (answering to the 'laments and moaning and woe' he must proclaim, as 27:31–32 show) and his rage are reflections of God's feelings toward Israel (cf. the thesis of Heschel, *The Prophets*, ch. 18), or his own distress over the dismal, thankless, and perhaps dangerous task imposed on him." He notes the similar ambiguity in the close parallel, Jer 15:17.

91. Glazov, *Bridling of the Tongue*, 236–38.

back to his peers, the bitterness of his task overwhelms him. He is bitterly distressed in the heat of his spirit. The prophet obeys, because it is Yahweh's word he is obeying. But what is entailed in that obedience may be a difficult task that causes pain and anguish. The sweetness lies in the fact of obedience, the bitterness and inner turmoil in what obedience entails. At no point is Ezekiel's *obedience* in doubt, for vv. 14–15 recount it: ‏ואלך...ואבוא אל־הגולה‏.

With regard to the word "stunned" (‏משמים‏), Block discusses the use of ‏שמם‏ at some length and notices some of the nuances: "silence, desolation, despair, distress, shock."[92] There have been four main interpretations of the word. The first is that it speaks of the disobedience of the prophet. His sitting for seven days was a reflection of his "resisting the call of God."[93] The second is that it speaks of the prophet being overwhelmed for seven days, in similar fashion to Ezra and Job (Ezra 9:4; Job 2:13), by the "initial shock and despair of the awesome judgment he had seen."[94] The third is that Ezekiel's sitting apart for seven days is part of his initiation ceremony into becoming a prophet, borrowing some of the imagery from the ordination of priests (cf. Lev 8:33).[95] The fourth is that Ezekiel is experiencing some of "the forthcoming overwhelming devastation of his people."[96]

There is no need to see, in ‏משמים‏, disobedience on the part of the prophet. Each of the other three interpretations has something to contribute. The sense of desolation comes from the task that he had to perform— he was one of the exiles, indeed he sat there "among them, desolate" for seven days. By the use of an oxymoron, the isolation of the prophet is brought to the fore, as is the distinction between the prophet and the people. Though he is among them, and is one of them, yet he is isolated from them. Indeed, it is precisely his obedience that isolates him. It is not his anger with Yahweh, nor his resistance that is in view here, but his isolation and devastation at the message of judgment. The "seven days" speaks not of his disobedience, sitting and doing nothing despite the charge, but of the separation of his consecration and preparation for the ministry lying ahead.

---

92. Block, *Ezekiel 1–24*, 138; see further Tyler F. Williams, "‏שמם‏," *NIDOTTE* 4:167–71.

93. Block, *Ezekiel 1–24*, 138.

94. Lamar E. Cooper, Sr., *Ezekiel* (NAC 17; Nashville, Tenn.: Broadman & Holman, 1994), 83.

95. Carl F. Keil, *Biblical Commentary on the Prophecies of Ezekiel* (trans. J. Martin; 2 vols.; Edinburgh: T. & T. Clark, 1876), 1:58; Odell, "You Are What You Eat," 236.

96. Duguid, *Ezekiel*, 70.

Commentators have discussed at great length the place of 3:16–21 within the narrative, and its relations to chs. 18 and 33.[97] Greenberg defends the authenticity and originality of its position here against Zimmerli, Cooke and Wevers. Block, while noting the awkwardness of these verses in terms of the change in language regards the unit as appropriate here. The "stern tone" and its "brutally direct warning" confirm, for Block, what he noted in 3:14–15—the stubbornness of the prophet.[98] While Block is right to emphasize the function of this passage in its context, there is an alternative view of its function here. Given the motif already established of the relationship between the prophet's obedience and the exiles' disobedience, this passage serves not only to anticipate the lack of repentance to Ezekiel's message, but also to demonstrate the *similarity of status* before Yahweh's word of both prophet and exiles. Failure to obey the word of Yahweh is a sentence of death for both prophet and people, though in different ways. The prophet, though given a specific and different task, is aligned with the exiles in terms of his situation. What matters is how he and they respond to that word of Yahweh.

In 3:22–27, Yahweh commands Ezekiel, "Rise up, go out into the valley, and there I will speak with you" (v. 22); the prophet responds, "So I rose up and went out into the valley…" What Yahweh had commanded, the prophet did. Though the power of Yahweh, as represented by the divine hand, has constrained the prophet, nonetheless, the prophet here is not just acted upon, he is subject too ("So *I* rose up and went out into the valley," v. 22). Unlike in 37:1, where the hand of Yahweh is upon him and the רוח of Yahweh brings him, here the prophet acts too. Here, again, the prophet's obedience is evident.

Later in the book, there are a number of other examples of the prophet's obedience. Within the vision in chs. 8–11, he is told to lift his eyes (8:5), which he does; he is told to dig through the wall that he has been shown (8:8), which he does; he is told to go in and see the vile abominations (8:9), which he does (8:10). In 12:1–6, the prophet is told to portray the exile, and so serve as a sign for the people. Ezekiel 12:7 recounts how "I did just as I was commanded." When instructed to act as a sign, the prophet is obedient. The same motif is found in ch. 24. There, the prophet is obedient, even to the point of not mourning in public for his wife (vv. 17–18), for "I did as I was commanded," an action that was to function as a "sign" for the exiles (v. 24). As Glazov comments,

97. See Allen, *Ezekiel 1–19*, 55–57; Block, *Ezekiel 1–24*, 140–43; Greenberg, *Ezekiel 1–20*, 87–97; Zimmerli, *Ezekiel 1*, 142–46.
98. Block, *Ezekiel 1–24*, 141.

The crucial point to grasp is that by retaining silence and suppressing lament, he shows compliance with, rather than resistance to, this stroke [מבפם, 24:16]: the destruction of the city and the exile, all that was in fact part and parcel of the message of doom to which he had to open his mouth at the start and retain quietly and obediently.[99]

In the vision in ch. 37, Ezekiel is commanded to prophesy to the bones (v. 4); in v. 5, he carries it out. In v. 9, he is commanded to prophesy to the breath. In v. 10, he relates how "I prophesied as he commanded me."

The picture generated throughout the book is clear: it is a picture of a prophet who suffers, who at points struggles with his call, yet who is obedient to the call of Yahweh. The costs personally and psychologically for him were immense (cf. 3:14–15; also, later, especially ch. 24)—yet these costs came *from*, rather than *despite*, his obedience. In view of these immense costs, we might expect reluctance in the prophet, but the text focuses not on his reluctance, but on his obedience: the prophet *did* heed the word of Yahweh.

These references are all the more remarkable when the paucity of narrative within the book is considered. Throughout the book, it is the word of Yahweh that is at the forefront. The prophet is rarely the subject of actions; instead, he is recipient of the divine word. This in itself is significant. The addressees of the book, the intended audience, *would have known* how the prophet had been obedient to the call that he had received. He *had* warned the exiles, he *had* uttered the words he was instructed to utter. That this is the case is clear from the fact that Yahweh speaks of the exiles' reactions to the words that he has uttered (e.g. 12:22, 27).

The exiles, then, are confronted both with the disobedience of Ezekiel's exilic audience, and with Ezekiel's own obedience. The book, however, does not simply present its addressees with the obedience of the prophet as an alternative way of responding to Yahweh's word. It also establishes him as a model of obedience for those addressees.

4.2. *The Establishment of the Prophet as a Model*
There are two main ways in which the narrative establishes the prophet as a model.[100] First, there are explicit instances where the prophet is described as such, in particular in the sign-acts. Secondly, the narrative as a whole points in that direction.

99. Glazov, *Bridling of the Tongue*, 273.

100. For the notion of Ezekiel as a "model" or "paradigm," see Sheldon H. Blank, "Prophet as Paradigm," in *Essays in Old Testament Ethics* (ed. James L. Crenshaw and John T. Willis; New York: Ktav, 1974), 123–24; Davis, *Swallowing the Scroll*, 83–84; Odell, "Genre and Persona," 208 (though she rightly points out that "Ezekiel is more than a moral exemplar"); Lapsley, *Can These Bones Live?*, 116–17.

4.2.1. *The prophet as a prescriptive sign (Ezekiel 24:15–27)*. In the book
of Ezekiel, the prophet is not just instructed to communicate by the
spoken word, he is also told to perform certain actions, or "sign-acts"
(sometimes designated by either אות or מופת). The precise role that
Ezekiel plays within the drama of these sign-acts varies.[101] In some,
Ezekiel's role is in no sense parallel with that of the people whom he is
addressing.[102] Other sign-acts within the book give a different picture.
They present the prophet as a paradigm for the house of Israel: what is
true of Ezekiel within the sign-act correlates closely with those whom the
sign-act depicts. Thus in Ezek 12:1–16, Ezekiel is to act out the process
of going into exile, for, Yahweh says, "I have made you a sign (מופת) for
the house of Israel" (v. 6). This self-understanding that the prophet is to
have is not merely a private one. He is to articulate it to the house of
Israel when they ask him (12:9–11).[103] In ch. 24, the prophet is again to
be seen as a sign. There, his lack of public mourning is to be interpreted
to the people as the prophet being a "sign" (מופת) to them (v. 24).[104] The
motif of the prophet and his actions being a sign, or paradigm, to "the
house of Israel" is an explicit one within the book of Ezekiel.

Understanding of Ezekiel as a "sign" or "paradigm" can be refined
further, though, since a paradigm can be either "descriptive" or "prescriptive."[105] Blank's focus on "prophet as paradigm," at least in his

---

101.   For the designation of these actions as signs, see especially Friebel, *Sign-
Acts*.

102.   There are four examples. First, in Ezek 4:1–3, the prophet is instructed by
Yahweh to portray the city of Jerusalem on a brick, which is then "besieged."
Yahweh explains to the prophet that this is a "sign" (אות) of what will happen to the
city of Jerusalem (v. 3); within the sign-act, the prophet represents Yahweh (and the
Babylonians), for he himself is to "lay siege" (v. 3) to the city (וצרת עליה). Secondly, in 5:1–4, he is to act as Yahweh, and the fate of the hair he has cut depicts the
fate of those in Jerusalem. Thirdly, in 21:23–29 (ET 21:18–23), Ezekiel is instructed
to portray the choice of two routes facing the king of Babylon, in order to make
more vivid the imminence of the destruction of Jerusalem. Fourthly, in the sign-act
of 37:15–28, the prophet is instructed to join together two sticks in order to symbol-
ize the reunification of the northern and southern kingdoms after the restoration.

103.   Note here that he is particularly a sign of what will happen to the "prince"
(vv. 12–13), though his experience will be the experience of the house of Israel in
general (vv. 10–11).

104.   See also 4:4–15; 5:1–4 (his hair); 12:17–20; 21:11–12, for other sign-acts
where the prophet's experience parallels that of the house of Israel.

105.   The distinction is not always made. Klein (*Ezekiel*, 37), for example, says
that "the exiles *are to* copy Ezekiel's stoic response" to his wife's death, yet just a
few lines later says of Ezekiel that "his actions at his wife's death *will* be echoed by
the exiles" (my emphasis).

discussion of the book of Ezekiel, deals exclusively with the prophet as a descriptive paradigm.[106] What is true of the prophet will be true, by analogy, of the people. While not wanting to minimize this dimension of Ezekiel as a "descriptive" paradigm, I want to contend that, with regard to the prophet's portrayed response to the word of Yahweh, Ezekiel functions as a prescriptive paradigm—his behaviour is a model that should be followed. It is not necessarily that what is true of the prophet *will* be true of the house of Israel, but that what is true of the prophet *ought* to be true of the house of Israel. That this is not a concept foreign to the book of Ezekiel is clear from the sign-act of Ezekiel's lack of mourning for the death of his wife,[107] though it may also be evident in Ezekiel's release from speechlessness.[108] In this sign-act, I shall argue that Ezekiel is portrayed as a prescriptive paradigm.

In 24:16–17, Yahweh announces that he will take away Ezekiel's wife in death, and he instructs Ezekiel, "yet you shall not mourn or weep, nor shall your tears run down." Instead, he is to "groan (but) be silent (when doing so)."[109] In addition, Yahweh charges him, "Bind on your turban, and put your sandals on your feet; do not cover your upper lip or eat the bread of mourners." In v. 18, although the timing is somewhat unclear, Ezekiel narrates how he did as he was instructed, and how his wife died.

106. Blank, "Prophet as Paradigm," 123–24.

107. For recent discussions in addition to commentaries, see Renz, *Rhetorical Function*, 148–55; Friebel, *Sign-Acts*, 329–51; Odell, "Genre and Persona."

108. Ezekiel's release from speechlessness is also described in terms of Ezekiel being a sign to the exiles (24:27). The motif of his "speechlessness" or "dumbness" (3:25–27; 24:25–27; 33:21–22) has been much debated. Its difficulty is evident from that fact that there is still nothing approaching scholarly consensus. See in particular the recent treatments by Friebel, *Sign-Acts*, 169–95; Renz, *Rhetorical Function*, 156–60; Glazov, *Bridling of the Tongue*, 238–74. See also Greenberg, "On Ezekiel's Dumbness"; Robert R. Wilson, "An Interpretation of Ezekiel's Dumbness," *VT* 22 (1972): 91–104; idem, "Prophecy in Crisis"; Greenberg, *Ezekiel 1–20*, 120–21; N. Tromp, "The Paradox of Ezekiel's Prophetic Mission: Towards a Semiotic Approach of Ezekiel 3,22–27," in Lust, ed., *Ezekiel and His Book*, 201–13; Allen, *Ezekiel 1–19*, 61–64. Conclusions depend on the answers to four questions: whether Ezekiel's dumbness is simply informative (i.e. tells the readers *about* the prophet's ministry, and a limitation on it) or also communicative (i.e. is part of the *message* of Ezekiel's ministry); whether Ezekiel's dumbness is literal or metaphorical; of whose behaviour Ezekiel is a "sign"; whether Ezekiel's release from speechlessness should be understood as a descriptive or prescriptive sign. Tentatively, I follow Friebel in seeing Ezekiel's speechlessness as a literal, divinely enabled but voluntary, communicative action giving a prescriptive paradigm of how his audience should respond. They should not talk back to Yahweh.

109. Friebel, *Sign-Acts*, 336.

In 24:19–27, for the only time in the book, the narrative that has centred around the word of Yahweh coming to the prophet changes perspective. Here, Ezekiel's addressees ask him the meaning of his actions which he has obediently carried out in response to Yahweh's command. Then the prophet actually addresses the exiles, recounting to them "the word of Yahweh" which he has received.

In this word, it is apparent that the prophet's behaviour with regard to the death of his wife is to be a "sign" (מוֹפֵת, v. 24) to the exiles concerning their response to news of the fall of Jerusalem. This parallel between Ezekiel and the exiles is reinforced in a number of ways. First, explicitly, there are the phrases "and you will/shall do just as I have done" (וַעֲשִׂיתֶם כַּאֲשֶׁר עָשִׂיתִי, v. 22) and "according to all that he has done you shall do" (כְּכֹל אֲשֶׁר־עָשָׂה תַעֲשׂוּ, v. 24). Secondly, there is the almost identical expression used to describe the one lost, whether Ezekiel's wife or Jerusalem: "delight of your (מַחְמַד עֵינֶיךָ)/their eyes (מַחְמַד עֵינֵיהֶם)." Thirdly, there are a number of identical verbs or phrases used to describe the reactions to the loss (e.g. עַל־שָׂפָם לֹא תַעְטוּ, v. 22 [cf. v. 17]; וְלֶחֶם אֲנָשִׁים לֹא תֹאכֵלוּ, v. 22 [cf. v. 17]), although the order is inverted.[110]

It has been debated whether Ezekiel is a sign in a descriptive or prescriptive sense. Since both predictive and instructional discourse tend to be marked by *w^{e}qatal*, and *yiqtol* often has a modal nuance when referring to the future, syntax alone is not determinative. Most commentators favour the descriptive sense: just as the prophet was struck dumb before the death of his wife, so too the exilic community would be struck with shock and would not mourn.[111]

There are potentially two main pieces of evidence in favour of the descriptive interpretation. First, the word מוֹפֵת only occurs four times in the book (12:6, 11; 24:24, 27). In ch. 12, Ezekiel clearly acts as a *descriptive* sign of what will happen to the "prince in Jerusalem and all the house of Israel in it" (12:10). In view of the different roles that Ezekiel plays in the different acts, however, this link is not conclusive. Secondly, in 33:10 the exiles seem to do exactly what Ezekiel has declared they will do, and there is no hint that such an action is an obedient one. In

---

110. These parallels make it clear that Ezekiel is not a sign representing Yahweh, a view that might otherwise seem possible because Ezekiel's wife mirrors Jerusalem. See Friebel, *Sign-Acts*, 339. The awkwardness of the order and the change in person has led some (e.g. Zimmerli, *Ezekiel 1*, 504; Wevers, *Ezekiel*, 192–93; cf. Eichrodt, *Ezekiel*, 345) to see vv. 22–23 as secondary. Both Block (*Ezekiel 1–24*, 787) and Allen (*Ezekiel 20–48*, 58), however, give good reasons to keep them.

111. E.g. Allen, *Ezekiel 20–48*, 61; Cooke, *Ezekiel*, 269–71; Eichrodt, *Ezekiel*, 344, 350; Wevers, *Ezekiel*, 194; Zimmerli, *Ezekiel 1*, 508.

24:23, Yahweh instructs Ezekiel to declare, "but you shall pine away in your iniquities" (ונמקתם בעונתיכם). In 33:10, Yahweh recounts what his addressees have been saying: "Our transgressions and our sins weigh upon us, and we pine away because of them" (כי פשעני וחטאתנו עלינו ובם אנחנו נמקים).[112] Such a correspondence does not, however, preclude a "prescriptive" understanding. Greenberg suggests the "disputational" form of the clause shows Yahweh's verdict, not on their *appropriate* reaction to their sins, but on their inappropriate despair.[113] In fact, it is possible to go further and question whether their reaction is in fact appropriate and obedient. The exiles' protest in 33:17, 20 that "the way of the Lord is not just" shows that they are still protesting their innocence; they have at best only superficially accepted responsibility.[114] In fact, most commentators do not marshal this evidence. Mostly, the decision that the sign is descriptive arises from the view that the exiles' grief at the destruction or loss of temple, sons and daughters will be so overwhelming that the exiles will be unable to carry out the usual mourning rituals. This explains Yahweh's declaration that they will not mourn (ספד) or weep (בכה).

There are three factors, however, which provide clear evidence either against the descriptive view or in favour of the prescriptive.

First, the notion that the grief would be so great that the exiles would be unable to perform the customary mourning rituals fails to deal with the fact that "rarely is grief so debilitating that no formal mourning customs are adhered to."[115]

Secondly, the descriptive view fails to distinguish between "grief," the emotional response, and "mourning," the public, social response.[116] This distinction is essential both in the command to Ezekiel, where public acts of mourning are prohibited while inward groaning is sanctioned

---

112. An almost identical phrase occurs in 4:17, where Yahweh declares that the inhabitants of Jerusalem will "waste away under their punishment" (ונמקו בעונם). See Renz, *Rhetorical Function*, 155, for the translation. Cf. Lev 26:39.

113. Greenberg, *Ezekiel 21–37*, 673.

114. Cf. Joyce, *Divine Initiative*, 144. He suggests that "פשעינו וחטאתינו" in v. 10 should be taken to refer not to (acknowledged) sins but rather to (undeserved) punishments (cf. Dan 8.12, 13; 9.24; Zech 14.19)." Mein criticizes this point (*Ezekiel and the Ethics of Exile*, 207), since it is hardly the most "natural reading." It is hard, however, to evade the force of the continued complaints of injustice in vv. 17 and 20.

115. Friebel, *Sign-Acts*, 340. Friebel identifies seven other variants within the descriptive (he terms it "predictive") view, and convincingly refutes each. See ibid., 340–42.

116. See Renz, *Rhetorical Function*, 153–55; Odell, "Genre and Persona," 198–202.

(הֵאָנֵק דֹּם, v. 17), and in the command to the exiles in v. 23, where mourning and weeping are proscribed (v. 23a), but pining away on account of their sins and groaning to one another is permitted (v. 23b).[117] Odell concludes after surveying the David narratives in Samuel, the deaths of Aaron's sons in Lev 10 and prophetic commands to mourn, "the act of mourning appears to have little to do with the expression of grief; rather, it is concerned with establishing and severing ties between the living and the dead. Prohibitions against mourning reflect an attempt to dissociate from the deceased."[118]

Thirdly, the context of the book as a whole makes it very difficult to see Ezekiel's lack of mourning as a descriptive sign: "the concern of the book of Ezekiel is not so much the emotional reaction of the exilic community to the fall of Jerusalem, but the manner in which the community identifies with Jerusalem."[119]

It is better, then, to see Ezekiel's behaviour as paradigmatic in a prescriptive sense. The exiles are to feel "joint responsibility" with those in Jerusalem for the fate of Jerusalem. Mourning as an expression of grief is wrong, because Yahweh was right to judge. Their groaning (v. 23b) was not to be a mark of sorrow, but of their culpability. Understood in this way, it provides "a contrast as to the focal point of the people's interests, shifting it from the tragedy of the judgment (the destruction of Jerusalem) to their own responsibility for their personal fate (their iniquities)."[120]

---

117. Renz (*Rhetorical Function*, 153–54) points out that the descriptive interpretation demands a "break" between v. 23a and v. 23b, since "you shall pine away in your iniquities and groan to one another" (v. 23b) is hardly compatible with shock and numbness, if they are both simply descriptions of what will happen (though Renz notes the dangers of arguing from psychological probability). As he points out, attempts to discern different layers within the text at this point to alleviate this difficulty appear "an attempt to save an interpretation even against the text" (p. 154).

118. Odell, "Genre and Persona," 201.

119. Renz, *Rhetorical Function*, 155. In similar vein, Boadt comments, "The prophet is forbidden to perform any sign of grief at the death of his wife. It is a very strong prophetic warning to the people. *They are not to mourn for the loss of Jerusalem because it deserved the punishment it received* (vv. 20–24)"; see Lawrence Boadt, "Ezekiel," in *The New Jerome Bible Commentary* (ed. R. E. Brown, J. A. Fitzmyer and R. E. Murphy; London: Chapman, 1989), 321 (my emphasis).

120. Friebel, *Sign-Acts*, 344. From a different perspective, that of Ezekiel "symbolically foreshadowing, but by the same token also bearing, the punishment of exile to be meted out to his people," Glazov (*Bridling of the Tongue*, 272–73) also sees Ezekiel's behaviour, as commanded in 24:17, as a prescriptive paradigm: "Here Ezekiel is told that he is to suffer the death of his wife, the 'delight of his eyes' without complaint as a sign to his fellow exiles that they ought to do as he has done when God takes away Jerusalem, the 'delight of their eyes.'"

This also fits in well with the theme of the release of Ezekiel from his speechlessness, which is also a "sign" (מופת) to them (24:27). There is a sense in which news of the destruction of Jerusalem signals a new era.

In summary, Ezekiel's lack of mourning, in particular,[121] presents "this living, breathing, radical-acting, flesh-and-blood prophet"[122] as a prescriptive sign of how the people "*should* respond to the circumstances, not predictive of how they *would* respond."[123] The prophet as a prescriptive paradigm of how the exiles should behave is not a concept alien to the book.

4.2.2. *The narrative's portrayal of the prophet as a model.* The conclusion that the prophet functions as a model is not based merely on the explicit instances of the prophet as a "sign." The narrative as a whole portrays the prophet as a model. This can be demonstrated by focusing on the ways in which the narrative identifies the prophet with the exiles —the similarities between the two—and on the ways in which the narrative distinguishes them in their response to the word of Yahweh—the distancing of the two.

4.2.2.1. *The similarities between Ezekiel and the exiles.* Though it is of course true that there are many experiences that are clearly unique to the prophet (such as the extraordinary visions), there are three main ways in which the prophet and the exiles are similar.

First, there are similarities as people. Though Ezekiel was to be a prophet "among them" (2:5), and sat desolate "among them" (3:15), he was not an alien among them. Twice in the book, Ezekiel is spoken of as a sentinel (3:16–21; 33:1–20). In 33:2, in the word of Yahweh that the prophet was to recount to the people, it is said in passing that the people selected the watchman. The people would "take one of their number as their sentinel (איש אחד מקציהם)." The word מקציהם here "connotes scanning the entire populace to pick the best man."[124] What is significant is that the sentinel comes from within, not from outside. Just as the people would take one from their own number as a sentinel to guard the city, so Yahweh had taken one from their number to warn the exiles. Ezekiel belonged to the exilic community. Closely paralleling this is Yahweh speaking of Ezekiel going to בני עמך ("the sons of your people,"

---

121. I suggested above that Ezekiel's release from speechlessness should also be understood in the same way. In addition, Friebel (*Sign-Acts*, 289–307) regards 21:11 (groaning) and 21:17 (crying out, striking the thigh) in a similar way.
122. Klein, *Ezekiel*, 37.
123. Friebel, *Sign-Acts*, 52 (original emphasis).
124. Greenberg, *Ezekiel 21–37*, 672.

3:11; also 13:17; 33:2, 12, 17, 30; 37:18). The force of the phrase can be seen in Lev 19:17–18, where it is juxtaposed with "your brother" (אָחִיךָ), "your relation" (עֲמִיתֶךָ) and "your neighbour" (רֵעֶךָ): the prophet is explicitly identified with the people whom he is addressing. The way in which Ezekiel is addressed also indicates the similarity between prophet and exiles as people. Throughout the book, he is never addressed as "Ezekiel," but always as "son of man" (בֶּן־אָדָם). The phrase occurs ninety-three times in the book of Ezekiel. Twenty-three times, the focus is further emphasized with "and you" (וְאַתָּה). Block argues that this phrase emphasizes his humanity rather than his mortality, his identifica- tion with his audience and the distance from the one who has commis- sioned him.[125] Though the gap between him and Yahweh is narrowed by Yahweh addressing him, the gap is re-established by the form of address.[126] Though the prophet may speak for Yahweh, he stands with the people.

The second similarity between the prophet and the exiles is in the similarities in their experiences. What I mean by this is not that Ezekiel was in exile, like those whom he was addressing, though this is obviously true. What I mean is that, within the context of the book, events that are true of the prophet are (or will be) seen to be true of the people too. We have already looked at one of the sign-acts that ought to be interpreted prescriptively. To this should be added other signs acts which are illus- trative of the experience of those in exile. For example, in 4:9–15, the diet that Ezekiel is to have, and the mode of cooking that he is to adopt, will parallel the experience of those in exile (v. 13).

The third similarity between Ezekiel and the exiles is the similarity in situation with regard to the word of Yahweh. There are two ways in which this similarity in relation to the word of Yahweh is evident. First, they both face the same fate for obedience and for disobedience. Though it is of course true in 3:16–21 and 33:1–20 that Yahweh's word to Ezek- iel as sentinel (i.e. "discharge this commission and warn") is different from his word to the exiles (i.e. "be warned, the enemy is coming"), their destiny based on their response is the same. For both, disobedience brings death, while obedience brings life. The second way in which the prophet and his addressees correspond in their relationship to Yahweh's word is

---

125.   Block, *Ezekiel 1–24*, 31; cf. Zimmerli, *Ezekiel 1*, 131; also Renz, *Rhetorical Function*, 140, who comments, "Ezekiel is the human representative, not only as distinct from God ('only human'), but also as the first of many who are to follow his receptiveness of the word (a 'proto-human')."

126.   Ehud Ben Zvi, Maxine Hancock and Richard Beinert, *Readings in Biblical Hebrew* (New Haven, Conn.: Yale University Press, 1993), 118.

one created by the narrative as a whole. Yahweh encountering the prophet both in word and vision dominates the book of Ezekiel. Of secondary importance is the prophet's uttering the words he has been told, and the reaction of the addressees. This stress on the prophet as recipient, not as speaker, as object, not as subject, causes the word of Yahweh (and Yahweh himself) to be the focus of the book. As Renz comments, "the prophet is cast in the role not of a mediator between Yahweh and his people, but of the first audience."[127] Thus "by portraying himself as a listener rather than an initiator of speech, Ezekiel…through representation of his own impressions and behavior…shows how hearers of God's word are to understand it and respond."[128] This is reinforced by instances where the "word" that comes to Ezekiel is clearly meant for a wider audience, without any hint that the prophet is meant to convey it (e.g. ch. 18, where Ezekiel is given no instruction to speak the words he is given). When the word of Yahweh comes to the prophet without instruction to speak, it is still in a public dialogical context. Finally, it is further reinforced by the prominence of the particle הִנֵּה, which moves the hearer from hearing to seeing, and to participating in what the prophet saw.[129]

In summary, the book portrays clearly the similarities between the prophet Ezekiel and his exilic addressees as people, in their experiences, and in the fact that they are both portrayed as recipients of Yahweh's word.

4.2.2.2. The distancing of Ezekiel and the exiles. The previous section showed how the narrative highlights similarities between the prophet and the exiles. If it is to be demonstrated that the book of Ezekiel portrays the prophet's response to the word of Yahweh, and not his addressees', as the model, the other necessary task is to show how the narrative clearly contrasts them with regard to their response to that word.

There are three motifs, all occurring within the commissioning of the prophet, that serve in particular to contrast the two responses. First, there is that of "rebelliousness." In 2:3–8, the house of Israel, Ezekiel's addressee, is clearly pictured as rebellious.[130] Yahweh, however, makes it very clear that the prophet is to respond differently to the word of

127. Renz, *Rhetorical Function*, 137.

128. Davis, *Swallowing the Scroll*, 83; cf. Block, *Ezekiel 1–24*, 112.

129. Cf. Meir Sternberg, *The Poetics of Biblical Narrative: Ideological Literature and the Drama of Reading* (Bloomington, Ind.: Indiana University Press, 1985), 255–56.

130. They are described as "rebellious" (מְרִי) in 2:5, 6, 7, 8 (cf. 3:9); the verb מרד is predicated of their ancestors, and clearly of the exiles too ("to this day") in 2:3.

Yahweh that comes to him: "But you, mortal, hear what I say to you; do not be rebellious (מרי) like that rebellious house…" (2:8). Here, "the prophet is warned not to let himself be infected by the Israelite disease— insubordination to the covenant Lord…"[131] The author of the book leads the addressees of the book to ask the question throughout the commissioning, and, indeed the rest of the book, "Is Ezekiel being like that rebellious house?"

Secondly, there is the motif of "hearing (with their ears)." This is closely related to the theme of rebelliousness, since rebellion consists in not listening to the word of Yahweh. In 2:8, the prophet is instructed, "Hear (שמע) what I say to you." Again, in 3:10, the prophet is told to "hear with your ears" (ובאזניך שמע) (cf. also 3:17). The prophet's response to the word of Yahweh was to "hear" the word that Yahweh spoke to him. The exiles' response was different. Already in the commissioning there has been an anticipation that the exiles will not hear (שמע), reflected in the repeated "whether they hear or refuse to hear" (2:5, 7; 3:11, 27; cf. 3:6, 7). In the narrative itself, as we have seen, they do not "hear." In 12:2, they, like the prophet, have ears to hear. Unlike the prophet, however, they do not hear. The same is true in 33:30–33. It is with irony that the narrative recounts their call to each other, "Come and hear what the word is that comes from Yahweh!" Again, their hearing is valueless, because it does not penetrate their hearts.

The third motif is that of the "heart." In 3:10, Ezekiel is instructed, "receive in your heart" (קח בלבבך) all the words that Yahweh shall speak to him. The order of the phrases, "receive in your heart and hear with your ears" is a strange one.[132] Blenkinsopp sees the order as reflecting "the way in which prophetic communications were thought to be received: first, as an impulse in the heart (we would say, mind), then in a form that is intelligible and communicable."[133] A more plausible explanation comes from Greenberg, who suggests that the strange order is explicable as a *hysteron proteron* "in which what (chrono)logically is last in a series is placed first owing to its importance."[134] Another possible reason, he suggests, is "the desire to resume the topic *leb* (*ab*) 'heart,' which has been suspended since vs. 7."[135] In view of the other contrasts established between the prophet and the exiles, both of Greenberg's

131. Block, *Ezekiel 1–24*, 123.
132. Allen (*Ezekiel 20–48*, 13) describes it as "awkward," and notes Ehrlich's comment that it is a mark of Ezekiel's "inelegant diction."
133. Blenkinsopp, *Ezekiel*, 27.
134. Greenberg, *Ezekiel 1–20*, 69.
135. Ibid., 69–70.

explanations are likely. The receptivity of Ezekiel's heart is to contrast with the hard-heartedness of the exiles (2:4; 3:7), a contrast that is developed throughout the book.

5. *Summary/Conclusions*

We have seen, then, that the book of Ezekiel does not simply portray the disobedience of the exiles to Yahweh's word and a future obedience to that word; it also presents to its addressees the prophet Ezekiel as a prescriptive paradigm of obedience—the exiles are to respond to Yahweh's word as he has done. Such a paradigmatic role is apparent both from the book's presentation of the prophet's obedience and from its clear establishment of him as a model, both by explicit references to him as a (prescriptive) sign, and the similarities and differences between Ezekiel and his audience. Only then will the vision of the future be a present reality for the exiles.

At this point the objection might be raised that it is most implausible for a prophet to have such a significant role in a book that focuses on his oracles. A number of scholars, however, have highlighted the prominence of the *persona* Ezekiel in the book. Collins observes that "*Ezekiel* is remarkable for the important place it gives to the individuality of the prophet whose name it bears," and he notes in particular the strong connections between the portrayal of Ezekiel, on the one hand, and Elijah and Elisha on the other.[136] Similarly, McKeating identifies a number of parallels between Moses and Ezekiel, both of structure (the three visionary experiences) and content (especially in chs. 40–48).[137] Odell, too, in her examination of the prohibition against Ezekiel's mourning, notes the important part played by the prophet's persona, and suggests that at least part of the impetus for such characterization may lie in Esarhaddon's Babylonian inscriptions.[138] Finally, Patton explores what it means for the central figure of the book, Ezekiel, to be portrayed as a priest, and why there is such a portrayal.[139] It is certainly plausible, then, for the *persona* Ezekiel within the book to be a model. Whether this was at his own instigation, or was the work of the author of the book, is harder to say.

---

136. Collins, *Mantle of Elijah*, 100.
137. McKeating, "Ezekiel the 'Prophet Like Moses'?," 99–103.
138. Odell, "Genre and Persona."
139. Corrine L. Patton, "Priest, Prophet and Exile: Ezekiel as a Literary Construct," in *Ezekiel's Hierarchical World: Wrestling with a Tiered Reality* (ed. Stephen L. Cook and Corrine L. Patton; SBLSymS 31; Atlanta: Society of Biblical Literature, 2004), 73–89.

Collins does not commit himself.[140] That it *could* come from the prophet himself is apparent from the role Ezekiel plays in the restoration of the dry bones: "in ch. 37 of Ezekiel the prophet is invited to stop being a mere spectator and to become an active participant in the drama he is describing. The restoration of the bones to life only happens, and happens in at least two stages, *at the instigation of Ezekiel himself*."[141]

There is also a different kind of problem that needs addressing. This is a problem for the addressees of the book. The history of the house of Israel that the book portrays is that of rebellion from first to last (ch. 20). The vision of restoration portrays a return to the land on a permanent basis (cf. chs. 38–39), which is accompanied by, and dependent upon, a renewed obedience for continued residence in the land. The critical questions for the readers of the book are precisely *how* such obedience would come about, and *how* it would be ensured, given this catalogue of failure which extended even to Ezekiel's intended audience (cf. Ezek 33:10, "How then can we live?").

140.   Collins, *Mantle of Elijah*, 101.

141.   McKeating, "Ezekiel the 'Prophet Like Moses'?," 106 (original emphasis). Fox ("The Rhetoric of Ezekiel's Vision," 9) sees Ezekiel as "an essentially passive spectator" here; so too Lapsley, *Can These Bones Live?*, 171. This, however, downplays the significance of Ezekiel's speaking. See Klein, *Ezekiel*, 155. Renz (*Rhetorical Function*, 205) adopts something of a mediating position, regarding the *w^{e}qatal* verb forms which describe Ezekiel's actions (vv. 7, 8, 10) as marking statements that are "off-line." This is possible given the prominence of *wayyiqtol* forms elsewhere in the narrative. It is difficult to be certain, since v. 2 opens with a *w^{e}qatal* (וְהַעֲבִירַנִי) where a *wayyiqtol* might have been expected, and the move away from *wayyiqtol* to *w^e* with the simple *qatal* is evident in Ezekiel (e.g. 11:6; 18:10) and characteristic of Late Biblical Hebrew. See Rooker, *Biblical Hebrew in Transition*, 101.

Chapter 6

RESPONDING TO YAHWEH'S WORD:
THE ACTION OF YAHWEH'S SPIRIT

In this chapter, I shall expand further on the paradigmatic nature of the prophet's experience. Ezekiel provides not just a paradigm of future obedience, but also points to the way by which such a vision of the future becomes a reality. I shall argue first that רוח is essential for the prophet's obedience to Yahweh's word, and that, in turn, רוח provides the link between the present disobedience of the exiles and their future obedience.

1. רוח *and Ezekiel's Obedience*

There are three main places where the impact of רוח on the prophet and his obedience can be seen. All are within those passages that we have already examined from the perspective of prophetic inspiration. This should not be surprising, since our discussion of "word-communicating" inspiration and "potentiating" inspiration focused on those instances where רוח is intimately linked not with the content of the prophet's message, but with his life.

The first, and the most important, instance is that in Ezek 2:2. Confronted with a vision of a figure which was "the appearance of the likeness of the glory of Yahweh" (1:28), Ezekiel had fallen on his face. Then he heard "the voice of someone speaking" (1:28). The voice commanded him, "Son of man, stand up on your feet, and I will speak with you." Verse 2 continues, "And when he spoke to me, רוח entered into me and set me on my feet; and I heard him speaking to me."

I have already examined in some detail the nature of רוח here and its relationship to the word that Yahweh spoke.[1] I concluded that, while the use of רוח is deliberately ambiguous here, Yahweh is still the source of its action, and that רוח functions not to communicate the words, but to

---

1. See Chapters 2 and 3 above.

revive the prophet, so that he is *enabled* to hear and to respond to Yahweh's word. It is, in fact, possible to go further than this. A comparison between v. 1 and v. 2 points to the fact that רוח *brings about* Ezekiel's obedience to the command that Yahweh has given.

The command to "stand" in v. 1 is answered directly in v. 2 by "רוח entered me...and stood me up." Of the eighty-five instances of the Hiphil of עמד in the Old Testament, this instance and Ezek 3:24 are the only ones where there is what would otherwise be understood as an "impersonal" subject. Here, explicitly, רוח is the agent that brings about Ezekiel's obedience to the command that Yahweh has uttered, and sets the prophet on his feet before Yahweh, so that he may serve him.[2] At the outset of the book, in response to the first command that the prophet receives from Yahweh, רוח brings about obedience to that command.[3] Redpath has expressed succinctly the nature of the work of רוח here: "Man cannot fulfil God's word without His Spirit 'preventing' him (in the old sense of the word)."[4]

The second instance is the similar phrase in 3:24, where again רוח sets the prostrate prophet on his feet. Though this is not a response to Yahweh's command, the agency of Yahweh's "hand" (v. 22) and רוח (v. 24) follows directly from the commission in 3:16–21, where the question is raised for the readers of the book, "Will Ezekiel be obedient to his commission?" Here, Ezekiel "is empowered by the spirit to stand and so assume the prophetic position of a servant standing in the presence of his divine master, like Elijah and other prophets."[5] As the readers of the book will know, Ezekiel was indeed obedient both to the immediately subsequent commands (3:25–27), and to his commission in general.

The third place, or better, way, in which רוח can be seen to be integral to the prophet's obedience is the compelling action of רוח within the visions that Ezekiel receives (3:12, 14; 8:3; 11:1, 24; 37:1; 43:5). This is particularly evident in 3:14–15. In 3:11, Ezekiel had been told, "then go to the exiles..." (ולך בא אל־הגולה). The narrative account of his movement once Yahweh's speech finishes highlights the agency of רוח. In

---

2. For the Hiphil of עמד being used of someone presenting another before Yahweh, see, e.g., Gen 47:7; Lev 14:11; Num 5:16. For the notion of a prophet "standing" before Yahweh, see 1 Kgs 17:1; 18:15; 2 Kgs 3:14; 5:16; Jer 15:19.

3. Cf. Hildebrandt's comment (*Spirit of God*, 189): "The task of Ezekiel as presented in 2:3–8 is clearly a difficult one that will bring much opposition and thus requires much divine help. In 2:2 the *rûah* is described as coming into Ezekiel, implying possession by the Spirit for the completion of his role (3:1–11)."

4. Henry A. Redpath, *The Book of the Prophet Ezekiel* (London: Methuen, 1907), 8; cf. Lys, *Rûach*, 131; Schwartz, "Concentric Structure," 110.

5. Allen, *Ezekiel 1–19*, 60–61.

3:14, Ezekiel relates, "The spirit (רוח) lifted me up and bore me away; I went (ואלך)…and I came to the exiles…(ואבוא אל־הגולה)." The fact that the action of רוח in transporting Ezekiel opens the narrative in 3:12 after the commissioning speech and is then repeated in 3:14 highlights not the movement of Yahweh's glory (3:12aβ–13), which is "parenthetical," but the action of רוח, which is "paramount."[6] These instances, along with Yahweh's hand and verbs expressing Yahweh's acting upon Ezekiel, point to Yahweh bringing about the prophet's obedience to him. The prophet is one constrained by Yahweh. Sometimes explicitly mentioned, but always present, Yahweh is one who generates the obedience of his prophet.

The picture, then, is of רוח being intimately involved in bringing about the prophet's obedience to Yahweh. This is not to say that the book portrays the prophet as passive (cf. 3:22–24). Nonetheless, the involvement of רוח in the ministry of the prophet, especially in 2:2, points to a prophet constrained by Yahweh, and whose obedience is effected by רוח.[7] Further, the agency of רוח is clearly at the initiative of Yahweh—it is at the instigation of Yahweh that רוח brings about the prophet's obedience. Finally, and perhaps most strikingly, the action of רוח as agent in 2:2 and 3:24 is not simply external, seizing the prophet like an object, but is now *internal*.[8]

2. רוח *and the Exiles' Obedience*

When we turn to the exiles and to their (future) obedience, we are at once faced with a tension created by two apparently contradictory facts. The tension requires exploration because Yahweh's word and Yahweh's רוח are closely bound up with it. In this section, I shall argue that the action of רוח, rightly understood, sheds some light on a possible synthesis.

The first fact is that the book of Ezekiel presents the call to repentance not as something which simply belonged to a phase in Ezekiel's ministry, but as something which still applies to its exilic addressees.

---

6. Schwartz, "Concentric Structure," 110.

7. *Pace* Schüngel-Straumann, *Rûaḥ bewegt die Welt*, 43–44. She argues that "*rwḥ* ersetzt nicht einfach die persönliche Initiative des Propheten. Ezechiel kann auf Befehl Gottes an anderen Stellen auch selbst handeln." For her, it is only when his own power is lacking that רוח enters. Then it should be translated not as "spirit" but as "(God's) vital force" ([*Gottes*] *Lebenskraft*). We have seen how, however, this רוח *brings about* Ezekiel's obedience and sets him on his feet. Further, the open-ended entering of רוח in 3:24 can be seen to pertain to the rest of Ezekiel's ministry, particularly when comparisons with Ezek 37:1–14 are borne in mind.

8. Cf. Lys, *Rûach*, 131.

Restoration, however, is the result of Yahweh's sovereign initiative. The book of Ezekiel makes this sovereign initiative clear in a number of ways. First, as Joyce, in particular, has pointed out, Yahweh's motive for delivering Israel is not a quality or an action of Israel upon which Yahweh is contingent, but is something within Yahweh himself. He delivers them for the sake of his "name" (36:22).[9] This contrasts with the picture found in Lev 26, where blessings are contingent on the obedience of the people.[10]

Secondly, while it is a mistake to distinguish between a "spiritual restoration" and a "physical, national one," or to regard them as strictly sequential,[11] since both are inextricably linked[12] and the order is not maintained consistently in the book,[13] the images used to describe the restoration of Israel—that of "a creation,[14] resurrection, exodus,[15] or a new gift of the land"—are "activities which by definition are solely the work of God."[16]

Thirdly, in chs. 40–48, neither Israel nor the new king of 34:23–24 are involved in the building of the new temple, the design of the worship or the appointment of priests.[17] As Ackroyd comments, "reorganization depends upon the presence of God and is not a prerequisite of it."[18] The

9.   See Joyce, *Divine Initiative*, 97–103.
10.   Compare Lev 26:3 and Ezek 36:26–27; also Lev 26:9 and Ezek 36:9. See Greenberg, *Ezekiel 21–37*, 720; Lapsley, *Can These Bones Live?*, 162; Wong, *Idea of Retribution*, 110–11.
11.   As Greenberg (*Ezekiel 21–37*, 735) does when he comments "first, the dispersed would be gathered and brought to their land, while still in their unregenerate state…there they would be purged of their pollution—absolved from their guilt—by a unilateral act of God."
12.   Von Rad, *Old Testament Theology*, 2:235–37.
13.   So 36:24–27 seems to envisage restoration to the land, followed by "spiritual renewal," while 37:14 envisages a new רוח before restoration to the land. See Renz, *Rhetorical Function*, 207.
14.   The two stages of Ezek 37:1–10 parallel those of Gen 2:7. So Allen, *Ezekiel 20–48*, 185; Block, *Ezekiel 25–48*, 379; Hals, *Ezekiel*, 269; Bruce Vawter and Leslie J. Hoppe, *A New Heart: A Commentary on the Book of Ezekiel* (ITC; Grand Rapids: Eerdmans, 1991), 167; Zimmerli, *Ezekiel 2*, 261.
15.   As reflected in the language of the exodus tradition (36:24; 37:12); cf. Hals, *Ezekiel*, 270.
16.   Klein, *Israel in Exile*, 84.
17.   Daniel I. Block, "Bringing Back David: Ezekiel's Messianic Hope," in *The Lord's Anointed: Interpretation of Old Testament Messianic Texts* (ed. P. E. Satterthwaite, R. S. Hess and G. J. Wenham; Grand Rapids: Baker, 1995), 187; Duguid, *Ezekiel and the Leaders of Israel*, 50–55.
18.   Ackroyd, *Exile and Restoration*, 115.

presence of Yahweh (43:1–5), in turn, follows from the temple built by Yahweh (chs. 40–42); it is "his building."[19] It is not an exaggeration, then, to say that chs. 34–48 as a section "describes the kingship of Yahweh as the beginning and end of Israel's transformation"[20] or that "the promised future in Ezekiel is solely the product of God's monergistic actions."[21]

Precisely how calls to repentance can be related to Yahweh's sovereign initiative at every stage has taxed many scholars. Such a question is particularly relevant for our purposes because, as Joyce's *Divine Initiative* explores, this apparent antinomy is encapsulated by the command for the exiles to get for themselves a "new heart and a new spirit" (18:30–31) and the promise of Yahweh to give to the exiles "one/a new heart and a new spirit" (11:19; 36:26).

Commentators naturally have addressed this tension between the promise and the command. Calvin sees the call in 18:31 as God showing the people "their duty" such that when "they acknowledge that they cannot discharge it, they fly to the aid of the Holy Spirit, so that the outward exhortation becomes a kind of instrument which God used to confer the grace of his Spirit."[22] Cooke reconciles the different perspectives by suggesting that "the full truth is arrived at by combining the two statements,"[23] and he points to Phil 2:12–13. Greenberg, commenting on 18:31, sees this as "a human capacity" to get "a new heart and a new spirit." He observes that Ezekiel is alone in ascribing to man such a capacity, that it is unique within Ezekiel, and that, elsewhere, the people's incorrigibility is stressed (chs. 16; 20). He comments: "This singular empowering of the people, so contrary to the general mood of the book, is of a piece with the liberating, encouraging tidings of this oracle,

---

19. Ibid.

20. Renz, *Rhetorical Function*, 60. For further discussion on Yahweh's kingship and the relationship to human kings, see Paul M. Joyce, "King and Messiah in Ezekiel," in *King and Messiah in Israel and the Ancient Near East: Proceedings of the Oxford Old Testament Seminar* (ed. J. Day; JSOTSup 270; Sheffield: Sheffield Academic Press, 1998), 323–37.

21. Klein, *Israel in Exile*, 95; cf. Ackroyd's comment (*Exile and Restoration*, 115), "All this is effected by divine action and by that alone. The new life is divinely given (cf. ch. 36, 37); the reordered land is made what it is by God; the new Temple is his building"; more recently, see also Mein, *Ezekiel and the Ethics of Exile*, 239–55, and Lapsley, *Can These Bones Live?*, 160–73.

22. John Calvin, *Commentaries on the First Twenty Chapters of the Book of the Prophet Ezekiel* (trans. Thomas Myers; repr., Grand Rapids: Eerdmans, 1999 [1849]), 265–66.

23. Cooke, *Ezekiel*, 391.

designed as an antidote to despair."[24] With regard to 36:26–27, Greenberg sees that human freedom is curtailed by Yahweh's action, such that
there is "enforced obedience."[25] Rather than attempt to reconcile the two,
he says that Ezekiel "vacillates between calling on the exiles to repent
and despairing of their capacity for it."[26] Nonetheless, "there is no question that for him the change of human nature was not an act of grace."[27]
Greenberg's approach does not allow for any reconciliation of the two
perspectives. Instead, the exigencies of the situation in ch. 18 justify the
unique emphasis on human responsibility. In similar vein, Block maintains that the use of the imperative in 18:30–31 "does not mean that
Ezekiel believes his audience capable of moral and spiritual self-transfor-
mation. The command…is a rhetorical device, highlighting the responsibility of the nation for their present crisis and pointing the way to the
future."[28] Thus it is "the contextual emphasis on personal human
responsibility"[29] in 18:30–31 that gives rise to that call to repentance,
while the dominant perspective is on Yahweh's restorative actions.[30]
Zimmerli comments that 18:31 "offers to faith, as something to be taken
hold of, what is promised as a gift in 11:19."[31] The "logical tensions"
serve to show that "in the divine salvation man never appears simply as a
vague object, but always as the purposeful subject of grace for a new
beginning."[32] Four other contributions to the debate also merit particular
attention: those of Joyce, Matties, Mein and Lapsley.[33]

---

24.   Greenberg, *Ezekiel 1–20*, 341.

25.   Greenberg, *Ezekiel 21–37*, 735.

26.   Ibid., 737; similarly idem, "Salvation of the Impenitent," 271.

27.   Greenberg, *Ezekiel 21–37*, 737.

28.   Block, *Ezekiel 1–24* (Grand Rapids: Eerdmans, 1997), 588.

29.   Block, *Ezekiel 25–48*, 355.

30.   Cf. Verhoef's comment, "This admonition does not suggest what they *can*
do, but what they *ought* to do: what God requires from everyone of them. God alone
can give them a new heart and spirit"; Pieter A. Verhoef, "חדשׁ," *NIDOTTE* 2:36
(original emphasis).

31.   Zimmerli, *Ezekiel 1*, 262.

32.   Ibid., 386.

33.   See also Michael Fishbane, "Sin and Judgment in the Prophecies of Ezekiel,"
Interpretation 38 (1984): 131–50; Benjamin Uffenheimer, "Theodicy and Ethics in
the Prophecy of Ezekiel," in *Justice and Righteousness: Biblical Themes and Their
Influence* (ed. H. G. Reventlow and Y. Hoffman; JSOTSup 137; Sheffield: JSOT
Press, 1992), 200–27; Baruch J. Schwartz, "Repentance and Determinism in Ezek-
iel," in *Proceedings of the Eleventh World Congress of Jewish Studies, Jerusalem,
June 22–29, 1993: Division A, The Bible and its World* (Jerusalem: The World
Union of Jewish Studies, 1994), 123–30.

Joyce, in defending a pre-587 date for ch. 18, suggests two reasons for calls to repentance before the final disaster. The first is to "underline Israel's responsibility for the inevitable punishment." The second is to say that "this is not what Yahweh would wish for Israel."[34] Joyce denies, however, that an aversion of the final disaster is possible. The call functions as a rhetorical device, with no expectation of success. In his diachronic solution to the tension between the calls to repentance and Yahweh's sovereign initiative, it is only after the fall of Jerusalem that Yahweh acts in a sovereign way to bring about restoration without the repentance or involvement of the exiles. He concludes that, since "obedience is guaranteed, it would seem that the responsibility of Israel has been subsumed in the overriding initiative of Yahweh."[35]

Joyce is right to say that repentance would not avert disaster for Jerusalem,[36] but he underestimates the significance of the fact that the oracle in ch. 18, and indeed the other calls to repentance, are directed towards the *exiles*. Repentance, leading to life, is a possibility, indeed a necessity, for the exiles. Even if, with Raitt, such calls to repentance were not part of Ezekiel's preaching to the exiles after the fall of Jerusalem, still the *book* portrays repentance as necessary for its exilic addressees.

Matties focuses on ch. 18 as a "hinge text, offering a way of being in the liminal moment between judgment and transformation."[37] Given this perspective, it is not surprising that he gives particular weight to the "call to conversion" in 18:30–32.[38] He argues that "the call to repentance is a fundamental facet of Hebrew moral discourse."[39] This call should neither be misunderstood as indicating that repentance would avert judgment, nor as indicating that salvation is guaranteed. "Rather, the exhortation serves as the basic statement of human responsibility in a cosmos that is characterized by order."[40] Yet this call is a real "call to life," with a real "possibility of action."[41] He tries to reconcile this with "divine action" by observing that "keeping *tôrâ* is based ultimately on the prior act of God in deliverance."[42] The ambiguity that he discerns in the place of human moral responsibility, however, also characterizes his own treatment. In his discussion of the relationship between "divine enablement and human

34. Joyce, *Divine Initiative*, 57.
35. Ibid., 127.
36. Ibid., 55–60.
37. Matties, *Ezekiel 18*, 208.
38. Ibid., 105–9.
39. Ibid., 108.
40. Ibid., 109.
41. Ibid.
42. Ibid.

responsibility,"[43] he observes "the fact that people are not capable of responding faithfully" (cf. 33:10; 37:11).[44] He comments, rightly,

> By offering the human alternative in chap. 18, in the midst of judgement, the prophet suggests that divine intervention beyond the present experience is not the only option for the exilic community. By fashioning its own character as a *tôrâ*-keeping peoplehood, Israel in exile is already participating in the divine intention of restoration.[45]

The relationship between present and future is not as sharply delineated as most commentators argue. It is, however, neither clear why he has privileged ch. 18 in this fashion, nor is it clear *how* divine enablement relates to human responsibility.

Mein reconciles the two in carefully argued fashion. For him, the calls to repentance found particularly in chs. 14 and 18 represent genuine calls to repentance to those in exile.[46] For him, however, the language of "life" that is at stake in these chapters is not related directly to life in the land that is spoken of in the salvation that is Yahweh's act, and Yahweh's alone. Rather, it is related to the temple and worship there.[47] To the extent that Yahweh is a sanctuary in the exile (cf. 11:16), the now powerless Jerusalem elite can experience some kind of "life" in exile. Noting the comparisons with 1 Kgs 8:50, he comments, "it looks as if repentance will bring blessing in exile rather than a return from exile."[48] The exilic community remain wholly passive in the "promises of salvation" that "appear extravagant and unrealistic" when set alongside the oracles of judgment and the "present status of the exiles."[49] Mein argues persuasively that there is in chs. 14 and 18 (and 33) a more "domestic" purview reflecting the change of circumstances in exile.[50] He is also right to note

43. Ibid., 205–8.

44. Ibid., 207.

45. Ibid., 207. See further below.

46. Mein, *Ezekiel and the Ethics of Exile*, 207. Although he overstates the degree of responsibility claimed by the exiles in 33:10, given the protest in vv. 17 and 20, he rightly observes the importance of the phrase "turn and live" in ch. 18 and the greater emphasis on the wicked man who repents in ch. 33 over against the one in ch. 18. Recently, Darr also argues that ch. 18 allows for the possibility of repentance, as "a means" for the exiles "to survive their *present* circumstances." See Katheryn Pfisterer Darr, "Proverb Performance and Transgenerational Retribution in Ezekiel 18," in Cook and Patton, eds., *Ezekiel's Hierarchical World*, 222.

47. So Zimmerli, "'Leben' und 'Tod,'" and idem, *Ezekiel 1*, 382, followed by Mein, *Ezekiel and the Ethics of Exile*, 210.

48. Mein, *Ezekiel and the Ethics of Exile*, 208–11 (quotation from p. 211).

49. Ibid., 220.

50. Cf. n. 14 on p. 178 above.

the lack of explicit links between "life" and "land" in ch. 18.[51] Within the context of the *book* of Ezekiel, however, "life" in ch. 18 is associated with the acquisition of "a new heart" and "a new spirit" (18:31–32). In ch. 36, these are explicitly part of Yahweh's eschatological gift to his people. Further, in ch. 37:12–14, "life" is clearly associated directly with return to the land. Mein provides no obvious reason for the shift in the solution for the exiles' hopelessness, from calls to repentance (after the cry, "Our transgressions and our sins weigh upon us, and we waste away because of them; how then can we live?," 33:10) to the declaration of unconditional salvation in 37:1–14 (in response to the cry, "Our bones are dried up, and our hope is lost; we are cut off completely," 37:11).[52]

Lapsley's work is aimed directly at the question of the relationship between calls to repentance and declarations of divine sovereign initiative in restoration. She surveys in depth the tension between these two perspectives, and concludes that the "inconsistencies" found in Ezekiel provide evidence of a tension that is fundamentally irreconcilable between two different anthropologies.[53] The call to the exiles to repent and get for themselves a new heart and a new spirit (18:30–32) reveals an anthropology that conflicts with the anthropology implicit in the deterministic language evident both in chs. 16; 20; 23; 24, and in the promises that Yahweh will give his people a new heart and a new spirit (11:19; 36:26). The former anthropology, which she sees as the dominant one to before Ezekiel's time, but as "waning"[54] in Ezekiel, regards people as "capable of understanding their moral failings and transforming them-selves."[55] The latter anthropology sees this capacity for moral virtue as available *only* as a gift from Yahweh. The need for an "organ transplant" (11:19; 36:26) provides evidence that their moral "equipment" is "not right."[56] In chs. 1–33, Ezekiel is "vacillating principally between two

51. Mein, *Ezekiel and the Ethics of Exile*, 209.

52. Mein does speak of the shift "from responsibility to passivity" (ibid., 216–56), but he ties *both* the (albeit limited) possibility of repentance *and* passivity to the circumstances of the exile. That the fall of Jerusalem is not the reason for the shift is clear, for "Ezekiel's community in exile have *already* experienced this loss [of insti-tutions that serve to mediate between the people and Yahweh], and their situation before 587 in some ways anticipates that of the whole nation after the disaster" (p. 214 [my emphasis]).

53. Lapsley, *Can These Bones Live?* (quotation from p. 15). Her particular con-tribution is to focus on the tension not so much for what it reveals about Ezekiel's theology, but for what it reveals about his anthropology.

54. Ibid., 106.

55. Ibid.

56. Ibid., 104–5.

models of the moral self.""[57] In chs. (34? 36? 37?) 35–48,[58] the new moral self is portrayed as a gift from Yahweh. Further, this new moral self has its focus not in action, in doing the right thing, but in knowledge of Yahweh. This is critical for her understanding of human freedom. The main places where action is predicated of the new moral self are 11:20 and 36:27. This action, however, arises *willingly* out of the newly created moral self. She quotes Fox with approval, "When one has God's spirit in him he does God's will because he *wants* to do God's will."[59] Yahweh is directly involved in obedience, insofar as he is the giver of the new moral identity. For Lapsley, however, "the right moral actions of these newly created people will flow naturally out of this knowledge."[60] Human freedom, then, is in a profound sense preserved.[61]

Lapsley argues clearly and, particularly in her analysis of the new moral identity, persuasively. At the same time, the polarization of the two anthropologies that she sees in the book is a bit too neat, and it hardly helps the rhetorical persuasiveness of the book, even if the more deterministic view, giving rise to the new moral self as Yahweh's gift, prevails. The "over-neatness" can be seen, for example, if we consider the question, "How 'virtuous' is the 'moral self' in passages which call the exiles to repentance?" In 18:31, the call to "get for yourselves a new heart and a new spirit" implies, for Lapsley, an ability to respond. The fact, however, that they need "a new heart and a new spirit" is, according to Lapsley, *itself* evidence that their moral equipment is corrupt.[62] In other words, on Lapsley's reasoning, these verses do not in fact call for the possible, but for the impossible. Once this is recognized, calls to repentance elsewhere cannot be seen necessarily as implying an underlying anthropology which speaks of the virtuous moral self.

It will be helpful at this moment to pause and reflect. The picture of restoration that the book paints is one where Yahweh's restoration is not

---

57. Ibid., 157.

58. Lapsley (ibid.) speaks of vacillation in chs. 1–36. In her summary on p. 183, however, Ezekiel's "struggle" is evident in chs. 1–33. On p. 159, the final section of the book is characterized as chs. 36–48. On p. 186, the final chapters are chs. 35–48.

59. Fox, "Rhetoric of Ezekiel's Vision," 15, cited in Lapsley, *Can These Bones Live?*, 182.

60. Lapsley, *Can These Bones Live?*, 182.

61. Though not in a total sense, because there is also an "absence of human freedom" implicit, for her, in the fact that "the people in Ezekiel who are transformed by God's action are for the most part not depicted as possessing the freedom to choose or refuse this gracious gift." Ibid., 188.

62. Ibid., 103–6.

established or precipitated by renewed obedience as a self-initiated act of the exiles. Rather, renewed obedience is established and maintained by Yahweh's restoration, and is part of that restoration. Since Ezekiel's promises present a picture of future security, Yahweh's intervention cannot merely provide a renewed stage on which Israel will have another opportunity to repeat its history of rebellion and failure.[63] Yahweh's intervention, bringing about a change in attitudes and behaviour, will ensure that the history of rebellion and failure will never be repeated.

Since the calls to repentance are for the exiles, and point to "a wholesale reorientation of life *and* an internal change in disposition" as "prerequisites for positive divine action,"[64] yet the exiles are "dead," a self-initiated response to Yahweh is inconceivable, and future salvation seems to be the work of Yahweh alone, the readers of the book would need to know *how* such a future vision could become a reality.

The importance of the route from the present to the future is not always acknowledged. Mein argues from a sociological perspective for Ezekiel's salvation oracles being an example of "the use of dramatic future hopes as a focus of communal solidarity"[65] that is characteristic of communities that have experienced disaster, deprivation and not comprised of those "at the very bottom of the social ladder."[66] Further, he suggests that Ezekiel instantiates a wider phenomenon, whereby "activism" in the face of domination tends to give way to "passive revolutionism" when it becomes apparent that action on the part of those dominated is impossible or will make no impact.[67] This "passive revolutionism" is marked by "reliance…entirely on supernatural action."[68] The shaping of communities by such oracles is an important observation, as is the emphasis on "supernatural action." For Ezekiel's addressees, and, by extension, for the book's addressees, however, the expansive vision of the future alone is not sufficient. The burning question for the exiles is *how* to be part of that future. This is clear from their question in 33:10—"How then can we live?"—a pertinent question in view of the sifting evident in 20:32–44

---

63. Though the careful guarding of access in chs. 40–48 and the presence of a renewed sacrificial system indicates that "the possibility of error remains," though at a "level" that is "presumably tolerable." Ibid., 188.

64. Block, *Ezekiel 1–24*, 588.

65. Mein, *Ezekiel and the Ethics of Exile*, 219.

66. Ibid., 227.

67. Ibid., 241.

68. Bryan R. Wilson, *Magic and the Millennium: A Sociological Study of Religious Movements of Protest Among Tribal and Third-World Peoples* (New York: Heinemann, 1973), 272, cited in Mein, *Ezekiel and the Ethics of Exile*, 241.

and 34:17–22.[69] In what follows, I shall argue that Ezekiel's vision of the dry bones does just that. Integral in this vision, and indeed integral in Yahweh's intervention for the sake of his name, is רוח.

2.1. *How the Vision of the Future Becomes a Present Reality: Ezekiel 37:1–14*

This is almost certainly the most well-known part of the book, and has received extensive attention.[70] The hand of Yahweh picks Ezekiel up, and brings him by רוח of Yahweh to a valley that is full of bones. After Yahweh has shown him the full extent of the bones, Yahweh asks the prophet whether they can live, a question "calculated to heighten wonder."[71] Though Ezekiel answers "politely,"[72] his answer should not be interpreted as evasive.[73] The dialogical approach has rhetorical force, engaging the readers. Yahweh's words are an invitation, a question, that confronts not just Ezekiel but the book's hearers as they look around: "Can these bones live?" "How can they live?" "Who will make them live?" The emphasis should be focused not on the locutionary act, but on the illocutionary: "What is Yahweh doing in asking the question?" Similarly, the lack of closure in Ezekiel's reply, with neither a positive nor negative answer, induces reader involvement. At one level, of course, there was no possibility (cf. Job 14:14). At the same time, Yahweh both "kills and makes alive" (1 Sam 2:6). More than that, he is the creator.[74] The barely believable possibility is left open.[75]

---

69. Cf. also the despairing cry of 37:11, "Our bones are dried up, and our hope is lost; we are cut off completely." In a different context, compare the words of the man who ran up to Jesus in Mark 10:17, "What must I do to inherit eternal life?"

70. In addition to the commentaries, see, e.g., Wagner, *Geist und Leben*; Fox, "Rhetoric of Ezekiel's Vision"; Peter Höffken, "Beobachtungen zu Ezechiel XXXVII 1–10," *VT* 31 (1981): 305–17; Adrian Graffy, *A Prophet Confronts His People: The Disputation Speech in the Prophets* (AnBib 104; Rome: Biblical Institute Press, 1984), 83–86; Bernhard Lang, "Street Theater, Raising the Dead, and the Zoroastrian Connection in Ezekiel's Prophecy," in Lust, ed., *Ezekiel and His Book*, 297–316; Ohnesorge, *Jahwe gestaltet sein Volk neu*, 283–338; Christopher R. Seitz, "Ezekiel 37:1–14," *Int* 46 (1992): 53–56; Leslie C. Allen, "Structure, Tradition and Redaction in Ezekiel's Death Valley Vision," in Davies and Clines, eds., *Among the Prophets*, 127–42; Harald M. Wahl, "'Tod und Leben.' Zur Wiederherstellung Israels nach Ez. XXXVII 1–14," *VT* 49 (1999): 218–39.

71. Fox, "Rhetoric of Ezekiel's Vision," 11.

72. Ibid.

73. *Pace* Ohnesorge, *Jahwe gestaltet sein Volk neu*, 326.

74. See further below and Kutsko, *Between Heaven and Earth*, 138–39.

75. So Schüngel-Straumann, *Rûaḥ bewegt die Welt*, 56.

Then Yahweh gives a prophetic word for Ezekiel to utter to the bones. That word stresses the רוח that Yahweh will "bring" (מביא, v. 5) and "give" (ונתתי, v. 6), for the revivifying רוח is mentioned twice. In v. 5, the essence of the revivification is spelled out, "I will cause breath to enter you, and you shall live." In v. 6, the entire process is outlined. After being embodied, the bones shall "live" (וחייתם) and shall, by way of climax "know that I am Yahweh" (וידעתם כי־אני יהוה). The actual events in the vision, however, in response to that first prophetic word, culminate in a puzzling, even astonishing, anti-climax at the end of v. 8, which seems to interrupt the flow: "but there was no breath in them" (ורוח אין בהם).[76] Within the vision, there needs to be another word uttered, summoning הרוח to come from the four winds, before the embodied bones can be on their feet, alive. Such an anti-climax demands an explanation.[77]

The two-stage vision of life for the bones resonates with the creation account in Gen 2:7 and its context; the presence of two stages (forming, then in-breathing), the repetition of נפח (Gen 2:7; Ezek 37:9), the goal of becoming "living" (לנפש חיה, Gen 2:7; וחייתם, Ezek 37:6),[78] the "setting" (נוח, Gen 2:15; Ezek 37:14)[79] in their "land" (אדמה, Gen 2:5; Ezek 37:12, 14)[80] and the "movement from chaos to order"[81] point in this direction. The fact that "breath" in Gen 2:7 is נשמה should not be seen as significant, since the need to exploit the polysemous nature of רוח in 37:1–14 makes it impossible for the breath that entered the bones to be נשמה, and by the time of the exile, the two words clearly had overlapping semantic

76. Allen's translation can accidentally miss out this phrase "but there was no breath in them," yet it still makes sense! Allen, *Ezekiel 20–48*, 181.

77. I am not persuaded by those who appeal to redactional activity to explain the two stages (e.g. Höffken, "Beobachtungen," 307–8; Ohnesorge, *Jahwe gestaltet sein Volk neu*, 290–93; Wahl, "'Tod und Leben,'" 224–31; Pohlmann, *Hesekiel 20–48*, 497–99). I am similarly unconvinced by those who attribute the shift in form between vision and oracle or the imagery between "bones" and "graves" to redactional activity (e.g. Wevers, *Ezekiel*, 277–79; Graffy, *A Prophet Confronts His People*, 83–84; Pohlmann, *Hesekiel 20–48*, 493). See Zimmerli, *Ezekiel 2*, 256–58; Allen, "Structure, Tradition and Redaction," 138–39; Wagner, "Geist und Leben," 153; Schüngel-Straumann, *Rûaḥ bewegt die Welt*, 60.

78. Schüngel-Straumann, *Rûaḥ bewegt die Welt*, 56.

79. Kutsko, *Between Heaven and Earth*, 133–34.

80. Schüngel-Straumann, *Rûaḥ bewegt die Welt*, 61. The phrase אדמת ישראל occurs seventeen times in Ezekiel, once in Ezek 37:1–14 (v. 12) and nowhere else in the Old Testament. The notion of "working" (עבד) the ground is present in Gen 2:5 and Ezek 36:34 (though there "ground" is ארץ).

81. Fox, "Rhetoric of Ezekiel's Vision," 10.

domains (cf. Gen 7:22; Isa 42:5).[82] Hals sees this link with creation as a sufficient explanation. The two-staged approach, he argues, is one of two ways of introducing a message of salvation; specifically, it is "the establishment of the continuity of divine action."[83] The new creation corresponds to the old creation (Gen 2:7); the same God can do a similar thing one more time.

Others, while acknowledging the links with Genesis, stress the drama: Greenberg remarks, "unexpectedly the process halts before life is restored to the reconstituted bodies, delaying, and thus highlighting, the climax."[84] All attention will now be focused on the "'very, very great army' standing on its feet, ready—for what?"[85] Allen says that "the process accentuates the power of God even as it concedes the difficulty of the enterprise,"[86] and Fox comments in a similar vein that such a failure parallels that of "the magician who invariably 'fails' once or twice…in order to intensify suspense and to focus attention on the climactic success to follow."[87]

Kutsko explains the two stages rather differently, although preserving the creational links. Drawing on what he maintains is the common understanding of Ezekiel's audience concerning the Mesopotamian imperial practices towards cult statues of vanquished foes, Ezekiel "fills the old pattern with new content" in chs. 36–37.[88] He deliberately "parodies" for rhetorical purposes the refashioning of cult images before their return, evinced in inscriptions, in order to emphasize the cleansing and removing of idolatry from Yahweh's people.[89] It is within this framework that Kutsko interprets 37:1–14. The vision of the reformed bones he sees as reversing the punishment for idolatry declared by Yahweh in 6:4–6, where Yahweh announces, "I will scatter your bones around your altars" (v. 5). The phrase in v. 8 speaking of the lack of breath in the refashioned

---

82. Albertz and Westermann (*TLOT* 3:1209) see the occurrences here as the earliest instances of רוח as "breath of life," and regard them as instrumental in the semantic shift. It is not easy, however, to see how this observation relates to their comment on p. 1208, in discussing the ancient notion of רוח as "vitality": "it is unthinkable that the Israelites could conceive of the force of vitality without a perceptible expression." LXX makes the link explicit by reading πνεῦμα ζωῆς at the end of v. 5.

83. Hals, *Ezekiel*, 269.

84. Greenberg, *Ezekiel 21–37*, 747.

85. Ibid.

86. Allen, *Ezekiel 20–48*, 185.

87. Fox, "Rhetoric of Ezekiel's Vision," 11.

88. Kutsko, *Between Heaven and Earth*, 101–49 (quotation from p. 124).

89. Ibid., 134.

bones (ורוח אין בהם) Kutsko sees as echoing the prophetic mocking of idols (e.g. ולא־רוח בם, Jer 10:14; cf. Hab 2:19). He summarizes, "It appears that the vision in Ezekiel 37 halts (in v. 8) at a point that leaves Israel equal to its idols—and no better. Neither they nor the intermediate formation of bodies has רוח. Thus the re-creation process must continue, as it did at creation, with God's breathing life into them."[90]

The link between ch. 6 and ch. 37 is more tenuous than Kutsko maintains, since the only significant verbal link is that of "bones," and ch. 6 relates to events in the land, not in exile, so the reversal is not exact. The bones belong to different people. His point about the language of idols being reflected in the salvation oracles in chs. 36–37, however, is more persuasive. There are strong echoes of idols, both in the language of 37:8b, and in the language of a "stone heart" which is, Kutsko proposes, a figurative way of speaking of Israel's attraction to foreign idols (cf. 20:32, "serve...stone").[91] Within the critique of those who worship idols becoming in some sense like those idols (cf. Ps 115:5–8),[92] the clear implication, which Kutsko does not draw, is that the "bones" addressed by Ezekiel are *still* idolatrous. This fits with the book's portrayal of Ezekiel's addressees. I shall return to this below, but need first to look at another scholar's analysis which in many ways complements that of Kutsko.

Renz states that "37:1–11a expose the prophetic word as achieving at first only a gathering of bones without giving those bones life."[93] He suggests that the first stage looks like "a failure of the prophetic word,"[94] for Ezekiel's word has not yet come to pass; it has not had the powerful impact that might have been expected. He does not think that the increased drama is adequate to account for such a serious issue. After refuting arguments that the two-stage restoration might be "something to do with Yahweh"[95] or a "spiritual restoration following a physical restoration,"[96] he argues that the two-stage restoration is a way of reassuring the audience of the power and efficacy of the prophetic word.

He observes that the prophetic word was often accused of being slow to come into effect (e.g. Ezek 12:21–28), and proposes, "by affirming

90. Ibid., 137.
91. Ibid., 128–29. He also draws particular attention to 20:16 and 14:4.
92. Cf. ibid., 137–38. Cf. Isa 41:29 where images are רוה, and 44:9, where those who make idols are similarly תהו.
93. Renz, *Rhetorical Function*, 207.
94. Ibid.
95. Ibid., 206.
96. Ibid., 207.

that a second step will complete what was lacking after the first step, the text claims that Yahweh will bring about what he promised, in spite of the ineffectiveness experienced so far."[97] If the experience of people is that the prophetic word is not coming to pass, then it is more effective to portray the two stages than simply to reaffirm dogmatically the power of the prophetic word. He sees confirmation of this in the behaviour of the audience portrayed in 33:30–33. The editor, Renz comments, clearly regards the fall of Jerusalem as the confirmation of Ezekiel's prophetic authority, but the original audience of the prophet is presented as still unconvinced about the claims Ezekiel makes: "The prophetic word has, so to speak, gathered 'the bones' without yet breathing life into them."[98] He then reapplies Hals' understanding: the link to Gen 2:7 points not to failure because of the two stages, but to the continuity of divine action. The "small things" that shaped and formed the community in exile should not be seen as a failure, but as "the first step towards full restoration."[99] A prophet is present. The hopeless sentiment expressed in 37:11 is precisely, Renz suggests, because the audience does not believe the prophetic word. "The book presents the vision as Yahweh's reassurance to his prophet that the prophetic word will accomplish its task."[100]

Renz's argument has much to commend it. First, it makes sense psychologically. Since Ezekiel was not instructed initially to report the vision,[101] any explanation of the two-staged vision must account for the effect of the vision on Ezekiel himself. Here, it serves to reassure him that his prophetic word will do its work, even though it appears feeble and frail at the moment, and people are not listening to him. They are still, to borrow Kutsko's phrase, "equal to…idols"[102] because they are still idolatrous.

Secondly, it explains the sense of anti-climax. Purely "dramatic" explanations underestimate the anti-climax and downplay the significance of the "failure" of the prophetic word. If initially the vision served to reassure the prophet, it reappears in the book of Ezekiel with the same perlocutionary aim, that of reassurance, but with different addressees: it aims to provide reassurance and confidence to the readers that this seeming delay in the restoration was part of God's purposes—the two stages are *part* of Yahweh's vision.

97. Ibid.
98. Ibid., 208.
99. Ibid.
100. Ibid., 209.
101. Cf. Zimmerli, *Ezekiel 2*, 262.
102. Kutsko, *Between Heaven and Earth*, 137.

Thirdly, the correspondence between Ezekiel's ministry to the bones and to the exilic addressees fits this picture. The goal of the proclamation in the vision was that the bones would "live" and "know that I am Yahweh" (vv. 5, 6). Ezekiel prophesied to the bones (v. 7). He has prophesied to the exiles, as instructed (vv. 12–14). The goal is the same, that they "live" and "know that I am Yahweh" (v. 14). The exiles are not yet alive, nor do they yet "know that I am Yahweh." The purpose of the oracle is to convince them that the next stage is coming. They are located at the end of v. 8, gathered but lifeless. It is an interesting point whether Kutsko and Renz differ in how positive this stage is. It might seem that Kutsko is more negative, because Israel are effectively still idols, having "no breath in them." Against the backdrop, however, of the refashioning being an unfinished process, with the next stage coming, there is no reason to think Kutsko would regard this stage as wholly negative. What both Renz and (my extrapolation of) Kutsko have in common is that this perspective is entirely *realistic*. Ezekiel has prophesied to the bones. They have to a degree been reformed, in that they are gathered around the prophet, but they are still rebellious. There is something transitional about this stage.

Finally, Renz is right to refute the notion that the two stages correspond to "*consecutive* acts" of physical, and then spiritual, restoration, both because it does not fit with what is said elsewhere in the book (e.g. 11:17–20, where removal of idols implies some internal workings by the exiles, yet it precedes the giving of a new heart and a new spirit), and because "the order in 37:14 is reversed."[103]

The role of the divine רוח, however, needs revisiting. Renz says that "the present text does not support the contention that Yahweh needs... the help of the Spirit (understood as an independent entity) to accomplish his task."[104] He goes on to point out that "Yahweh's spirit is Yahweh's efficacy" which "makes life possible" and "enables people to accomplish deeds they could not otherwise do."[105] Further, "winds and breath are completely at Yahweh's disposal."[106] He concludes that the two stages are not explicable in terms of Yahweh, and therefore must be to do with Israel. While Renz is right to stress Yahweh's authority over רוח, such that he does not need the help of the Spirit, yet Yahweh may *choose* to use רוח as his instrument. After the bones have been formed into lifeless

---

103. Renz, *Rhetorical Function*, 207 (original emphasis); see further p. 216 above.
104. Ibid., 206.
105. Ibid.
106. Ibid.

bodies, there is no further word addressed to them. A further word to them is not needed for them to come to life. In that sense, the vision is an *apologia* for the book of Ezekiel itself; no further word beyond the words of the prophet Ezekiel, as recorded in the book, is necessary.[107] It is at this point, though, that my understanding diverges from Renz's, for it is of great significance that the vision calls neither for a passive waiting, nor for an active response on the part of the reformed bodies (i.e. repentance of the exiles), until the apparently weak, "failed" word proves itself to be powerful by bringing about the desired effects in due time. What *is* needed is something different, something radical, something from the outside breaking in to bring to completion what the word has started. What is needed is רוח. It is this רוח that will move the exiles from being in their idolatry like idols to the final goal of knowing that "I am Yahweh."

In other words, what is at issue in the two stages is not so much the power of the word per se, but *how that word can become effective in their experience*. Ezekiel 37:1–14 is not about "affirming the absurd."[108] Rather, it explains *how* the absurd will happen, and makes it seem less absurd by using language redolent of creation. While it is true, with Renz, that the exiles are the bones gathered and re-formed by the prophetic word of the prophet, they are still idolatrous and still disobedient to that word. They are awaiting not a further word, nor a fulfilment of the original word, but רוח to come and make that word effective in their experience. Further, the agent of this change is not simply רוח as "life-breath" that will revivify the "dead" exiles, for in 37:14 there is the dynamic shift in meaning from רוח as "breath of life" to רוח as Yahweh's spirit. "Ezekiel introduces a new idea by subterfuge just by adding the possessive suffix."[109] In ch. 37, רוח moves beyond the *Lebenskraft*, the "vitality" that was lost, to *Lebensodem*, the "breath of life" for those who were dead. In 37:14, it moves beyond *Lebensodem* to *Geist Gottes*, echoing 36:27.[110] Not simply revivification, but moral transformation and a new community united in their knowledge of Yahweh are in view. It is as the

---

107.   For v. 9, see below.

108.   Fox, "Rhetoric of Ezekiel's Vision," 1.

109.   Ibid., 15.

110.   Cf. D. M. G. Stalker, *Ezekiel: Introduction and Commentary* (Torch Bible Commentaries; London: SCM, 1968), 257; Schüngel-Straumann, *Rûaḥ bewegt die Welt*, 63–64. The clear link with 36:27, noted particularly by Allen ("Structure, Tradition and Redaction"), suggests that it is more simply than his own "breath" that he gives to them in analogous fashion to Ps 104:29–30, *pace* Koch, *Geist Gottes*, 125, and Woodhouse, "'Spirit,'" 18.

exiles respond in repentance to the call made to Ezekiel's audience, and now made, indirectly, through the book, to the addressees of the book, that Yahweh's רוח works to bring about precisely that response, breathing new life into them, as part of the holistic restoration.

The continuity in divine action that Hals maintains, and that can be seen in the disputation oracle that explains the vision (37:12–14), highlights two points. From a divine perspective, it shows the intimate link between the prophet speaking the word and the response that is both desired and will be produced by Yahweh's רוח. From the perspective of the exilic addressees of the book, it shows how their response to Yahweh's word is appropriate, indeed essential, as an integral part of one event—the revivifying of the "dead" that they themselves are. Here, then, Yahweh's word and Yahweh's רוח are intimately related. Here, too, divine initiative and sovereignty, expressed in the action of רוח, are held together with human responsibility, expressed in the ongoing need for repentance. The response to their helpless complaint, "How shall we live?" (33:10), was met there by the call to repent (33:11). The response to their helpless complaint, "Our bones are dried up" (37:11), is that Yahweh will put his spirit *qua* breath in them (v. 14). The two passages provide complementary perspectives. The initiative lies with Yahweh. It is he who commands Ezekiel to address הרוח while the reformed bodies are still not alive. But the image of רוח revivifying the bones should not be interpreted as obviating the need for a response.

Before we look at evidence that supports such a view, it is necessary to address one notion that would invalidate such an understanding, and that is the notion that the word itself is inherently powerful. Were this the case, then there would be no need for רוח to effect Yahweh's word.

It has often been said that the ancient Israelites had a different conception of the word from that of modern Western thinking. So, for example, Eichrodt has written that it "possessed an importance quite different from that which it enjoys today."[111] This different perspective is, exponents say, seen particularly in the power that the ancients supposedly saw as inherent in the word.[112] So Koch comments, "in the prophet's view the dynamic aspect of the word, which calls forth historical events, is more important than the dianoetic information it contains."[113]

---

111. Eichrodt, *Theology*, 2:69.
112. Von Rad, *Old Testament Theology*, 2:80–98; Isaac Rabinowitz, *A Witness Forever: Ancient Israel's Perception of Literature and the Resultant Hebrew Bible* (Bethesda, Md.: Capital Decisions Limited, 1993).
113. Koch, *The Prophets*, 2:94; also pp. 165–66.

Such a notion could potentially be seen in both the first and the second stages of the vision in 37:1–10. Thus Rabinowitz argues that speech directed to inanimate objects such as dry bones reflected ancient Israel's understanding that "the speech was designed to create a physical reality."[114] In similar vein, Eichrodt says that the prophet "has experience of the effectiveness of the divine word of power which he has been ordered to proclaim."[115] What the word has declared in vv. 4–6, comes to pass in vv. 7–8, even as Ezekiel is prophesying. Further, in v. 9, the divine word spoken by the prophet summons רוח, and רוח comes.

Such a view, however, of the inherent power of words in general in the ancient world, and of the power of the word in Ezek 37, is mistaken. The notion that words in general in ancient Israel were understood to be powerful has been subject to a devastating critique by Thiselton.[116] Of particular significance is his criticism that proponents of the "powerful word" do not give adequate attention to the fact that often it is Yahweh (or, in the ancient Near East, the deity) who speaks the word, thus confounding the issue of where the power actually lies. More significant even than that for our purposes is the fact that it is not Yahweh's word *per se* that is seen to be powerful in Ezek 37 at all. Thus in the first stage, although Ezekiel addressees the bones, the word that he utters in vv. 5–6 is a declaration of what Yahweh, not Yahweh's word, will do for the bones. There is silence on *how* the bones came together; Yahweh's word reveals Yahweh's will, and no more; it shows that Yahweh's actions are not arbitrary.[117] In the second stage, it is true that the prophetic word spoken by Ezekiel summons הרוח, but that does not mean that the word itself is powerful to act independently of Yahweh, whose word it is. What it does serve to show is that the action of רוח is intimately linked with the prophetic word spoken through the prophet Ezekiel, and now re-presented to the exilic addressees. רוח comes in and through the words of the prophet.[118] There is no hope for revival and renewal separate from the words of the prophet; neither is there hope for revival and renewal separate from the revivifying work of רוח. Schüngel-Straumann comes close to summarizing it neatly, though her strict distinction of roles is unwarranted: "The all-powerful word of Yahweh admittedly brings the *rwh*, but the making alive happens through the power of God, *rwh*, alone;

114.   Rabinowitz, *A Witness Forever*, 55.
115.   Eichrodt, *Ezekiel*, 508.
116.   Anthony C. Thiselton, "The Supposed Power of Words in the Biblical Writings," *JTS* 25 (1974): 283–99.
117.   Cf. Fretheim, "Word of God," 6:965.
118.   Schüngel-Straumann, *Rûaḥ bewegt die Welt*, 59.

so neither a super- nor a sub-ordination between *rwh* and word can be maintained, rather something like a complementarity."[119]

Though arguments about the power of Yahweh's word do not refute the understanding put forward above, that רוח effects the word in the experience of those who hear it, such an understanding still needs positive evidence. Three pieces of evidence, taken together, point in this direction.

First, a penitent response to the prophet's call elsewhere in the book yields an identical result to that produced by the action of רוח in ch. 37. In a number of places (e.g. 13:22; 18:32; 33:11), "life" for the exiles is explicitly portrayed as the product of Ezekiel's addressees' repentance or of obedience to Yahweh's laws (e.g. 20:11). In ch. 37, "life" is clearly the outcome of the action of רוח that comes in and through the words of the prophet. I have argued above that the addressees of the book are still confronted with calls to repent. From the perspective of the book as a whole, as it confronts its exilic addressees, רוח can be seen to bring about in their own experience the response that is required of them.

Secondly, the parallel with creation traditions, already noted in the presence of the two stages in the process of restoration, extends further, as evinced in the relationship between the divine word and the divine רוח in Gen 1.[120] Yahweh's רוח acts to bring about Yahweh's word. Such an interpretation of Gen 1 is by no means universally accepted. The phrase רוח אלהים in 1:2 has been interpreted in three main ways, as a "great

---

119.   Ibid., 65: "Das vollmächtige Jahwewort bringt zwar die *rwh* herbei, aber das Lebendigmachen geschieht durch die Gotteskraft *rwh* allein; so läßt sich weder eine Über- noch eine Unterordnung zwischen *rwh* und Wort behaupten, eher so etwas wie eine Komplementarität."

120.   Caution over speaking of allusions to creation in Ezekiel has been rightly expressed by Petersen. See David L. Petersen, "Creation in Ezekiel: Methodological Perspectives and Theological Prospects," in Cook and Patton, eds., *Ezekiel's Hierarchical World*, 169–78. He is, however, unduly sceptical about the presence and significance of creation traditions in Ezekiel. Some parallels with the Genesis creation account attributed to J (2:4b–3:24) have already been noted; see further Levenson, *Theology of the Program*, 25–36; Kutsko, *Between Heaven and Earth*, 129–34; Steven S. Tuell, "Contemporary Studies of Ezekiel: A New Tide Rising," in Cook and Patton, eds., *Ezekiel's Hierarchical World*, 248–49. Although Zimmerli (*Ezekiel 1*, 52) states that "the specific theological ideas of the historical outline of P…find no echo in Ezekiel" and Kutsko's argument that Ezekiel knew and built on the notion of humans as "in the image of God" relies perhaps too much on circumstantial evidence, there are still pointers towards common ideas (e.g. ורבו ופרו, 36:11); the role of רוח in (re-)creation; the emphasis on Yahweh's spoken word (Zimmerli, "'Leben' und 'Tod,'" 507). My argument is not that Ezekiel is alluding to Gen 1. Rather, there is a similarity of ideas present in both places.

wind,"[121] as "the wind/breath of God"[122] and as "the spirit of God."[123] The difference between the first of these interpretations and the other two cannot be underestimated. The first suggests that רוח אלהים refers to the substance out of which God creates the universe, while the others suggest that this phrase refers in some sense to the creator of the universe. The difference between the second and third interpretations lies not in the source of רוח, since all agree that the phrase refers to the deity as origin, but in the primary referent. The second interpretation, while acknowledging that God may be responsible for the wind, sees the text as describing what is essentially a meteorological phenomenon. The third interpretation sees God's רוח being portrayed as separate from God, not in the sense of being independent of God, but rather speaking of "the impending creative activity of the deity."[124] The Targumim capture some of the difficulty. *Targum Onqelos* has "a wind from before the Lord,"[125] while *Targum Pseudo-Jonathan* and *Targum Neofiti* 1 have "a wind/spirit of mercy from before God/the Lord."[126]

121. So, e.g., von Rad, who comments that "this 'spirit of God' takes no more active part in creation"; see Gerhard von Rad, *Genesis: A Commentary* (trans. J. H. Marks; 3d ed.; London: SCM, 1972), 49; also Harry M. Orlinsky, "The Plain Meaning of *RÛAḤ* in Gen. 1.2," *JQR* 48 (1957–58): 174–82; E. A. Speiser, *Genesis* (AB 1; New York: Doubleday, 1964), 5; Claus Westermann, *Genesis 1–11: A Commentary* (trans. J. J. Scullion; London: SPCK, 1984), 79, 107–8; P. J. Smith, "A Semotactical Approach to the Meaning of the Term *rûaḥ ʾĕlōhîm* in Genesis 1:2," *JNSL* 8 (1980): 99–104.

122. N. H. Ridderbos, "Gen. 1.1 und 2," *OtSt* 12 (1958): 214–60; Gordon J. Wenham, *Genesis 1–15* (WBC 1; Dallas: Word, 1987), 16–17; Dion, "La *rwḥ* dans l'Heptateuch," 172; Tengström, 7:405–7.

123. Brevard S. Childs, *Myth and Reality in the Old Testament* (London: SCM, 1960), 35; van Imschoot, *Theology*, 187; Aubrey R. Johnson, *The Cultic Prophet in Ancient Israel* (2d ed.; Cardiff: University of Wales Press, 1962), 32–33; Neve, *Spirit of God*, 64–71; Victor P. Hamilton, *The Book of Genesis Chapters 1–17* (NICOT; Grand Rapids: Eerdmans, 1990), 111–14; Michael DeRoche, "The *rûaḥ ʾĕlōhîm* in Gen 1:2c: Creation or Chaos," in *Ascribe to the Lord: Biblical and Other Studies in Memory of Peter C. Craigie* (ed. Lyle Eslinger and Glen Taylor; JSOTSup 67; Sheffield: JSOT Press, 1988), 303–18; Dreytza, *Der theologische Gebrauch von RÛAḤ*, 173–75.

124. DeRoche, "*rûaḥ ʾĕlōhîm* in Gen 1:2c," 318.

125. Bernard Grossfeld, *The Targum Onqelos to Genesis* (The Aramaic Bible 6; Edinburgh: T. & T. Clark, 1988), 42. In the quotation, I have removed Grossfeld's square brackets from "and a wind." His brackets indicate that the text is missing from Vatican Manuscript 448, but present in the Sabbioneta text (see p. 36).

126. McNamara renders the phrase "a spirit of mercy from before the Lord." See Martin McNamara, *Targum Neofiti 1: Genesis* (The Aramaic Bible 1A; Edinburgh: T. & T. Clark, 1992), 52. Maher, on the other hand, prefers "a merciful

Syntactically, the phrase parallels "the earth was desert-like and empty"[127] and "darkness covered the deep." The parallelism is further enhanced by the virtual synonymity of "deep" and "waters" in v. 2b and v. 2c. Thus v. 2 consists of three parallel clauses which describe the situation prior to God speaking in v. 3.

This parallelism leads some scholars, such as Westermann, to see any kind of positive connotations in רוח אלהים as inappropriate. Thus they prefer the translation "a fearful wind."[128]

This view, however, is not without its problems. There are six main arguments against this, the first interpretation. First, this interpretation regards אלהים as expressing a superlative, yet אלהים is never elsewhere used with "wind" to express a superlative.[129] Secondly, such a rendering ignores the parallels with the next occurrence of the phrase in Exod 31:3, where Bezalel is filled with the רוח אלהים. According to Hamilton (who follows Fishbane), "this key phrase unites...via an intertextual allusion, world building and tabernacle building."[130] Thirdly, of the thirty-five occurrences of אלהים in Gen 1:1–2:3, thirty-four clearly refer to the deity; it is unlikely that its occurrence in this clause would have a different meaning.[131] More particularly, אלהים in v. 2 would hardly have a different meaning from that in v. 1 and v. 3 without any indication.[132] Fourthly, there are other unambiguous ways of expressing "a mighty wind." Fifthly, wind is usually an opponent of the waters, drying them out, rather than a cobelligerent.[133] Finally, the main argument in favour of

wind." See Michael Maher, *Targum Pseudo-Jonathan: Genesis* (The Aramaic Bible 1B; Edinburgh: T. & T. Clark, 1992), 16 (original emphasis). Maher notes the possibility of translating as "a spirit *of mercy*," but expresses his preference for "wind" because of the verb "blow" (p. 16 n. 5). Both note that there is the same phrase in 8:1.

127.   David T. Tsumura, *The Earth and the Waters in Genesis 1 and 2: A Linguistic Investigation* (JSOTSup 83; Sheffield: JSOT Press, 1989), 42. Tsumura argues cogently that "both the biblical context and extra-biblical parallels suggest that the phrase *tōhû wābōhû* in Gen 1:2 has nothing to do with 'chaos' and simply means 'emptiness' and refers to the earth which is an empty place, i.e. 'an unproductive and uninhabited place'" (p. 43).

128.   Westermann, *Genesis 1–11*, 107, 206.

129.   Wenham, *Genesis 1–15*, 16–17.

130.   Hamilton, *Genesis 1–17*, 112; so too J. H. Sailhamer, *The Pentateuch as Narrative: A Biblical-Theological Commentary* (Grand Rapids: Zondervan, 1992), 32–33; idem, "Genesis," in *The Expositor's Bible Commentary*. Vol. 2, *Genesis–Numbers* (Grand Rapids: Zondervan, 1990), 25.

131.   DeRoche, "*rûaḥ ʾĕlōhîm* in Gen 1:2c," 307.

132.   Childs, *Myth and Reality*, 35.

133.   Cf. Gen 8:1; Exod 14:21; 15:8; Isa 17:13; 50:2; Ps 18:16 (ET 18:15). So especially Ridderbos, "Gen. 1.1 und 2," 244.

this position, the textual one based on the parallelism in v. 2, can be answered by saying that simultaneity rather than synonymity is in view.[134]

Distinguishing between the other two interpretations is more difficult. Comparisons with texts elsewhere in Genesis or the Pentateuch are suggestive of "the wind of God." In Gen 8:1, "God made a wind blow (ויעבר אלהים רוח) over the earth, and the waters subsided." This is clearly an echo of Gen 1, pointing to the unstated action of רוח in the separating of the waters, a prelude to Noah as an Adam figure with a renewed Adamic mandate. The close relationship between the wind as a meteorological phenomenon sent by God, God's own breath, and water, is apparent from the parallels between Exod 14:21 and 15:8, 10. In Exod 14:21, "Yahweh drove the sea back by a strong east wind (ברוח קדים עזה) all night." The same action is expressed in 15:8 with the words, "At the blast of your nostrils (וברוח אפיך) the waters piled up," an unmistakable reference to Yahweh's breath. Yahweh is again involved when the sea swamps Pharaoh's army, "You blew with your wind/breath (נשפת ברוחך), the sea covered them" (15:10). Further evidence for the parallels between the two, and with Gen 1, are found in the effects of this רוח in revealing "dry ground" (Gen 1:9; Exod 14:22; 15:19). In addition, other places in the Old Testament speak metaphorically of the creative power of רוח *qua* Yahweh's breath (e.g. Ps 33:6; Job 26:13).

On the other hand, there are two factors which make it preferable to see the primary referent here not as a meteorological phenomenon, the wind of God, but as theological, the creative "spirit of God." First, the Piel participle which qualifies רוח אלהים in v. 2 points towards this. It comes from the verb רחף, which only occurs in the Piel elsewhere in the Old Testament in Deut 32:11. There Yahweh's guiding is like an eagle "hovering" (רחף Piel) over the wilderness (תהו).[135] Clearly, the verb in Deuteronomy has nurturing, rather than confrontational, connotations. This makes parallels with texts where the wind confronts the water less determinative for interpretation. The next occurrence of the phrase, in Exod 31, also supports this understanding, for there is a striking parallel between the making of the world and the making of the tabernacle. As Sailhamer comments, "in both accounts the work of God (*mᵉlākāh*, Gen 2:2; Exod 31:5 [also v. 3]) is to be accomplished by the 'Spirit of God' (*rûaḥ ᵉlōhîm*). As God did his 'work' (*mᵉlākāh*) of creation by means

---

134.   DeRoche, "*rûaḥ ᵉlōhîm* in Gen 1:2c," 315. He also notes that appeals to ancient Near Eastern cosmogonies have proved indecisive. See ibid., 307–8.

135.   Cf. Meredith G. Kline, *Images of the Spirit* (repr., Eugene: Wipf & Stock, 1999 [1980]), 14–15.

of the 'Spirit of God' (*rûaḥ ʾelōhîm*), so Israel was to do their 'work' (*meláḵāh*) by means of the 'Spirit of God.'"[136]

These contrasting pieces of evidence point to an ambiguity in Gen 1:2 that is surely deliberate. There is a reference to a wind sent by Yahweh, to Yahweh's breath, and to Yahweh's spirit. It should of course be noted that רוח in Ezek 37 is at one moment the wind summoned by the prophetic word (v. 9), at the next moment the creative revivifying breath of life (vv. 5, 6, 8, 10), a breath that is itself interpreted as God's spirit (v. 14).

In Gen 1, while רוח as "wind" never reappears, רוח as breath/spirit "joins the God of creation in v. 1 to the same God in v. 3, maintaining the continued action of the creative God," and can be seen, in parallel with Ps 33:6, to have a close link with the creative word.[137] "The spirit of God is the creative power of God which joins with the word, bearing and articulating it, in the creative act."[138] In other words, the spirit of God *makes effective* the spoken word; it has an integral function within creation. Fretheim expresses such a point in discussing the role of God's word in creation. He maintains that "God's creative activity" should be understood not just in terms of what God said, but also with reference to "the work of the Spirit of God" in Gen 1:2.[139] At this point, his reference to Isa 34:16[140] is particularly significant. The function of רוח there is to give "expression" to the word not by uttering it, nor by gathering it into the book of Yahweh, but "by executing it."[141] For Fretheim, then, spirit and word go together: "it is not suggested that there was no divine activity apart from speaking. God's spirit and power follow in the train of the word and produce certain effects."[142] The same view has been articulated

136. Sailhamer, "Genesis," 25.

137. Neve, *Spirit of God*, 69; Montague, *Holy Spirit*, 67–68.

138. Neve, *Spirit of God*, 69.

139. Fretheim, "Word of God," 6:965. In his commentary on Genesis (Terence E. Fretheim, "Genesis," *NIB* 1:343), he comments, "God's speaking does not stand isolated from God's making (e.g. 1:6–7, 14–16; see also Ps 33:6; Isa 48:3). This speaking-doing rhythm may reflect earlier forms of the text that have now been decisively integrated. Hence, the word itself does not explain sufficiently what comes to be; the word is accompanied by the deed. God does not create by 'word events' but by 'word–deed events.'" Cf. Westermann, *Genesis 1–11*, 82–87.

140. Isa 34:16 reads: "Seek and read from the book of Yahweh: // Not one of these shall be missing; // none shall be without its mate. // For the mouth of Yahweh has commanded (כי־פי הוא צוה), // and his spirit has gathered them (ורוחו הוא קבצן)."

141. Ma, *Until the Spirit Comes*, 77–78 (quotation from p. 77). Ma is swift to add that "they are not separate actions by different agents."

142. Fretheim, "Word of God," 6:965.

clearly by Warfield: "God's thought and will and word take effect in the world, because God is not only over the world, thinking and willing and commanding, but also in the world, as the principle of all activity, *executing*."[143] In Gen 1, God's רוח is the power by which Yahweh brings to effect what his word expresses. Ezekiel 37:14 mirrors the creation accounts not just at the point of "two stages," but also with regard to the relationship between divine word and divine רוח. Yahweh's רוח makes effective the word that has been uttered.[144]

The third piece of evidence pointing to רוח making effective Yahweh's word is the symmetry between Ezekiel, in his commissioning, and the experience of the dry bones of the exilic community. In 2:2, the prophet, prostrate before the vision of the likeness of the glory of Yahweh, is set on his feet by רוח that enters him. In 37:10, the hopeless exiles (cf. 33:10b; 37:11) stand on their feet because of רוח that enters them. The similar wording in the two points strongly to conceptual links.

Before the prophet himself can have a hope for the future, before he can stand in Yahweh's presence, hear his word and obey, he himself must experience the divine רוח;[145] the same is true of the exiles. It is רוח that makes effective the divine word in 2:2; in the same way, in ch. 37, what the re-formed bones of the exiles need is Yahweh's רוח to come so that they can stand on their feet—to make effective in their experience the word that has been spoken to them by the prophet, and which is recorded for them in the book.

Similar links are present in 3:22–24. There, רוח enters Ezekiel and sets him on his feet (ותבא־בי רוח ותעמדני על־רגלי). What is particularly striking is that this happens in the "valley" (הבקעה). The only other occurrences of this word in the book are in 8:4, where Ezekiel refers to

---

143.   Warfield, "The Spirit of God," 108 (original emphasis).

144.   Note how a similar understanding of the work of God's spirit has been combined with speech act theory by Vanhoozer, such that God's spirit brings about the perlocutionary effects of an illocutionary act of speaking. He comments, "there is a connection…between pneumatology and perlocutions…a perlocution is what one brings about *by* one's speech act. Speech frequently presents an argument, but arguments are intended to produce assent. Perlocutions have to do with the effect on the hearer of a speech act"; see Kevin J. Vanhoozer, "Effectual Call or Causal Effect? Summons, Sovereignty and Supervenient Grace," *TynBul* 49 (1998): 248. Cf. idem, "God's Mighty Speech-Acts: The Doctrine of Scripture Today," in *A Pathway Into the Holy Scriptures* (ed. Philip E. Satterthwaite and David F. Wright; Grand Rapids: Eerdmans, 1994), 143–81; idem, *Is There a Meaning in This Text?* (Leicester: Inter-Varsity Press, 1998); idem, "From Speech Acts to Scripture Acts."

145.   That it is divine is clear not from the immediate context, but only retrospectively. See pp. 115–20 above.

the vision that he saw "in the valley," and in 37:1–2, where it is referred to again as "the valley" (הבקעה). Just as רוח caused Ezekiel to stand in the valley (3:22–24), so רוח enables the refashioned bones to stand "in the valley" (37:1–2, 10).[146] Such parallels between the experience of the prophet and the experience of the exiles are reinforced by three further links, all internal to ch. 37.

The first can be derived from structural observations about the construction of the unit 37:1–14.[147] Although it is not necessary to agree with Fishbane that there is a chiastic structure in these verses, he notes several *inclusio*s which serve to tie the prophet's experience to the exiles': "(A) the text opens with a reference to Ezekiel's inspiration by means of the divine spirit (רוח) and his relocation (ויניחני) in a death valley (vv. 1–2), and it concludes (A') with references to Israel's resuscitation through YHWH's spirit-breath (רוח) and its relocation (והנחתי) in its ancestral homeland (v. 14)."[148]

Secondly, and derived from the first point, there is the link between רוח יהוה in 37:1 and רוחי in 37:14. Carley sees the occurrence of the explicit "spirit of Yahweh" as being something significant at this point in the book.[149] He argues that throughout the rest of the book, רוח is not specifically Yahweh's רוח. This enables Yahweh's רוח to be used exclusively in the book "in connection with the restoration of the nation, or the revival of the people as those who 'know Yahweh.'" The shift marked

---

146. The reason for the move from רוח as subject in 2:2 and 3:24 of עמד (Hiphil) to the refashioned bones being the subject of עמד (Qal) in 37:10 is not certain. It could be to encourage the possibility of a theological understanding in 2:2 and 3:24 (cf. Ohnesorge, *Jahwe gestaltet sein Volk neu*, 303), generating deliberate ambiguity. The alternative is that it serves to stress the action, not the mere passivity, of the refashioned bones in 37:10. Enabled by רוח, they, as agents, stand on their feet.

147. That these verses form a literary unit is clear from both the start and the conclusion. See Block, *Ezekiel 25–48*, 370; Allen, "Structure, Tradition and Redaction." The start is marked by the "hand of Yahweh" coming upon the prophet and bringing him out, something that is clearly distinct from what has preceded. The conclusion is marked by a combination of the recognition formula, the formulaic "I have spoken and I will do it," by the concluding signatory formula in v. 14 and by the word-event formula introducing a new unit in 37:15.

148. Michael Fishbane, *Biblical Interpretation in Ancient Israel* (Oxford: Clarendon, 1985), 452. Allen (*Ezekiel 20–48*, 183) also draws attention to the *inclusio*s. Fox ("Rhetoric of Ezekiel's Vision," 14), however, disagrees, arguing that the author does not conspicuously draw attention to v. 1 in v. 14 and that the two occurrences of רוח "function too differently to be able to combine into such a summary." This is not compelling, since the presence of the other links (נוח and the theme of "place") do establish the links.

149. Carley, *Ezekiel Among the Prophets*, 28–31.

by the introduction of "spirit of Yahweh" is due, in Carley's view, to the "difference between the old and the new Israel... In the context of the hope of restoration, common phenomena no longer served as satisfactory images to describe the new, dynamic power which would enable the people to honour Yahweh's name."[150] Thus, in 37:1, "the promise of the future is realized in the prophet's own experience."[151] Carley's basic observation about the relationship between prophet and people stands, even if the self-evidently theological references to רוח in 11:5 and 11:24 are accepted. Within the prophet's experience, there is a move from רוח as the breath of life that enters and restores the prophet and sets him on his feet (2:2), to the spirit of Yahweh that explicitly is seen to transport him (within his vision) in 37:1. In the same way, the meaning of רוח with regard to the exiles permutes within ch. 37 from רוח as revivifying "breath" (v. 5) through to רוח as Yahweh's "spirit" in v. 14.

Thirdly, it has already been noted how the prophet is addressed by Yahweh throughout the book of Ezekiel as "son of man." The Targum of Ezekiel does not render it with a phrase that connotes the "mortal unworthiness of the prophet,"[152] such as the Aramaic *bar ʾĕnāš* or its variants, but on every occasion translates it with *bar ʾādām*. Levey comments, "the Targumic phrase can only mean 'son of Adam' or 'Adamite,'"[153] for in Aramaic, *ʾādām* is a proper name. Levey notes that "while it seems evident that the intent is deliberate, we can only conjecture as to the purpose of the phrase." One way of reading it might be derived from Ezek 37. We have already observed how the two distinct stages of resuscitation parallel closely the two phases of the creation of Adam in Gen 2:7; as Block observes, "the two-phased process of resuscitation also serves a theologico-anthropological function, emulating the paradigm of Yahweh's creation of *ʾādām*."[154] If the prophet is a paradigm of the people in his experience of the divine רוח, then he can be seen as the first human in Yahweh's new work of creation among the exiles.[155] Twice, he is addressed as בן־אדם in these verses (vv. 3, 9). In the context of these

---

150.	Ibid., 31.

151.	Ibid.

152.	Samson H. Levey, *The Targum of Ezekiel: Translated, with a Critical Introduction, Apparatus, and Notes* (The Aramaic Bible 13; Edinburgh: T. & T. Clark, 1987), 6.

153.	Ibid., 7.

154.	Block, *Ezekiel 25–48*, 379.

155.	*Targum Onqelos* reads אדם in Gen 2:7. Grossfeld (*Targum Onqelos to Genesis*, 43) observes in his comment on אנשא in Gen 1:26, "from the moment of his actual creation, depicted in this verse, the Targum treats this term as referring to an actual individual, hence Adam."

verses, the prophet, as the first one who has received the life-giving רוח of Yahweh, is indeed "son of Adam" in another sense.[156]

In summary, we have seen that Ezek 37:1–14 serves to show to the exilic addressees of the book *how* the vision of the future, modelled by the prophet, can become "real" in their experience, despite a history of constant failure to respond aright to Yahweh's word, right up to their fathers, Ezekiel's addressees. If the gathered, but lifeless, exilic community is to follow the prophet's call to repentance, רוח, intimately linked to the word spoken by the prophet, is essential. Only then can it be the revivified, restored, united house of Israel in the land once again, knowing that "I am Yahweh." Further, just as Ezekiel, in contrast to his intended audience, is paradigmatic for the readers in his response to Yahweh's word, so too he is paradigmatic in his experience of Yahweh's רוח as that which enables an appropriate response. Seitz asks quizzically, "Are the condemned people now to undergo the same transformation that the prophet experienced at his call?"[157] We can answer in the affirmative.

This picture of רוח as essential for the obedience of the exiles is not restricted, however, to their response to Yahweh's word as spoken by the prophet; רוח is also essential for their ongoing obedience to Yahweh's statutes and ordinances, as can be seen from 36:26–27.

2.2. *How Israel's Long-term Future is Secured: Ezekiel 36:26–27*
In view of the organic link between the behaviour of those in Jerusalem and the judgment that had come, future obedience would be essential if the exiles' long-term future back in the land was to be secure. Ezekiel 36:26–27 speaks directly of an effected future obedience. In v. 26, Yahweh promises to the exiles, in words very similar to the promise in 11:19 and the command in 18:31, "A new heart I will give you, and a new spirit I will put within you; and I will remove from your body the heart of stone and give you a heart of flesh." This promise is then extended in words not found elsewhere: "I will put my spirit within you, and make you follow my statutes and be careful to observe my ordinances" (v. 27).

The context of the promised רוח is the literary unit from 36:16 to 36:38, marked at the beginning by the characteristic word-event formula.[158] Verses 17–21, in which "Ezekiel appears to function as Yah-

---

156. Cf. Renz, *Rhetorical Function*, 140. Renz suggests Ezekiel is a "proto-human" in view of his designation "son of man." This suggestion is not tied specifically to ch. 37. Cf. Lys, *Rûach*, 143–44.

157. Seitz, "Ezekiel 37:1–14," 53.

158. The oldest LXX manuscript, Papyrus 967, does not have 36:23b–38. It also follows a different order in chs. 36–39 from the MT. Wevers (*Ezekiel*, 273) explains the omission as parablepsis. This is unlikely given the length and the significant

weh's confidant and friend,"[159] outline the crisis for Yahweh's honour brought about by profanation of his holy name among the nations (cf. v. 20). In vv. 22–32, framed by two *inclusio*s, "not for your sakes" and "house of Israel," Yahweh explains *how* he will restore the honour of his name. If his name is not to be profaned again, it is vital that the "deity–nation–land" relationship is fully restored once more.[160] This requires two things. First, Yahweh must make sure that the fundamental problem of Israel's disobedience is tackled. It was their behaviour that had caused the land to be defiled (vv. 17–18) and had led to Yahweh pouring out his wrath upon them and scattering them (vv. 18–19). Therefore Yahweh must effect their cleansing and obedience. Secondly, the land must be restored, so that the nations will not be appalled at it (cf. Ezek 36:30; Lev 26:32–33). Both these things are dealt with in vv. 24–32. There follow two other oracles that are marked off as separate by the citation formulae in v. 33 and v. 37. They are not out of place in the current literary context, however, since they have a number of themes in common with the preceding material,[161] and עוד זאת in v. 37 clearly assists integration.

The significance of these two verses, and of v. 27 in particular, for our analysis of the relationship between Yahweh's word and Yahweh's רוח, can be summed up by answering two questions. First, "What is understood by רוח in these verses?" Secondly, "How does what is being promised relate to the word of Yahweh?'

2.2.1. רוח *in Ezekiel 36:26–27*. Without v. 26, Yahweh's promise that he would give "my spirit" (רוחי) in the midst of the exiles (v. 27) could be nothing other than a promise of revivifying breath within the reconstituted "person" that is the new house of Israel;[162] in so far as Yahweh is the source of רוח, it is Yahweh's while it remains outside the person, but

content (Block, *Ezekiel 25–48*, 340). Papyrus 967, however, is probably not a reflection of the original text, since the *inclusio* (v. 22 and v. 32) points towards the MT as being correct; further, the announcement that Yahweh will "act" (v. 22) and will "sanctify" his great name (v. 23) is left hanging, if Yahweh's actions themselves are not present (see Zimmerli, *Ezekiel 2*, 245). For a fuller discussion, bibliography of the issue, and defence of the authenticity of the MT, see Block, *Ezekiel 25–48*, 337–43; Greenberg, *Ezekiel 21–37*, 739–40; Allen, *Ezekiel 20–48*, 177–78.

159.   Block, *Ezekiel 25–48*, 344.

160.   Cf. ibid., 347–49.

161.   Links from the first oracle (vv. 33–36) include: "cleanse" (v. 25); "resettle/rebuild" (v. 10b); "tilled" (v. 9b). See Greenberg, *Ezekiel 21–37*, 732. There is also the reaction of the nations (v. 30). Links from the second oracle include the increase in population (36:10–11, 33, 35) and "sheep" (ch. 34).

162.   The language is better understood as corporate, rather than individual. See Joyce, *Divine Initiative*, 112–13.

becomes that person's once it is "inside" them.[163] It would then be a picture of new life coming to what is dead. The close correspondence in the wording of v. 26 and v. 27, however, points in a different direction: the new רוח promised in v. 26 is further identified as none other than Yahweh's רוח.

To understand what is meant by Yahweh's רוח in v. 27, then, we need to do two things. First, we need to explore the significance of רוח חדשה in v. 26 and, in particular, its relation to לב. Secondly, we need to look at how the two occurrences of רוח in these verses relate to one another.

As we turn to the significance of רוח חדשה in v. 26, we shall look first at לב, since how לב is understood will affect our interpretation of רוח חדשה.[164]

In 11:19 and 36:26, Yahweh promises to give the exiles "one heart"[165] (לב אחד) or a "new heart" (לב חדש). This is expanded upon later in both verses by the promise that Yahweh will change the "heart of stone" (לב האבן) for a "heart of flesh" (לב בשר). The heart here stands neither for the whole "person," since this "heart" is removed and replaced, nor for the seat of emotions (cf. 36:5), since obedience not emotional response is in view, nor even for the intellectual faculty, the mind (cf. 3:10; 38:10), since it is not their understanding, but their response that is wrong, as is evident from the words qualifying "heart" here. Rather, it speaks metonymically of the human will, especially the moral will, the deepest orientation in a person for a particular direction.[166] It is this heart

---

163. Cf. Ps 104:29–30; see p. 116 above.

164. For more on לב, see Johnson, *Cultic Prophet*, 75–87; Wolff, *Anthropology of the Old Testament*, 40–58; F. Stolz, "לֵב *lēb* heart," *TLOT* 2:638–42; Alex Luc, "לֵב," *NIDOTTE* 2:749–54. For לב in Ezekiel, see especially Joyce, *Divine Initiative*, 108–9, 119–21. I follow his categories in what follows.

165. The reading אחד is debated, because LXX reads here καρδίαν ἑτέραν (suggesting a Vorlage with אחר), Syriac reads "new," and Targum ("fearful," "fearing") could be a paraphrase of either אחר (cf. LXX) or חדש (cf. Syriac) but not אחד (MT). Further, the MT of Jer 32:39 reads ונתתי להם לב אחד, giving a close parallel here, while the LXX of Jer 39:39 reads δώσω αὐτοῖς ὁδὸν ἑτέραν καὶ καρδίαν ἑτέραν, paralleling the LXX of Ezek 11:19. In addition, 1 Sam 10:9 has לב אחר which LXX renders with καρδίαν ἄλλην. Those who favour "another" include Allen, *Ezekiel 20–48*, 129; H. L. Ellison, *Ezekiel: The Man and His Message* (London: Paternoster, 1956), 48; Wolff, *Anthropology*, 54; Zimmerli, *Ezekiel 1*, 230; Dominique Barthélemy, "'Un seul', 'un nouveau' ou 'un autre'? À propos de l'intervention du Seigneur sur le coeur de l'homme selon Éz 11,19a et des problèmes de critique textuelle qu'elle soulève," in Mosis and Ruppert, eds., *Der Weg zum Menschen*, 329–38. Those who favour the MT reading here include Block, *Ezekiel 1–24*, 342, 353; Greenberg, *Ezekiel 1–20*, 190 (he speaks of "rich overtones"); Joyce, *Divine Initiative*, 160–61. If the MT is allowed to stand, "one" speaks of an undivided heart

that is hard to Yahweh's word (2:4; 3:7), yet welcoming to idols (14:3; 20:16) and greedy for gain (33:31). The significance of the heart being "of stone" lies in part in the figurative way of speaking about Israel's unresponsiveness in Ezekiel's initial commissioning, where their heart is hard (חזקי־לב, 2:4). This adjective is used in 3:9 in conjunction with "flint" and "rock." The precise significance, however, needs to be derived also from the heart with which it is replaced: a "heart of flesh." This positive sense of בשר is "absolutely unique."[167] Greenberg accounts for this by suggesting that the heart will now be "of the same element as its body."[168] This certainly suggests that the house of Israel is currently in some sense *less than human*. This may be because to have a heart of stone is to be like an animal, for Leviathan has a heart like stone (Job 41:16 [ET 41:24]).[169] There it is used positively, however, speaking of a quality of invincibility, impenetrable to any weapon, rather than pejoratively, of the impossibility of Leviathan being tamed. More likely is Kutsko's suggestion that Israel takes on the characteristics of the idols they have taken into their heart.[170] On both these readings, there is something profoundly deficient in the very humanity of the person Israel. There may also be a further nuance here, which certainly fits with 37:1–14. In 1 Sam 25:37, the narrator comments on Nabal's death, "when Nabal's heart died within him, he became like stone." The exiles' heart is not simply "hard" in the sense of unresponsive, but even dead to Yahweh.[171]

---

in two possible senses that overlap. First, it "could possibly reflect hopes of renewed national unity," suggesting a singleness of purpose (Joyce, *Divine Initiative*, 161; also noted but not adopted by Ellison, *Ezekiel*, 49; cf. Ezek 37:22). This usage is found in 1 Chr 12:39 (ET 12:38). The alternative is that of an undivided heart as the antithesis of insincerity (cf. Deut 6:4–5; 1 Chr 12:34; 2 Chr 30:12 and especially Ps 12:3 [ET 12:2], "they speak with double-heart" [ידברו בלב ולב]). See Block, "Prophet of the Spirit," 45–46; Greenberg, *Ezekiel 1–20*, 190. On the other hand, Barthélemy argues that the MT reading reflects a deliberate and straightforward scribal change from אחר to אחד because of perceived negative connotations in the word אחר (cf. אלהים אחרים), and positive connotations in אחד (cf. שמע ישראל יהוה אלהינו יהוה אחד, Deut 6:4).

166. Cf. Joyce, *Divine Initiative*, 108–9. Joyce suggests (p.109) that in 11:19–20 and 36:26, לב is the "the locus of the moral will" (cf. 2:4; 3:7) and "the symbol of inner reality as distinct from mere outward appearance" (cf. 14:3; 33:31).

167. Wolff, *Anthropology*, 29.

168. Greenberg, *Ezekiel 21–37*, 730.

169. Lapsley, *Can These Bones Live?*, 104.

170. Kutsko, *Between Heaven and Earth*, 128–29.

171. In this regard, it is interesting in the case of Nabal that the body's turning to stone is associated with the death of the לב; though his heart died, he went on living for another ten days. See 1 Sam 25:38.

In this way, while the main thrust of the picture in 36:26 is that Israel will be responsive and malleable now to Yahweh and his word, the "heart of flesh" might also suggest that one who was less than human will now be truly human, and the one dead to Yahweh will now be alive again.[172]

When we turn our attention to רוח חדשה, it is clear that the "new spirit" in 11:19, 18:31 and 36:26 is anthropological.[173] Many scholars regard לב and רוח here as synonymous, chiefly because they "both refer primarily to the gift of a renewed capacity to respond to Yahweh in obedience."[174] Further evidence pointing to synonymy here comes from the fact that רוח elsewhere in Ezekiel can be the seat of moral thinking: in 11:5 of those in Jerusalem, and in 20:32 of those in exile (cf. Jer 51:50). This clearly parallels the usage of לב (e.g. 2:4; 3:7; 6:9; 14:3; 38:10; cf. also the parallels in 13:2–3).[175]

Others, however, see לב and רוח as complementary (cf. Deut 2:30).[176] Wolff maintains that "the new *rūaḥ* brings to the perception and will of the heart the *new vital power* to hold on steadfastly in willing obedience,"[177] and Knierim comments that "the 'heart' is the anthropological complementation to the cosmological or theological 'spirit' and as such is structured to be susceptible to the influences of 'spirit' and its notions."[178]

172. Cf. Dieter Baltzer, *Ezechiel und Deuterojesaja: Berührung in der Heilserwartung der beiden großen Exilspropheten* (BZAW 121; Berlin: de Gruyter, 1971), 76.

173. See pp. 82–83 above for my preliminary discussion.

174. Joyce, *Divine Initiative*, 111; cf. Johnson, *Vitality of the Individual*, 86; Verhoef, *NIDOTTE* 2:35; Albertz and Westermann, *TLOT* 3:1212. So too Daniel I. Block, "Gog and the Pouring Out of the Spirit: Reflections on Ezekiel xxxix 21–29," *VT* 37 (1987): 45–46, on 11:19 and 18:31; cf. van Imschoot, "L'esprit de Jahvé et l'alliance nouvelle," 219: "Ici l'esprit est, comme le coeur, le siège ou l'organe des sentiments, des pensées, de la vie morale; c'est l'esprit humain, qui doit être transformé et, pour ainsi dire, créé à neuf."

175. For the close links between anthropological uses of רוח and לב, see Schüngel-Straumann, *Rûaḥ bewegt die Welt*, 48–51.

176. Schoemaker, "The Use of רוח," 29; Cooke, *Ezekiel*, 125; Lys, *Rûach*, 141; Eichrodt, *Ezekiel*, 499; Wevers, *Ezekiel*, 97; Wolff, *Anthropology*, 38, 54; Donald E. Gowan, *Eschatology in the Old Testament* (Philadelphia: Fortress, 1986), 70–71; Knierim, *Task*, 282; Ohnesorge, *Jahwe gestaltet sein Volk neu*, 269–70; Lapsley, *Can These Bones Live?*, 104–5; Matties (*Ezekiel 18*, 206) notes the synonymity elsewhere, but suggests that the presence of the "new spirit here seems to nuance the parallelism to suggest a holistic personhood."

177. Wolff, *Anthropology*, 54 (my emphasis).

178. Knierim, *Task*, 282. Knierim makes this point based on his understanding of רוח and of the differences between the לב and רוח. For him, רוח is perceived "not only as the vitalizing power as such, but also as that endowment which disposes human(s) toward the fulfillment of God's manifold purposes for the world and for

With Block, I think it likely that they are not synonymous in 36:26.[179] Block gives three reasons: first, synonymy is rarely exact in Hebrew poetry; secondly, different prepositions are used (לכם, "to you"; בקרבכם, "within you"); thirdly, and most significantly for him, the distinction is confirmed by the elaboration. Although Yahweh supplies both the new heart and the new spirit, the new heart is not said to be Yahweh's, but a "heart of flesh"; the new רוח, however, is Yahweh's. To this can be added the observation that while the "new heart" involves replacing something that is *present* and defective, the "new spirit," while hinting at something present because of the parallel with "new heart," seems to involve supplying something that had once been present but now is *absent*, for there is no mention of an old "driving force" being removed. Care, however, should be taken in overstating the case based on the third reason, because the elaboration plays on the different meanings of רוח. The shift in the meaning of רוח evident when moving from v. 26 to v. 27 should not then be read back into v. 26.

The implication, then, is that the "new רוח" of 36:26 is not so much the "new center of volition necessary for repentance and new obedience to the commandments,"[180] as something like the new "driving force" that empowers the locus of the moral will, the heart of flesh.[181]

We turn our attention, then, to how Yahweh's רוח (v. 27) relates to the new "driving force" within Israel. There are three main choices.

First, it is logically possible to view these two different uses of רוח as *univocal*.[182] This understanding obtains if the רוח of the house of Israel is used in the same literal[183] way of the personified Israel as רוח is used (anthropomorphically) of Yahweh. One of those who seems to regard the

the life of humans..." (p. 277). The differences between לב and רוח reside in the fact that לב is created, while רוח exists. רוח "signifies the concept of life, God's life, its coming *to* humans and their dependence on it," while לב "signifies the concept of the central relay-station *in* humans in which the inspired life—or the influences of other 'spirits'—can be received" (p. 282 [original emphasis]).

179. Block, *Ezekiel 25–48*, 355–56.
180. Albertz and Westermann, *TLOT* 3:1212.
181. Cf. Fohrer's "treibende Kraft" (*Ezechiel*, 205).
182. Univocal: "any word or phrase used in the same way on two or more occasions is used univocally" (Edward L. Schoen, "Anthropomorphic Concepts of God," *RelS* 26 [1990]: 134). This is the opposite of equivocal: "terms used in more than one sense which bear no relation to one another" are used "equivocally" (Janet Martin Soskice, *Metaphor and Religious Language* [Oxford: Clarendon, 1985], 65).
183. The distinction between "literal" and "non-literal" is "assumed to be determined by the actual practices of linguistic communities. Words or phrases are used literally if they are used in accustomed, standardized ways" (Schoen, "Anthropomorphic Concepts of God," 134).

relationship between the two senses as univocal is Greenberg. Yahweh "will replace Israel's hopelessly corrupted spirit with *his own* impulsion to goodness and righteousness."[184] Univocal explanations require that the "new spirit" of v. 26 corresponds directly with Yahweh's רוח in v. 27. If רוח is "the driving force in a person," then it is essential to see רוח in v. 27 as something akin to "the driving force in a person," and that "person" is Yahweh. Another who seems to regard the two senses as univocal is Lapsley, though she speaks of רוח as "mind" here. For her, "Yahweh is not simply the *source* of the new spirit; in 36:27 it is *Yahweh's* spirit (רוחי) that will animate and suffuse the people. In a sense, then, the *people will receive the 'mind' of God...*"[185] Lapsley's first sentence is straightforwardly true. It is Lapsley's final statement, treating the two uses as univocal, that is more debatable. While it is true that the book of Ezekiel is accustomed to bold anthropomorphisms,[186] it is unlikely that language of Yahweh's רוח should be understood of as simply univocal at this point. This is chiefly because 36:27a anticipates 37:1–14.[187]

A second way is to regard the two uses of רוח in vv. 26–27 as *equivocal*. In other words, the two instances need to be clearly differentiated, although happening to use the same word (רוח). Lind seems to see the two in this light, when he comments, "God's fourth act is to put the divine *Spirit* within them (36:27). This is to be distinguished from the *new spirit* of 36:25 [*sic*]."[188] The correspondence, then, is at the level of words chosen, but not at the level of what the words denote or connote. This, however, is unlikely, for the two instances of רוח are "quite clearly intended to refer to the same reality,"[189] because of the almost identical wording in the two phrases.

The third way of regarding the two senses is as *analogical*.[190] This presupposes some kind of correspondence between the two different instances of רוח, but not that of univocity. Yahweh's רוח that he will put in the people is analogous to their own רוח. This must be partly correct, since, as we have seen, the two uses of רוח are clearly meant to speak of

184.   Greenberg, *Ezekiel 21–37*, 730 (my emphasis).
185.   Lapsley, *Can These Bones Live?*, 166 (my emphasis in the final phrase).
186.   Cf. Rimmon Kasher, "Anthropomorphism, Holiness and Cult: A New Look at Ezekiel 40–48," *ZAW* 110 (1998): 192–208.
187.   See further below.
188.   Lind, *Ezekiel*, 291.
189.   Joyce, *Divine Initiative*, 110–11.
190.   "Analogical": according to Soskice's understanding of Aquinas, a way of talking "between" univocal and equivocal (such as "Tom is happy"; "this song is happy"); see Soskice, *Metaphor and Religious Language*, 64–66. Soskice wants to affirm that analogy is not a form of metaphorical speech, but a form of literal speech.

the same reality. 36:27, however, expands the horizon limited by 36:26 (and 11:19; 18:31). Though the house of Israel's "driving force" is in view in 36:26–27, רוח as the absent "breath of life" lies beneath the surface, only to appear in 37:1–14.[191] Such a view is supported by Hals' observations about the strong links between 36:26–27 and 37:1–14, to be seen in the shift from "spirit" to "my spirit," in the language of the exodus tradition (36:24; 37:12), and in the language of covenant restoration (36:28; 37:2–13).[192] It is also supported by the fact that there is no mention of the old רוח being taken away, although mention of "a new spirit" in 36:26 leads us to believe there *is* an old one, and we have already met the exiles' corrupt רוח in 20:32.[193] If רוח in 36:26 was simply "breath" that was absent, there would be no need to qualify it with the adjective "new."

This analysis of רוח should not be seen as a case of "illegitimate totality transfer,"[194] adding the semantic value of a word in one context ("breath of life," 37:5–10) to its semantic value in another context ("driving force," 36:26), then reading the sum of these values into a particular case. While Nida is right to say that as a general principle that "the correct meaning of any term is that which contributes least to the total context,"[195] the fact that רוח as "driving force" in v. 26 is not described as "corrupt" or "hard," but seems to be absent here, points to a deliberate play on רוח as "driving force" and רוח as "breath of life." In 36:26, then, רוח as "driving force" merges seamlessly with רוח as absent "life-breath." Just as in 37:1–14, where רוח shifts from "breath of life" to Yahweh's life-giving רוח, so here there is a shift from רוח as "human driving force" to רוח as Yahweh's spirit. This development, caused by the juxtaposition of v. 26 and v. 27, means that the presence of 11:19–20

She comments that "analogical usage…from its inception…seems appropriate" (p. 65), for it is concerned with "stretched uses, not figurative ones" (p. 66). In her example, if we came across a Martian who could not speak, but arranged its fibres in a particular way such that it could communicate, then we could say, by *analogy*, that the Martian "told me."

191.   Cf. Block ("Prophet of the Spirit," 39), who proposes that 37:1–14 serve as an expansion of 36:27; also Lys, *Rûach*, 133; Allen, "Structure, Tradition and Redaction," 140–41.

192.   Hals, *Ezekiel*, 270.

193.   In Ezek 20:32, Ezekiel is to declare concerning their idolatrous desires to worship wood and *stone* like the other nations, "What is in your mind (והעלה על־רוחכם) shall never happen."

194.   James Barr, *The Semantics of Biblical Language* (Oxford: Oxford University Press, 1961), 218.

195.   Eugene A. Nida, "The Implications of Contemporary Linguistics for Biblical Scholarship," *JBL* 91 (1972): 86.

is not an "insoluble problem"[196] because of its anticipation of the very similar passage in 36:26–27. Rather, there is a dimension of רוח that is absent in 11:19 and 18:31. The addressees of the book, faced with the already prominent role of רוח within the ministry of Ezekiel, are left to wonder at the significance of רוח in 11:19, and its ultimate identity.[197] It is only in 36:27a that this identity is revealed. The stubborn, rebellious house of Israel has no "driving force" to obey. It needs Yahweh's dynamic, potentiating, revivifying רוח.

2.2.2. *Relating the word of Yahweh and* רוח. We have just observed how the "empowering spirit of Yahweh"[198] will come as the "new spirit," the new "driving force" acting on the "heart of flesh." In the second part of 36:27, Yahweh declares that he will "make" the exiles "follow" his "statutes" and "be careful to observe" his "ordinances" and do them (ועשיתי את אשר־בחקי תלכו ומשפטי תשמרו ועשיתם).

The syntax at the start of v. 27b, of עשה followed by את אשר, usually entails a description of the subject "doing that which" had been said.[199] את אשר introduces a noun clause which serves as the object of the verb עשה. The construction here is unique for yielding the meaning "cause."[200] Cooke cites Eccl 3:14 as the only other instance of עשה followed by the relative having the same meaning ("cause"), but notes that there is no sign of the accusative there.[201] Although the syntax is unusual, the force of the sentence is clear. Yahweh declares that he will cause obedience to his word, expressed in his statutes and judgments.

Most scholars judge that it is by the action of the "new spirit," Yahweh's רוח (36:27a) (and the new heart) that the new obedience of the house of Israel will be ensured.[202] Allen, however, while acknowledging

---

196. Eichrodt, *Ezekiel*, 111.
197. Cf. also the ambiguity surrounding רוח in 2:2 and the transporting רוח.
198. Cf. the role of רוח within the book of Judges. See Block, "Empowered by the Spirit of God."
199. E.g. Gen 28:15; 1 Sam 16:4.
200. For the construction more generally, see GKC 157c.
201. Cooke, *Ezekiel*, 395.
202. E.g. Fohrer, *Ezechiel*, 205; John B. Taylor, *Ezekiel: An Introduction and Commentary* (TOTC; London: InterVarsity Press, 1969), 232; Wevers, *Ezekiel*, 275; Zimmerli, *Ezekiel 2*, 249; Joyce, *Divine Initiative*, 127; Blenkinsopp, *Ezekiel*, 168; Bernard J. Lee, "God as Spirit," in *Empirical Theology* (ed. R. Miller; Birmingham, Ala.: Religious Education Press, 1992), 135–36; Gary V. Smith, *An Introduction to the Hebrew Prophets: The Prophets as Preachers* (Nashville, Tenn.: Broadman & Holman, 1994), 23; Hildebrandt, *Spirit of God*, 95; Greenberg, *Ezekiel 21–37*, 730. Ohnesorge (*Jahwe gestaltet sein Volk neu*, 234), however, links renewed obedience

the role of the "new spirit,"[203] puts much greater emphasis on the correspondence between 36:27 and ch. 37. He regards the first half of 36:27 as
resumed in 37:1–13, highlighted with v. 14a, and the second half as
resumed in 37:15–24a, highlighted with 37:24b. His conclusion is that

> the editorial function of 37.1–13 in its present position is to throw light
> on the gift of the spirit in 36.27a. That of 37.15–23 is to clarify a means
> by which Yahweh would bring about the obedience of 36.27b, namely via
> a Davidic king who would impose order among God's people, uniting
> southern and northern elements with his royal staff or scepter.[204]

This observation concerning how 36:27 relates to ch. 37, confirmed by
the shift in meaning in רוח between 36:26 and 36:27 for which I argued
above, and the right recognition of the role of the Davidic king in obedience, might suggest a diminution in the role of the new heart and the new
spirit in the renewed obedience.

This, however, is not so. First, the Davidic king[205] in the book of Ezekiel plays no part in the restoration of the nation; he neither gathers the
people nor leads them back; he is not an agent of peace or righteousness
(cf. Isa 9:6–7); these are Yahweh's prerogative. Renewed obedience has
already been ascribed to the work of Yahweh in giving a "heart of flesh"
and a "new spirit" (11:19–20). In that sense, the king is not an agent of
the transformation, but a feature of the transformed people. The declaration in 37:24b that the united people of Israel will follow Yahweh's
ordinances and be careful to observe his statutes under the new מלך does
not specify *how* they will do them, although it does give a role to the
Davidic king.

Secondly, the link between נשיא/מלך and renewed obedience depends
ultimately on the action of Yahweh's רוח. In the lamentation of ch. 19,

directly to Yahweh because of the "I will cause." As with the transporting רוח,
however, Yahweh's actions are mediated by רוח as the agent (so, e.g., 37:1).

203.   Allen (*Ezekiel 20–48*, 179) comments, "thanks to him [Yahweh], their lives
would be governed by a new impulse that was to be an expression of Yahweh's own
spirit."

204.   Allen, "Structure, Tradition and Redaction," 140.

205.   Though LXX reads ἄρχων in 37:22, 24 and 25, while MT has מלך in 37:22,
24, and elsewhere Ezekiel is reluctant to use מלך of the Israelite monarchy, thus
suggesting a possible original נשיא, Block defends the MT on two main grounds.
First, LXX varies in rendering מלך; secondly, the presence of "kingdoms" (ממלכות,
v. 22) and "nation" makes מלך preferable here, for it "highlights the restoration of
Israel to full nationhood." See Block, "Bringing Back David," 179. See also
Zimmerli, *Ezekiel 2*, 269, 275, 277–78; Allen, *Ezekiel 20–48*, 190; Block, *Ezekiel
25–48*, 413–15.

any hope envisaged for the exiled King Jehoiachin dies;[206] indeed, the lamentation means "a judgement upon all existing members of the Davidic dynasty."[207] Death pervades the scene.[208] As Duguid argues, however, the end is not permanent: "it is an end which does not inherently rule out the possibility of a new beginning by means of divine intervention and for the sake of the divine name."[209] He sees the heart of this divine intervention in 37:1–14, "where a scene redolent with death gives way to unexpected new life through the intervention of the spirit of Yahweh."[210] In other words, where life comes out of death, there Yahweh's רוח can be seen; the vision of the future for the Davidic dynasty should be seen to depend on the operation of the divine רוח, though רוח itself is not explicitly linked with the renewal of Davidic promises. Such a view makes good sense when we also observe the role of רוח within the Davidic tradition: "the spirit of Yahweh" "rushed" (צלח) upon David when Samuel anointed him king (1 Sam 16:13); the spirit of Yahweh speaks through David (2 Sam 23:2); Isaiah's vision of an eschatological, Davidic, ruler gives רוח great prominence (Isa 11:1–5).[211] It also makes good sense when it is remembered that the Davidic king, Yahweh's anointed, was described as "the breath of our life" (רוח אפינו, Lam 4:20).

206.   For the identification of the second cub as Jehoiachin, see Greenberg, *Ezekiel 1–20*, 355–56, who notes the parallels with Jer 22:10–12 (Jehoahaz) and 22:24–30 (Jehoiachin).

207.   Duguid, *Ezekiel and the Leaders*, 45–46.

208.   Cf. Hals' comment (*Ezekiel*, 130), "To conduct a dirge beside the hospital bed of a still living patient would be incredibly crass. Something of that dimension of bizarre crudity is inherent in prophetic dirges."

209.   Duguid, *Ezekiel and the Leaders*, 46.

210.   Ibid.

211.   Ma (*Until the Spirit Comes*, 201) sees this pre-exilic passage describing the coming king (Isa 11:1–5) as "redactionally deroyalized" because of subsequent references to רוח in the servant figure (42:1–4) and the "prophet-like person" in 61:1. At the same time, he notes how "the רוח of Yahweh…becomes an eschatological element in the 'messianic' expectation" (ibid., 42). Blenkinsopp (*Ezekiel*, 176–77) suggests a correspondence between the reduced role of the eschatological ruler in Ezekiel (as reflected both in the common title for this ruler, נשיא, and in the designation עבדי) and the servant in the first "servant song" in Isa 42:1–4. There, too, רוח is prominent in the servant's ministry. The reduced role of Ezekiel's future Davidic ruler should not be exaggerated, though. He will not simply be "among" them as a servant (34:24; cf. Klein, *Israel in Exile*, 123), but he will also be king "over" them (37:24; cf. Duguid, *Ezekiel and the Leaders*, 49); his rule will be for ever (לעולם), "a continuous state of righteous rule" (ibid.); he will be a "powerful ruler" but also a "gentle shepherd" (ibid., 55); his work will be to unite a divided country (cf. Werner E. Lemke, "Life in the Present and Hope for the Future," *Int* 38 [1984]: 180).

In summary, the obedience which is made possible by "one heart and a new spirit" in 11:19, and which will be the case under the new king (מלך) in 37:24 will be brought about by the divine רוח in 36:27a. Here, again, the apparent antinomy of divine initiative and human responsibility reappears. The house of Israel is to be marked by repentant shame (36:32), even in the present; yet the obedience that is envisaged (36:27b) is clearly brought about by the initiative of Yahweh. The presence of a new heart and a new driving force, in fact Yahweh's own רוח, within the house of Israel, points to willing action by them in obedience—yet the fact that both are the gift of Yahweh points to Yahweh's sovereign initiative. Yahweh's action is more than simply "creating the conditions for human responsibility,"[212] for Yahweh "causes" obedience (v. 27). Yahweh's רוח moves Israel to go (הלך) where he wills, just as in the chariot vision the living creatures would "go" (הלך) "where the spirit (הרוח) would go" (1:12, 20; 36:27). Davis is right to say, however, that "it is no more true that the divinely given heart of flesh obviates human responsibility than that the first bestowal removed Israel's culpability."[213] Both are held together. Further, and critical for our study, is the observation that, as in 37:1–14, Yahweh's רוח is instrumental in bringing about obedience to Yahweh's word, though this time it is Yahweh's word as seen in his statutes and ordinances.

2.3. *The Outpouring of Yahweh's* רוח
In 39:29, there is the third and final instance of Yahweh speaking of "my spirit" (רוחי) in the book. It occurs in the conclusion of the Gog oracle, from 39:21–29, a conclusion that was shaped with the whole of chs. 38–39 in view, and that gives integrity to the whole.[214] Verses 21–24 focus

212.   Davis, *Swallowing the Scroll*, 115.
213.   Ibid., 116.
214.   The connection between these verses and the Gog oracle has been disputed (as indeed are many things about the Gog oracle). Cooke (*Ezekiel*, 422) comments, "These verses have nothing to do with the apocalypses 38¹–39¹⁶ and 39¹⁷⁻²⁰; they give a summary of Ezekiel's teaching and form a conclusion to Part III.b., chs. 34–37." Eichrodt (*Ezekiel*, 521) regards 39:25–29 as a conclusion not of the Gog oracle, to which it "shows no acquaintance," but of chs. 34–37. Zimmerli (*Ezekiel 2*, 319) sees some connection. He notes the links between 39:21–22 and the Gog oracle, but regards 39:23–29 as "*a final oracle looking back on Ezekiel's total message*," linking "directly" to 39:21–22. Block, however, makes a strong case for the structural unity of chs. 38–39 as a whole, as well as of 39:21–29; see Block, "Gog," 257–70. Further, he notes several significant links between 39:21–29 and 38:1–39:20 (pp. 265–66): the link of Yahweh's glory and the concern for his holy name (v. 21 paralleling 39:13; v. 25 paralleling 39:7); the temporal, historical "now" (עתה) of v. 25 which contrasts with the eschatological phrases to be found in 38:1–39:20; the transitional

on the impact of Yahweh's acting in judgment, both in the future, on
Gog (39:21–22), and in the past, on the house of Israel (vv. 23–24). The
temporal sphere of this impact lies the other side of the anticipated salvation.[215] With v. 25, there is a shift in focus back to the present, to the
scene of the exile, highlighted by עתה. In vv. 25–29, Yahweh again
speaks of the future restoration, and the effect that it will have on the
house of Israel (vv. 26, 28). As with the destruction of Gog, Israel's
restoration shall prove to Israel Yahweh's covenant relationship with
them.[216] It is in this context that Yahweh declares, "I shall not leave any
of them still there [i.e. in exile], and I shall not again hide my face from
them, when I pour out my spirit upon (אשר שפכתי את־רוחי) the house of
Israel—oracle of the Lord Yahweh."[217]

There are two questions that are important for our purposes. The first
one is about the authenticity of the phrase: the textual question. I shall
argue, against Lust, that the MT should be retained. The second is about
the scope of the phrase, its relation to 36:27 and 37:14 and hence its relation to Yahweh's word: the significance question. I shall argue, principally against Block, that the more concrete imagery of the pouring of
Yahweh's רוח does not indicate a significant shift in meaning from the
"giving" of Yahweh's רוח. It is not simply the "presence" of Yahweh's

---

vv. 21–22 presuppose what has gone before. More recently, Cook has argued, as part
of his thesis that "deprivation" is not essential for the production of "apocalyptic"
literature (p. 86), that there is essential continuity in "idioms, style and theology"
(p. 103) between the book of Ezekiel and chs. 38–39 (pp. 97–105), and that Ezek
39:21–29 "presupposes" the rest of the Gog narrative because of many links between
them (pp. 117–21) and is probably "one of the last layers in the book, postdating the
proto-apocalyptic redaction" (p. 120). See Stephen L. Cook, *Prophecy and Apocalypticism: The Postexilic Social Setting* (Minneapolis: Fortress, 1995). His analysis
of the links is persuasive, even if his dating (as mostly post-exilic) and genre
classification (as apocalyptic [p. 109]) can be challenged (see Block, *Ezekiel 25–48*,
424–32), and if his thesis on the insignificance of "deprivation" needs qualification
(see Mein, *Ezekiel and the Ethics of Exile*, 228–31).
   215.   So Block, *Ezekiel 25–48*, 480.
   216.   Allen, *Ezekiel 20–48*, 209.
   217.   The syntax of the phrase is somewhat awkward. אשר is treated in one of
three ways: *causal*, "because" = יען אשר; cf. LXX ἀνθ' οὗ; Vulgate *eo quod* (so
Cooke, *Ezekiel*, 424, and Block, *Ezekiel 25–48*, 478; but they point to Ezek 12:12
whose occurrence and meaning is disputed [see Zimmerli, *Ezekiel 1*, 267]; a better
example is 21:9 [ET 21:4]); *temporal*, "after" (so Zimmerli, *Ezekiel 2*, 295; Hals,
Ezekiel, 280); *relative*, "(I) who will have…" (so Allen, *Ezekiel 20–48*, 202; he sees
the relative as giving the literal meaning, but translates more idiomatically [and
temporally], "once I have" [p. 199]). The perfect שפכתי may be explicable in terms
of "relative time" (for which term, see especially Goldfajn, *Word Order*), indicating
an event preceding that of Yahweh not hiding his face again (cf. Vulgate *effuderim*).

רוח among the people that assures their future,[218] but the permanent transformation effected by the outpouring.

2.3.1. The textual question. With regard to the textual question, most scholars accept the reading of the MT, as cited above. Lust, however, noting that the LXX speaks of Yahweh pouring out his "wrath" here (ἐξέχεα τὸν θυμόν μου), argues strongly for a different *Vorlage* from the MT.[219] He observes that the phrase "I pour out my spirit" is "transformed" from one of Ezekiel's favourite phrases ("I pour out my wrath," אשפוך חמתי, Ezek 7:8; 9:8 et al.), and that רוח can function as a synonym for both חמה and זעם.[220] He acknowledges that, on these grounds, the different readings in MT and LXX could be explained by the LXX translator treating the (unusual) "I pour out my spirit" as if it were the more usual Ezekielian phrase. He disagrees, however, for two reasons. First, he states that the LXX translator does not tend to increase the stereotypical character of the language—rather, he uses synonyms, avoids repetition and stereotypical language. His second argument is based on the sequence of Papyrus 967, which he regards as a trustworthy witness of the LXX in its early form. In that papyrus, ch. 37 follows ch. 39. Lust says that it is unlikely that the writer, seeing what was coming up with the significant role of Yahweh's רוח (in what is now 37:1–14) would have translated רוח with θυμός. He integrates this observation with a number of other observations about 39:26–29, and suggests that the LXX worked initially from a different *Vorlage* from our Hebrew text, where רוח had not yet replaced either חמה or זעם. It was in a later period that "more hopefilled connotations were added."[221] One of these "hopefilled connotations" that was added was the replacement of חמה or זעם by רוח.

While Lust's arguments are plausible, Allen is probably right that the explanation for the LXX variant is "exegetical."[222] There are a number of

218.   Block, "Gog," 48.
219.   Johan Lust, "The Final Text and Textual Criticism: Ez 39,28," in Lust, ed., *Ezekiel and His Book*, 48–54.
220.   Lust ("Final Text," 52) notes, first, that the two Hebrew words, חמה and זעם, can act in "parallel" (i.e. as synonyms) in the Ezekielian phrase "pour out my wrath" (Ezek 7:8; 9:8; cf. 21:36; 22:31); secondly, that רוח is translated by θυμός in Job 15:13; Isa 59:19; Zech 6:8 (though Lust's reference is 9:8); thirdly, that in Zech 6:8, רוח is the object of נוח (Hiphil); in four places in Ezekiel, this same verb has חמה as its object (5:13; 16:42; 21:22; 24:13). To these points it can be added that often the LXX of Ezekiel renders חמה by θυμός (e.g. 5:15; 9:8). This also happens once with the noun זעם (22:31), which itself occurs only three times in Ezekiel.
221.   Lust, "Final Text," 53.
222.   Allen, *Ezekiel 20–48*, 202.

strands of evidence to support this conclusion, which need to be taken together. Some explain the appearance of the LXX variant, while others support the originality of רוח.

First, as Lust himself notes, the semantic domains of רוח and θυμός overlap. Thus רוח is sometimes translated by θυμός (though it should be noted that this is only when רוח is used in an anthropological sense (Zech 6:8; Job 15:13; Prov 18:14; 29:11; cf. Isa 59:19).[223]

Secondly, as Allen notes, the LXX translation "relates v 29bα to" Israel's "experience of past judgement and defeat" (cf. vv. 23–24), and to 36:17–19, in the middle of which the phrase "pour out my wrath" occurs (36:18). This linking is also apparent from the language of uncleanness that is found in 36:17 and 39:24.[224] If Lust is right about Papyrus 967 (that this is a "trustworthy witness" of the early LXX, and therefore likely to be trustworthy as an indicator of the order of the *Vorlage* from which the LXX was derived), then that in fact strengthens the "exegetical" case, since 39:29 occurs even closer to 36:17–19.

Thirdly, Allen makes the point that the whole context is positive. Even if it were granted that some of the more "hopeful connotations" were added later, the context at the start of v. 29 and of vv. 25–29 as a whole (especially v. 25) is sufficiently positive that it is probable v. 29a had a positive sense.[225] As it stands, this argument might make it all the more puzzling that the LXX translator should have misinterpreted the phrase so drastically. There was, however, a clear strand of thought especially after the exile that the exile had been necessary in order to participate in the new age (2 Chr 36:21; cf. Lev 26:43),[226] so it would not be strange for the LXX translator to link Yahweh's not hiding his face with the experience of Yahweh's outpoured wrath.

Finally, elsewhere in the Old Testament, there are striking links between Yahweh hiding his face, and the presence of רוח. In Ps 104:29–30, Yahweh's hiding his face (סתר פנים Hiphil) occurs in parallel with Yahweh taking away (אסף) breath (רוח) (v. 29); it also occurs as the opposite of Yahweh sending forth his רוח, a sending forth that creates (v. 30). In Ps 143:7, the psalmist's lament that his רוח is failing is closely

---

223.   This is not surprising. Isaacs has noted that "by the time the O.T. came to be translated, the normal Greek vocabulary employed would be θυμός for man's emotions, and ψυχή when indicating his thought or determination"; see Marie E. Isaacs, *The Concept of Spirit* (Heythrop Monograph 1; London: Heythrop College, 1976), 11.

224.   Allen, *Ezekiel 20–48*, 202.

225.   Ibid.

226.   Sklba, "'Until the Spirit,'" 16–17.

linked with Yahweh hiding his face from him. These references suggest that Yahweh's sending his life-giving רוח is effectively the opposite of Yahweh's hiding his face. In Ps 139:7, going from Yahweh's spirit (מרוחך) is in parallel with fleeing from his face (מפניך) (cf. Ps 51:13). Therefore, Yahweh not hiding his face in Ezek 39:29 points to the authenticity of the MT, and the originality of רוח. It could, of course, be argued in reverse, that the presence of Yahweh hiding his face suggested to a scribe the possibility of רוח here. It is more likely, however, that רוח was original, fitting appropriately both with the notion of Yahweh hiding his face (as a contrast) and with Yahweh "pouring out" his spirit, not his wrath, than that there were two, independent, reasons why רוח fitted so naturally into this context when it was not there originally.

In conclusion, though it is possible that there was an alternative Hebrew reading from which the LXX acquired its ἐξέχεα τὸν θυμόν μου, it is more probable that the MT reading, "I pour out my spirit" (שפכתי את־רוחי), is original, and LXX represents an interpretative development.

2.3.2. *The significance question.* The precise relationship of the phrase, "when I pour out my spirit" (אשר שפכתי את־רוחי), to Yahweh's promise that he will "give" (נתן) his רוח "within them" (בקרבכם) or "in you" (בכם) in 36:27 and 37:14 has been disputed. In particular, the debate revolves around the significance of the different verbs and prepositions found in chs. 36 and 37, on the one hand, and in ch. 39, on the other. This is reinforced by the fact that this "pouring out" (שפך) of Yahweh's רוח is more closely paralleled externally (in Joel) than internally (within the book of Ezekiel).

Zimmerli sees the promise of Yahweh "giving his רוח" (36:27; 37:14) as being transformed by "the late redactional formulation of 39:29 to the more concrete image of the pouring out of the spirit by Yahweh,"[227] which "paves the way" for Joel 3:1–5. This concept of "pouring out" "must envisage the concept of the fructifying, beneficent rain from heaven giving growth and nourishment."[228] He contrasts this with "the inner transformation of man, which enables him to keep the commandments" in 36:27 (and 37:14).[229] Yahweh's spirit in 39:29 serves "as the final irrevocable union of Yahweh with his people."[230] For Zimmerli, there is, then, a shift in meaning of רוחי from 36:27 and 37:14 to 39:29.

---

227. Zimmerli, *Ezekiel 2*, 567. The *terminus ad quem* of the redaction is the date of Joel 3:1–5.
228. Ibid., 567.
229. Ibid.
230. Ibid., 321.

Block, too, sees a shift in meaning between the occurrences.[231] While he regards the vision of the dry bones coming to life in 37:1–14 as an exposition of 36:27 (where Yahweh promises Israel that "I will put my spirit within you"), he says that there is a "fundamental difference in significance"[232] between 36:27 and 39:29. In 36:27 and 37:14, רוחי was "within" or "in their midst" (בכם/בקרבכם). He notes that this was "obviously associated with the renewal of the covenant,"[233] but "it seems to relate more immediately to the rebirth of the nation, her receiving new life."[234] He sees this as very different from "pour my spirit upon" in 39:29, which he regards as "a sign and seal of the covenant."[235] He then goes on to look at the other contexts of Yahweh "pouring out" his רוח (Isa 32:15; 44:3; Joel 3:1; Zech 12:10). He comments,

> it would appear from all these references that the pouring out of the Spirit of Yahweh upon his people signified the ratification and sealing of the covenant relationship. It represented the guarantee of new life, peace and prosperity. But it signified more than this. It served as the definitive act whereby he claimed and sealed the newly gathered nation of Israel as his own.[236]

Thus, he interprets this "pouring out" of Yahweh's רוח in the Gog oracle to be the divine mark of ownership, accounting for Yahweh's intervention before Israel is touched. The focus is on the presence of Yahweh's רוח, not on the transformation effected by his רוח. This is one argument that he brings in favour of the integration of the Gog oracle at this point. The destruction of Gog functions as visible evidence of the truthfulness of Yahweh's word "for the prophet."[237]

Eichrodt and Allen, however, see the reference to Yahweh's רוח in 39:29 as fundamentally similar to those in 36:27 and 37:14. For Eichrodt, the outpouring of the spirit on the house of Israel "serves as a guarantee of their being continual objects of divine favour and of the future unbroken fellowship between God and his people."[238] That this is not different from the promise of Yahweh's רוח in 36:27a and 37:14 is evident from his comments on 36:27. There he sees Yahweh "giving" his רוח as referring to the "outpouring of the spirit."[239]

231. Block, "Gog"; also idem, *Ezekiel 25–48*, 488–89.
232. Block, "Gog," 267.
233. Ibid.
234. Ibid.
235. Ibid., 268.
236. Ibid., 269.
237. Ibid.
238. Eichrodt, *Ezekiel*, 529.
239. Ibid., 502.

Allen regards the outpouring of the spirit as forming a contrast with the outpouring of wrath (a phrase which occurs twelve times in the book of Ezekiel, and most recently in 36:18). His interpretation thus gives the phrase a "different nuance"[240] than in the other instances of the "pouring out" of Yahweh's רוח (Isa 44:3; Joel 3:1 [ET 2:28]; Zech 12:10).[241] "The new age would be characterized by the gift of Yahweh's enabling spirit, as 36:26 and 37:14 had proclaimed."[242] Israel is now secure from the onslaught of nations from afar.

While scholars are agreed that the outpouring of Yahweh's רוח serves to guarantee the future of the exiles, in that never again will Yahweh hide his face from them, as he had done (39:23–24), it is preferable, with Allen and Eichrodt, not to see a shift in essential meaning between Yahweh "pouring out his רוח" and Yahweh "giving his רוח (with)in them" for three reasons.

First, an analysis of Yahweh "giving" רוח and Yahweh "pouring" רוח points to them describing essentially similar actions. In the Old Testament, there are sixteen instances of Yahweh giving (נתן) רוח. The phrase can be used with different senses of רוח (and our categorizations may serve to mask the fluidity and flexibility of the word), and, more significantly, with different prepositions following.[243] In particular, Yahweh can נתן his רוח "upon" (על) a person, where רוח is Yahweh's רוח.

These observations about Yahweh "giving" רוח need to be juxtaposed with observations about the pouring of רוח, a phrase that itself needs to be set within a wider context, since in the Old Testament, רוח in a number of places is associated with a "fluid" metaphor, without always necessarily being used of Yahweh's spirit.[244]

On five occasions, רוח is linked to the language of "filling" (Exod 28:3; 31:3; 35:31; Deut 34:9; Mic 3:8). Of these, Exod 28:3 and Deut

---

240. Allen, *Ezekiel 20–48*, 209.

241. He does not mention Isa 32:15.

242. Allen, *Ezekiel 20–48*, 209.

243. Different senses of רוח: (a) Yahweh's spirit (Num 11:25, 29; Isa 42:1; Ezek 36:27; 37:14); (b) "a lying spirit" (1 Kgs 22:23); (c) "an interior disposition" (van Imschoot, *Theology*, 184 n. 28) (2 Kgs 19:7); (d) the breath of life (Ezek 37:6); (e) the "driving force" within a person (Ezek 11:19). Different prepositions used with the phrase נתן רוח (with sense of רוח in each phrase indicated by the letter in brackets): ב, Ezek 37:14 (a); 1 Kgs 22:23 (b); 2 Kgs 19:7 (c); Ezek 37:6 (d); בקרב, Ezek 36:27 (a); Ezek 11:19 (e); על, Num 11:25, 29; Isa 42:1 (a); ל, Isa 42:5 (d); אל, Eccl 12:7; Isa 42:5; Ezek 37:6 (d).

244. Cf. van Imschoot, *Theology*, 184; Lys, *Rûach*, 154; Albertz and Westermann, *TLOT* 3:1218; Dreytza, *Der theologische Gebrauch von RUAH*, 224–26; Koch, *Geist Gottes*, 33; Schüngel-Straumann, *Rûaḥ bewegt die Welt*, 26.

34:9 speak of being filled with "the spirit of wisdom." That this "spirit" is somehow independent of the recipient, external to him, and not merely an anthropological description, seems clear from the fact that Joshua has this רוח through the laying on of Moses' hands.[245] Exodus 31:3 and 35:31 speak of being filled with רוח אלהים. Here, too, this is linked to being filled with wisdom. The fifth occurrence, which we examined above, is Mic 3:8.

On two other occasions, apart from the language of pouring, רוח is associated particularly with liquid (Isa 4:4; 30:28).[246] First, in Isa 30:28, in strongly anthropomorphic language, Yahweh's "breath" (רוח) is likened to an overflowing wadi. The picture is of a once dry wadi bursting its banks, overpowering all that goes before it. There is no reason why Yahweh's רוח *sensu* "breath" could not be thought of in liquid terms. Therefore, language of Yahweh pouring out his רוח (Ezek 39:29) should not *necessarily* be distinguished from language of Yahweh giving his spirit *qua* vivifying רוח-breath (Ezek 37:14). Secondly, in Isa 4:4, everyone will be called holy "once the Lord has washed away the filth of the daughters of Zion and cleansed the bloodstains of Jerusalem from its midst by a spirit (רוח) of judgment and by a spirit (רוח) of burning." It is not certain what is meant at this point by רוח—whether it refers to the storm wind that is at Yahweh's disposal (there has been storm imagery used of the coming day in Isa 2:19, 21), or to an independent spirit at Yahweh's disposal (cf. 1 Kgs 22:21–23) or to Yahweh's own spirit. What is striking to notice is that this רוח (Yahweh's agent) is involved with cleansing and washing the people of Jerusalem. This liquid metaphor is very close in thought to Ezek 36:17–19 and 39:24. In Isa 4:4 (indeed from 3:16), Zion has been personified in her "daughters." Though the reference to "blood" is probably a reference to Zion's bloodshed, it is possible that it is deliberately ambiguous, and could refer to the unclean menstrual flow. If that were so, that would provide a close semantic link to Ezek 36:17–19, where Israel's behaviour has been likened to a woman's uncleanness (v. 17), a behaviour that in v. 18 is identified in terms of "bloodshed" (הדם).[247] The רוח that is at Yahweh's disposal is involved in cleansing the people from their uncleanness and filth.[248]

---

245.   Deut 34:9; though cf. Num 27:18.

246.   There are other instances which are close to the "fluid" metaphor. In Num 11:17, Yahweh "sets aside" (אצל) some of the רוח which is on Moses and puts (שים) it on the elders. In Isa 63:11, Yahweh puts (שים) his רוח within (בקרב) his people.

247.   Though the LXX does not have Ezek 36:18b. Allen (*Ezekiel 20–48*, 176) and Zimmerli (*Ezekiel 2*, 241) regard this explanation as secondary. Cf. Block, *Ezekiel 25–48*, 344; Greenberg, *Ezekiel 21–37*, 728. MT provides a striking parallel

For our purposes, though, it is the instances of Yahweh "pouring" רוח that are of particular significance. Again, as with Yahweh "giving" רוח, there is variation both in the nature of רוח poured, and in the prepositions associated with the verb of pouring. There is also variation in the verbs for "pour."[249]

Two observations can be made about "giving" רוח and "pouring" רוח that point to their essential similarity. First, the sphere of operation is similar because the prepositions are to some extent interchangeable. Yahweh can "pour" רוח "in the midst" (בקרב), though "pour upon" (על) is much more common. In the same way, Yahweh can "give" (נתן) רוח "in the midst" (בקרב), but Yahweh also can "give" (נתן) רוח "upon" (על). Secondly, the desired democratization of prophecy that in Num 11 is due to Yahweh "giving" רוח "upon" (על) all people, is promised in terms of Yahweh "pouring" רוח "upon" (על) in Joel 3:1–2; "giving" and "pouring" are not fundamentally different. This essential similarity is not to say that they are always identical. Language of pouring implies an extravagance to Yahweh's action not necessarily self-evident in "giving."[250] In Ezek 39, this extravagance is appropriate both as a reversal of the pouring out of wrath and as the climax of the section that is full of hope, culminating in Yahweh showing mercy for the first time in the book (v. 25). It is, however, to deny that there is a "fundamental difference" (Block) between the two. It is better to account for the variation in Ezekiel's usage by seeing a deliberate exploitation of the ambiguity inherent in רוח, as it moves from the new driving force (36:26) and the new life-breath (37:4–10) to Yahweh's "spirit" (36:27; 37:14). This "play" requires that רוח is "within" or "in" because that is the locus both of the anthropological "driving force" and of the "life-breath."

between the crime, of pouring out (שפך) blood, and the punishment, of pouring out (שפך) wrath.

248.   Cf. Ma, *Until the Spirit Comes*, 136–39.

249.   Different senses of Yahweh's רוח (cf. n. 243 above) with different verbs of "pouring": (a) Yahweh's spirit (Isa 32:15 [ערה Niphal "be emptied out"]; 44:3 [יצק]; Ezek 39:29 [שפך]; Joel 3:1–2 [ET 2:28–29] [שפך]); (c) "an interior disposition" (Isa 19:14 [מסך]; 29:10 [נסך]; Zech 12:10 [שפך]). Prepositions used with occurrences of Yahweh "pouring" רוח: בקרב (Isa 19:14 [c]; על, Isa 32:15; 44:3; Ezek 39:29; Joel 3:1–2 [a]; Isa 29:10; Zech 12:10 [c]).

250.   It is striking in this regard to note that the link with "rain" and a verb of pouring is only explicit in Isa 44:3. שפך is never used of rain (see Schüngel-Straumann, *Rûaḥ bewegt die Welt*, 26–27; also Dreytza, *Der theologische Gebrauch von RUAH*, 225). What seems to be in view is the metaphorical unreserved boundless giving of Yahweh's רוח rather than the connotations of rain. See Dreytza, *Der theologische Gebrauch von RUAH*, 224–46; Schüngel-Straumann, *Rûaḥ bewegt die Welt*, 26; *pace* Lys, *Rûach*, 154; Zimmerli, *Ezekiel 2*, 567; Koch, *Geist Gottes*, 33.

The second reason why it is preferable to see the conceptual similarity of the three instances of Yahweh bestowing his spirit, despite the different fientive verb in 39:29, comes from the links with the notion of Yahweh hiding his face. Such a concept, not found elsewhere in the book of Ezekiel apart from the three instances in ch. 39 (vv. 23, 24, 29),[251] "implies a break in communication"[252] with Yahweh. Such a break came because of Israel's "iniquity" (בעונם, v. 23), because they had "dealt treacherously" (מעלו, v. 23) with him, because of their uncleanness (כטמאתם, v. 24), and because of "their transgressions" (כפשעיהם, v. 24). Here, then, is the organic link between Israel's behaviour and Yahweh's judgment, reflected in his hiding his face. In v. 29, Yahweh promises that he will never hide his face again "אשר I pour out my spirit..." Whether אשר is taken temporally or causally, there is clearly a link between the pouring out of the spirit, and the result that Yahweh will no longer hide his face. The clear implication is that the pouring out of Yahweh's רוח will serve to reverse what caused the hiding of his face, according to vv. 23–24. In other words, Yahweh's רוח will ensure the obedience of the restored people. This is precisely the force of Yahweh's רוח in 36:27. These links are further buttressed by the fact that Yahweh's "face" (פנים) as Yahweh's presence[253] is linked elsewhere with Yahweh's spirit. In Ps 104:29–30, Yahweh's hiding his face is tantamount to death, to the taking away of a person's breath (רוח). Hence, Yahweh's turning his face towards a person is tantamount to the giving of רוח, or the giving new life (cf. Ezek 37:14). In Ps 51:13, the taking away of the "holy spirit" is parallel to being cast from Yahweh's presence (פנים);[254] it is likely, then, that the reverse is also true—being in Yahweh's presence is to have Yahweh's רוח. In other words, the linking of רוח with פנים points to the fact that the "pouring out" of Yahweh's רוח in 39:29 should be seen in the same terms as that in 36:27 and 37:14; it also points to the life-giving, as well as the "obedience-ensuring" dimension of רוח.

Thirdly, although there is scholarly debate about the relationship between 39:21–29 and the Gog oracle of 38:1–39:20, it is clear that the "now" (עתה) of v. 25 shifts the focus from the future back to the present.[255] Verses 25–29 have the same provenance and perspective as the

---

251. Though Yahweh "turns away" (סבב Hiphil) his face in 7:22.
252. Allen, *Ezekiel 20–48*, 208–9.
253. Cf. Exod 33:14; see Montague, *Holy Spirit*, 56–58.
254. Cf. Ps 139:7: "Where can I go from your spirit (מרוחך)? Or where can I flee from your presence (מפניך)?"
255. Block, *Ezekiel 25–48*, 485, states that "the divine speech...opens abruptly with *ʿattâ*, 'Now,' snatching the hearers' attention away from the distant utopian

earlier salvation oracles, looking forward to a return to the land and to
restoration. It is unlikely, therefore, that the "pouring out of Yahweh's
spirit" speaks of something other than the same promise of Yahweh's
רוח mentioned already.

In conclusion, the change in terminology expresses both a symmetry
with the pouring out of Yahweh's anger and the extravagance of Yahweh's actions, but does not signify something fundamentally new or
different from that which is envisaged in 36:27a or 37:14.[256] This being
so, here again Yahweh's רוח is directly linked with Yahweh's word. It is
Yahweh's רוח that ensures that a rebellious people (cf. 39:23–24) will
never again experience Yahweh turning his face away. This can only be
ensured by the renewed obedience of the exiles. Yahweh's רוח is the
means whereby transformation is effected.

2.4. *Summary*

If Yahweh's רוח in 37:14 served to show *how* it would be that the "dead"
exiles would come to respond in repentance to Yahweh's word, the
references in 36:27a and 39:29 (partially, in view of the links with Yahweh "hiding" his face) point to the role of Yahweh's רוח in effecting obedience: "I will put my spirit within you, and make you follow my statutes
and be careful to observe my ordinances" (36:27a). What Jeremiah sees
as achieved by Yahweh writing the Torah on the hearts of the house of
Israel (Jer 31:33), what Deuteronomy ascribes to Yahweh circumcising
the hearts of Israel (Deut 30:6–8), Ezekiel ascribes to the giving of the
divine רוח.

---

future, and returning them to the very real needs of the present." Cf. Allen, *Ezekiel
20–48*, 209.

256.   If there is after all an echo of "rain" brought by the wind (רוח), then this
would provide a neat reversal with the scorching רוח that Yahweh has sent in judgment (Ezek 17:10; 19:12).

Chapter 7

SUMMARY AND CONCLUSIONS

1. *Summary*

This study began by pointing out the striking prominence of both Yahweh's word and Yahweh's רוח in the book of Ezekiel, and by positing that an examination of the theological relationship between these two enables significant contributions to a number of questions within current רוח and Ezekiel scholarship. These include the more general question of רוח-inspiration within the diverse phenomenon of Old Testament prophecy, and some issues that are particularly related to the study of the book of Ezekiel, notably the tension in the book between divine sovereignty and human responsibility, the reason(s) for the marked prominence of (theological uses of) רוח, the place of the prophetic persona and the rhetorical function of the book as a whole.

The investigation has fallen into three main parts.

In Part I: Gathering the Data, there were two chapters. Chapter 1 did four things. First, it introduced the subject of the study, emphasizing its exploratory nature. Secondly, it outlined the approach that this work has taken to the book of Ezekiel. The approach has been synchronic, recognizing a redactional unity that arises out of a communicative intent, and principally theological in focus. Thirdly, it embedded this study within its various contexts, including study of רוח in the Old Testament and in the book of Ezekiel, with the final context being the scholarly study of word and רוח in Ezekiel. It was noted that there has been significant attention on both the prophetic and the transforming רוח in Ezekiel. Scholars examining the former have tended to interpret references within the framework of prophetic (self-)authentication, while those exploring the latter have tended to focus on the obvious tension raised by the call to the exiles to make for themselves a new רוח (18:31), a call that coexists in the book with unconditional promises by Yahweh that he will give to the exiles a new רוח (11:19; 36:26). There has been less attention to the function of references to רוח as an integrated whole. Finally, it outlined the argument, which can be summarized as follows: *The relationship between Yahweh's* רוח *and Yahweh's word in the book of Ezekiel is to be understood not so much in terms of the inspiration and authentication of the prophet but in terms of the transformation of its addressees.*

Chapter 2 looked more closely at "word" and רוח in Ezekiel, gathering and classifying the somewhat scattered data, and focusing on them separately before exploring the relationship in the rest of the study. First, it discussed where Yahweh's word is to be found in the book of Ezekiel. In order to see how Yahweh's רוח is related to Yahweh's word, it was essential to see where that word is found, and how it should be understood. Although the book itself is dominated by reports expressed in the first person of the word coming to the prophet, I identified and explored four distinct types of speech event: Yahweh addressing Ezekiel; Ezekiel addressing his audience; Yahweh's ordinances and statutes; the book of Ezekiel itself. I argued that the book's addressees are the exiles in Babylon, with a date probably before 538 B.C.E. As part of thinking further about Yahweh's word and its addressees, I drew on insights from speech act theory to show how the illocutionary force of Ezekiel's oracles can shift by virtue of their being re-presented within the book of Ezekiel. In the second part of this chapter, I analyzed all 52 instances of רוח in the book, identified those occurrences where there is significant scholarly disagreement over meaning and discussed important cases which would not be discussed later in the study (e.g. 1:12, 20–21). It became apparent that the wide semantic range of רוח, combined with the fluidity in categories, created the potential for significant deliberate or unintended ambiguity, and made closer analysis a necessity. Part I concluded by arguing that there a number of places where there is some kind of relationship between word and רוח.

In Part II: Word, Spirit and Inspiration, I turned to the question of inspiration and prophecy. Part II set out to explore some of the issues surrounding the prominence of רוח within the ministry of Ezekiel, a prominence that is particularly striking when set against the absence in other classical prophets. Three questions shaped the discussion. The first was whether in Ezekiel רוח is or can be understood as Yahweh's breath on which his word is carried. The second was whether Ezekiel recovers רוח as foundational in prophetic inspiration. The third was whether the emphasis on רוח within the prophet Ezekiel's ministry is best explained in terms of the authentication of the prophet. This is the usual explanation for the importance of רוח within the ministry of Ezekiel.

Chapter 3 surveyed the different scholarly perspectives on the place of רוח within classical prophecy. Next, it examined the concept of inspiration, and suggested two theoretical distinctions should be acknowledged. The first was that between "potentiating" inspiration, where רוח inspires the prophet, and "word-communicating" inspiration, where רוח inspires words. The second was that between the prophetic event, of Yahweh's word coming to the prophet, and the rhetorical event, of the prophet speaking Yahweh's word. The chapter then examined רוח-inspiration within the book of Ezekiel, and argued that there is evidence of both "potentiating" and "word-communicating" inspiration, although more evidence of the former, and that each can be found in both the prophetic and the rhetorical events.

Chapter 4 examined the relationship between רוח and prophetic inspiration in the pre-classical prophets, the classical prophets and in selected post-exilic works. With regard to the pre-classical prophets, I argued that there is strong evidence both of "potentiating" inspiration and of "word-communicating" inspiration, but that רוח is not especially prominent. With regard to the classical prophets, I argued that, while it is certainly true that רוח-inspiration is not prominent, both "potentiating" inspiration and "word-communicating" inspiration as concepts may be found. The classical prophets did not repudiate רוח in their own inspiration, but downplayed their own inspiration by רוח for rhetorical reasons. In post-exilic literature, again both "potentiating" and "word-communicating" inspiration may be found. In terms of the three questions raised, I concluded that רוח as the "breath" of Yahweh's mouth is not explicitly linked with Yahweh's word in Ezekiel. Secondly, Ezekiel cannot be said to "recover" רוח as foundational in his inspiration because the pre-classical prophets are not depicted as inspired as often as is sometimes said and because the classical prophets are more inspired than is sometimes allowed. Ezekiel does have a greater emphasis on רוח in his own inspiration, but that is one of degree, not of kind. Thirdly, regarding language of רוח as part of the prophet's own attempt at self-authentication fails to account for the reasons for the almost total silence on רוח in the classical prophets. Regarding it as part of the *book's* attempt at authenticating the prophet makes more sense, but does not do justice to the book's overriding purpose of transforming its addressees.

Part III: Word, Spirit and Transformation, turned to the question of the role of רוח in the transformation of the people, effecting obedience to Yahweh's word. In Chapter 5, we observed how there is symmetry in the book of Ezekiel between the portrayals of judgment and restoration. We saw how it depicts the disobedience of Ezekiel's addressees as something that endures throughout the prophet's ministry. At the same time, we noted how the book also looks forward to a day when the exilic house of Israel will again be characterized by a renewed obedience. I argued that this dichotomy serves both to demonstrate to the exilic addressees of

the book that the unresponsiveness of Ezekiel's addressees was not surprising, hence did not discredit his ministry. Further, it provides a powerful call to the book's addressees to distance themselves from the past
response of Ezekiel's addressees, and to identify with the future, if they
are to live and not die (Ezek 18:31; 33:11). Finally, I argued that the book
portrays the prophet Ezekiel as a prescriptive paradigm of the obedience
that is both desired and required. The chapter closed by observing that,
for the readers of the book, the vision of restoration and renewed obedience does not rest easily with the history of the house of Israel, characterized by rebellion from first to last (ch. 20). The critical questions for
them are precisely *how* such obedience would come about, and *how* it
would be ensured, given this catalogue of failure which extended even to
Ezekiel's intended audience, and given their current plight in exile (cf.
33:10; 37:11).

Chapter 6 argued that רוח is fundamental for renewed and long-term
obedience to Yahweh's word, whether it is the prophet's word, or Yahweh's statutes. It is precisely in this context that רוח within the book
assumes its greatest significance. The chapter began by contending that
the book of Ezekiel portrays not just the prophet's obedience, but also his
experience of רוח as paradigmatic. In the rest of the chapter, I argued
that רוח is essential for the obedience of the prophet, and that this is
mirrored in the future vision for the exiles: רוח provides the key to how
the vision of the future becomes a present reality (Ezek 37:1–14). The
two-staged vision points to the need of רוח to effect a penitent response
to the prophetic word, now written in the book of Ezekiel, in those who
hear it. It also provides the key to how the vision of the future will remain
a permanent reality (Ezek 36:27a; 39:29). Yahweh's רוח will so infuse
the house of Israel, acting upon its new heart, that it will cause the people
to obey in a permanent way—a way that will ensure they are never cast
from the land again, even if the renewed sacrificial system points to the
possibility of sin. Yahweh's רוח transforms the people by effecting
Yahweh's word in their experience.

2. *Conclusions and Implications*

2.1. רוח-*Inspiration and Prophecy*
It has been axiomatic among many Old Testament scholars that רוח does
not really relate to the prophetic word until the exile. According to this
reading of the evidence, רוח was associated with prophecy in the pre-
classical period only insofar as it gave rise to what is loosely called
"ecstatic prophetic behaviour." Later, the classical prophets either

repudiated רוח or would not have attributed their prophetic inspiration to רוח. It was after the exile, when רוח had been subject to a number of developments, that the pre-exilic prophets were said to have prophesied under the inspiration of רוח (Neh 9:30; Zech 7:12). This viewpoint usually takes its place within a wider narrative in which there is a clear distinction between, on the one hand, the professional נביאים, who went around in groups, who were marked by stereotypical, sometimes extravagant, prophetic manifestations, who were prophets announcing success and salvation and who were prophets of רוח, and, on the other, the "dissident intellectuals"[1] or "protest movement,"[2] represented in the Old Testament by Amos, Hosea, Isaiah, Micah, Zephaniah and Jeremiah (and, obviously to a lesser extent, Ezekiel). These have traditionally been described as writing prophets, but, in this narrative, they neither wrote anything nor were prophets (נביא). Rather, they protested against the behaviour and the message of the נביאים. One significant line of evidence that is adduced for this argument is the profile of the occurrences of the word נביא in the books that bear their names. The term is strikingly absent from the earlier books, when these figures speak of their own ministry, and only in the exile starts to be a designated description of these figures, principally on the lips of others.[3] The most sceptical form of this narrative is that these figures are essentially later literary creations.[4] A less sceptical one sees these figures as repudiating the designation נביא and those known as נביאים, but nonetheless fulfilling the task that a נביא had, of mediating the word of Yahweh to the people.[5]

Such an analysis should be modified in the light of our investigation into רוח.

While it is certainly true that רוח was associated with ecstatic behaviour, such prophets did produce words which were clearly understood as related to the activity of רוח (1 Kgs 22:6, 10–11). Whether it was Yahweh's רוח or an evil רוח sent from Yahweh was a matter of debate, but רוח was related to prophetic speech even in early times. For the classical prophets, while prophetic behaviour clearly changed, and clear

---

1. Joseph Blenkinsopp, *Sage, Priest, Prophet: Religious and Intellectual Leadership in Ancient Israel* (Louisville, Ky.: Westminster John Knox, 1995), 144–45.

2. Fenton, "Israelite Prophecy," 137.

3. See especially the influential article, Auld, "Prophets Through the Looking Glass."

4. See, e.g., Carroll, "Poets Not Prophets"; idem, "Whose Prophet?"; Davies, "The Audiences of Prophetic Scrolls."

5. E.g. Terry L. Fenton, "Deuteronomistic Advocacy of the *nābîʾ*: 1 Samuel IX 9 and Questions of Israelite Prophecy," *VT* 47 (1997): 36–38; idem, "Israelite Prophecy," 138–41.

statements of their own inspiration are very rare, there is no evidence of their repudiating רוח, and there is sufficient evidence to point towards their own רוח-inspiration, albeit downplayed for rhetorical reasons. The prophet Ezekiel is not a strange anomaly in his consciousness of רוח-inspiration, any more than he is a strange anomaly in aspects of his prophetic behaviour. There is a difference in degree, but not a difference in kind. Rather, the change in rhetorical situation, the message of transformation, and the carefully constructed prophetic persona in the book of Ezekiel explain the prominence of רוח in the book.

Once this is granted, we can revisit the wider narrative outlined above. The general absence of the term נביא from the canonical prophets should not be interpreted in terms of wholesale repudiation or a clear distinction. While it is certainly true that the canonical prophets repudiated the message of the נביאים, we have encountered enough similarities between the canonical prophets and the נביאים, particularly in terms of רוח-inspiration, dramatic sign-acts and their consciously performing the function of a נביא (cf. Amos 7:14–16, where Amos' apparent denial that he is a נביא is juxtaposed with Yahweh's command to Amos, הנבא), to acknowledge that the canonical prophets saw themselves as fulfilling a similar function in bringing Yahweh's word, and would surely have been recognized as such by society, even if they were rejected,[6] and even if the precise title was something they were reluctant to own for themselves. The apparent repudiation of the term נביא by Amos may in reality be a rhetorical device to avoid particular commonly held associations.

2.2. *The Study of the Book of Ezekiel*

2.2.1. רוח *in the book of Ezekiel*. Although references to רוח are undoubtedly based in the personal experience of the prophet,[7] their place in the book needs to be understood within the ferment in thinking precipitated by the exile. By its very fluidity, רוח is able to fuse a number of elements that resonate not simply with the personal experience of the prophet, but also with the transformation of the people. Although of necessity these have to be discussed in linear fashion in a book, these instances are better characterised as exhibiting a network of connections.

---

6. So Gordon, "Where Have All the Prophets Gone?" Barstad makes the point, while ceding the possibility that Auld and Carroll are correct in some respects, that what we have in the prophetic books is similar to prophetic utterances found elsewhere in the Old Testament and in the wider ancient Near East. See Barstad, "No Prophets?," 51–52.

7. Volz, *Der Geist Gottes*, 69; cf. Carley, *Ezekiel Among the Prophets*, 71–76.

There is רוח as the breath of life for those who see themselves "dead," "separated from Yhwh's beneficent acts" and "forgotten by him"[8] (Ezek 37; cf. 2:2; 3:24). By the agency of this רוח the exiles can and will live again. Yet the problem is not simply that they are dead, for they also have a "mind" (רוח), synonymous with their לב, that is corrupt (11:5; 20:32; cf. 13:3) and needs replacing. There is, though, another anthropological רוח, for רוח is also the "driving force" that acts upon Israel's לב (Ezek 11:19; 18:31; 36:26; cf. Deut 2:30), rather than being simply synonymous with it. These notions of "life-breath" that is absent, "mind" that is corrupt and "driving force" that needs renewing are all answered by the multi-faceted gift of Yahweh's own רוח, promised to the exiles. Yet that by no means exhausts the polyvalency of רוח.

As the power that transports Ezekiel from place to place (37:1 et al.), רוח encapsulates the action of Yahweh (by his רוח) in transporting the people back to their land from exile (37:14). As the means by which Yahweh brings about obedience to his word (2:2; 3:24; cf. 36:26–27; 37:1–14), the action of Yahweh's רוח echoes the equipping power that clothed the judges, enabling them to fulfil Yahweh's will.[9] Further, it points to the transforming power by which the book's addressees can share in Ezekiel's vision of the future, and by which Yahweh himself can "participate directly in man's new obedience."[10] As the inspiring power that takes Ezekiel, though in visions, to the place of revelation where he comes to know Yahweh and his will, so רוח will bring the book's addressees to a true knowledge of Yahweh (cf. 36:27; 37:6, 14).[11] As the outpoured רוח of Yahweh, "fécondante"[12] in its effects (39:29), an end is signalled to the scorching רוח of Yahweh's judgment, metaphorically represented by the storm wind (13:11, 13) or east wind (17:10; 19:12). As the means by which a divine act of recreation, replicating the creation of Adam, is accomplished, רוח points towards the recreation of a new people (37:1–14). In addition, the role played by רוח in effecting Yahweh's spoken word mirrors that found in Gen 1:2. The importance of Yahweh as creator, and of the role of Yahweh's רוח in creation, is often highlighted in discussions of exilic Isaianic theology.[13] The same emphasis is present in Ezekiel.

8. Olyan, "'We Are Utterly Cut Off,'" 48.
9. Cf. Block, *Ezekiel 1–24*, 12.
10. Zimmerli, *Ezekiel 2*, 249. For Lapsley (*Can These Bones Live?*, 62) it is this divine dimension that separates the promise of renewal in Ezekiel from that in Jeremiah, a reflection of Ezekiel's greater pessimism about human ability.
11. Cf. Lapsley, *Can These Bones Live?*, 167.
12. Lys, *Rûach*, 154.
13. Cf. Ma, *Until the Spirit Comes*, 96–101.

In the exilic and post-exilic periods, רוח begins to be seen "as a representative or manifestation of Yahweh on earth"[14] (cf. Isa 63:7–14; Hag 2:5). There are nascent signs in the book of Ezekiel of רוח acting as a means by which a transcendent deity is present and acts immanently (1:12; 20; cf. 39:29 and the links with פנים).[15] Although for Ezekiel as a priest, divine presence is clearly focused in the mobile כבוד יהוה, yet Ezekiel is not simply a priest, he is a prophet, inspired by רוח. The cultic and the charismatic merge. The fructifying and life-giving effect of the stream flowing from the temple in 47:1–12, where כבוד יהוה is present (cf. 43:1–5), is not far from the thought of the life-giving effects of רוח in 37:1–14 and the renewal of the land in Edenic fashion that accompanies the renewal of the people.[16] Such connections are closer after the exile, where רוח is said to have performed actions that are predicated elsewhere of Yahweh's glory in the cloud (Neh 9:19–20; Isa 63:11–14; Hag 2:5).[17] With Ezekiel, then, it seems that new ways of speaking about Yahweh's presence are appearing; in particular, רוח, which has not until this point been associated with temple or cult (hence the absence from Leviticus), now becomes an accepted way to speak about Yahweh's presence in a prophetic book that focuses on the rebuilding of the temple (Hag 2:5). Brueggemann states that after the destruction of the temple in 587 B.C.E., there were "two ways to formulate 'presence' that could no longer be flatly in Jerusalem" and goes on to identify these as "the priestly theology of glory" and the "deuteronomic theology of name."[18] Without entering into questions of whether these two really do arise as a result of the fall of Jerusalem, this analysis also needs to give account of a theology of רוח-presence.

---

14. Lindblom, *Prophecy*, 413–14; cf. Schoemaker, "The Use of רוח," 28; Ronald E. Clements, *God and Temple: The Idea of the Divine Presence in Ancient Israel* (Oxford: Blackwell, 1965), 132–34; idem, *Old Testament Theology: A Fresh Approach* (London: Marshall, Morgan & Scott, 1978), 69–70; Sklba, "'Until the Spirit,'" 15; Ma, *Until the Spirit Comes*, 152.

15. Although there are some moves towards personification of רוח, such as the participle עמדת being predicated of רוח in Hag 2:5 (cf. Meyers and Meyers, *Haggai, Zechariah 1–8*, 52), רוח is not hypostatized, and the categories of transcendent and immanent themselves can skew the discussion. For the last point, see John W. Wright, "Beyond Transcendence and Immanence: The Characterization of the Presence and Activity of God in the Book of Chronicles," in *The Chronicler as Theologian: Essays in Honor of Ralph W. Klein* (ed. M. Patrick Graham, Steven L. McKenzie and Gary N. Knoppers; JSOTSup 371; London: T. & T. Clark, 2003), 240–67.

16. Cf. Zimmerli, *Ezekiel 2*, 516.

17. Kline, *Images of the Spirit*, 15.

18. Brueggemann, *Theology of the Old Testament*, 670–75.

Finally, in terms of the number of occurrences related to the prophet himself, Ezekiel deserves the title, "prophet of the spirit." Discussion of רוח in Ezekiel, however, needs to be carried out not by isolating the prophetic רוח from the transforming רוח, for the book of Ezekiel takes the prophetic רוח and marshals it not chiefly for the authentication of Ezekiel as prophet, but as an integral part of the book's wider rhetorical function of transforming its addressees.

2.2.2. *The prophet as persona*. This study has highlighted the significance of Ezekiel the prophet as a *persona* with an important role to play in the message of the book. It can hardly be said that the portrait of the prophet is a comprehensive one. There is not much in the way of biographical detail about the prophet that can be gleaned from reading the book. As Mein observes, "the prophet is hidden behind the role he performs as mediator between YHWH and Israel."[19] Further, as a literary character in the book, there is neither a developed nor a rounded portrayal. It is not surprising that Ezekiel does not feature in standard works exploring biblical characterization.[20] Scholarship, however, which already has given significant attention to the characterization of Jeremiah,[21] has begun to explore the characterization of prophets more generally,[22] and Ezekiel in particular.[23] Patton even goes so far as to say, "the storytelling in the book is so artful that it draws the reader into assuming what it says about Ezekiel reflects a historical person's real experience."[24] Although the

19. Andrew Mein, "Ezekiel as a Priest in Exile," in de Moor, ed., *The Elusive Prophet*, 201.

20. E.g. Robert Alter, *The Art of Biblical Narrative* (London: George Allen & Unwin, 1981); Adele Berlin, *Poetics and Interpretation of Biblical Narrative* (Bible and Literature Series 9; Sheffield: Almond, 1983); Sternberg, *Poetics of Biblical Narrative*; Richard L. Pratt, Jr., *He Gave Us Stories* (repr., Phillipsburg, N.J.: P. & R., 1993 [1990]); Shimon Bar-Efrat, *Narrative Art in the Bible* (trans. Dorothea Shefer-Vanson; JSOTSup 70, Bible and Literature Series 17; Sheffield: Sheffield Academic Press, 2000).

21. See, e.g., Childs, *Introduction*, 349–50; Gowan, *Theology of the Prophetic Books*, 98–112; and, most recently, Kathleen M. O'Connor, "The Prophet Jeremiah and Exclusive Loyalty to God," *Int* 59 (2005): 130–41.

22. See, e.g., Moor, ed., *The Elusive Prophet*.

23. E.g. Odell, "You Are What You Eat"; idem, "Genre and Persona"; Patton, "Priest, Prophet and Exile." This attention to Ezekiel is anticipated with von Rad's comment, "With Jeremiah and Ezekiel at least, the prophetic 'I' suddenly becomes very much more prominent," although his continuation, "indeed, the book of Ezekiel is practically a long prophetic autobiography" hardly accounts for the prominence on the word of Yahweh or the paucity of biographical details; see von Rad, *Old Testament Theology*, 2:265.

24. Patton, "Priest, Prophet and Exile," 74.

recurrent dates and the account of the death of Ezekiel's wife make Patton's judgment on historical value unduly sceptical, for it is hardly likely these were created purely as a literary construct, Patton is perceptive in highlighting in her thoughtful study the art of the narrator in Ezekiel.[25]

Generally speaking, recent focus has been on the characterization of Ezekiel as prophet[26] or priest,[27] with general agreement that Ezekiel is not portrayed as performing any of the priestly duties associated with the temple,[28] and some disagreement over whether Ezekiel is depicted as acting as priest in exile at all.[29] Chapters 40–48 tend to polarize the discussion, with some seeing Ezekiel as priest and law-giver here, while others stress the prophetic nature of the vision. Duguid captures the view of a number of scholars well, when he comments rightly, "Ezekiel 40–48 presents a *vision*, not legislation. To be sure, part of the vision is in legislative form, but it is vision in the form of legislation, not legislation in the form of vision."[30] After all, although in many ways the book of Ezekiel clearly seems to have impacted post-exilic life back in the land,[31] yet the building programme was not taken up.[32] There are, however, clear similarities between Ezekiel and Moses as law-giver that have been observed.[33] Attention has also been paid recently to the characterization

25. Cf. also Renz, *Rhetorical Function*, 132–37, for more on Ezekiel as narrator.

26. Odell, "You Are What You Eat"; Baruch J. Schwartz, "A Priest Out of Place: Reconsidering Ezekiel's Role in the History of the Israelite Priesthood," in Cook and Patton, eds., *Ezekiel's Hierarchical World*, 61–71.

27. Mein, "Ezekiel as a Priest"; Iain M. Duguid, "Putting Priests in Their Place: Ezekiel's Contribution to the History of the Old Testament Priesthood," in Cook and Patton, eds., *Ezekiel's Hierarchical World*, 43–60; Patton, "Priest, Prophet and Exile."

28. Although Fechter suggests that the authors of 43:18–27 portray Ezekiel as the one who "initiates postexilic sacrifice in the temple"; see Friedrich Fechter, "Priesthood in Exile According to the Book of Ezekiel," in Cook and Patton, eds., *Ezekiel's Hierarchical World*, 34.

29. Mein ("Ezekiel as a Priest," 201–8), in particular, highlights Ezekiel's priestly ministry as a teacher of instruction (תורה, Ezek 7:26) who makes distinctions, even in exile (Ezek 22:36; cf. Lev 10:10–11). See also Corrine L. Patton, "'Should Our Sister Be Treated Like a Whore?' A Response to Feminist Critiques of Ezekiel 23," in Odell and Strong, eds., *The Book of Ezekiel*, 84–85, for "priestly activities related to the community," such as bearing the people's punishment, that Ezekiel performs. Schwartz ("Priest Out of Place"), however, denies this to Ezekiel, and emphasizes discontinuity between priest and prophet.

30. Duguid, *Ezekiel*, 522; cf. Schwartz, "Priest Out of Place," 63.

31. Renz, *Rhetorical Function*, 229–47.

32. A point made strongly by Moshe Greenberg, "Design and Themes."

33. See, e.g., Levenson, *Theology of the Program*, 37–53; Greenberg, "Design and Themes," 183; McKeating, "Ezekiel the 'Prophet Like Moses'?"

of Moses as law-giver in the Pentateuch, and its rhetorical function.[34] Watts comments, "the force of law depends on the authority of its promulgator. Self-characterizations by lawgivers play a vital role in persuading hearers and readers to accept law and in motivating them to obey it. Pentateuchal laws therefore join narratives in characterizing law-speakers as part of a rhetoric of persuasion."[35] Additional work on the prophet Ezekiel's characterization as law-giver would be fruitful in exploring further the rhetorical function of the book as a whole, and the means by which the book seeks to persuade.

If the first dimension of attention to the prophetic persona relates to Ezekiel as a bringer of Yahweh's word, the second dimension is that of Ezekiel as paradigmatic persona in his response to Yahweh's word. I argued that the book presents the prophet as a prescriptive paradigm in his obedience to Yahweh's word as it came to him. This is apparent through Ezekiel being termed a מופת (24:24) in his response to his wife's death, and from the narrative portrayal of the similarities and differences between Ezekiel and his addressees, a portrayal that extends to experience of Yahweh's רוח. What O'Connor writes perceptively of the portrayal of Jeremiah could equally be predicated of Ezekiel,

> Jeremiah symbolizes what his community ought to be. His behavior shows them how they must behave if they are to endure the present suffering and reconstitute themselves as God's covenant community in the future. Like them, he is wounded, but he is also the ideal survivor who, even as he opposes his people and is opposed by them, exhibits virtues they must practice to regain their life together. They should relate to God in the same manner he does. Like him, they must be utterly devoted to God...[36]

This second function of the characterization of Ezekiel, not just as bringer of the word of Yahweh, but also as recipient and obedient respondent, relates directly to the rhetorical function of the book of Ezekiel. In the face of the trauma of exile,[37] Ezekiel mirrors for the readers, in his questioning of Yahweh and in his oracles, the puzzled but necessary realization that Jerusalem fell because of Yahweh's judgment. Yet the focus is

---

34. See James W. Watts, "The Legal Characterization of Moses in the Rhetoric of the Pentateuch," *JBL* 117 (1998): 415–26; idem, *Reading Law: The Rhetorical Shaping of the Pentateuch* (The Biblical Seminar 59; Sheffield: Sheffield Academic Press, 1999).

35. Watts, "Legal Characterization," 415.

36. O'Connor, "Prophet Jeremiah," 138.

37. For which, see especially Daniel L. Smith-Christopher, *A Biblical Theology of Exile* (Minneapolis: Fortress, 2002).

not retrospective. For the exiles, the burning question is "How can we live?" (Ezek 33:10). Ezekiel, in his experience of רוח and the ensuing obedience to Yahweh's word, embodies and depicts the answer.

Together, these two dimensions of the characterization of Ezekiel are essentially pastoral in focus. This is not usually the first word that is associated with the portrayal of the prophet. Ezekiel himself, one scholar argues, "died as he had lived: wretched, hateful, tormented by rages and longings which he could not possibly have understood."[38] The pastoral purpose is clearly present, however, notwithstanding the ordeal that may well have shaped some of his words and actions.[39] To exiles troubled with issues of loss of land, Ezekiel addresses them with words of reassurance (Ezek 11:15; 33:24); elders came to consult him, and his words, while hard, command an understanding of the fall of Jerusalem that would not have severed the artery of their religion, but rather preserved Yahweh as one who has acted rightly. To exiles concerned about the future, despairing and rebellious in equal measure, the prophet does not just call to repentance, or speak words of hope, but shows how Yahweh will make the future present, and is depicted as embodying that change, as the first human in the new creation.

Again, the words of O'Connor, which were written to describe the function of the portrait of Jeremiah, could equally be applied to the portrayal of the prophet Ezekiel:

> His calling is rooted in the community in the obvious sense that the community is his primary audience, but it is also rooted in the community because the survival and future reclamation of the community are the book's most thoroughgoing concern. To help the community to endure its present suffering, to understand and absorb what has happened to it, and, finally, to reconstitute itself as God's covenant people is the book's large rhetorical purpose. The book's portrait of Jeremiah's life contributes to that purpose.[40]

Study of the canonical prophets should continue to take seriously the narrative portrayal of the prophet with a view to understanding further the means by which the books that bear their names set out to shape their readers and hearers.

2.2.3. *Calls to repentance*. Both the polyvalency of רוח, functioning as symbol, and the twofold characterization of the prophet point towards the

---

38. David J. Halperin, *Seeking Ezekiel: Text and Psychology* (University Park, Pa.: Pennsylvania State University Press, 1993), 225.

39. Cf. Smith-Christopher, *Biblical Theology of Exile*, 89–104.

40. O'Connor, "Prophet Jeremiah," 137.

essential unity of the book, and give indicators towards the communicative intent of the book. The third area that this study impinges on, in particular, is that of the place of calls to repentance, not so much within the historical context of Ezekiel's ministry, as the book depicts it, but within the book that bears his name. This again serves to illuminate the communicative intent of the book.

The place of calls to repentance in the book and how such calls relate to apparently unilateral and unconditional declarations of salvation by Yahweh have been much debated. Whether the product of different layers, chronological development, rhetorical technique, different moral worlds, conflicting anthropologies or something else, within the *book* of Ezekiel the two remain side-by-side, with neither revoked. Indeed, oracles not originally aimed at eliciting repentance have been re-presented within the book of Ezekiel, as indirect speech acts with different illocutionary force, to bring the exilic addressees to repentance. Within the framework of the book of Ezekiel, I have argued for a different perspective on this antinomy, that they provide *complementary* perspectives on the same event, albeit with divine initiative working through רוח enabling a response impossible for the inveterately rebellious nation. These calls fit within the wider purpose of the book of Ezekiel, which is not so much to give an explanation for the fall of Jerusalem, though it does do that, inviting its readers to share its view that it was Yahweh's just punishment, but to foster the recreation of the nation, and to highlight the importance of repentance within that recreation. In that respect, it resonates with the portrayal of repentance in exile that is found in Lev 26:40–46 and Deut 30:1–6.[41] It also resonates with the Deuteronomistic History as a whole, which, as Albertz points out, focuses less on the theological rationale for the fall of the southern kingdom, and more on the appropriate response now, a response that, as with significant positive moments in this history recounted, entails repentance expressed in the repudiation of idolatry and an unswerving, undivided worship of Yahweh.[42] Finally, the possibility and positive value of repentance is also evident, after the exile, in

41. The parallel between the divine call of Deut 10:5, to "Circumcise, then, the foreskin of your heart," answered by the promise of Deut 30:6, "Moreover, the LORD your God will circumcise your heart," and the divine call of Ezek 18:31, "Get yourselves a new heart and a new spirit," answered by the promise of Ezek 36:26, "A new heart I will give you, and a new spirit I will put within you," is a graphic illustration of this resonance.

42. Rainer Albertz, *A History of Israelite Religion in the Old Testament Period.* Vol. 2, *From the Exile to the Maccabees* (trans. John Bowden; London: SCM, 1994), 388–99. This is not, of course, to flatten distinctions between Ezekiel and Deuteronomistic History.

Chronicles, especially 2 Chr 10–36.[43] Scholarship needs to acknowledge the place of calls to repentance within the communicative intent of the book of Ezekiel as a whole.

The book of Ezekiel, then, highlights the effecting power of רוח as it calls its readers to reorient their lives around the word of Yahweh, whether statutes or prophetic word spoken through Ezekiel. Yahweh, by his רוח, brings about moral and ethical transformation and renewal, creating a new community obedient to his word, with Ezekiel, בן אדם, as its first member.

---

43. Kelly, "'Retribution,'" 217–18.

BIBLIOGRAPHY

Ackroyd, Peter R. *Exile and Restoration*. OTL. London: SCM, 1968.

Aitken, K. T. "Hearing and Seeing: Metamorphoses of a Motif in Isaiah 1–39." Pages 12–41 in Davies and Clines, eds., *Among the Prophets*.

Albertz, Rainer. *A History of Israelite Religion in the Old Testament Period*. Vol. 2, *From the Exile to the Maccabees*. Translated by John Bowden. London: SCM, 1994.

Albright, W. F. "The Oracles of Balaam." *JBL* 63 (1944): 207–33.

Allen, Leslie C. *The Books of Joel, Obadiah, Jonah and Micah*. NICOT. Grand Rapids: Eerdmans, 1976.

—*Ezekiel 1–19*. WBC 28. Waco, Tex.: Word, 1994.

—*Ezekiel 20–48*. WBC 29. Dallas: Word, 1990.

—"The Structure and Intention of Ezekiel 1." *VT* 43 (1993): 145–61.

—"Structure, Tradition and Redaction in Ezekiel's Death Valley Vision." Pages 127–42 in Davies and Clines, eds., *Among the Prophets*.

Alter, Robert. *The Art of Biblical Narrative*. London: George Allen & Unwin, 1981.

—*The Art of Biblical Poetry*. New York: Basic Books, 1985.

Anderson, Arnold A. *2 Samuel*. WBC 11. Dallas: Word, 1989.

Applegate, John. "Narrative Patterns for the Communication of Commissioned Speech in the Prophets: A Three-Scene Model." Pages 69–88 in *Narrativity in Biblical and Related Texts*. Edited by G. J. Brooke and J.-D. Kaestli. BETL 149. Leuven: Leuven University Press, 2000.

Aquinas, Thomas. *Summa Theologiae*. Vol. 45, *Prophecy and Other Charisms*. Edited by Roland Potter. London: Blackfriars, 1970.

Auld, A. Graeme. "Prophets Through the Looking Glass: Between the Writings and Moses." *JSOT* 27 (1983): 3–23.

Austin, J. L. *How to Do Things With Words*. Edited by J. O. Urmson. Oxford: Oxford University Press, 1962.

Bailey, Lloyd R. *Biblical Perspectives on Death*. OBT 5. Philadelphia: Fortress, 1979.

Baker, David W. "Israelite Prophets and Prophecy." Pages 266–94 in *The Face of Old Testament Studies: A Survey of Contemporary Approaches*. Edited by David W. Baker and Bill T. Arnold. Grand Rapids: Baker, 1999.

Baltzer, Dieter. *Ezechiel und Deuterojesaja: Berührung in der Heilserwartung der beiden großen Exilspropheten*. BZAW 121. Berlin: de Gruyter, 1971.

Bar-Efrat, Shimon. *Narrative Art in the Bible*. Translated by Dorothea Shefer-Vanson. JSOTSup 70. Bible and Literature Series 17. Sheffield: Sheffield Academic Press, 2000.

Barr, James. *The Semantics of Biblical Language*. Oxford: Oxford University Press, 1961.

Barstad, Hans M. "No Prophets? Recent Developments in Biblical Prophetic Research and Ancient Near Eastern Prophecy." *JSOT* 57 (1993): 39–60.

Barthélemy, Dominique. "'Un seul', 'un nouveau' ou 'un autre'? À propos de l'intervention du Seigneur sur le coeur de l'homme selon Éz 11,19a et des problèmes de critique textuelle qu'elle soulève." Pages 329–38 in Mosis and Ruppert, eds., *Der Weg zum Menschen.*

Bartholomew, Craig, Colin Greene and Karl Möller, eds. *After Pentecost: Language and Biblical Interpretation.* Scripture and Hermeneutics Series 2. Carlisle: Paternoster, 2001.

Ben Zvi, Ehud, Maxine Hancock and Richard Beinert. *Readings in Biblical Hebrew.* New Haven, Conn.: Yale University Press, 1993.

Berlin, Adele. *Poetics and Interpretation of Biblical Narrative.* Bible and Literature Series 9. Sheffield: Almond, 1983.

Bertholet, Alfred. *Hesekiel, mit einem Beitrag von Kurt Galling.* HAT 13. Tübingen: J. C. B. Mohr (Paul Siebeck), 1936.

Birch, Bruce C. "The Development of the Tradition on the Anointing of Saul in 1 Sam. 9:1–10:16." *JBL* 90 (1971): 55–68.

Bjørndalen, A. J. "Zu den Zeitstufen der Zitatformel...כה אמר im Botenverkehr." *ZAW* 86 (1974): 393–403.

Blank, Sheldon H. "Prophet as Paradigm." Pages 111–30 in *Essays in Old Testament Ethics.* Edited by James L. Crenshaw and John T. Willis. New York: Ktav, 1974.

Blenkinsopp, Joseph. *Ezekiel.* Interpretation. Louisville, Ky.: Westminster John Knox, 1990.

—*A History of Prophecy in Israel.* Rev. and enl. ed. Louisville, Ky.: Westminster John Knox, 1996.

—*Sage, Priest, Prophet: Religious and Intellectual Leadership in Ancient Israel.* Louisville, Ky.: Westminster John Knox, 1995.

Block, Daniel I. *The Book of Ezekiel Chapters 1–24.* Grand Rapids: Eerdmans, 1997.

—*The Book of Ezekiel Chapters 25–48.* Grand Rapids: Eerdmans, 1998.

—"Bringing Back David: Ezekiel's Messianic Hope." Pages 167–88 in *The Lord's Anointed: Interpretation of Old Testament Messianic Texts.* Edited by P. E. Satterthwaite, R. S. Hess and G. J. Wenham. Grand Rapids: Baker, 1995.

—"Empowered by the Spirit of God: The Holy Spirit in the Historiographic Writings of the Old Testament." *SBJT* 1 (1997): 42–61.

—"Gog and the Pouring Out of the Spirit: Reflections on Ezekiel xxxix 21–29." *VT* 37 (1987): 257–70.

—"The Prophet of the Spirit: The Use of *RWḤ* in the Book of Ezekiel." *JETS* 32 (1989): 27–49.

—Review of Ellen F. Davis, *Swallowing the Scroll. JBL* 110 (1991): 144–46.

Boadt, Lawrence. "Ezekiel." Pages 305–28 in *The New Jerome Bible Commentary.* Edited by R. E. Brown, J. A. Fitzmyer and R. E. Murphy. London: Chapman, 1989.

—"The Function of the Salvation Oracles in Ezekiel 33 to 37." *Harvard Annual Review* 12 (1990): 1–21.

—"Rhetorical Strategies in Ezekiel's Oracles of Judgment." Pages 182–200 in Lust, ed., *Ezekiel and His Book.*

Breck, John. *Spirit of Truth: The Holy Spirit in Johannine Tradition.* Vol. 1, *The Origins of Johannine Pneumatology.* Crestwood, N.Y.: St. Vladimir's Seminary Press, 1991.

Briggs, Charles A. "The Use of רוח in the Old Testament." *JBL* 19 (1900): 132–45.

Briggs, Richard S. *Words in Action.* Edinburgh: T. & T. Clark, 2002.

Bright, John. *Jeremiah.* AB 21. Garden City, N.Y.: Doubleday, 1965.

Brownlee, William H. *Ezekiel 1–19*. WBC 28. Waco, Tex.: Word, 1986.

Brueggemann, Walter. *Theology of the Old Testament: Testimony, Dispute, Advocacy*. Minneapolis: Fortress, 1997.

Budd, Philip J. *Numbers*. WBC 5. Waco, Tex.: Word, 1984.

Calvin, John. *Commentaries on the First Twenty Chapters of the Book of the Prophet Ezekiel*. Translated by Thomas Myers. Repr., Grand Rapids: Eerdmans, 1999 (1849).

Carley, Keith W. *Ezekiel Among the Prophets: A Study of Ezekiel's Place in Prophetic Tradition*. SBT 2d Series 31. London: SCM, 1975.

Carroll, Robert P. *Jeremiah*. OTL. London: SCM, 1986.

—"Poets Not Prophets: A Response to 'Prophets Through the Looking Glass.'" *JSOT* 27 (1983): 25–31.

—"Prophecy and Society." Pages 203–25 in *The World of Ancient Israel: Sociological, Anthropological and Political Perspectives*. Edited by R. E. Clements. Cambridge: Cambridge University Press, 1989.

—"Whose Prophet? Whose History? Whose Social Reality? Troubling the Interpretative Community Again: Notes Towards a Response to T. W. Overholt's Critique." *JSOT* 48 (1990): 33–49.

Cazelles, Henri. "Prolégomenes à une étude de l'esprit dans la Bible." Pages 75–90 in *Von Kanaan bis Kerala*. Edited by W. C. Delsman et al. AOAT 211. Neukirchen–Vluyn: Neukirchener, 1982.

Chevallier, Max-Alain. *Souffle de Dieu: Le Saint-Esprit Dans le Nouveau Testament*. Le Point Théologique 26. Paris: Editions Beauchesne, 1978.

Childs, Brevard S. *Introduction to the Old Testament as Scripture*. London: SCM, 1979.

—*Myth and Reality in the Old Testament*. London: SCM, 1960.

—"Speech-Act Theory and Biblical Interpretation." *SJT* 58 (2005): 375–92.

Clements, Ronald E. "The Chronology of Redaction in Ezekiel 1–24." Pages 283–94 in Lust, ed., *Ezekiel and His Book*.

—*Ezekiel*. Louisville, Ky.: Westminster John Knox, 1996.

—"The Ezekiel Tradition: Prophecy in a Time of Crisis." Pages 145–58 in *Old Testament Prophecy: From Oracles to Canon*. Louisville, Ky.: Westminster John Knox, 1996. Repr. from pages 119–36 in Coggins, Phillips and Knibb, eds., *Israel's Prophetic Tradition*.

—*God and Temple: The Idea of the Divine Presence in Ancient Israel*. Oxford: Blackwell, 1965.

—*Old Testament Prophecy: From Oracles to Canon*. Louisville, Ky.: Westminster John Knox, 1996.

—*Old Testament Theology: A Fresh Approach*. London: Marshall, Morgan & Scott, 1978.

Cody, Aelred. *Ezekiel, With an Excursus on Old Testament Priesthood*. Old Testament Message 11. Wilmington, Del.: Glazier, 1984.

Cogan, Mordechai. *I Kings*. AB 10. New York: Doubleday, 2001.

Cogan, Mordechai, and Hayim Tadmor. *II Kings*. AB 11. New York: Doubleday, 1988.

Coggins, Richard, Anthony Phillips and Michael Knibb, *Israel's Prophetic Tradition: Essays in Honour of Peter R. Ackroyd*. Cambridge: Cambridge University Press, 1982.

Cohen, Ted. "Illocutions and Perlocutions." *Foundations of Language* 9 (1973): 492–503.

Collins, Terence. *The Mantle of Elijah: The Redaction Criticism of the Prophetical Books.* The Biblical Seminar 20. Sheffield: JSOT Press, 1993.

Conrad, Edgar W. *Zechariah.* Readings: A New Biblical Commentary. Sheffield: Sheffield Academic Press, 1999.

Cook, John A. "The Semantics of Verbal Pragmatics: Clarifying the Roles of *Wayyiqtol* and *Weqatal* in Biblical Hebrew Prose." *JSS* 49 (2004): 247–73.

Cook, Stephen L. *Prophecy and Apocalypticism: The Postexilic Social Setting.* Minneapolis: Fortress, 1995.

Cook, Stephen L., and Corrine L. Patton, eds. *Ezekiel's Hierarchical World: Wrestling with a Tiered Reality.* SBLSymS 31. Atlanta: Society of Biblical Literature, 2004.

Cooke, G. A. *A Critical and Exegetical Commentary on the Book of Ezekiel.* ICC. Edinburgh: T. & T. Clark, 1936.

Cooper, Lamar E., Sr. *Ezekiel.* NAC 17. Nashville, Tenn.: Broadman & Holman, 1994.

Couturier, Guy. "L'Esprit de Yahweh et la Fonction Prophétique en Israël." *Science et Esprit* 42 (1990): 129–65.

Craigie, Peter C. *Ezekiel.* DSB. Edinburgh: The Saint Andrew Press, 1983.

Craigie, Peter C., Page H. Kelley and Joel F. Drinkard, Jr. *Jeremiah 1–25.* WBC 26. Dallas: Word, 1991.

Crenshaw, James L. *Prophetic Conflict: Its Effect Upon Israelite Religion.* BZAW 124. New York: de Gruyter, 1971.

Dafni, Evangelia G. "רוח שקר und falsche Prophetie in 1 Reg 22." *ZAW* 112 (2000): 368–85.

Darr, Katheryn Pfisterer. "The Book of Ezekiel: Introduction, Commentary and Reflections." *NIB* 6:1073–1607.

—"Ezekiel Among the Critics." *Currents in Research: Biblical Studies* 2 (1994): 9–24.

—"Proverb Performance and Transgenerational Retribution in Ezekiel 18." Pages 199–223 in Cook and Patton, eds., *Ezekiel's Hierarchical World.*

Davies, Eryl W. *Numbers.* NCB. Grand Rapids: Eerdmans, 1995.

Davies, G. I. *Hosea.* NCB. London: Marshall Pickering, 1992.

Davies, Philip R. "The Audiences of Prophetic Scrolls: Some Suggestions." Pages 48–62 in *Prophets and Paradigms: Essays in Honor of Gene M. Tucker.* Edited by Stephen B. Reid. JSOTSup 229. Sheffield: Sheffield Academic Press, 1996.

Davies, P. R., and D. J. A. Clines, eds. *Among the Prophets: Language, Image and Structure in the Prophetic Writings.* JSOTSup 144. Sheffield: JSOT Press, 1993.

Davis, Ellen F. *Swallowing the Scroll: Textuality and the Dynamics of Discourse in Ezekiel's Prophecy.* JSOTSup 78. Bible and Literature Series 21. Sheffield: Almond, 1989.

DeRoche, Michael. "The *rûaḥ ʾĕlōhîm* in Gen 1:2c: Creation or Chaos." Pages 303–18 in *Ascribe to the Lord: Biblical and Other Studies in Memory of Peter C. Craigie.* Edited by Lyle M. Eslinger and Glen Taylor. JSOTSup 67. Sheffield: JSOT Press, 1988.

DeVries, Simon J. *1 Kings.* WBC 12. Waco, Tex.: Word, 1985.

—*Prophet Against Prophet: The Role of the Micaiah Narrative (1 Kings 22) in the Development of Early Prophetic Tradition.* Grand Rapids: Eerdmans, 1978.

Dion, Paul-Eugène. "La *rwḥ* dans l'Heptateuque." *Science et Esprit* 42 (1990): 167–91.

Dreytza, Manfred. *Der theologische Gebrauch von RUAH im Alten Testament: Eine wort- und satzsemantische Studie.* Giessen: Brunnen, 1990.

Driver, S. R. *An Introduction to the Literature of the Old Testament.* 9th ed. Edinburgh: T. & T. Clark, 1913.

Duguid, Iain M. *Ezekiel*. NIVAC. Grand Rapids: Zondervan, 1999.

—*Ezekiel and the Leaders of Israel*. VTSup 56. Leiden: Brill, 1994.

—"Putting Priests in Their Place: Ezekiel's Contribution to the History of the Old Testament Priesthood." Pages 43–60 in Cook and Patton, eds., *Ezekiel's Hierarchical World*.

Eichrodt, Walther. *Ezekiel*. Translated by C. Quin. OTL. London: SCM, 1970.

—*Theology of the Old Testament*. Translated by J. A. Baker. 2 vols. London: SCM, 1961–67.

Ellison, H. L. *Ezekiel: The Man and His Message*. London: Paternoster, 1956.

Endo, Yoshinobu. *The Verbal System of Classical Hebrew in the Joseph Story: An Approach from Discourse Analysis*. Studia Semitica Neerlandica 32. Assen: Van Gorcum, 1996.

Eslinger, Lyle M. *Kingship of God in Crisis: A Close Reading of 1 Samuel 1–12*. Bible and Literature Series 10. Sheffield: Almond Press, 1985.

Fechter, Friedrich. "Priesthood in Exile According to the Book of Ezekiel." Pages 27–41 in Cook and Patton, eds., *Ezekiel's Hierarchical World*.

Fensham, F. Charles. *The Books of Ezra and Nehemiah*. NICOT. Grand Rapids: Eerdmans, 1982.

Fenton, Terry L. "Deuteronomistic Advocacy of the *nābî'*: 1 Samuel Ix 9 and Questions of Israelite Prophecy." *VT* 47 (1997): 23–42.

—"Israelite Prophecy: Characteristics of the First Protest Movement." Pages 129–41 in de Moor, ed., *The Elusive Prophet*.

Fishbane, Michael. *Biblical Interpretation in Ancient Israel*. Oxford: Clarendon, 1985.

—"Sin and Judgment in the Prophecies of Ezekiel." *Int* 38 (1984): 131–50.

Fohrer, Georg. *Die Hauptprobleme des Buches Ezechiel*. BZAW 72. Berlin: Töpelmann, 1952.

—*Ezechiel, mit einem Beitrag von Kurt Galling*. 2d ed. HAT 13. Tübingen: J. C. B. Mohr (Paul Siebeck), 1955.

Fokkelman, J. P. *Narrrative Art and Poetry in the Books of Samuel: A Full Interpretation Based on Stylistic and Structural Analyses*. 4 vols. Studia Semitica Neerlandica 20. Assen: Van Gorcum, 1981–93.

Fox, Michael V. "The Rhetoric of Ezekiel's Vision of the Valley of the Bones." *HUCA* 51 (1980): 1–15.

Fretheim, Terence E. "Genesis." *NIB* 1:319–674.

—*The Suffering of God: An Old Testament Perspective*. OBT 14. Philadelphia: Fortress, 1984.

—"Word of God." *ABD* 6:961–68.

Friebel, Kelvin G. *Jeremiah's and Ezekiel's Sign-Acts*. JSOTSup 283. Sheffield: Sheffield Academic Press, 1999.

Fritz, Volkmar. *1 & 2 Kings*. Translated by A. Hagedorn. Continental Commentaries. Minneapolis: Fortress, 2003.

Garscha, Jörg. *Studien zum Ezechielbuch: eine redaktionskritische Untersuchung von 1–39*. Europäische Hochschulschriften 23. Frankfurt: Lang, 1974.

Gass, Erasmus. "Genus und Semantik am Beispiel von 'theologischem' *rûḥ*." *BN* 109 (2001): 45–55.

Glazov, Gregory Y. *The Bridling of the Tongue and the Opening of the Mouth in Biblical Prophecy*. JSOTSup 311. Sheffield: Sheffield Academic Press, 2001.

Goldfajn, Tal. *Word Order and Time in Biblical Hebrew Narrative*. Oxford Theological Monographs. Oxford: Clarendon, 1998.

Gordon, Robert P. *1 & 2 Samuel: A Commentary*. Exeter: Paternoster, 1986.

—"Where Have All the Prophets Gone? The 'Disappearing' Prophet Against the Background of Ancient Near Eastern Prophecy." *BBR* 5 (1995): 67–86.

Gowan, Donald E. *Eschatology in the Old Testament*. Philadelphia: Fortress, 1986.

—*Theology of the Prophetic Books: The Death and Resurrection of Israel*. Louisville, Ky.: Westminster John Knox, 1998.

Graffy, Adrian. *A Prophet Confronts His People: The Disputation Speech in the Prophets*. AnBib 104. Rome: Biblical Institute Press, 1984.

Graham, M. Patrick, Steven L. McKenzie and Gary N. Knoppers, eds. *The Chronicler as Theologian: Essays in Honor of Ralph W. Klein*. JSOTSup 371. London: T. & T. Clark, 2003.

Gray, G. B. *A Critical Introduction to the Old Testament*. Studies in Theology 10. London: Duckworth, 1913.

Gray, John. *I & II Kings*. 3d ed. OTL. London: SCM, 1977.

Greenberg, Moshe. "The Design and Themes of Ezekiel's Program of Restoration." *Int* 38 (1984): 181–208.

—*Ezekiel 1–20*. AB 22. New York: Doubleday, 1983.

—*Ezekiel 21–37*. AB 22A. New York: Doubleday, 1997.

—"On Ezekiel's Dumbness." *JBL* 77 (1958): 101–5.

—"Salvation of the impenitent *ad Majorem Dei Gloriam*: Ezek 36:16–32." Pages 263–71 in *Transformations of the Inner Self in Ancient Religion*. Edited by Jan Assmann and Guy G. Stroumsa. Studies in the History of Religions 83. Leiden: Brill, 1999.

—"The Use of the Ancient Versions for Understanding the Hebrew Text." Pages 131–48 in *Congress Volume, Göttingen 1977*. Edited by J. A. Emerton. VTSup 29. Leiden: Brill, 1978.

—"What Are Valid Criteria for Determining Inauthentic Matter in Ezekiel?" Pages 123–35 in Lust, ed., *Ezekiel and His Book*.

Greene, John T. *The Role of the Messenger and Message in the Ancient Near East*. Brown Judaic Studies 169. Atlanta: Scholars Press, 1989.

Grossfeld, Bernard. *The Targum Onqelos to Genesis*. The Aramaic Bible 6. Edinburgh: T. & T. Clark, 1988.

Habel, Norman C. "The Form and Significance of the Call Narratives." *ZAW* 77 (1965): 297–323.

Halperin, David J. *Seeking Ezekiel: Text and Psychology*. University Park, Pa.: Pennsylvania State University Press, 1993.

Hals, Ronald M. *Ezekiel*. FOTL 19. Grand Rapids: Eerdmans, 1989.

Hamilton, Victor P. *The Book of Genesis Chapters 1–17*. NICOT. Grand Rapids: Eerdmans, 1990.

Harrison, Roland K. *Numbers*. WEC. Chicago: Moody, 1990.

Hatch, Edwin, and Henry A. Redpath. *A Concordance to the Septuagint*. 2d ed. Grand Rapids: Eerdmans, 1998.

Hehn, Johannes. "Zum Problem des Geistes im Alten Orient und im Alten Testament." *ZAW* 43 (1925): 210–25.

Heider, George C. "A Further Turn on Ezekiel's Baroque Twist in Ezek 20:25–26." *JBL* 107 (1988): 721–24.

Hengstenberg, E. W. *The Prophecies of Ezekiel Elucidated.* Translated by A. C. Murphy and J. G. Murphy. Edinburgh: T. & T. Clark, 1869.

Herntrich, Volkmar. *Ezechielprobleme.* BZAW 61. Giessen: Töpelmann, 1932.

Heschel, Abraham J. *The Prophets.* 2 vols. Repr., Peabody, Mass.: Prince, 2000 (1962).

Hildebrandt, Wilf. *An Old Testament Theology of the Spirit of God.* Peabody, Mass.: Hendrickson, 1995.

Hillers, Delbert R. *A Commentary on the Book of the Prophet Micah.* Hermeneia. Philadelphia: Fortress, 1984.

Höffken, Peter. "Beobachtungen zu Ezechiel XXXVII 1–10." *VT* 31 (1981): 305–17.

Holladay, William L. *Jeremiah 1: A Commentary on the Book of the Prophet Jeremiah.* Hermeneia. Minneapolis: Fortress, 1986.

Hölscher, Gustav. *Hesekiel, der Dichter und das Buch.* BZAW 29. Giessen: Töpelmann, 1924.

Horn, F. W. "Holy Spirit," *ABD* 3:260–80.

Hosch, Harold E. "*RÛAḤ* in the Book of Ezekiel: A Textlinguistic Analysis." *JOTT* 14 (2002): 77–125.

Houston, Walter. "What Did the Prophets Think They Were Doing? Speech Acts and Prophetic Discourse in the Old Testament." *Biblical Interpretation* 1 (1993): 167–88.

Howie, C. G. *The Date and Composition of Ezekiel.* JBL Monograph Series 4. Philadelphia: Society of Biblical Literature, 1950.

Hurvitz, A. *A Linguistic Study of the Relationship Between the Priestly Source and the Book of Ezekiel: A New Approach to an Old Problem.* CahRB 20. Paris: Gabalda, 1982.

Imschoot, Paul van. "L'action de l'esprit de Jahvé dans l'Ancient Testament." *RSPT* 23 (1934): 553–87.

—"L'esprit de Jahvé et l'alliance nouvelle dans l'Ancient Testament." *ETL* 13 (1936): 201–20.

—"L'esprit de Jahvé, principe de vie morale dans l'Ancient Testament." *ETL* 16 (1939): 457–67.

—"L'esprit de Jahvé, source de la piété dans l'Ancient Testament." *Bible et Vie Chretienne* 6 (1954): 17–30.

—"L'esprit de Jahvé, source de la vie dans l'Ancient Testament." *RB* 44 (1935): 481–501.

—"Sagesse et esprit dans l'Ancient Testament." *RB* 47 (1938): 23–49.

—*Theology of the Old Testament*, vol. 1. Translated by K. Sullivan and F. Buck. Tournai: Desclée, 1965.

Isaacs, Marie E. *The Concept of Spirit.* Heythrop Monograph 1. London: Heythrop College, 1976.

Jacob, Edmond. *Theology of the Old Testament.* Translated by A. W. Heathcote and P. J. Allcock. London: Hodder & Stoughton, 1958.

Johnson, Aubrey R. *The Cultic Prophet in Ancient Israel.* 2d ed. Cardiff: University of Wales Press, 1962.

—*The One and the Many in the Israelite Conception of God.* Cardiff: University of Wales Press, 1961.

—*The Vitality of the Individual in the Thought of Ancient Israel.* 2d ed. Cardiff: University of Wales Press, 1964.

Jones, Douglas R. *Jeremiah.* NCB. London: Marshall Pickering, 1992.

Jones, Gwilym H. *1 and 2 Kings: Based on the Revised Standard Version.* 2 vols. NCB. London: Marshall, Morgan & Scott, 1984.

Joyce, Paul M. "Dislocation and Adaptation in the Exilic Age and After." Pages 45–58 in *After the Exile: Essays in Honour of Rex Mason*. Edited by John Barton and David J. Reimer. Macon, Ga.: Mercer University Press, 1996.

—*Divine Initiative and Human Response in Ezekiel*. JSOTSup 51. Sheffield: JSOT Press, 1989.

—"Ezekiel and Individual Responsibility." Pages 317–21 in Lust, ed., *Ezekiel and His Book*.

—"King and Messiah in Ezekiel." Pages 323–37 in *King and Messiah in Israel and the Ancient Near East: Proceedings of the Oxford Old Testament Seminar*. Edited by J. Day. JSOTSup 270. Sheffield: Sheffield Academic Press, 1998.

Kaiser, Otto. *Isaiah 13–39*. Translated by R. A. Wilson. OTL. London: SCM, 1974.

Kapelrud, Arvid S. "The Spirit and the Word in the Prophets." *ASTI* 11 (1977–78): 40–47.

Kasher, Rimmon. "Anthropomorphism, Holiness and Cult: A New Look at Ezekiel 40–48." *ZAW* 110 (1998): 192–208.

Kaufmann, Yehezkel. *The Religion of Israel: From Its Beginnings to the Babylonian Exile*. Translated and edited by Moshe Greenberg. London: George Allen & Unwin Ltd, 1961.

Keil, Carl F. *Biblical Commentary on the Prophecies of Ezekiel*. Translated by J. Martin. 2 vols. Edinburgh: T. & T. Clark, 1876.

—*The Books of Ezra, Nehemiah, and Esther*. Translated by S. Taylor. Edinburgh: T. & T. Clark, 1873.

—*Commentary on the Old Testament*. Vol. 10, *The Minor Prophets*. Translated by James Martin. Repr., Peabody, Mass.: Hendrickson, 1996 (1861–99).

Kelly, Brian E. "'Retribution' Revisited: Covenant, Grace and Restoration." Pages 206–27 in Graham, McKenzie and Knoppers, eds., *The Chronicler as Theologian*.

Kinlaw, Pamela E. "From Death to Life: The Expanding רוח in Ezekiel." *PRSt* 30 (2003): 161–72.

Kissling, Paul J. *Reliable Characters in the Primary History: Profiles of Moses, Joshua, Elijah and Elisha*. JSOTSup 224. Sheffield: Sheffield Academic Press, 1996.

Klein, Ralph W. *1 Samuel*. WBC 10. Waco, Tex.: Word, 1983.

—*Ezekiel: The Prophet and His Message*. Columbia: University of South Carolina Press, 1988.

—*Israel in Exile: A Theological Interpretation*. OBT. Philadelphia: Fortress, 1979.

Klement, Herbert H. *II Samuel 21–24: Context, Structure and Meaning in the Samuel Conclusion*. European University Studies. Frankfurt: Lang, 2000.

Kline, Meredith G. *Images of the Spirit*. Repr., Eugene: Wipf & Stock, 1999 (1980).

Knierim, Rolf P. *The Task of Old Testament Theology*. Grand Rapids: Eerdmans, 1995.

Koch, Klaus. *The Growth of the Biblical Tradition: The Form-Critical Method*. Translated by S. M. Cupitt. London: A. & C. Black, 1969.

—"The Language of Prophecy: Thoughts on the Macrosyntax of the *děbar YHWH* and Its Semantic Implications in the Deuteronomistic History." Pages 210–21 in *Problems in Biblical Theology: Essays in Honour of Rolf Knierim*. Edited by Henry T. C. Sun, Keith L. Eades, James M. Robinson and Garth I. Moller. Grand Rapids: Eerdmans, 1997.

—*The Prophets*. Translated by M. Kohl. 2 vols. London: SCM, 1982–83.

Koch, Robert. *Der Geist Gottes im Alten Testament*. Frankfurt: Lang, 1991.

—*Geist und Messias*. Freiburg: Herder, 1950.

Koehler, Ludwig. *Old Testament Theology.* Translated by A. S. Todd. London: Lutter-worth, 1957.

Kutsko, John F. *Between Heaven and Earth: Divine Presence and Absence in the Book of Ezekiel.* Biblical and Judaic Studies 7. Winona Lake, Ind.: Eisenbrauns, 2000.

—"Ezekiel's Anthropology and Its Ethical Implications." Pages 119–41 in Odell and Strong, eds., *The Book of Ezekiel.*

Lang, Bernhard. "Street Theater, Raising the Dead, and the Zoroastrian Connection in Ezekiel's Prophecy." Pages 297–316 in Lust, ed., *Ezekiel and His Book.*

Lapsley, Jacqueline E. *Can These Bones Live? The Problem of the Moral Self in the Book of Ezekiel.* BZAW 301. Berlin: de Gruyter, 2000.

—"Shame and Self-Knowledge: The Positive Role of Shame in Ezekiel's View of the Moral Self." Pages 143–73 in Odell and Strong, eds., *The Book of Ezekiel.*

Lee, Bernard J. "God as Spirit." Pages 129–41 in *Empirical Theology.* Edited by R. Miller. Birmingham, Ala.: Religious Education Press, 1992.

Lemke, Werner E. "Life in the Present and Hope for the Future." *Int* 38 (1984): 165–80.

Levenson, Jon D. *Theology of the Program of Restoration of Ezekiel 40–48.* HSM 10. Missoula, Mont.: Scholars Press, 1976.

Levey, Samson H. *The Targum of Ezekiel: Translated, with a Critical Introduction, Apparatus, and Notes.* The Aramaic Bible 13. Edinburgh: T. & T. Clark, 1987.

Levitt Kohn, Risa. "Ezekiel at the Turn of the Century." *CBR* 2 (2003): 9–31.

—*A New Heart and a New Soul: Ezekiel, the Exile and the Torah.* JSOTSup 358. London: Sheffield Academic Press, 2002.

Lind, Millard C. *Ezekiel.* Believers Church Bible Commentary. Scottdale, Pa..: Herald, 1996.

Lindblom, Johannes. *Prophecy in Ancient Israel.* Oxford: Blackwell, 1962.

Lust, Johan, ed., *Ezekiel and His Book: Textual and Literary Criticism and Their Inter-relation.* BETL 74. Leuven: Leuven University Press, 1986.

—"The Final Text and Textual Criticism: Ez 39,28." Pages 48–54 in Lust, ed., *Ezekiel and His Book.*

—"Notes to the Septuagint: Ezekiel 1–2." *ETL* 75 (1999): 5–31.

Lyons, John. *Linguistic Semantics: An Introduction.* Cambridge: Cambridge University Press, 1995.

Lys, Daniel. *Rûach: Le Souffle dans L'Ancien Testament.* Études D'Histoire et de Philosophie Religieuses. Paris: Presses Universitaires de France, 1962.

Ma, Wonsuk. *Until the Spirit Comes: The Spirit of God in the Book of Isaiah.* JSOTSup 271. Sheffield: Sheffield Academic Press, 1999.

Mackintosh, A.A. *Hosea.* ICC. Edinburgh: T. & T. Clark, 1997.

Maher, Michael. *Targum Pseudo-Jonathan: Genesis.* The Aramaic Bible 1B. Edinburgh: T. & T. Clark, 1992.

Matties. Gordon H. *Ezekiel 18 and the Rhetoric of Moral Discourse.* SBLDS 126. Atlanta: Scholars Press, 1990.

Mays, James L. *Hosea: A Commentary.* OTL. London: SCM, 1969.

—*Micah.* OTL. London: SCM, 1976.

McCarter, P. Kyle, Jr. *I Samuel.* AB 8. New York: Doubleday, 1980.

—*II Samuel.* AB 9. New York: Doubleday, 1984.

McConville, J. Gordon. "Priests and Levites in Ezekiel: A Crux in the Interpretation of Israel's History." *TynBul* 34 (1983): 3–31.

McKane, William. *The Book of Micah: Introduction and Commentary*. ICC. Edinburgh: T. & T. Clark, 1998.

—*Jeremiah*. 2 vols. ICC. Edinburgh: T. & T. Clark, 1986–96.

McKeating, Henry. *Ezekiel*. OTG. Sheffield: Sheffield Academic Press, 1993.

—"Ezekiel the 'Prophet Like Moses'?" *JSOT* 61 (1994): 97–109.

McKenzie, Steven L. *The Trouble With Kings: The Composition of the Book of Kings in the Deuteronomistic History*. VTSup 42. Leiden: Brill, 1991.

McNamara, Martin. *Targum Neofiti 1: Genesis*. The Aramaic Bible 1A. Edinburgh: T. & T. Clark, 1992.

Meier, Samuel A. *The Messenger in the Ancient Semitic World*. JSM 45. Atlanta: Scholars Press, 1988.

—*Speaking of Speaking: Marking Direct Discourse in the Hebrew Bible*. VTSup 46. Leiden: Brill, 1992.

Mein, Andrew. *Ezekiel and the Ethics of Exile*. Oxford Theological Monographs. Oxford: Oxford University Press, 2001.

—"Ezekiel as a Priest in Exile." Pages 199–213 in de Moor, ed., *The Elusive Prophet*.

Meyers, Carol L., and Eric M. Meyers. *Haggai, Zechariah 1–8*. AB 25B. New York: Doubleday, 1987.

Milgrom, Jacob. *Numbers*. JPS Torah Commentary. New York: The Jewish Publication Society of America, 1990.

Miller, Cynthia L. *The Representation of Speech in Biblical Hebrew Narrative: A Linguistic Analysis*. HSM 55. Atlanta: Scholars Press, 1996.

Miller, Patrick D. *Sin and Judgment in the Prophets*. SBLMS 27. Chico, Calif.: Scholars Press, 1982.

Moberly, R. W. L. "Does God Lie to His Prophets? The Story of Micaiah Ben Imlah as a Test Case." *HTR* 96 (2003): 1–23.

Möller, Karl. *A Prophet in Debate: The Rhetoric of Persuasion in the Book of Amos*. JSOTSup 372. London: Sheffield Academic Press, 2003.

—"Words of (In-)evitable Certitude? Reflections on the Interpretation of Prophetic Oracles of Judgment." Pages 352–86 in Bartholomew, Greene and Möller, eds., *After Pentecost*.

Montague, George T. *Holy Spirit: Growth of a Biblical Tradition*. New York: Paulist Press, 1976.

Montgomery, J. A., and H. S. Gehman. *A Critical and Exegetical Commentary on the Books of Kings*. ICC. Edinburgh: T. & T. Clark, 1951.

Moor, Johannes C. de, ed. *The Elusive Prophet: The Prophet as a Historical Person, Literary Character and Anonymous Artist*. OtSt 45. Leiden: Brill, 2001.

Mowinckel, Sigmund. "A Postscript to the Paper 'The Spirit and the Word in the Pre-Exilic Reforming Prophets'." *JBL* 56 (1937): 261–65.

—"The 'Spirit' and the 'Word' in the Pre-Exilic Reforming Prophets." *JBL* 53 (1934): 199–227. Repr. pages 83–99 in *The Spirit and the Word: Prophecy and Tradition in Ancient Israel*. Edited by K.C. Hanson. Minneapolis: Fortress, 2002.

Mosis, Rudolf, and Lothar Ruppert, eds. *Der Weg zum Menschen: Zur philosophischen und theologischen Anthropologie*. Freiburg: Herder, 1989.

Myers, Jacob M. *Ezra–Nehemiah*. AB 14. New York: Doubleday, 1965.

Neve, Lloyd. *The Spirit of God in the Old Testament*. Tokyo: Seibunsha, 1972.

Nida, Eugene A. "The Implications of Contemporary Linguistics for Biblical Scholarship." *JBL* 91 (1972): 73–89.

Niditch, Susan. "Ezekiel 40–48 in a Visionary Context." *CBQ* 48 (1986): 208–24.

Noth, Martin. *Numbers: A Commentary.* Translated by J. D. Martin. OTL. London: SCM, 1968.

O'Connor, Kathleen M. "The Prophet Jeremiah and Exclusive Loyalty to God." *Int* 59 (2005): 130–41.

Odell, Margaret S. "Genre and Persona in Ezekiel 24:15–24." Pages 195–219 in Odell and Strong, eds., *The Book of Ezekiel.*

—"The Inversion of Shame and Forgiveness in Ezekiel 16:59–63." *JSOT* 56 (1992): 101–12.

—"You Are What You Eat: Ezekiel and the Scroll." *JBL* 117 (1998): 229–48.

Odell, Margaret S., and John T. Strong. *The Book of Ezekiel: Theological and Anthropological Perspectives.* SBL Symposium Series 9. Atlanta: Society of Biblical Literature, 2000.

Ohnesorge, Stefan. *Jahwe gestaltet sein Volk neu: Zur Sicht der Zukunft Israels nach Ez 11,14–21; 20,1–44; 36,16–38; 37,1–14. 15–28.* Forschung zur Bibel 64. Würzburg: Echter, 1991.

Olmo Lete, G. del. "David's Farewell Oracle (2 Samuel xxiii 1–7): A Literary Analysis." *VT* 34 (1984): 414–37.

Olyan, Saul M. "'We Are Utterly Cut Off': Some Possible Nuances of נגזרנו לנו in Ezek 37:11." *CBQ* 65 (2003): 43–51.

Orlinsky, Harry M. "The Plain Meaning of *RÛAḤ* in Gen. 1.2." *JQR* 48 (1957–58): 174–82.

Oswalt, John N. *The Book of Isaiah Chapters 1–39.* NICOT. Grand Rapids: Eerdmans, 1986.

Overholt, Thomas W. "Prophecy in History: The Social Reality of Intermediation." *JSOT* 48 (1990): 3–29.

Patton, Corrine L. "Priest, Prophet and Exile: Ezekiel as a Literary Construct." Pages 73–89 in Cook and Patton, eds., *Ezekiel's Hierarchical World.*

—"'Should Our Sister Be Treated Like a Whore?' A Response to Feminist Critiques of Ezekiel 23." Pages 221–38 in Odell and Strong, eds., *The Book of Ezekiel.*

Petersen, David L. "Creation in Ezekiel: Methodological Perspectives and Theological Prospects." Pages 169–78 in Cook and Patton, eds., *Ezekiel's Hierarchical World.*

—*Haggai & Zechariah 1–8.* OTL. London: SCM, 1984.

—*Zechariah 9–14 & Malachi.* OTL. London: SCM, 1995.

Pohlmann, Karl-Friedrich. *Das Buch des Prophet Hesekiel (Ezechiel) Kapitel 1–19.* ATD 22/1. Göttingen: Vandenhoeck & Ruprecht, 1996.

—*Das Buch des Prophet Hesekiel (Ezechiel) Kapitel 20–48.* ATD 22/2. Göttingen: Vandenhoeck & Ruprecht, 2002.

Porter, J. R. "The Origins of Prophecy in Israel." Pages 12–31 in Coggins, Phillips and Knibb, eds., *Israel's Prophetic Tradition.*

Pratt, Richard L., Jr. *He Gave Us Stories.* Repr., Phillipsburg, N.J.: P. & R., 1993 (1990).

Preuss, Horst D. *Old Testament Theology.* Translated by L. G. Perdue. 2 vols. Edinburgh: T. & T. Clark, 1995–96.

Rabinowitz, Isaac. *A Witness Forever: Ancient Israel's Perception of Literature and the Resultant Hebrew Bible.* Bethesda, Md.: Capital Decisions Limited, 1993.

Rad, Gerhard von. *Genesis: A Commentary.* Translated by J. H. Marks. 3d ed. London: SCM, 1972.

—*Old Testament Theology.* Translated by D. M. G. Stalker. 2 vols. Edinburgh: Oliver & Boyd, 1962–65.

Raitt, Thomas M. *A Theology of Exile: Judgment / Deliverance in Jeremiah and Ezekiel.* Philadelphia: Fortress, 1977.

Redpath, Henry A. *The Book of the Prophet Ezekiel.* London: Methuen, 1907.

Rendtorff, R. "Botenformel und Botenspruch." *ZAW* 74 (1962): 165–77.

—"Ezekiel 20 and 36:16ff. in the Framework of the Composition of the Book." Pages 190–95 in Rendtorff, *Canon and Theology: Overtures to an Old Testament Theology.* Translated and edited by M. Kohl. Edinburgh: T. & T. Clark, 1993.

Renz, Thomas. *The Rhetorical Function of the Book of Ezekiel.* VTSup 76. Leiden: Brill, 1999.

Richardson, H. Neil. "The Last Words of David: Some Notes on II Sam. 23, 1–7." *JBL* 90 (1971): 257–66.

Ridderbos, N. H. "Gen. 1.1 und 2." *OtSt* 12 (1958): 214–60.

Roberts, J. J. M. "The Hand of Yahweh." *VT* 21 (1971): 244–51.

Rooker, Mark F. *Biblical Hebrew in Transition: The Language of the Book of Ezekiel.* JSOTSup 90. Sheffield: JSOT Press, 1990.

Rosenberg, Joel. "Jeremiah and Ezekiel." Pages 194–206 in *The Literary Guide to the Bible.* Edited by Robert Alter and Frank Kermode. London: Fontana, 1987.

Rowley, H. H. "The Book of Ezekiel in Modern Study." Pages 169–210 in idem, *Men of God.* London: Nelson, 1963. Repr. from *BJRL* 36 (1953–54): 146–90.

Sailhamer, J. H. "Genesis." Pages 1–284 in *The Expositor's Bible Commentary.* Vol. 2, *Genesis–Numbers.* Grand Rapids: Zondervan, 1990.

—*The Pentateuch as Narrative: A Biblical-Theological Commentary.* Grand Rapids: Zondervan, 1992.

Satterthwaite, Philip E. "The Elisha Narratives and the Coherence of 2 Kings 2–8." *TynBul* 49 (1998): 1–28.

Scharbert, Josef. "Der 'Geist' und die Schriftpropheten." Pages 82–97 in Mosis and Ruppert, eds., *Der Weg zum Menschen.*

Schniedewind, William M. "Prophets and Prophecy in the Book of Chronicles." Pages 204–24 in *The Chronicler as Historian.* Edited by M. Patrick Graham, Kenneth G. Hoglund and Steven L. McKenzie. JSOTSup 238. Sheffield: Sheffield Academic Press, 1997.

—*The Word of God in Transition: From Prophet to Exegete in the Second Temple Period.* JSOTSup 197. Sheffield: Sheffield Academic Press, 1995.

Schoemaker, William R. "The Use of רוּחַ in the Old Testament, and of πνεῦμα in the New Testament." *JBL* 23 (1904): 13–67.

Schoen, Edward L. "Anthropomorphic Concepts of God." *RelS* 26 (1990): 123–39.

Schüngel-Straumann, Helen. *Rûaḥ bewegt die Welt: Gottes schöpferische Lebenskraft in der Krisenzeit des Exils.* Stuttgarter Bibelstudien 151. Stuttgart: Katholisches Bibelwerk, 1992.

Schwartz, Baruch J. "The Concentric Structure of Ezekiel 2:1–3:15." Pages 107–14 *Proceedings of the Tenth World Congress of Jewish Studies, Jerusalem, August 16–24 1989.* Edited by David Assaf. Jerusalem: The World Union of Jewish Students, 1990.

—"Ezekiel's Dim View of Israel's Restoration." Pages 43–67 in Odell and Strong, eds., *The Book of Ezekiel.*

—"A Priest Out of Place: Reconsidering Ezekiel's Role in the History of the Israelite Priesthood." Pages 61–71 in Cook and Patton, eds., *Ezekiel's Hierarchical World.*

—"Repentance and Determinism in Ezekiel." Pages 123–30 in *Proceedings of the Eleventh World Congress of Jewish Studies, Jerusalem, June 22–29, 1993: Divsion A, The Bible and its World*. Jerusalem: The World Union of Jewish Studies, 1994.

Searle, John R. *Expression and Meaning: Studies in the Theory of Speech Acts*. Cambridge: Cambridge University Press, 1979.

—*Speech Acts: An Essay in the Philosophy of Language*. Cambridge: Cambridge University Press, 1969.

—"What is a Speech Act?" Pages 39–53 in *The Philosophy of Language*. Edited by John R. Searle. London: Oxford University Press, 1971.

Searle, John R., and Daniel Vanderveken. *Foundations of Illocutionary Logic*. Cambridge: Cambridge University Press, 1985.

Seitz, Christopher R. "Ezekiel 37:1–14." *Int* 46 (1992): 53–56.

Shaw, Charles S. *The Speeches of Micah: A Rhetorical-Historical Analysis*. JSOTSup 145. Sheffield: JSOT Press, 1993.

Simon, László T. *Identity and Identification: An Exegetical and Theological Study of 2 Sam 21–24*. Tesi Gregoriana Serie Teologia 64. Rome: Gregorian University Press, 2000.

Sklba, Richard J. "'Until the Spirit from on High is Poured Out on Us' (Isa 32:15): Reflections on the Role of the Spirit in Exile." *CBQ* 46 (1984): 1–17.

Smith, Gary V. *An Introduction to the Hebrew Prophets: The Prophets as Preachers*. Nashville, Tenn.: Broadman & Holman, 1994.

Smith, P. J. "A Semotactical Approach to the Meaning of the Term *rûaḥ ʾĕlohîm* in Genesis 1:2." *JNSL* 8 (1980): 99–104.

Smith, Ralph L. *Micah–Malachi*. WBC 32. Waco, Tex.: Word, 1984.

Smith-Christopher, Daniel L. *A Biblical Theology of Exile*. Minneapolis: Fortress, 2002.

Snaith, Norman H. *The Distinctive Ideas of the Old Testament*. London: Epworth, 1944.

Soskice, Janet Martin. *Metaphor and Religious Language*. Oxford: Clarendon, 1985.

Speiser, E. A. *Genesis*. AB 1. New York: Doubleday, 1964.

Spiegel, Shalom. "Ezekiel or Pseudo-Ezekiel." *HTR* 24 (1931): 245–321.

Stalker, D. M. G. *Ezekiel: Introduction and Commentary*. Torch Bible Commentaries. London: SCM, 1968.

Sternberg, Meir. *The Poetics of Biblical Narrative: Ideological Literature and the Drama of Reading*. Bloomington, Ind.: Indiana University Press, 1985.

Stevenson, Kalinda R. *The Vision of Transformation: The Territorial Rhetoric of Ezekiel 40–48*. SBLDS 154. Atlanta: Scholars Press, 1996.

Stiver, Dan R. "Ricoeur, Speech-Act Theory, and the Gospels as History." Pages 50–72 in Bartholomew, Greene and Möller, eds., *After Pentecost*.

Stuart, Douglas. *Ezekiel*. MOT. Dallas: Word, 1988.

—*Hosea–Jonah*. WBC 31. Waco, Tex.: Word, 1987.

Sweeney, Marvin A. *Isaiah 1–39*. FOTL 16. Grand Rapids: Eerdmans, 1996.

Talstra, E. "Text Grammar and Hebrew Bible. II: Syntax and Semantics." *BO* 39 (1982): 26–38.

Taylor, John B. *Ezekiel: An Introduction and Commentary*. TOTC. London: InterVarsity Press, 1969.

Thiselton, Anthony C. *New Horizons in Hermeneutics*. London: Marshall Pickering, 1992.

—"Speech-Act Theory and the Claim that God Speaks: Nicholas Wolterstorff's Divine Discourse." *SJT* 50 (1997): 97–110.

—"The Supposed Power of Words in the Biblical Writings." *JTS* 25 (1974): 283–99.

Thomson, J. G. S. S. *The Word of the Lord in Jeremiah*. London: Tyndale Press, 1959.
Throntveit, Mark A. *Ezra–Nehemiah*. Interpretation. Louisville, Ky.: John Knox, 1989.
Torrey, Charles C. "Notes on Ezekiel." *JBL* 58 (1939): 69–86.
—*Pseudo-Ezekiel and the Original Prophecy*. New Haven, Conn.: Yale University Press, 1930.
Tov, Emanuel. "Recensional Differences Between the MT and LXX of Ezekiel." *ETL* 62 (1986): 89–101.
—*Textual Criticism and the Hebrew Bible*. Rev. ed. Minneapolis: Fortress, 2001.
Tromp, N. "The Paradox of Ezekiel's Prophetic Mission: Towards a Semiotic Approach of Ezekiel 3,22–27." Pages 201–13 in Lust, ed., *Ezekiel and His Book*.
Tsumura, David T. *The Earth and the Waters in Genesis 1 and 2: A Linguistic Investigation*. JSOTSup 83. Sheffield: JSOT Press, 1989.
Tucker, Gene M. "Prophetic Superscriptions and the Growth of a Canon." Pages 56–70 in *Canon and Authority: Essays in Old Testament Religion and Theology*. Edited by G. W. Coats and B. O. Long. Philadelphia: Fortress, 1977.
Tuell, Steven S. "Contemporary Studies of Ezekiel: A New Tide Rising." Pages 241–54 in Cook and Patton, eds., *Ezekiel's Hierarchical World*.
—"Haggai–Zechariah: Prophecy After the Manner of Ezekiel." Pages 263–86 in *SBL Seminar Papers, 2000*. Society of Biblical Literature Seminar Papers 39. Atlanta: Society of Biblical Literature, 2000.
—*The Law of the Temple in Ezekiel 40–48*. HSM 49. Atlanta: Scholars Press, 1992.
Uffenheimer, Benjamin. "Theodicy and Ethics in the Prophecy of Ezekiel." Pages 200–27 in *Justice and Righteousness: Biblical Themes and Their Influence*. Edited by H. G. Reventlow and Y. Hoffman. JSOTSup 137. Sheffield: JSOT Press, 1992.
Vanhoozer, Kevin J. "Effectual Call or Causal Effect? Summons, Sovereignty and Supervenient Grace." *TynBul* 49 (1998): 213–51.
—"From Speech Acts to Scripture Acts: The Covenant of Discourse and the Discourse of the Covenant." Pages 1–49 in Bartholomew, Greene and Möller, eds., *After Pentecost*.
—"God's Mighty Speech-Acts: The Doctrine of Scripture Today." Pages 143–81 in *A Pathway Into the Holy Scriptures*. Edited by Philip E. Satterthwaite and David F. Wright. Grand Rapids: Eerdmans, 1994.
—*Is There a Meaning in This Text?* Leicester: InterVarsity Press, 1998.
Vawter, Bruce. "Were the Prophets *Nābî*'s?" *Bib* 66 (1985): 206–20.
Vawter, Bruce, and Leslie J. Hoppe. *A New Heart: A Commentary on the Book of Ezekiel*. ITC. Grand Rapids: Eerdmans, 1991.
Volz, Paul. *Der Geist Gottes und die Verwandten Erscheinungen im Alten Testament und im anschließenden Judentum*. Tübingen: J. C. B. Mohr (Paul Siebeck), 1910.
Vos, Geerhardus. *Biblical Theology: Old and New Testaments*. Grand Rapids: Eerdmans, 1948.
Vriezen, Th. C. *An Outline of Old Testament Theology*. Oxford: Blackwell, 1958.
Wagner, Siegfried. "Geist und Leben nach Ezechiel 37,1–14." Pages 151–68 in *Ausgewählte Aufsätze zum Alten Testament*. Edited by D. Mathias. Berlin: de Gruyter, 1996. Repr. from pages 53–65 in *Theologische Versuche X*. Edited by Joachim Rogge and Gottfried Schille. Berlin: Evangelische Verlagsanstalt, 1979.
Wahl, Harald M. "'Tod und Leben.' Zur Wiederherstellung Israels nach Ez. XXXVII 1–14." *VT* 49 (1999): 218–39.
Walsh, Jerome T. *1 Kings*. Berit Olam. Collegeville, Minn.: Liturgical Press, 1996.

Warfield, Benjamin B. "The Spirit of God in the Old Testament." Pages 101–29 in idem, *Biblical Doctrines*. Edinburgh: Banner of Truth, 1988 (1929).

Watts, James W. "The Legal Characterization of Moses in the Rhetoric of the Pentateuch." *JBL* 117 (1998): 415–26.

—*Reading Law: The Rhetorical Shaping of the Pentateuch*. The Biblical Seminar 59. Sheffield: Sheffield Academic Press, 1999.

Weinfeld, Moshe. *Deuteronomy 1–11*. AB 5. New York: Doubleday, 1991.

Weisman, Zeʿev. "The Personal Spirit as Imparting Authority." *ZAW* 93 (1981): 225–34.

Wendland, Ernst R. " 'Can These Bones Live Again?': A Rhetoric of the Gospel in Ezekiel 33–37, Part I." *AUSS* 39 (2001): 85–100.

—" 'Can These Bones Live Again?': A Rhetoric of the Gospel in Ezekiel 33–37, Part II." *AUSS* 39 (2001): 241–72.

Wenham, Gordon J. *Genesis 1–15*. WBC 1. Dallas: Word, 1987.

Wenk, Matthias. "The Holy Spirit and the Ethical/Religious Life of the People of God in Luke–Acts." Ph.D. diss., Brunel University, 1998.

Westermann, Claus. *Basic Forms of Prophetic Speech*. Translated by H. C. White. London: Lutterworth, 1967.

—*Elements of Old Testament Theology*. Translated by D. W. Scott. Atlanta: John Knox, 1982.

—"Geist im Alten Testament." *EvT* 41 (1981): 223–30.

—*Genesis 1–11: A Commentary*. Translated by J. J. Scullion. London: SPCK, 1984.

—*Isaiah 40–66*. Translated by D. M. G. Stalker. OTL. London: SCM, 1969.

Wevers, John W. *Ezekiel*. NCB. London: Nelson, 1969.

White, Hugh C. "Introduction: Speech Act Theory and Literary Criticism." *Semeia* 41 (1988): 1–24.

Whybray, R. Norman. *The Making of the Pentateuch: A Methodological Study*. JSOTSup 53. Sheffield: JSOT Press, 1987.

Williams, P. J. "Lying Spirits Sent by God? The Case of Micaiah's Prophecy." Pages 58–66 in *The Trustworthiness of Scripture: Perspectives on the Nature of Scripture*. Edited by P. Helm and C. R. Trueman. Grand Rapids: Eerdmans, 2002.

Williamson, H. G. M. *1 and 2 Chronicles*. NCB. London: Marshall, Morgan & Scott, 1982.

—*Ezra, Nehemiah*. WBC 16. Waco, Tex.: Word, 1985.

—"A Response to A. Graeme Auld." *JSOT* 27 (1983): 33–39.

Wilson, Robert R. "An Interpretation of Ezekiel's Dumbness." *VT* 22 (1972): 91–104.

—"Prophecy in Crisis: The Call of Ezekiel." *Int* 38 (1984): 117–30.

—*Prophecy and Society in Ancient Israel*. Philadelphia: Fortress, 1980.

Wolff, Hans W. *Anthropology of the Old Testament*. Translated by M. Kohl. London: SCM, 1974.

—*A Commentary on the Book of the Prophet Hosea*. Translated by Gary Stansell. Hermeneia. Philadelphia: Fortress, 1974.

—*Joel and Amos: A Commentary on the Books of the Prophets Joel and Amos*. Translated by W. Janzen, S.D. McBride Jr. and C.A. Muenchow. Hermeneia. Philadelphia: Fortress, 1977.

—*Micah: A Commentary*. Translated by Gary Stansell. Minneapolis: Augsburg, 1990.

Wolterstorff, Nicholas. *Divine Discourse: Philosophical Reflections on the Claim That God Speaks*. Cambridge: Cambridge University Press, 1995.

—"The Promise of Speech-act Theory for Biblical Interpretation." Pages 73–90 in Bartholomew, Greene and Möller, eds., *After Pentecost*.

Wong, Ka Leung. *The Idea of Retribution in the Book of Ezekiel*. VTSup 87. Leiden: Brill, 2001.

Wood, Leon J. *The Holy Spirit in the Old Testament*. Contemporary Evangelical Perspectives Series. Grand Rapids: Zondervan, 1976.

Woodhouse, John. "The 'Spirit' in the Book of Ezekiel." Pages 1–22 in *Spirit of the Living God Part One*. Edited by B. G. Webb. Explorations 5. Sydney: Lancer, 1991.

Wright, John W. "Beyond Transcendence and Immanence: The Characterization of the Presence and Activity of God in the Book of Chronicles." Pages 240–67 in Graham, McKenzie and Knoppers, eds., *The Chronicler as Theologian*.

Yule, George. *Pragmatics*. Oxford: Oxford University Press, 1996.

Zimmerli, Walther. *Ezekiel 1: A Commentary on the Book of the Prophet Ezekiel Chapters 1–24*. Translated by R. E. Clements. Hermeneia. Philadelphia: Fortress, 1979.

—*Ezekiel 2: A Commentary on the Book of the Prophet Ezekiel Chapters 25–48*. Translated by J. D. Martin. Hermeneia. Philadelphia: Fortress, 1983.

—"I Am Yahweh." Pages 1–28 in *I Am Yahweh*.

—*I Am Yahweh*. Edited by W. Brueggemann. Translated by D.W. Stott. Atlanta: John Knox, 1982.

—"Knowledge of God According to the Book of Ezekiel." Pages 29–98 in idem, *I Am Yahweh*.

—"'Leben' und 'Tod' im Buche des Propheten Ezechiel." *TZ* 13 (1957): 494–508.

—*Old Testament Theology in Outline*. Translated by D. E. Green. Edinburgh: T. & T. Clark, 1978.

—"Plans for Rebuilding After the Catastrophe of 587." Pages 111–33 in idem, *I Am Yahweh*.

—"The Special Form- and Traditio-Historical Character of Ezekiel's Prophecy." *VT* 15 (1965): 515–27.

—"The Word of Divine Self-Manifestation (Proof-Saying): A Prophetic Genre." Pages 99–110 in *I Am Yahweh*.

—"The Word of God in the Book of Ezekiel." Pages 3–13 in *History and Hermeneutic*. Edited by R. W. Funk. JTC 4. New York: Harper & Row, 1967.

INDEXES

INDEX OF REFERENCES

INDEX OF AUTHORS